UNIVERSITIES UNDER DICTATORSHIP

UNIVERSITIES UNDER DICTATORSHIP

John Connelly and Michael Grüttner, editors

The Pennsylvania University State University Press
University Park, Pennsylvania

Library of Congress Cataloging-in-Publication Data

Universities under dictatorship / John Connelly and Michael Grüttner, editors.
p.   cm.
Includes bibliographical references and index.
ISBN 978-0-271-05862-7 (pbk : alk. paper)
1. Higher education and state—History—20th century.
2. Academic freedom—History—20th century.
3. Dictatorship—History—20th century.
I. Connelly, John. II. Grüttner, Michael.

LC171.U55 2005
378'.00917—dc22
2004028124

Copyright © 2005
The Pennsylvania State University
All rights reserved
Printed in the United States of America
Published by
The Pennsylvania State University Press,
University Park, PA 16802-1003

The Pennsylvania State University Press is a member of the
Association of American University Presses.

It is the policy of
The Pennsylvania State University Press to use acid-free paper
This book is printed on stock that
meets the minimum
requirements of American National Standard for
Information Sciences—Permanence of Paper for Printed
Library Materials, ANSI Z39.48–1992.

CONTENTS

Preface   vii
Abbreviations   ix
Introduction   1
JOHN CONNELLY

1 Russian Universities Across the 1917 Divide   15
MICHAEL DAVID-FOX

2 Italian Universities Under Fascism   45
RUTH BEN-GHIAT

3 German Universities Under the Swastika   75
MICHAEL GRÜTTNER

4 Spanish Universities Under Franco   113
MIGUEL ÁNGEL RUIZ CARNICER

5 The Communist Idea of the University: An Essay Inspired by the Hungarian Experience   139
GYÖRGY PÉTERI

6 Czech Universities Under Communism   167
JAN HAVRÁNEK

7 Polish Universities and State Socialism, 1944–1968   185
JOHN CONNELLY

8 Resistance to the Sovietization of Higher Education in China   213
DOUGLAS STIFFLER

9 Between Control and Collaboration: The University in East Germany   245
RALPH JESSEN

Concluding Reflections: Universities and Dictatorships   283
MICHAEL GRÜTTNER

Index   297

PREFACE

The following collection of essays had its origin in an international conference that took place at the University of California, Berkeley on 13–14 May 2000. The contributions that grew out of this meeting can be read in varying ways. Those interested primarily in the history of the universities of a particular country will find case studies of nine different dictatorships, all of which appear for the first time. They are written by the leading experts in their respective fields. We had wanted to add a contribution devoted to the Japanese case, but were unsuccessful in finding an author.

We hope, however, to have collected more than just a group of single-country studies. The decision to organize this conference was based on our belief in the value of a comparative study that would dissect similar structures and behaviors across national boundaries and permit deeper understanding of the peculiarities of specific cultures and their institutions. This volume is thus also a contribution to the comparative analysis of the dictatorships that have shaped the face of the twentieth century. In order to enhance the comparability of the separate cases, authors were asked to address common questions, which are discussed in detail in the introduction and conclusion.

For generous support we thank the Institute for European Studies; the Institute for Slavic, East European, and Eurasian Studies; and the Center for Studies in Higher Education, all at the University of California at Berkeley; as well as the German Academic Exchange Service (DAAD) in New York. Michael Grüttner would also like to thank the Deutsche Forschungsgemeinschaft for their generous support of his research. Many persons have contributed to the completion of this project, but we would like to thank especially Britta Baron, Gerald D. Feldman, Anne J. Maclachan, Andrej Milivojevic, and Barbara Motyka.

Our meeting in 2000 was enriched by the participation of Jan Havránek and Reggie Zelnik, professors of history in Prague and Berkeley, who did not live to see this final outcome. In the 1960s both men took active roles in defending universities from threats to academic freedom: Jan in the Prague Spring, Reggie in the Free Speech Movement. Both risked their careers. In 1969 Jan was denied professorship. That same year the Regents of the University of California attempted to overturn the decision of the University of California at Berkeley and deny Reggie tenure. Because of the vigorous protest of the Berkeley chancellor they failed. The outer circumstances of their struggles differed, but both men were joined by uncompromising devotion to free inquiry. This book is dedicated to them.

John Connelly
Michael Grüttner

ABBREVIATIONS

AAUP	American Association of University Professors
ACNP	Asociación Católica Nacional de Propagandistas (National Catholic Association of Propagandists)
ANSt	Working Community of National Socialist Women Students
CCP	Chinese Communist Party
CPSU	Communist Party of the Soviet Union
CSIC	Consejo Superior de Investigaciones Científicas (Higher Council of Scientific Research)
DDP	German Democratic Party
DNVP	German National People's Party
DVP	German People's Party
DVV	German Education Administration in Berlin
FE de las JONS	Falange Española de las Juntas de Ofensiva Nacional-Sindicalista (Spanish Falange of National Syndicalist Shock Groups)
FNUF	National Federation of Fascist Universitarians
FUCI	University Federation of Italian Catholics
FUDE	Federación Universitaria Democrática de Estudiantes (Democratic University Student Federation)
FUE	Federación Universitaria Escolar (University Student Federation)
Glavprofobr	Main Committee on Professional Education
GMD	Guomindang
GUF	Fascist University Groups
JAE	Junta de Ampliación de Estudios e Investigaciones Científicas (Board for the Promotion of Scientific Study and Research)
KOR	Commitee for the Protection of Workers
KPD	German Communist Party
KSČ	Communist Party of Czechoslovakia
LOU	Law of the Organization of Universities (Spain)
MCP	Ministry of Popular Culture
Narkompros	Commissariat of Enlightenment
NEP	New Economic Policy
NSDAP	National Socialist German Workers Party
NSDDB	National Socialist German League of Lecturers
NSDStB	National Socialist German Student League
PNF	Fascist National Party
PZPR	Polish United Workers' Party
rabfaki	workers' faculties (Russia)
REM	Reich Ministry of Education (Germany)
SDE	Sindicatos Democráticos de Estudiantes (Democratic Student Unions)

SED	Socialist Unity Party of Germany
SEPES	Servicio Español del Profesorado de Enseñanza Superior (Spanish Association of Professors of Higher Education)
SEU	Sindicato Español Universitario (Spanish University Union)
SMAD	Soviet Military Administration in Germany
SVS	Students' Central Organization (Czechoslovakia)
TEU	Teatro Español Universitario (Spanish University Theater)
TseKUBU	Central Commission for Improving the Life of Scholars
Vesenkha	All-Union Council of the National Economy
VTUZy	higher technical institutes (Soviet Union)
ZLP	Union of Polish Writers
ZMP	Union of Polish Youth
ZMS	Union of Socialist Youth (Poland)

Introduction

JOHN CONNELLY

In the twentieth century both "dictatorship" and "university" acquired dimensions that had previously been unthinkable. In the turmoil following World War I, dictatorships emerged that marshaled resources, mass movements, and ideologies that had antecedents but no precedents. Because of the theoretically unlimited resolve of these new regimes to establish controls over societal life, some of them were described as totalitarian.[1] At the same time, the functions of universities expanded far beyond the "idea" of the university known in John Henry Newman's time.[2] Whether state-run or private, universities were called upon to serve "public" interests, and therefore shifted from elite to mass institutions, with heavy emphases on teaching. In the United States, where these trends have gone furthest, fourteen hundred institutions of higher education are devoted entirely to teaching students majoring in everything from classics (ever fewer) to business administration (ever more). Though room remains for disinterested research, it is dwarfed by capacities serving the military industrial complex, and many

---

1. On the rise of such states, see Abbott Gleason, *Totalitarianism: The Inner History of the Cold War* (New York: Oxford University Press, 1995), and Mark Mazower, *Dark Continent: Europe's Twentieth Century* (New York: Vintage Books, 2000).

2. On the expansion of the university, see the essays in Sheldon Rothblatt and Björn Wittrock, eds., *The European and American University Since 1800: Historical and Sociological Essays* (Cambridge: Cambridge University Press, 1993); Clark Kerr, *The Great Transformation in Higher Education* (Albany: State University of New York Press, 1991); and Steven Muller, ed., *Universities in the Twenty-First Century* (Providence, R.I.: Berghahn, 1996).

bemoan the gradual severing of teaching from research—an ideal of the "Humboldtian" university.[3]

What seems to make the juxtaposition of dictatorship and university interesting is academic freedom: dictatorships destroy it, universities need it. This is a proposition that most students of politics would readily accept.[4] Students of higher education quickly recognize a problem, however: academic freedom has no generally accepted meaning. Is it freedom of the academy from outside interference—for example, from the state—or freedom of the individual academic from outside interference—for example, from the academy itself? Does it protect freedom of inquiry on all subjects, or only on the specialty of the scholar? Does it embrace the entire university community, or only professors? And what happens when one goes beyond the Anglo-Saxon world? Within their own contexts, French tend to say "liberté des enseignements" or "liberté de recherche"[5] and Germans "Freiheit der Wissenschaft" when they mean something like "academic freedom." But universities are not the sole preserves of instruction, research, or science. Teaching takes place at a range of institutions with little to no interest in free inquiry, and there are scientists and scientific research at workplaces carefully controlled by the state—such as defense laboratories.[6] Taken singularly, teaching and science do not touch the university mission that academic freedom supposedly safeguards. They do not involve the "idea" of the university.

But the issue of linguistic equivalency may be deceptive. Regardless of whether the German language has a precise counterpart for "academic freedom" (which is translated as "akademische Freiheit"),[7] it is to

---

3. On the fate of Wilhelm von Humboldt's ideas on the university, see Mitchell G. Ash, ed., *German Universities Past and Future: Crisis or Renewal* (Providence, R.I.: Berghahn, 1997).

4. For example, Columbia University political philosopher Robert M. MacIver wrote in 1955 that the Communist Party "wherever it has gained control, has totally suppressed academic freedom and the right of free inquiry." *Academic Freedom in Our Time* (New York: Gordian Press, 1967), 199–200.

5. The term "liberté académique" is also used, but in France primarily to denote the freedom of the Academy. In Belgium, Switzerland, and Canada it functions more often as a counterpart to the English "academic freedom." I thank Richard Wagner for this information.

6. John Turner, "The Price of Freedom," in *Academic Freedom and Responsibility*, ed. Malcolm Tight (Milton Keynes: Open University Press, 1988), 107.

7. Germans have been saying "akademische Freiheiten" (usually the plural) since the nineteenth century, but mostly to refer to the famous as well as notorious student freedoms: the freedom to spend one's time studying or doing other things of one's choosing—like drinking or dueling—the freedom to select seminars of one's preference, the freedom to choose when one wanted to be examined and by whom, and so on.

German culture that America owes its idea and practice of academic freedom. The 1915 founding statements of the American Association of University Professors (AAUP) on academic freedom cite the German notion of *Lehrfreiheit* (freedom of teaching), whose value was recognized by the thousands of Americans who had studied in Germany in the late nineteenth century.[8] But this idea took new form on American soil. The freedom of professors to pursue scholarship and teaching without external interventions was recognized in both Germany and the United States; yet in the United States scholars also asserted rights to extramural utterance, and it was here that the major contests with "society" — in the form of university trustees — occurred. In Germany, university teachers did not claim this right.[9] But unlike their American counterparts, German universities also explicitly recognized the sovereign independence of students, something called *Lernfreiheit* (freedom of learning). American universities, with their frequent examinations and rigid degree requirements, have long impressed observers from Central Europe as being more like secondary schools (*verschult*).

The point is that academic freedom varies according to the place of higher education in civil society. German universities have been and remain state institutions, for which ministers of education bear ultimate responsibility. The campus is the preserve of the professors, however: through their institutions of self-governance, they run the university. In Wilhelmine Germany universities were protected islands in an otherwise highly regimented society.[10] In the United States, by contrast, universities operate under boards of trustees. Professors, therefore, do not owe their academic freedom to the state, but rather gained it through political agitation and legal battles with trustees and administrators. Because trustees threatened them with dismissal, the professors' defense of academic freedom was couched in terms focused on tenure of employment. As Walter Metzger wrote in 1969, the "key to crime prevention lay in the adoption

---

8. Richard Hofstadter and Walter P. Metzger, *The Development of Academic Freedom in the United States* (New York: Columbia University Press, 1955), 386–87; Robert K. Poch, *Acdemic Freedom in American Higher Education: Rights, Responsibilities, and Limitations*, ASHE-ERIC Higher Education Report No. 4 (Washington, D.C.: The George Washington University School of Education and Human Development, 1993), 6–7.

9. Charles E. Curran, *Catholic Higher Education, Theology, and Academic Freedom* (Notre Dame: University of Notre Dame Press, 1990), 11.

10. For example the Prussian constitution of 1850 guaranteed that "science and its teaching shall be free." Cited in Louis Joughin, *Academic Freedom and Tenure: A Handbook of the American Association of University Professors* (Madison: University of Wisconsin Press, 1967), 179.

of regulations that would heighten the security of the office-holder and temper the arbitrariness of the 'boss.'"[11] Its principal safeguards—tenure, peer review, and academic due process—were enshrined in the AAUP's 1915 founding statements. This organization reflected and furthered the American approach: nowhere else did a lobbying group have the specific purpose of safeguarding academic freedom.

Since 1915, dismissals of faculty for their political opinions have become exceptional in the United States. Despite witch hunts that all but silenced the left in the McCarthy era, relatively few tenured professors lost their jobs, and in subsequent years professors have defended tenure despite persistent threats.[12] For example, in 1967 a resolution to the regents of the University of Wisconsin to dismiss faculty for boycotting classes after a police incursion on campus (in the wake of an antiwar rally) failed by a vote of 5 to 4.[13] Confessional colleges, a comparatively large part of U.S. higher education, still presume to restrict what their professors may teach,[14] but here too dismissals of tenured faculty are rare. The one case in Catholic higher education occurred in the late 1980s, when the Congregation of the Doctrine of the Faith determined

---

11. "Academic Freedom in Delocalized Academic Institutions," in *Dimensions of Academic Freedom*, ed. W. P. Metzger et al. (Urbana: University of Illinois Press, 1969), 3.

12. In 1949 three tenured professors (Herbert Phillips, Joseph Butterworth, and Ralph Gundlach) at the University of Washington were fired for alleged membership in the Communist Party. http://www.washington.edu/alumni/columns/dec97/red1.html. In August 1950, thirty-one tenured University of California faculty were fired for not signing an oath that they were not members of the Communist Party. In October 1952 the California State Supreme Court ordered that they be reinstated; two years later sixteen sued successfully for back pay. http://sunsite.berkeley.edu/uchistory/archives_exhibits/loyaltyoath/ timelinesummary.html. For other cases of dismissals of tenured faculty, see Ellen Schrecker, *No Ivory Tower: McCarthyism and the Universities* (New York: Oxford University Press, 1986).

13. Arthur Debardeleben, "The University's External Constituency," in Metzger et al., *Dimensions of Academic Freedom*, 71.

14. For example, the Lutheran Church (Missouri Synod) has an official statement titled "Limitations on Academic Freedom," and the Mormon Church requires that professors at Brigham Young University do not contradict church teaching. According to its mission statement, "All students at BYU should be taught the truths of the gospel of Jesus Christ. . . . BYU's faculty, staff, students, and administrators should be anxious to make their service and scholarship available to The Church of Jesus Christ of Latter-day Saints in furthering its work worldwide." http://unicomm.byu.edu/about/mission. *Ex Corde Ecclesiae*, the apostolic constitution on Catholic universities issued by Pope John Paul II in 1990, defends institutional autonomy and academic freedom, but also (n. 27) requires adherence to the teaching authority of the church in matters of faith and morals. Academic freedom is limited by the "confines of the truth and the common good" (n. 29). Charles Curran, "Church, Authority, Law: Personal Reflections," in *Issues in Academic Freedom*, ed. George Worgul (Pittsburgh: Duquesne University Press, 1992), 107–8.

that Charles E. Curran, tenured at the Catholic University of America, was "neither suitable nor eligible to be a professor of Catholic theology." Two years later he lost his position.[15]

If dismissals of tenured professors are marginal, other threats remain, directed in particular against those who do not enjoy security of employment. In the 1950s, of all the junior professors who refused to cooperate with committees investigating Communism on campus, only one managed to keep his job.[16] In recent years nontenured faculty and students have come under pressures of speech codes. Almost all U.S. colleges and universities have "verbal behavior" provisions in their codes, but their wording tends to be vague and flexible. To cite just two cases from the top of the alphabet: at Bowdoin College students can be held liable for "harassment" for telling jokes and stories "experienced by others as harassing," and at Brown University, students can be disciplined for "verbal behavior" that causes "feelings of impotence," "anger," or "disenfranchisement," whether "intentional or unintentional."[17]

As a result of these and other codes, dozens of students and faculty have been censured, suspended, and encouraged to undergo reeducation for supposedly creating a "hostile environment" for women and minorities. In the view of critics, the codes themselves have engendered a "totalitarian atmosphere" on U.S. campuses. Most controversial was a case at the University of Pennsylvania in 1993, in which a white student faced disciplinary procedures for calling late-night revelers who were disturbing his work "water buffalo." They were black.[18] But there are numerous other instances. In 1992, student protesters ransacked the premises of the student newspaper at the University of Massachusetts. It was accused of racism for having referred to "riots" in Los Angeles after the acquittal of the police officers who had beaten Rodney King. Refused protection by university authorities, the editors tried to publish from a secret location, but successive editions of the newspaper were stolen and destroyed. In the end, the newspaper's

---

15. It was made possible by the unique relation between the Catholic University of America and the Vatican. Curran, *Catholic Higher Education*; Richard P. McBrien, "Academic Freedom and the Catholic Theologian," in Worgul, *Issues in Academic Freedom*, 140–41.

16. Ellen Schrecker, "Political Tests for Professors: Academic Freedom During the McCarthy Years." http://sunsite.berkeley.edu/uchistory/archives_exhibits/loyaltyoath/ symposium/schrecker.html.

17. Alan Kors and Harvey Silverglate, *The Shadow University: The Betrayal of Liberty on America's Campuses* (New York: HarperCollins, 1999), 147.

18. Ibid., 12ff. In the end the university lost this case in court.

editors surrendered, and agreed to a new editorial structure with special editors and sections for "historically oppressed" minorities on campus.[19]

The question is how to ground intellectually and juridically the academic freedom threatened by such practices. Alan Kors and Harvey Silverglate argue that speech codes infringe upon rights protected under the First Amendment, and they cite court decisions protecting academic freedom as derivative of these rights. In 1967 the Supreme Court wrote that the Constitution did not "tolerate laws that cast a pall of orthodoxy over the classroom," which should remain a "marketplace of ideas."[20] In recent years courts have struck down speech codes at the University of Michigan and the University of Wisconsin precisely because they violate constitutional rights.

Legal scholar Robert Post takes a different approach: for him academic freedom is not an individual right. "Insofar as freedom of extramural expression is a right that should theoretically accrue to all faculty," he writes, "it cannot be justified by the general civil liberties guaranteed by the First Amendment or by the civil law generally."[21] For Post, "the function of academic freedom is not to liberate individual professors from all forms of institutional regulation, but instead to ensure that faculty within the university are free to engage in professionally competent forms of inquiry and teaching, which are necessary for the realization of the social purposes of the university." Academic freedom is a "professional freedom."[22] Academics require it because of their "primary responsibility . . . to the public itself." Universities are not a "private proprietorship" but rather a "public trust."[23] The German, more specifically Humboldtian, origins of such thoughts tend to be neglected in the American context.

---

19. In 1994 the university chancellor wrote that seizure of the newspapers could hardly be called "theft because the paper is distributed to the public free of charge." The following year he proposed a new harassment code proscribing not only epithets and slurs, but also "negative stereotyping." Anthony Lewis of the *New York Times* predicted the new guidelines would "create a totalitarian atmosphere" on campus and asked, "Do the drafters have no knowledge of history? No understanding that freedom requires 'freedom for the thought that we hate'?" Ibid., 150–51.

20. Ibid., 57.

21. Robert Post, "The Structure of Academic Freedom," in *Academic Freedom After September 11*, ed. Beshara Doumani (New York: Zone Books, 2005).

22. Ibid. In Post's view, this professional understanding of academic freedom was already enshrined in the classic statement of 1915.

23. Ibid. From the 1915 Declaration, printed in AAUP *Policy Documents* (2001), 294, in Post, "Structure of Academic Freedom": "In this sense academic freedom does not now, nor has it ever, protected the autonomy of professors autonomously to pursue their own individual work, free from university restraints. Instead academic freedom is designed to create the liberty

Beyond dismissals of faculty and students, there are deeper, structural challenges to freedom in American academia. In a 1969 essay Metzger cautioned against global processes beyond academic control. The major culprit was the federal government, which began subcontracting research work to universities after World War II, and by 1969 was funding up to three-quarters of all academic research. As a consequence, most of the research at universities served the interests of agencies outside academia.[24] Most objectionable in Metzger's eyes was military research, which is carried out in secret and encourages deceit. Such "intrusion of lock-and-key research into an ostensibly open enterprise" injures "academic integrity."[25] To his own dismay, Metzger failed to formulate a general theory that would intellectually ground the university's defense against the perversions caused by such injuries to academic freedom. Existing regulations protected the academic rights of individuals, but not of institutions.

Government control, reeducation, infringements on speech, obligations to the public—these all sound familiar to students of dictatorship. And so the question arises: are universities under democracies really so different from universities under dictatorships? Regardless of regime, politics in modern settings is invasive, and that means that academic freedom is never absolute. Following sociologist Zygmunt Bauman, some historians conceptualize the modern state as a "gardening state," which, regardless of constitutional form, prunes unwanted growth in civil society with little moral scruple.[26] Arguably, the intrusiveness of the modern state has shaped and necessitated academic freedom: the premodern state, recognizing universities as legally independent corporations, did not raise

---

necessary to facilitate the advancement of knowledge, understood as the unimpeded application of professional norms of inquiry." The Declaration does not understand academic freedom as "absolute freedom of utterance of the individual scholar, but the absolute freedom of thought, of inquiry, of discussion and of teaching, of the academic profession." Academics have the right of self-regulation because of their "privilege of expertise," and in order to protect the "mission of the university to advance knowledge," which would be "impaired if research were subject to the application of standards other than those of professional scholarship." By implication, then, academics must recognize the validity of corporate judgments of the professoriate: they have "no right of immunity from such judgments." There is no freedom against the academic community.

24. "Academic Freedom in Delocalized Academic Institutions," 23.

25. Ibid., 28. Other cases of federal interference that concerned Metzger included attempts by the Department of State to gain appointment for its own employees at universities, "the better to defend our foreign policy," or the decision of the Selective Service Administration to defer men who achieved a certain grade or higher.

26. See Zygmunt Bauman, *Modernity and the Holocaust* (Ithaca: Cornell University Press, 1989).

concerns about the freedom of academics. Academic freedom is thus a quintessentially modern concept: both defense of it and challenges to it issue from modern regimes. Yet university policies do reveal a difference between democracies and dictatorships: the two sorts of regime come at questions of academic freedom from opposite ends of the spectrum. Liberal democratic regimes honor this principle in all but exceptional circumstances; modern dictatorships honor it only in exceptional circumstances.

In the United States the debate over whether academic speech is shielded by some transcendent public duty or by First Amendment rights seems to have strengthened each side of the question: they are not mutually exclusive, but rather mutually reinforcing. Those who stress one do not rule out the other. A cultural and legal context has emerged in which university communities are deeply sensitive and take quick recourse to institutional safeguards when they feel threatened. The general attitude has been described well by Columbia University president Lee C. Bollinger, who acknowledged in the wake of controversies over speech codes that tolerance is never absolute; every institutional setting ultimately requires and enforces some commitment to belief, a point recognized even by such skeptics as John Stuart Mill, Isaiah Berlin, and Oliver Wendel Holmes. Nevertheless, the task of the university is more the "correction of the impulse to intolerance than the need for commitment to belief . . . the defining characteristic of the university ought to be the extraordinary degree to which it is open to ideas."[27]

There is also a practical problem for those who would restrict academics' extramural utterances. Who is to say when controversial speech is based on professional competence, and when not? Post sketches the dilemma:

> It is plain that universities would be placed in an extremely awkward position were they to refuse to accept responsibility for publication of faculty that relate to professional competence, but accept such responsibility for extramural expression that does not relate to professional competence. In such circumstances universities would virtually invite offended constituencies to argue that faculty publications should be censored because they are insufficiently related to scholarly expertise as to merit the protec-

---

27. Lee C. Bollinger, "The Open-Minded Soldier and the University," in *Unfettered Expression: Freedom in American Intellectual Life*, ed. Peggie J. Hollingsworth (Ann Arbor: University of Michigan Press, 2000), 39–40, 44–45.

tion of freedom of research. Universities would thus strengthen their ability to protect freedom of research if they were categorically to refuse to accept responsibility for the publications of their faculty, regardless of the precise connection between such publications and the academic expertise for which the faculty have been hired or trained.

He echoes Harvard president Abbott Lawrence Lowell, who wrote in his report for the 1916–17 academic year:

> If a university or college censors what its professors may say, if it restrains them from uttering something that it does not approve, it thereby assumes responsibility for that which it permits them to say. This is logical and inevitable, but it is a responsibility which an institution of learning would be very unwise in assuming.... If a university is right in restraining its professors, it has a duty to do so, and it is responsible for whatever it permits. There is no middle ground. Either the university assumes full responsibility for permitting its professors to express certain opinions in public, or it assumes no responsibility whatever, and leaves them to be dealt with like other citizens by the public authorities according to the laws of the land.[28]

Though universities in Communist and fascist states also claimed to be fulfilling a duty to the public—referred to alternately as people, state, nation, or race—they came to radically different views on academic freedom. They branded it a fiction and spoke of "so-called freedom of scholarship."[29] They argued that academic freedom had a particular political or class content. After the Nazi seizure of power, as we learn from Michael Grüttner, Hitler's lawyer Hans Frank rejected Theodor Mommsen's idea that science should be "without precondition," asserting

---

28. Henry Aaron Yeomans, *Abbott Lawrence Lowell, 1856–1943* (Cambridge: Harvard University Press, 1948), 311–12, cited in Post, "Structure of Academic Freedom."

29. See, for example, correspondence of the department of science of the Central Committee of the Polish Communist Party (PZPR) of 15 December 1950 on awards for top scientists, in Archiwum Akt Nowych (Warsaw) KC PZPR 237/XVI/13 k. 27–31; or the letter from the Party Organization of the Socialist Unity Party of Germany (SED) to the Central Committee of 3 April 1952, about the unfortunate need to discuss "academic freedoms" with members of the university community, in Sächsisches Staatsarchiv (Leipzig), IV/4.14/64.

instead that it "must of necessity be in service to National Socialism." Following their own seizure of power in 1948, Communists in the Czech city of Brno maintained that professors had been discharged for "abusing academic freedom in order to incite students to act against the law."[30] In effect, professors had violated the freedom of the working class. Higher education always served the interests of the governing classes, and since the state is an instrument of these classes, universities do—and therefore should—serve the state.[31] This view had originated among Soviet functionaries and was faithfully transplanted. As Douglas Stiffler describes the Chinese case, the Soviet model in higher education involved removing politically offensive teachings and teachers, outright service to the cause of economic growth, placing important decisions on higher education in the hands of state functionaries, promoting the new classes—workers and peasants—in students admissions and faculty hiring, and establishing new courses in the social sciences for all students.[32]

These considerations lead to deeper questions about the "idea of the university." Did Communist reforms—which privileged technical education, punished free speech, and corroded academic autonomy—destroy the university? On the face of it, they did not. As we see in Michael David-Fox's contribution, Bolsheviks of the early 1930s vilified universities as "feudal relics" and seemed ready to cast them onto the dust heap of history. But at the crucial moment they backed off, and universities survived, despite radical transformations. Chinese and other Communists followed the Bolshevik cultural revolutionaries in reforming, not demolishing, universities. The question was how far reforms would go.

As we see in each of the chapters in this book, universities under duress were able to protect some of their traditional freedoms, more for example in the hard than in the social sciences, more in research than in teaching,

---

30. Letter of Seifert to Ministry of Education, 12 March 1948, in Státní Ústřední Archív (Prague) MŠK, č.k. 628, sign. 5Ia.

31. There was of course some recent historical experience to validate this view. Thomas Ellwein writes of universities in nineteenth-century Germany: "They took for granted a consensus with society. They did not want to be, and could not be, a critical voice; rather they wanted to take the leading role in bourgeois society." Thomas Ellwein, *Die deutsche Universität: Vom Mittelalter bis zur Gegenwart* (Königstein: Athenäum, 1985), 125.

32. This catalog comes very close to that recognized as a Soviet model by East European communists; see J. Connelly, "The Sovietization of Higher Education in the Czech Lands, East Germany, and Poland during the Stalinist Period, 1948–1954," in *Academia in Upheaval: The Origins and Demise of the Communist Academic Regime*, ed. György Péteri and Michael David-Fox (Westport, Conn.: Greenwood Press; London: Bergin & Garvey, 2000).

more in traditional institutions than in the newly founded. If in liberal regimes academic freedom is never completely protected, in the dictatorial states of the twentieth century it was never completely eroded. Can we speak of a core, of things so essential to a university that they became visible only under the pressures of states wielding unprecedented powers?

That conclusion might be drawn from the essays of Michael David-Fox on the Soviet Union and of György Péteri on Hungary. At the height of the assault on universities in 1932, professors at Leningrad State University were "most persistent in defending a component of advanced research in official definitions of the university's functions." Yet they did not attempt to "defend the research university on philosophical grounds." They argued instead in terms of "rational production of cadres, maintaining standards, and serving the industrialization drive more effectively." The issue was not freedom but rather function and performance. Péteri calls these professional standards. At the height of cultural revolution in Stalinist Hungary, Péteri notes that even the most ideologically correct faculties—those teaching Marxist-Leninist political economy—"could not remain totally unaffected by the norms and standards set by the economics profession in the country."

We seem confronted with an image of totalitarian failure, of desperate attempts to extinguish the flame of inquiry, which nevertheless continued to smolder in institutions of higher education, ready to reignite under proper circumstances. In Hungary, these reemerged after 1956, and as Péteri notes, Hungarian social sciences reattained international prominence in the relative openness of that time. In a sense, the traditional university returned to the buildings from which it had been banished, and with its regenerative capacities it grew over and limited the damage of ideology. Perhaps one can measure the degree of erosion of the university by the time it takes to recover after assault. In the early 1990s, an impatient West German establishment did not wait for native forces to reassert the university in the former German Democratic Republic, but instead hastily moved in with its own underemployed cadres. Local historians and social scientists were purged before they could recreate full academic life. But this is the exception: elsewhere, including the part of former Nazi Germany that became West Germany, academia was permitted to return to a less politicized identity on its own.

But should one conclude that universities are indestructible? Ralph Jessen cautions that academic work does not survive without a modicum of independence and willingness to take initiative. And what about the

Humboldtian notion that universities comprise teaching and research? Does one still have a university when the former has fully eclipsed the latter? Or where research is free, but teaching is not? Jessen notes that the East German regime compensated for the "politicization of teaching by granting freedom to research." And scholars colluded: the Communists may have opposed academic freedom but they were arguably pro-science. So were the Nazis: they made research possible in the biological sciences that was forbidden under liberal regimes.[33] Or what if one removes from the university most social science and humanities faculties and permits only one methodology in those that remain? This is what happened in China, the Soviet Union, and much of Eastern Europe. In Fascist Italy the opposite happened: technical and scientific disciplines were separated from universities, and separate higher schools were created to train Italians in pharmacology, architecture, and engineering. Ruth Ben-Ghiat calls this process "deprofessionalization." If the Italian state was eviscerating professionalism, it was destroying precisely that quality which had saved universities from ruin in Stalinist Hungary. This destruction went hand in hand with a devaluation of scientific and technical disciplines. How many faculties or degree programs can a university sacrifice before it becomes something else, or at best a university in name only?

Over these questions hovers a larger one, whether there is a generally valid understanding of the university. Does it not, like the idea of academic freedom, differ according to context? Péteri warns against "essentializing" the university, preferring to view it as something "socially embedded" that changes according to time and place; after Pierre Bourdieu he imagines it as a "dynamic social field which is inhabited by various agents of academic and science-political activities and where various ('orthodox' and 'heterodox') positions as to the idea of the university articulate themselves." The only thing eternal and universal about the university is the "never-ceasing contestation about what the 'idea of the university' should be."

The essays that follow do not pretend to give final answers to these questions. But by providing a comparative framework they permit readers to consider what happens to institutions of free inquiry that come under extreme political pressure. The essays were originally written for a conference that took place in Berkeley in May 2000, and describe the range of options that dictatorships pursued in order to make universities useful, but also a range of responses adopted by universities: from opposition and

---

33. I thank Michael Grüttner for making this point.

evasion to accommodation and active collaboration. For the sake of comparability, authors were encouraged to address the following groups of questions:

1. What role did universities play in the foundation period of the dictatorship. Were they defenders of autonomy, or pioneers of dictatorship? Or both? In some cases, academics began to doubt the idea of the university. Why? To what extent and why did they collude in the destruction of academic freedom?
2. To what extent did the dictatorship cause a personal and structural rupture with university tradition?
3. What influence did the political system have on the content of teaching and research? Did traditional ideals of autonomy or unity of teaching and research seem outmoded, a dangerous illusion? Did the regime recognize limits to intervention?
4. To what extent did dictatorships succeed in creating academic elites that identified with the interests of the regime? In some cases we see production of eminently loyal students, for example in the GDR, but in others, such as Hungary or Poland, even promises of massive upward social mobility failed to secure political loyalty. How can we account for the differences?
5. Were universities in the long run more a support for or a threat to the dictatorship? More aids in helping discipline society, or places that generated alternative visions?

All of these questions boil down to the issue of self-defense: what resources did universities possess to ward off incursions of the state? The answers are partly moral, involving perceptions of legitimacy. In the postwar period, professors in Hungary or East Germany appeared deeply compromised through collaboration with the previous regime, and could not make plausible cases for freedom and autonomy. They faced legacies of their own creation. In other cases, like China, the strength of a different moral imperative—nationalism—tended to overwhelm attempts by academics to band together in common defense. Finally there were cases of overwhelming political will on the part of the rising hegemon, and its power to corrupt (as in Italy) or destroy (as in Spain). Explanations for divergence divide between the role of the university in civil society and the contours of ideology. Neither was supreme; in no case do we see absolute power either of society or of idea, but rather a subtle interplay of both.

1

Russian Universities Across the 1917 Divide

MICHAEL DAVID-FOX

Most any visitor to Moscow will at some point view the monument to Soviet "university science" represented by the gargantuan, "wedding-cake" Stalinist Gothic building of Moscow State University. From its commanding perch atop the Lenin (now Sparrow) Hills, it is the grandest of the seven Stalin-era skyscrapers that even now define the capital's skyline. The picture of the university as a central, unambiguously celebrated facet of the Soviet dictatorial order, which one might deduce from the architectural symbolism of this postwar monumentalism, is in several ways misleading. For one thing, when the initial idea was raised for a massive new university building—proposed as part of the reconstruction of the city of Moscow as the showcase capital of socialism as early as 1931–32—the university's new home was explicitly intended as a grand facade, one that would also serve the function of impressing foreign dignitaries, who would judge the state of all Soviet universities from their Moscow visits.[1]

---

1. See Commissar of Enlightenment Andrei Sergeevich Bubnov's 1932 letter to the Council of People's Commissars outlining the proposal for the construction of a new Moscow University, in Gosudarstvennyi arkhiv Rossiiskoi Federatsii (State Archive of the Russian Federation, hereafter GARF) f. A-2307, op. 17, ed. khr. 169, l. 21–26. His initiative can be better understood in light of the Central Committee's 25 August 1931 resolution requiring the Commissariat of Enlightenment to create "model" (*obratsovye*) elementary schools. This was a measure clearly connected to the much broader repudiation of a range of iconoclastic tendencies in education and elsewhere during the "Great Break" (1928–31) period that this chapter will discuss in relation to the break-up of universities into specialized institutes. On model schools and the

Starting at the end of the 1930s, and especially in the postwar era, Soviet universities did come to assume the top place in a new, strict hierarchy specifically within the Soviet education establishment. However, while a good deal of research continued, especially at Moscow State, Soviet universities all remained very much downgraded into subordinated training institutions in comparison either to the research universities of the West or the thriving if persistently troubled universities of late imperial Russia. Even the showcase Moscow State University, which by the postwar era had become the unambiguously "central" university in the Soviet Union, could hardly compete with the bolshevized Academy of Sciences, the vast "empire of knowledge" in advanced research.[2] Finally, the grand plans for Moscow came only as part of a general renovation of universities in 1932 and after, a sharp change of course which followed right on the heels of a little-known episode of assault on universities as "feudal relics" that reached its apex in 1930. Although few in Russia or even scholars in the field of Russian history are aware of it today, universities in the USSR, some of which "withered away" completely as their departments were broken up into new specialized institutes under the aegis of state commissariats, were brought to the brink of extinction in the course of Stalin's "second revolution."[3]

This chapter seeks to explain in several contexts this startling reversal in the Soviet approach to universities before, during, and after Stalin's "Great Break" of 1928–31. The first will be a long-term if necessarily condensed consideration of the legacy of the Russian universities under

---

dominance of one showcase institution among them, see Larry E. Holmes, *Stalin's School: Moscow's Model School No. 25, 1931–1937* (Pittsburgh: University of Pittsburgh Press, 1999). On the cultural-ideological shifts from the Great Break to the later 1930s, see Katerina Clark, *Petersburg, Crucible of Cultural Revolution* (Cambridge: Harvard University Press, 1995). Central, dominant, showcase institutions embodied the values of gigantism and larger-than-life heroism that came to the forefront in Stalinist ideology after 1931–32, superseding the attacks on "old" institutions and groups connected to the class-war, iconoclastic, and centrifugal cultural tendencies that were at the forefront during the Great Break.

2. The Soviet-type system of higher learning made sharp distinctions between teaching and research, which was dominated by the academy and the "branch sector" of applied research institutes attached to industrial commissariats. The reference is to Alexander Vucinich, *Empire of Knowledge: The Academy of Sciences of the USSR (1917–1970)* (Berkeley and Los Angeles: University of California Press, 1984).

3. Both in Russia and the West the state of research on universities before 1917 remains far more advanced, and to this day Chanbarisov's Soviet-era study (cited in full in note 20) remains the only significant work on the making of the Soviet university system—despite the rise of the university sector after 1991 and a spate of new works on the contemporary status of Russian universities in the 1990s and 2000s.

tsarism, particularly since the Great Reforms of the mid-nineteenth century. An understanding of the late imperial period is crucial for appreciating the enduring conflicts, changing status, and fiercely fought autonomy movement of the Russian universities, all of which directly shaped their experience with successive revolutionary upheavals and their initial confrontation with Bolshevik state. This period of the most impressive flourishing of Russian universities never stabilized them or resolved their internal divisions, and it also witnessed the creation of revolutionary agendas toward higher learning that influenced the first fifteen years of the Soviet experience. The bulk of this chapter then attempts an interpretive analysis of the shifting place of universities in three successive and influential phases in the emergence of the Soviet cultural system in general and the universities in particular (1918–22, 1923–28, 1929–32).

My goal is to highlight those strains in Bolshevik thought and policy that most affected the development of Soviet universities during the volatile and formative interwar period. While there certainly was such a thing as Soviet university policy and at certain moments (such as during the imposition of the first Soviet university charter of 1922 and the decision to revive the universities in 1932) the universities were the object of focused consideration by the top political leadership, in general the forces shaping the place of the university under Soviet power were far broader than can be explicated by reference to university policy alone. They had to do most with the successive phases in the evolution of Soviet culture and the emergence of a broader academic regime, in which the fluctuating number of state universities within the higher education and research sectors was merely one, and at times almost peripheral part.[4]

In both Russia and the Soviet Union, unlike in many countries in the nineteenth and twentieth centuries, universities were never the dominant institutions of learning and research. In tsarist Russia, Peter the Great's Academy of Sciences was designated the "supreme" academic institution and predated the rise of the universities in the empire, which occurred largely in the nineteenth century; in revolutionary Russia, the same academy preserved its position through a compromise with the new regime in 1918 and, after violent and wrenching restructuring at the end of the 1920s, assumed a position of even greater centralized dominance at

---

4. See Michael David-Fox and György Péteri, "On the Origins and Demise of the Communist Academic Regime," in David-Fox and Péteri, *Academia in Upheaval*, 3–38 (cited in full in the introduction, note 32).

the apex of the research system. In addition, myriad specialized "scientific-research" and educational institutes and Communist Party institutions by the 1920s assumed the status of alternative and often new or "revolutionary" alternatives to "conventional" higher education. Thus the status of universities—embedded in higher education policy, competing agendas toward higher education, and ideology—assumes crucial importance in explaining the long-term changes leading up to the sudden attack on Soviet Russian universities in the late 1920s. Nonetheless, the kind of radical assault on universities followed by far-reaching reconstruction of them that took place largely in the Stalin era needs to be understood not only in terms of revolutionary and Soviet approaches toward "old" elites and institutions, but in terms of what since the mid-nineteenth century was a perennially troubled relationship between universities and the state. Indeed, the late imperial and early Soviet periods appear comparable in that they both witnessed rapid flux and unresolved internal and external tensions in the history of the Russian universities.

Late Imperial and Early Soviet Universities: A Comparative Overview

In the course of the imperial period, as in the Soviet, universities became noticeably more important to the regime even as it displayed highly ambivalent attitudes about their worth. Although in the Russian/Soviet field the dividing line 1917 has often been an insurmountable barrier for historians, the late imperial period between 1855 and 1917 is fruitfully viewed in tandem with the period between the October Revolution and the time the universities were finally reestablished as a permanent part of the Soviet order in the 1930s. For one thing, both the late imperial and the early Soviet period were times of rapid change and flux for the universities. The Great Reforms led to their rapid growth, diversification, and emergence as world-class institutions, but also to their persistent confrontation with the state, a confrontation that was repeated in less successful and more compressed form in the early postrevolutionary years. As this implies, in some ways the history of the universities after 1917 was an immediate, direct continuation of earlier, long-established patterns; in other ways, the late imperial movement for university autonomy as well as heavy state interference set the stage for the Soviet era either by setting precedents or shaping the agendas of the most important actors.

Second, in both late imperial and early Soviet Russia the universities were both heavily imprinted and shaped by the state and, at the same time, fit imperfectly into the existing, official social-political order. They did not completely fit into "official" Russia or the USSR, of course, in different ways: in the late nineteenth and early twentieth centuries, members of the intelligentsia, professions, and student movement formed part of an alternative, in part revolutionary, in part oppositionist, future-oriented movement; after 1917, universities were suddenly transformed into "old" institutions, partly yet damagingly associated with discredited liberal, moderate socialist, "anti-Soviet" or nonparty values. Despite these crucial distinctions, universities did not and could not become fully statist in important ways, either before 1917 or after, and this fact spurred on even more state intervention. In both periods, moreover, universities were affected by alternating phases in the state's approach. As the Russian university system grew in the late nineteenth century it was subject to bouts of reform and reaction, reform and counterreform. Similarly, in the first two decades after the revolution, universities were the objects of successive bouts of Bolshevik long-term transformation: first they struggled with the new regime, then they were almost destroyed, but finally they reemerged. In both periods and especially in the midst of revolution, in other words, the status and ultimate fate of the Russian universities was uncertain and not at all assured.

As my title implies, this consideration of universities and the Russian Revolution is pervaded with a sense of historical irony and paradox. The fate of the Russian universities was unusual not because it appears historically illogical or incomparable to the history of higher education in other countries, but because of the sharp reversals and ambiguous outcomes that this story reveals. The revolution offered no coherent answer to the question of what universities should be under socialism. In the early years, the Bolshevik revolutionaries, who frequently compared their own revolution with the French, often noted the destruction of the old universities and the birth of a new kind of system of education in the French Revolution, begun in the *cours révolutionnaires* and cemented in the *école polytechnique*.[5] The irony is not only that the old institutions in Russia ultimately did survive both the "revolution from below" in 1917

---

5. On the French case, see Janis Langins, *La république avait besoin de savants. Les débuts de l'école polytechnique: L'école centrale des travaux publiés et les cours révolutionnaires de l'an III* (Paris: Belin, 1987).

and Stalin's "revolution from above" of the late 1920s and early 1930s. It is that the Soviet order more generally, which became one of the most controlled, "planned," and statist systems of organized intellectual life ever developed, ultimately decided the shape of its universities based on a hodge-podge of radically different approaches in successive periods. Thus, in the case of the universities, as elsewhere, did the despised, "spontaneous" forces of history master even the willful "consciousness" of the Bolsheviks. An additional paradox was that those forces set in motion by the revolution and the development of the party-state did thoroughly subordinate and etatize the universities by the Stalin period; yet, all the same, "serving the state" meant different things in the different subperiods of Soviet history. It ranged from ideologizing the methodologies of science and learning, to making higher education highly "practical" in order to serve the industrialization drive, to pursuing significantly varied versions of making and enlightening the "new Soviet man." These were not always coherent or compatible forms of service.

An additional paradox, related to the first, is that Soviet communism adopted simultaneously scientistic/modernizing and antibourgeois/anti-Western features; the "unplanned" history of universities under it testifies to the volatility of that mix. Finally, the Bolsheviks, who talked about "contradictions" in bourgeois society, pursued a kind of socialism in which frequently warring repressive (negative) and transformative (constructive) agendas affected universities at once: sharp assaults on and wasteful repression of "bourgeois specialists" and lavish privileges for intelligentsia elites were both part of the Soviet phenomenon, as were extensive purges and the creation of the largest state-supported science system the world has known. The result of the first two decades after 1917 was indubitably a major rupture with university tradition, yet even here the situation is ironic. Despite all the twists and turns of a most thoroughgoing internal transformation, or in some cases in part because of them, various lines and elements of continuity are readily apparent before and after the most extreme period of assault.

Two Dictatorships, Three Revolutions, Three States

Crucial to understanding the postrevolutionary history of the universities is the legacy of their creation and development under tsarist autocracy and their evolution in the revolutions of 1905, February 1917, and October

1917. In Russia education and science were developed from the top down, from above and from abroad; the Imperial Russian Academy of Sciences was founded in 1724 as part of the Petrine Westernizing reforms and was stocked largely with German scholars; the first university, in Moscow, followed only in 1755.[6] More universities were founded during a later period of reform, under Alexander I in the early nineteenth century.[7] Like almost all the universities under dictatorships considered in this volume, Russian and Soviet universities were state institutions; but, arguably the role of the state here was greater than in other national contexts, as the very creation of the Russian university system in the nineteenth century was sponsored by an autocracy that was at once modernizing and repressive. Run strictly according to state charters, universities and the professions were therefore simultaneously developed and reined in. The universities played a large role in the growth of the intelligentsia and Russian national culture in the second quarter of the nineteenth century and experienced simultaneously a great expansion and intensive secret-police scrutiny under the "apogee of autocracy," Nicholas I, that in certain ways anticipated the Soviet combination of state sponsorship and repression.[8]

It was only the Great Reforms of Alexander II after 1855, however, that led to fundamental changes in the nature and status of the Russian universities. The reforms gave the universities a new charter granting significant internal autonomy and also led to the rapid growth of professional societies and public organizations of all types.[9] Some have viewed this in universalistic terms as a nascent civil society, but in the Russian context autonomy was never fully achieved, and state sponsorship and orientation toward the state remained crucial in the academic and other

---

6. Alexander Vucinich, *Science in Russian Culture*, vol. 1, *A History to 1860* (Stanford: Stanford University Press, 1963).

7. James T. Flynn, *The University Reform of Tsar Alexander I, 1802–1835* (Washington, D.C.: Catholic University of America Press, 1988). For a useful general history, see V. G. Kinelev, ed., *Vysshee obrazovanie v Rossii: Ocherki istorii do 1917 goda* (Moscow: NII VO, 1995).

8. Nicholas V. Riasanovsky, *A Parting of Ways: Government and the Educated Public in Russia, 1801–1855* (Oxford: Clarendon Press, 1976).

9. Here see especially Samuel D. Kassow, "The University Statute of 1863: A Reconsideration," in *Russia's Great Reforms, 1855–1881*, ed. Ben Eklof, John Bushnell, and Larisa Zakharova (Bloomington: Indiana University Press, 1994), 247–63. See also R. G. Eimontova, *Russkie universitety na putiakh reformy: 60-ye gody XIX veka* (Moscow: Nauka, 1993). On the broader situation, see especially Edith Clowes, Samuel Kassow, and James West, eds., *Between Tsar and People: Educated Society and the Quest for Public Identity in Late Imperial Russia* (Princeton: Princeton University Press, 1991).

professions.¹⁰ The counterreforms of Alexander III and the attempts to restrict university autonomy were only partially successful and could in no way resurrect a status quo ante. However, the struggle for institutional autonomy that ensued and lasted down until 1917 set the stage for early Soviet developments. By the period after the first failed revolution of 1905 it had led to the creation of the first fully private institutions in Russia, the "people's universities," which quite typically represented intelligentsia "enlightenment" initiatives and a coalition of the left. It also led to the famous standoff in 1911 between the Moscow University professoriate and minister of education L. A. Kasso, in which the cream of the academic intelligentsia resigned, many switching over the Shaniavskii People's University. When the universities were again subordinated to the state in the first Soviet-era charter of 1922, the rector of Moscow University likened the Bolshevik commissars of enlightenment, Anatolii Lunacharskii and Mikhail Pokrovskii, to the reactionary tsarist ministers Konstantin Pobedenotsev and Kasso.¹¹

In late imperial Russia the universities flourished as research centers; taken together they certainly began to rival the Academy of Sciences. Yet for all their growth and struggle for autonomy they were highly fragmented institutions, both socially and politically.¹² The peculiar Russian social estate (*soslovie*) system was not dying, but rather flourishing and evolving in the nineteenth century, and it embraced the professions as well as social and national groups that developed corporate consciousness persisting well into the late imperial era of ideological rejection and conservative defense of the estate structure.¹³ At the same time that the professoriate was caught between a radicalized student movement and the tsarist administration, the universities were intractably divided politically among revolutionaries, moderates and liberals, and conservatives. The complete closing of the universities during 1905, and standoffs and divisions of both corporate and "liberation movement" solidarities after

10. For a comparative approach that questions models developed in the Anglo-American context and reflects current research, see Harley D. Balzer, ed., *Russia's Missing Middle Class: The Professions in Russian History* (Armonk, N.Y.: M. E. Sharpe, 1996).

11. M. Novikov, "Moskovskii Universitet v pervom periode bol'shevistskogo rezhima," in *Moskovskii Universitet, 1755–1930: Iubileinyi sbornik*, ed. V. B. El'iashevich et al. (Paris: Sovremennye zapiski, 1930), 191.

12. The most important analytical study remains Samuel D. Kassow, *Students, Professors, and the State in Tsarist Russia* (Berkeley and Los Angeles: University of California Press, 1989).

13. Gregory Freeze, "The Estate (Soslovie) Paradigm and Russian Social History," *American Historical Review* 91, no. 1 (February 1986): 11–36.

the failed revolution, only fragmented the universities further.[14] In light of this half-century of growth, struggle, and discord, the renewed defense of autonomy in the half-decade after 1917, its failure, and the reemergence of a severe new fragmentation in the 1920s (as described below) make good historical sense.

Four aspects of the tsarist environment that shaped the Russian universities hold special relevance for understanding Bolshevik and postrevolutionary approaches. The first was a class or social dimension. Since the Westernization programs of Peter the Great, education was closely linked to elite status, and in imperial Russia the university diploma conferred rank (*chin'*). Tsarist investment in university education is hardly comparable to Bolshevik cadre policy, but both the imperial and Soviet states were committed to competition with the Western great powers while attempting to transform a social fabric very different from that of their European rivals. In both cases this lashed the attention of the state in higher education firmly to the creation of the elite. In broadest terms, late imperial policy attempted to increase the numbers of qualified candidates to the bureaucracy and the professions while maintaining the social hierarchy of the estate order, and to expand higher education without conceding more autonomy to the universities or intelligentsia.[15] Under late tsarism, the nobility was deliberately favored (although its numbers declined significantly at the end of the old regime); non-Russian national minorities, especially Jews and Poles, faced restrictions on entry to higher education that complemented those connected to class (estate). Instead of maintaining an old elite, as the tsarist government attempted to do in breaking the erosion of noble predominance, the new regime consciously aimed to create a new intelligentsia and political class. After the revolution, the nobles were dispossessed "former people," while those who could prove

---

14. On the student movement, an important recent study is Susan K. Morrissey, *Heralds of Revolution: Russian Students and the Mythologies of Radicalism* (New York: Oxford University Press, 1998); on the professoriate, academic culture, and higher education, see James C. McClelland, *Autocrats and Academics: Education, Culture, and Society in Tsarist Russia* (Chicago: University of Chicago Press, 1979). On universities and students in late imperial Russia, see the many works of Anatolii Evgenevich Ivanov, including *Vysshaia shkola Rossii v kontse XIX—nachale XX veka* (Moscow: Institut Istorii SSSR, 1991) and his latest study, *Studenchestvo Rossii kontsa XIX—nachalo XX veka: Sotsial'no-istoricheskaia sud'ba* (Moscow: ROSSPEN, 1999).

15. The theme is developed in a rare treatment of both sides of 1917 by Peter H. Kneen, "Higher Education and Cultural Revolution in the USSR," CREES Discussion Papers, Soviet Industrialization Project Series, no. 5, University of Birmingham, 1976, 4–27.

working-class credentials (and party members) soon had privileged access to higher education. Soviet power immediately erased all barriers to entry into higher education, but also aspired to far more than free access. True, the earliest Bolshevik pronouncements about higher education spoke of the "democratization" of the student body, but this was shortly turned into the goal of "proletarianization," which in practice launched an extensive and complicated history of quota policies that peaked in the late 1920s and early 1930s but persisted up until the mid-1930s.

Second was an academic or intellectual dimension. The ambivalent attitude of the tsarist authorities toward science (and materialism, a link made during the first wave of positivism and the revolutionary movement in the 1860s) held important consequences. Applied science, vocational training, and technology were very much underrepresented in Russian higher education, trends that were reinforced by the influence of Germanic notions of pure science as well as home-grown economic underdevelopment.[16] The Bolsheviks turned "praxis" and practicality into touchstones of their approach to academia, not merely in response to theoretical constructs, but also to reverse a concrete legacy.

Third, many revolutionaries were former students who had dropped out or been expelled from the universities, since the student movement was a prime recruiting ground for the revolutionary movement. There already existed a well-developed radical student/revolutionary critique of the moderate (and after 1905, liberal or Constitutional Democratic [Kadet]) professoriate; it condemned narrow, elitist privileging of institutional autonomy and freedom of thought over broader social and political aims. The moderate-radical split in what had been a coalition "liberation movement" became acute in the course of the Revolution of 1905, during which universities opened themselves to the "street" and unrest was so acute that universities were closed across the country. Fourth, the fact that tsarism opposed several alternative arrangements to official universities (ranging from projects to found applied institutes, to the people's universities, to adult education initiatives, not to mention, of course, the

---

16. However, significant expansion and improvements in higher technical and engineering education were made under Minister of Finance Sergei Witte, incorporating historically rare private input and operating outside the capital cities, during industrialization efforts after the turn of the twentieth century. See Harley D. Balzer, "Public-Private Partnerships in Russian Education: Historical Models and Lessons," in *Extending the Borders of Russian History: Essays in Honor of Alfred J. Rieber*, ed. Marsha Siefert (Budapest: Central European University Press, 2003), 457–79.

illegal study circles in the revolutionary movement known as *kruzhki*) implied that universities would not automatically become the sole or even primary venues for the pursuit of revolutionary agendas when the revolution finally came.

Yet it was only the brief interregnum of February to October 1917 that enshrined the position of the liberal academic intelligentsia as the definitive "bourgeois" foil for the evolution of Bolshevik views, setting the stage for a five-year struggle over university autonomy following October. Several Kadet-affiliated professors were catapulted to the heights of political power in the Provisional Government; the future rector of Moscow University when the Soviet charter was imposed, the zoologist Mikhail Novikov, headed the special commission for the reform of higher schools.[17] While the universities were not especially active in the midst of war and revolution, and many student activists of all kinds abandoned study, the fateful interlude ushered in by the February Revolution must have seemed to many a time when the long battle for university autonomy against the tsarist autocracy was finally won. When the Bolsheviks came to power in October 1917, they had many ideas and inclinations but no coherent plan for universities or higher education. The initial refusal to cooperate with the new regime—the vaunted intelligentsia "sabotage"—on the part of much of the professoriate and student body ratified a course of initial conflict between the universities and the Soviet authorities in the early years of Soviet power.

While many Bolsheviks in the course of the civil war came to view the academic opposition centered in universities as not merely bourgeois but reactionary, the clash might in some ways be seen as one between the impulses and implications of two revolutions, February and October. Academic disapproval, passive and active, of the Bolshevik–Left Socialist Revolutionary coalition government of October 1917–summer 1918 formed part of a larger phenomenon of negative sentiments toward the new regime among large segments of the intelligentsia.[18] This was something the Bolsheviks never forgot during the fragile stabilization and modus vivendi of the 1920s, and it further undermined the status of old institutions such as universities in Bolshevik plans for the future.

---

17. On this period, see O. N. Znamenskii, *Intelligentsiia nakanune velikogo oktiabria (fevral'–oktiabr' 1917 g.)* (Moscow: Nauka, 1988).

18. The literature on Bolshevik-intelligentsia relations and the "specialists" is large. See, for example, Kendall Bailes, *Technology and Society Under Lenin and Stalin: Origins of the Soviet Technological Intelligentsia* (Princeton: Princeton University Press, 1978).

Phase I: "The Struggle for the Higher School," 1918–1922

The era of the Russian civil war (1918–20) might be seen, not only as the time when a Bolshevik academic agenda took shape, but also as an era of chaotic yet influential flowering of manifold trends with "outsider" prerevolutionary roots, representing programs in all echelons of higher learning that had been stymied by the old regime. Despite war, hunger, and acute material hardship, the revolution provided impetus for movements with established impulses *not* formulated primarily by Bolsheviks. Just as the Italian Fascists embraced the 1923 Gentile reform that was rooted in late liberal pedagogical thought, and Chinese communist programs in some ways simply extended earlier Guomintang initiatives (both discussed in later chapters), so post-October developments reflected pre-October agendas. These included, notably, the founding of an array of specialized and applied "scientific-research institutes" that were largely alternatives to the university sector and initiatives in long-slighted higher technical education and applied research.[19] Other alternatives to the established old institutions included the exuberant mushrooming of all sorts of "enlightenment" initiatives with which Bolshevik agendas overlapped. This included the rapid if short-lived expansion of the conventional system of higher education—almost every province and major city tried to found its own university, and sixteen new state universities were founded in 1918 alone—as well as alternative "university" venues for adults and the underprivileged. One source claims 101 people's universities existed in the new Soviet republic in 1919.[20] The Bolsheviks also founded their own system of specifically Communist Party education in this period, which included by 1920 the emergence in Moscow of the first Communist university, named after the recently deceased Bolshevik leader Iakov Sverdlov, which clearly had pretensions of becoming a full-fledged party alternative to the higher school.[21] At the same time, the Academy of Sciences, in order to preserve itself as a unique institution at the apex of

---

19. For an overview, see F. N. Petrov, "Nauchno-issledovatel'skie instituty SSSR," *Molodaia gvardiia* 9–11 (October 1925): 146–49. The most significant scholarly study remains Loren R. Graham, "The Formation of Soviet Research Institutes: A Combination of Revolutionary Innovation and International Borrowing," *Social Studies of Science* 5, no. 3 (August 1975): 303–29.

20. David Currie Lee, *The People's Universities of the USSR* (New York: Greenwood Press, 1988), 20–47, 39 n. 29; Sh. Kh. Chanbarisov, *Formirovanie sovetskoi universitetskoi systemy* (Moscow: Vysshaia shkola, 1988), 41–45.

21. On Sverdlov Communist University and the rise of the entire system of party schools and Communist academic institutions, see Michael David-Fox, *Revolution of the Mind: Higher Learning Among the Bolsheviks* (Ithaca: Cornell University Press, 1997), 83–132.

Russian science, came to a formal understanding with the new regime in 1918.[22] In other words, at a time when the universities were proving resistant to change, alternatives to universities seemed possible both within the inherited academic system and from the new "revolutionary" alternatives that had emerged.

Although the roots of confrontation with the universities extended to events in 1918, the revolutionary authorities had much more pressing tasks during the Russian civil war and there was a great deal of de facto autonomy before 1920. Most old professors were reelected when elections became mandatory; few Marxists or Communist sympathizers (most of whom were off to the military or political, as opposed to the "cultural," front) succeeded in penetrating the higher schools, even in the social sciences. Attempts were made to exacerbate older conflicts by splitting junior faculty from the senior, but these also foundered. The Moscow University historian Iurii Vladimirovich Got'e, situated politically well to the right of the Kadets, and whose evaluations of Bolshevik intellectuals mingled with his anti-Semitism, noted in his diary that "our young people" showed "solidarity with us" in the reelections of 1919; only one professor, the future academician Pavel N. Sakulin, was blackballed for "his currying favors with the Bolsheviks, of course."[23] Early efforts by the Commissariat of Enlightenment (Narkompros) to alter the social and political composition of the universities through open admissions did not live up to their expectations; the student movement, with its strong corporate traditions and bastions of support for the other socialist parties, maintained its anti-Bolshevik activism up until the early 1920s.[24]

To be sure, several major initiatives of Soviet power in universities—both attacks on elements of the inherited system and efforts to twist it into a new one—did occur. They included the closing of the juridical faculties in 1918 and the foundation of a system of workers' faculties (*rabfaki*) after

22. The most complete explication of this is in Vera Tolz, *Russian Academicians and the Revolution: Combining Professionalism and Politics* (London: Macmillan, 1997).

23. Terence Emmons, ed., *Time of Troubles: The Diary of Iurii Vladimirovich Got'e* (Princeton: Princeton University Press, 1988), 251–52. In addition, see James C. McClelland, "The Professoriate in the Russian Civil War," in *Party, State, and Society in the Russian Civil War*, ed. Diane Koenker, William Rosenberg, and Ronald Suny (Bloomington: Indiana University Press, 1989), 243–51, and on Petrograd University in this period, Mary McCauley, *Bread and Justice: State and Society in Petrograd, 1917–1922* (Oxford: Oxford University Press, 1991), 330–50.

24. See the memoirs of Sergei Zhaba, *Petrogradskoe studenchestvo v bor'be za svobodnuiu vyshhuiu shkolu* (Paris: n.p., 1922). Literature on universities outside Moscow and Petrograd is extremely sparse.

1919 as preparatory institutes for working-class and pro-Soviet students attached to institutions of higher education. The years 1918–20—between Red Terror and economic collapse—was a time of crisis and misery for scholars and university professors in the red zone. It was inflamed by high-profile repressions. But as compared with later systematic initiatives, these measures fell short of the far-reaching "reform" of the higher school for which the Bolsheviks agitated. The irony of the war communism period for universities was that it combined threatening and often apocalyptic revolutionary rhetoric with de facto decentralization. The opposite might be said of universities in the 1920s: despite a range of conciliatory Bolshevik gestures and policies, it led to far-reaching transformation.

The protracted struggle to "win the higher school" really got off the ground after the civil war and lasted from 1920 to 1923. The chief issue was administrative command, and the 1921 university statute and the 1922 university charter achieved the aim of party-state appointment of rectors and administrations. The combination of the threat to autonomy and financial misery led faculty members of the prestigious Moscow Higher Technical School to go out on strike in 1921, and in early 1922 "professors' strikes" followed in the three most prestigious universities of Moscow, Petrograd, and Kazan'.

The growing number of "red" forces at the universities—*rabfak* students, Communist cells, and Komsomol activists—believed they were witnessing the long-anticipated destruction of the bourgeois higher school. Even two key Communist officials, the future leading Trotskyite Evgenii Preobrazhenskii, at the time head of the Main Committee on Professional Education (Glavprofobr) and the Marxist historian Mikhail Pokrovskii, the deputy commissar of enlightenment, both ended up with rebukes from the Politburo for their unwillingness to follow orders to compromise and their hard lines against the strikes.[25] The top leadership ended up preserving the old institutions and even offering them material incentives. The stick, of course, came along with the carrot: the closing in 1922 of independent intelligentsia organizations and deportation in the "philosophers boat" of hundreds of leading intellectuals, many of them leading lights in the universities.[26] The party thus curbed its militant left

25. See the Politburo resolutions from 6, 11, and 13 February 1922 in Rossiiskii gosudarstvenyi arkhiv sotsialno-politicheskoi istorii (Russian State Archive of Socio-Political History, the former Central Party Archive, hereafter RGASPI) *f.* 17, *op.* 3, *d.* 260, *ll.* 1; *d.* 261, *ll.* 2, 8; *d.* 263, *ll.* 2; *d.* 265, *ll.* 3, 10.

26. The most detailed archival consideration of the deportations, and their connections to the struggle over university autonomy, are in Stuart Finkel, "'The Brains of the Nation':

but did much to cement processes of change in the areas it deemed most important. In addition to establishing administrative control, priorities included social and political engineering (boosting the numbers of proletarians and party members among students, and increasing the numbers of the "red" professoriate), even if the speed and scope was under dispute. A campaign against "idealism" made open criticism of Marxism difficult at best. Efforts were made to introduce obligatory Marxist courses and alter the teaching personnel in the social sciences first and foremost (which in the Russian Marxist tradition tended to include fields considered humanities elsewhere). The pervasive Bolshevik preoccupation with revolutionary purity in the 1920s was expressed in the much greater concerns about teachers (of "youth") than about researchers, who could always be "kicked upstairs" to new institutes—a tendency that bolstered divisions between teaching and research.

In sum, the 1922 university settlement preserved the old institutions, forming an initial cyclical shift from a short-lived revolutionary "advance" to a 1920s mélange of preservation of old institutions, slow "reform" carried out by revolutionaries, and certain areas of rapid change on the "cultural front." The conflict set the stage for a stabilization that lasted until 1928.[27] As this scenario was unfolding in the RSFSR (Russian Soviet Federal Socialist Republic), however, a different outcome was achieved in the second most important union republic, Ukraine. Whereas the settlement in the Russian universities ended up as a compromise between champions of political, vocational/industrialist, and broad general education, as well as between militant and moderate approaches toward old institutions and elites, in Ukraine a strong strand of revolutionary vocationalism triumphed unimpeded.[28] The greater disruption of the education system in Ukraine during the civil war, as well as the association of professors and universities (in, for example, Kiev) with occupying White forces, allowed the republican commissariat of enlightenment to push for a more radical transformation. This turned out to favor a system more weighted to

---

The Expulsions of Intellectuals and the Politics of Culture in Soviet Russia, 1920–1924" (Ph.D. diss., Stanford University, 2001), and Finkel, "Purging the Public Intellectual: The 1922 Expulsions from Soviet Russia," *Russian Review* 62, no. 4 (October 2003): 589–613.

27. Michael David-Fox, "The Emergence of a 1920s Academic Order in Soviet Russia," *East-West Education* 18, no. 2 (fall 1997): 106–42.

28. On the compromises in approaches between vocational, political, and general education among Bolshevik policymakers in the early 1920s, see especially James McClelland, "Bolshevik Approaches to Education, 1917–1921," *Slavic Review* 30 (1971): 818–31.

"practical" specialization. Leninist nationalities policy in the 1920s also placed education and language policies outside the kind of strict centralization pursued in the realms of politics and economics. The Ukrainian commissar of enlightenment, G. F. Grinko, along with the head of the Ukrainian Glavprofobr, Ian Petrovich Riappo, were especially influential in engineering the breakup of the Ukrainian universities.

Forty-two separate, specialized institutes replaced the universities of Kiev, Odessa, Kharkov, and Ekaterinoslav. The phenomenon in both its ideological and organizational dimensions bears a striking resemblance to what happened on a union-wide scale after the party's "left turn" after 1928. Riappo called not for "reform" but for full-fledged revolution in higher education, including the destruction of those old "temples of science," whose professor-priests trained only intelligentsia dilettantes. So unchecked was his vocationalist-industrial hostility to "scholastic" learning that Riappo even opposed the creation of an Institute of Red Professors, the leading center for elite party-Marxist scholars and theoreticians in the 1920s, on Ukrainian soil.[29] In its link between revolutionary liquidationism and an extreme technical-industrial vocationalism, the Ukrainian precedent bears an uncanny resemblance to the breakup of Soviet universities that reached its height in 1930. There is some evidence of personal links between the two episodes, although this deserves further research; Riappo himself resurfaces in 1927 with ties to the Central Bureau of Proletarian Students, the Communist student organization that first advanced the attack on universities as feudal relics in the late 1920s.[30] But the return to revolutionary offensive would come only after a complex, ambiguous, yet influential interlude, the period of the New Economic Policy (NEP).

Phase II: Restabilization, Fragmentation, Transformation, 1922–1928

Once administrative command of the universities had passed to Communist rectors and state-appointed administrations, the status of the universities

---

29. Ia. Riappo, *Reforma Vysshei shkoly na Ukraine v gody revoliutsii (1920–1924): Sbornik statei i dokladov* (Kharkov: Gosizdat Ukrainy, 1924); Riappo, *Sovetskaia professional'naia shkola* (Kharkov: Gosizdat Ukrainy, 1926).

30. "Zasedanie Prezidiuma TsBPS VTsSPS ot 8-go fevralia 1927," in GARF f. A-2306, op. 69, ed. khr. 1221, l. 8.

in the "transition to socialism" was no longer seriously in doubt, and this situation persisted until the next period of "socialist offensive" unfolded in 1928. This stabilization entailed a curtailment or rechanneling of the transformative and militant agendas of many groups, from the Bolshevik intellectuals and cultural-policy officials to the Communist student movement. This was typical of many areas of culture during the 1920s. Indeed, the "student commissars" who had assumed political and even financial control during earlier periods, and who would rise again during the chaotic upheaval after 1928, would not threaten the power of either Communist or nonparty university elites in this period. Instead of immediate destruction or "revolution" in the surviving prerevolutionary institutions, this next phase in the history of Soviet universities triggered long-term attempts at what in retrospect might be called sovietization—except that the adjective "soviet," in the 1920s, referred specifically to the Soviet state, still dominated at the lower and middle levels by nonparty officials and experts, as opposed to the party hierarchy that shadowed the state institutions. The new situation triggered long-term adjustments in the social and political composition of higher schools, a circumscribed but significant injection of Marxism into the curriculum, and an often plodding pursuit of Bolshevik ideals of service and practicality in higher learning.

The NEP-era situation was part of a broader, fragile reconciliation with nonparty "bourgeois specialists," who were given a new, legitimized identity in the new order (as Lenin's "noncommunist hands" that would help to build socialism). A new wage scale was introduced, paving the way for old elites such as scholars to receive significantly higher salaries. A new "star" system gave lavish privileges to the most important scholars, and more generally approaches were differentiated in terms of how useful the given figure was deemed (which tended to decrease the importance of the humanities). The Central Commission for Improving the Life of Scholars (TSEKUBU) now provided special privileges such as facilities and sanatoria for scholars. In terms both of cultural policy and revolutionary plans, serious attempts at renewed assault that seriously threatened this stabilization were placed off limits—just as Lenin had explicitly forbidden "mischief-making" around the old Academy of Sciences in 1918, once it had agreed to cooperate with the new regime. Internationally, the new Soviet regime in the 1920s, although its cultural policies were vastly more transformational than those of Italian Fascism discussed by Ben-Ghiat in this volume, was also concerned with proving that the new system was not the enemy of culture and science that its opponents claimed, which in both cases was seemingly linked to long-standing anxieties about status vis-à-vis Western Europe.

To be sure, in Soviet higher education in the 1920s there were moments of no small tension, such as the large-scale 1924 purges of students that accompanied the anti-Trotskyite Communist student cell purges, but in general the formal indicators of change in an era of quantification mania remained relatively meager. Of the over 12,500 teaching personnel in seventeen universities and eighty-six institutions of higher education in 1925 in the Russian Federation, only 6.1 percent were party members. The figure had barely increased by 1928. Of the 1,590 Communists classified as "scientific workers" in 1929, 42 percent were in Moscow and 61.4 percent were in the social sciences. The so-called social minimum made some Marxism obligatory, but several institutional arrangements to foster change even in the social sciences in the old institutions were hardly great successes—something made clear if only in retrospect when in 1928 party forces rapidly swept them away. Outside the social sciences, the professoriate retained de facto control over most faculty appointments and the selection of graduate students. While the composition of the student body was an area of much greater concern to policymakers, even here data show what must have been seen as signs of slow "progress" and transformations yet to come: in 1925 the contingent of Communist and Komsomol students in the seventeen universities and eighty-six institutions of higher education was 10.3 and 10.0 percent respectively; the number of students classified as proletarian was 21.8 percent. This latter figure included the *rabfaki* expanded after 1920 as a way of proletarianizing higher education. While the *rabfaki* did contribute to a significant change in social composition, producing between 5,500 and 7,000 graduates per year between 1923 and 1929, they were plagued by endemic problems relating to quality of preparation and integration into host institutions.[31]

---

31. *Narodnoe obrazovanie v RSFSR* (Moscow: Izdatel'stvo "Doloi negramotnost'," 1925), 185; *Statisticheskii sbornik po narodnomu prosveshcheniiu RSFSR, 1926* (Moscow, 1928); "Nauchnye kadry VKP(b)," 1929, in GARF f. R-3145, op. 2, d. 10, ll. 35–61; on control over faculty appointments and graduate student admissions, see M. N. Pokrovskii, "O podgotovke nauchnykh rabotnikov," *Nauchnyi rabotnik* 1 (January 1929): 16–28. See also Sheila Fitzpatrick, *Education and Social Mobility in the Soviet Union, 1917–1934* (New York: Cambridge University Press, 1979); David-Fox, *Revolution of the Mind*, 78–79; and Harley D. Balzer, "Workers' Faculties and the Development of Science Cadres in the First Decade of Soviet Power," in *The Social Direction of the Public Sciences: Causes and Consequences of Co-operation Between Scientists and Non-Scientific Groups*, ed. Stuart Blume (Dordrecht and Boston: D. Reidel, 1987), 193–211.

While I will make the case that much indeed was changing even at the old universities in the NEP period, it is no wonder that all the factors preventing more revolutionary transformation in the 1920s made it seem that to many Bolsheviks the universities remained "alien" institutions (quite unlike the later case discussed by Douglas Stiffler, where the Chinese Communist Party was favorably disposed toward universities). "The higher school," Bukharin remarked at the height of NEP, "has not been won over by us one whit. I in no way demand the expulsion of all nonproletarian elements, but in front of us lies a very complex and difficult task."[32] It was not merely that the plans and activities of Bolshevik intellectuals, scholars, and students for a new socialist kind of higher education did not center around the old institutions or were partitioned off within them. The secret police developed a pattern of highly ideological reporting on the "bourgeois" professoriate, as V. S. Izmozik has shown. The "anti-Soviet" outlook and activities of the professors were standard fare in secret police reports on the "moods" of various segments of the population. Strong views in favor of preserving university autonomy as well as the non-Bolshevik political activities of students were recorded late into the 1920s, but more significant than any single set of activities is the way they were almost automatically and routinely reported as "anti-Soviet," "counterrevolutionary," and corrupting of proletarian youth.[33]

To be sure, on an official level ways were found to legitimize the universities in Soviet terms. As late as 1929 plans were proceeding for a gala jubilee for Moscow State University's 175th anniversary, and the rector, Ivan Udal'tsov boasted that with more than nine thousand students and thirteen hundred scientific workers, Moscow State was the country's most "enormous scientific-educational institution." Its size was matched by its "enormous political meaning," exemplified by the historic contributions of Moscow students and professors to the revolutionary movement.[34]

---

32. Nikolai Bukharin, "Rechi na XIII s"ezde RKP (Partiiia i vospitanie smeny)," in *Bor'ba za kadry: Rechi i stat'i* (Moscow-Leningrad: Molodaia gvardiia, 1926), 140.

33. V. S. Izmozik, *Glaza i ushi rezhima: Gosudarstvennyi politicheskii kontrol' za naseleniem Sovetskoi Rossii v 1918–1928 godakh* (St. Petersburg: Izdatel'stvo Sankt-Peterburgskogo Universiteta Ekonomiki i Finansov, 1995). Vladimir Brovkin, who was apparently unaware of Izmozik's work, uncritically takes the reports as largely nonideological and reflecting historical reality, but in the process provides a compendium of secret police materials on students and professors that indicate the information the party leadership was receiving on them. Vladimir Brovkin, *Russia after Lenin: Politics, Culture, and Society* (London: Routledge, 1998), 129–32.

34. Ivan Udal'tsov, "V kollegiiu Narkomprosa: 12 fevralia 1929," GARF f. A-2306, op. 69, d. 1720, l. 6.

Even so, in the divided academic order of the 1920s, plans for the research and education system of the future were made in reference to other kinds of institutions. These included the Academy of Sciences, which was declared the supreme scientific institution of the land in 1925, and influenced both in rejection and emulation its chief rival, the Communist Academy. The Bolshevik intellectuals at the helm of this rival academy later formulated plans for the creation of a new supreme institution of the future that would be made out of the building blocks of scientific-research institutes, and it was they who influenced the Soviet-type organization of research after the so-called bolshevization of the old academy after 1928.[35] In terms of higher education, an entire, separate, party system of "Communist universities" and "soviet-party schools" was developed after 1920 — in contrast to the lone project for an alternative Nazi higher school discussed by Michael Grüttner — and revolutionary agendas were often carried out here more than in what were by comparison the obstructed venues of the old universities.[36] To give but one example, revolutionary innovations in pedagogy — so-called active methods such as the Dalton or Laboratory plan, touted for their collectivism and the undermining of the authority of the old professoriate — were implemented much more broadly in Communist universities than in the old universities, and formed the basis for the "laboratory-brigade method" that swept through higher education in the era of the first Five-Year Plan. The old universities survived in the 1920s, and even flourished, retaining research institutes and a good deal of advanced research, but their ultimate place in the socialist order was, we can see, precarious.

The universities themselves, despite the post-1922 stabilization, remained fragmented along several lines. Power and university affairs were divided between the party-appointed administrations, the faculty, and the Communist student cells, as Sheila Fitzpatrick's study of higher education in the 1920s emphasizes.[37] Divisions between party minorities and nonparty majorities among students and professors were also acute. The most extensive study of the *studenchestvo* (student body) in this period, Peter Konecny's study of Leningrad, emphasizes the persistence of a range of subcultures (tellingly, he adopts the Soviet term "deserters") who opted

---

35. Michael David-Fox, "Symbiosis to Synthesis: The Communist Academy and the Bolshevization of the Russian Academy of Sciences, 1918–1929," *Jahrbücher für Geschichte Osteuropas* 46, no. 2 (1998): 219–43.
36. I have examined the many consequences of this in my *Revolution of the Mind*.
37. Fitzpatrick, *Education and Social Mobility*, 67 and passim.

out of the plans of all the various "builders" of socialism.[38] On the other side of the spectrum, students living in communes and the intense student interest in fashioning a new "everyday life" (*byt*) in this era testify to the younger generation's interests in collectivism and sexual mores that often revealed a gap with the often culturally puritanical Bolshevik authorities. Even the hyperpoliticized militancy of student Communists often went beyond the bounds of what the party leadership wished. From the point of view of official party ideologues and moralists, youth was at once a specially plastic group to be fashioned and protected, a source of deviation, and a potential force to be unleashed and mobilized.[39]

The Soviet universities thus went through a long and staggered process of sovietization *avant la lettre* before the two successive phases of radical assault and renovation that followed after 1929 and 1932. Unlike the cases of Hungary and Poland discussed in this volume, where a very brief period under the People's Democracies was immediately followed by an imitation of full-blown Stalinism, the contradictory revolutionary "breathing space" of the Soviet 1920s was drawn out and thus a crucial contribution to the emerging Soviet system even though NEP was ultimately rejected. Furthermore, unlike all the East European postwar communist reconstructions, there were obviously no extant models of sovietization for the Soviets themselves to follow. The resulting manner in which Soviet higher education and culture formed out of radically different subperiods would create historical ambiguities for any future import-export of the Soviet experience.

Phase III: Assault, Dismemberment, and Resurrection, 1928–1932

The 1920s order that had preserved the universities as the objects of gradual sovietization began to unravel in 1928. The Shakhtii show trial of alleged saboteurs among the technical specialists in the coal-mining region of

---

38. Peter Konecny, *Builders and Deserters: Students, State, and Community in Leningrad, 1917–1941* (Montreal: McGill-Queens University Press, 1999).
39. On these issues, see Anne E. Gorsuch, *Youth in Revolutionary Russia: Enthusiasts, Bohemians, Delinquents* (Bloomington: Indiana University Press, 2000); Hilary Pilkington, *Russia's Youth and Its Culture: A Nation's Constructors and Constructed* (London: Routledge, 1994); David-Fox, *Revolution of the Mind*, chap. 2; on communes, Ibeen-Shtrait, "Studencheskie kommuny," *Krasnyi student* 8–9 (August–September 1924): 44–45; and Richard Stites, *Revolutionary Dreams: Utopian Vision and Experimental Life in the Russian Revolution* (New York: Oxford University Press, 1989), 205–22.

Shakhtii set off a reevaluation of the entire stance toward old elites. The new period of "socialist offensive" that lasted through 1931 was marked by arrests and repressions of professionals and scholars previously considered protected—among them, the "academy" or Platonov affair at the Academy of Sciences during its "bolshevization," as well as show trials of agronomists and engineers. The "specialists of the old school," as Stalin put it, were rehabilitated only in 1932, not coincidentally the same year old institutions such as the universities began to be restored. The other side of the coin of the era of prolonged attack on the nonparty intelligentsia was a new party program, put forward by Stalin and Molotov in 1929, to rapidly train a new "proletarian" intelligentsia with special expertise in the technical disciplines. Policies rapidly promoting large numbers of workers and party members into higher education thus coincided with a reordering of the entire educational system in favor of technical and applied training ("ties to production") in the era of the first Five-Year Plan.

As the new antispecialist, vocationalist course assumed importance for all Communists, a number of other factors combined to undermine the fragile position of the old universities. The Commissariat of Enlightenment, which oversaw them, had entered the most vulnerable period of its existence. The commissar since 1917, Lunacharskii, was removed in 1929 along with many top Bolshevik cultural authorities of the 1920s; he was associated with a "soft" line on the intelligentsia. Within the universities and other institutions, outbreaks of "social purging" fanned political-class antagonisms among the students and faculty; Lunacharskii opposed the persecution of children of the former privileged classes, but more militant agencies such as the Central Committee's Agitprop turned a blind eye. A strong element of generational conflict was also present, and party cells and the proletarian student movement completely overturned the fragmented balance of power that had been established in the 1920s.

In this atmosphere, draconian proposals dormant or repressed between 1922 and 1928 now bubbled to the surface. In fact, the assault on the universities originated in the radical student movement, whose official organ, the Central Bureau of Proletarian Students, had been created in 1922, during the last great crisis for the universities, to oversee student party cells. Throughout 1929 the student organs lashed out at officials for caving in to the reactionary professoriate, for delaying measures that had assumed the status of the revolutionary, such as internships in factories throughout the academic year (the so-called uninterrupted production practice). In October 1929, a lone student writer in the journal *Krasnoe studenchestvo* (Red studentry) raised a startling question: "Are Universities Necessary?" The writer, a certain Markov, termed the universities a "medieval fortress" and a "monstrous conglomerate," evocative terms that suggested a bastion to be stormed by the Bolsheviks and an impervious capitalist trust. Markov attacked the "idol" of "pure science," calling for the transfer of traditionally large, multidisciplinary departments to relevant state commissariats (medical faculties to the Commissariat of Health, physical-mathematical faculties to the All-Union Council for the National Economy, and so on).[40]

Although on the basis of the evidence at my disposal I cannot establish the precise links between this first published sally and later events, what Markov proposed "for discussion" in 1929 was exactly the process that brought the universities to their knees in 1930. Given the role the Bureau of Proletarian Students played in advancing the ideological attack on universities in 1929–30, it can be concluded that this agency played a significant role in the radicalization of Communist agendas toward those parts of higher education associated with the prerevolutionary past. The broader significance of this is worth pondering. Although students in the USSR initially did not provide anything like the kind of broad-based support that the radical right-wing regimes in Germany, Italy, and Spain enjoyed, the Communist student movement in the 1920s was certainly a significant force pushing for militant policies against elites, politicization, and a range of more and less "official" projects connected to the idea of forging the "new person." However, what we observe in the Bureau of Proletarian Students differs from the postwar Czechoslovak "studentocracy" discussed by Jan Havránek; it is closer to a "pseudo-plebian mobilization" discussed in the East German context by Ralph Jessen. Because of the staggered nature of the Soviet transformation of higher education, representatives of the Communist student movement were integrated from the early 1920s on into the bureaucratic structures of the party-state, where they helped formulate agendas for the radical rupture of the late 1920s.

For thirteen issues after the proposal to liquidate the universities was made, silence reigned in *Krasnoe studenchestvo*. In January 1930, however, a flood of articles reinforced and amplified the original call. Demands to separate off faculties and bring them closer to "production" combined with attacks on the institutions as temples of pure science obsolete in the

---

40. M. Markov, "Nuzhny li nam universitety," *Krasnoe studenchestvo*, 10 October 1929, 10–11.

age of industrialization. The rector of Moscow University, the same man who as recently as three months before was gearing up to celebrate a "holiday of university science," now demanded the death of his institution by the deadline of its 175th jubilee.[41] By early 1930, the rhetoric of cultural assault had assumed an apocalyptic tinge.

The universities were thus weakened institutionally and ideologically during the most intensive period of cultural upheaval. But the actual breakup of the universities was a complicated process with many different facets. One was the long-standing conflict between party-Marxist scholars based in party institutions and their nonparty rivals in the humanities and the social sciences; this led to widespread infighting in the social sciences and the transfer, already in 1929, of the association of social-science research institutes (most associated with universities) to the Communist Academy. A second element was the rivalry between the All-Union Council of the National Economy (Vesenkha) and the Commissariat of Enlightenment over the jurisdiction of technical education, which was fought over the course of 1929 and 1930 and increasingly won by Vesenkha. The transfer of technical institutes to the industrial commissariats was the first step in a wave of transfers that caught up the university faculties as well. A key decision in March 1930 escalated processes already at work: a Politburo commission (headed by Politburo member Lazar' Kaganovich and including leading party scholars Pokrovskii and Otto Shmidt) ordered transfers of most institutions of higher education to the commissariats, and the breakup of "multifaculty" institutions such as universities into specialized institutes "in the shortest possible time."[42]

In the assault on the universities we can thus observe a shift from the successive blows of the proletarian student movement (concerned with social/political promotion policies and the old professoriate) to the Marxist-Leninist scholars (concerned with the social sciences and nonparty rivals) to industrializers based in the commissariats, who were first and foremost concerned with vocationalism, rapid cadre production, narrow specialization, and technical education. Of course, all three groups overlapped, but they did have their own institutional bases, and their agendas for

---

41. Ivan Udal'tsov, "175-letnii starets," and other articles in *Krasnoe studenchestvo*, January 1930, 12.

42. "O operedache vuzov, vtuzov i tekhnikumov v vedenie sootvetstvuiushchikh narkomatov (Utverzhdeno Politbiuro TsK VKP(b) 5. III.1930," in RGASPI *f.* 17, *op.* 3, *ed. khr.* 778, *l.* 11.

higher learning were either overtly hostile to or not centered on the old universities. The wave of transfers and struggles to split off the university faculties in spring and summer of 1930 resulted in a great deal of chaos and internecine infighting over buildings, laboratories, and resources. Moscow, Leningrad and Kazan' universities, the oldest and most prestigious institutions, managed to cling to more departments than all the others; some universities, like those in Saratov, Tomsk, Irkutsk, and Voronezh, retained two or three faculties, but they were not the same ones, indicating that central decrees were not at all carried out uniformly on the ground. Some, such as the Second Moscow University, by August 1930 had no more faculties left and thus ceased to exist. Thus, as the number of specialized, technical, and applied (industrial "branch") institutes shot up in this period, and as the newly bolshevized Academy of Sciences was set on a course of rapid expansion in the realm of advanced research, the university sector, on the verge of collapse, fed the other two with its scholars, students, or faculties. No doubt even more than the case of the Nazi-era flight from universities to industry in the 1930s, discussed by Grüttner in this volume, the university sector in the USSR lost the best personnel to better-funded research institutes under the aegis of the economic commissariats and the Academy of Sciences.

While the transfers of faculties were contested and chaotic, certain processes were widespread in affecting the content and curriculum in what remained of the old universities. The contours of this process seem strikingly similar to those shaping institutional reorganization. The decisions of the party leadership set the course in 1928 and 1929 privileging higher technical education. In the intense campaign mode of Stalin's Great Break, policies associated with the industrializing projects of cadres, "practice" and "production" then ballooned out of all previously imagined proportions. Just as this had begun with the transfer of a few technical institutes from the Commissariat of Enlightenment and ended with the virtual liquidation of the universities, what started in instantly canonic party decisions about ties to production and early, narrow specialization turned into the aping of new-model technical institutes in university faculties. Two ungainly terms arose to describe this phenomenon: "branchification" (*otraslirovanie*), the attempt to ensure higher education directly served the branches of industry, and "technification" (*vtuzirovanie*), the tendency to mimic the forms and methods of the higher technical institutes (VTUZy). Engineers were trained to specialize in oil-based paints and non-oil-based paints, as the new technical institutes pursued "specialties so limited they bordered on the absurd."⁴³ Medical faculties were instructed to cease the training of general practitioners, and universities became reluctant to declare they were training mathematicians and natural scientists, for "this smacks of the past. . . . The [new] profile in many cases corresponds to that of an engineer."⁴⁴ In pedagogy, two further developments show how "revolutionary" and "proletarian" initiatives went hand in hand with a profound integration into the industrialization drive's call for rapid-fire, low-quality training. A movement to make time spent in factory "production practice" equal academic study peaked as well in 1930, and the "laboratory-brigade" method ensured that teachers appeared only episodically, and collective evaluation of the brigades prevented penalization of weaker students. Brigades went through "themes" as if they were fulfilling production norms, "storming" them in concentrated periods of time.⁴⁵

There was, however, a good deal of opposition to both university breakup and the destruction of university higher education, which in retrospect may have delayed the universities' full destruction before the party leadership reversed course in 1932. The professoriate of Leningrad State University and its successive directors appear to have been the most persistent in defending a component of advanced research in official definitions of the university's functions. By disputing each transfer and clawing over equipment and buildings, the universities were fighting a rear-guard battle, but one that significantly delayed the breakup. By late 1930, moreover, the Commissariat of Enlightenment itself was becoming far more assertive about protecting its holdings and was galvanized to make the first, tentative defenses of general, theoretical, and advanced university education. However, while these efforts may have slowed the universities' destruction, it is hard to classify them as outright resistance. No attempts to openly defend the research university on philosophical grounds, and no open attack on "branch specialization" could be mounted; instead, opponents of the Great Break trends channeled their views into arguments about the rational production of cadres, maintaining standards,

---

43. Harley Balzer, "Engineers: The Rise and Decline of a Social Myth," in *Science and the Soviet Social Order*, ed. Loren Graham (Cambridge: Harvard University Press, 1990), 152.

44. "Uchebnye plany meditsinskikh fakul'tetov i Institutov," in GARF *f.* A-2307, *op.* 15, *ed. khr.* 128, *ll.* 12–14; "Plenum universitetskoi sektsii GUS'a," 8 May 1932, ibid., *op.* 17, *ed. khr.* 22, *l.* 12.

45. "O metodakh prepodavaniia i uchete uspevaemosti v universitetakh," 1932, in GARF *f.* A-2307, *op.* 17, *d.* 9, *ll.* 90–113; Konecny, *Builders and Deserters*, chap. 5.

and serving the industrialization drive more effectively. This minority view, which one might call a utilitarian-statist idea of the university, in fact reinforced the etatization of higher education.

In fact, one might say that the restoration of the universities in 1932 represented the triumph of the utilitarian-statist, cadres-oriented stance already established as an undercurrent in 1930–31. Indeed, the goal of restoring a scientific-research function to the universities, restoring internal discipline through "one-man management," and anointing university graduates as necessarily "highly qualified," came in 1931 after it was championed above all by Moscow and Leningrad universities. The resurrection of the universities could best be achieved by taking two additional drastic steps facilitated by all of the upheaval that had already occurred. The first was to make yet another series of transfers, lopping off the social sciences and humanities as the least "practical" disciplines and the ones the most jealously guarded by the Marxist-Leninist scholars and ideologists. The second was to sever pedagogical faculties from the universities, because they were most associated with low-level cadres. These measures were recommended by the Commissariat of Enlightenment in mid-1931.[46]

The 1932 shift was prompted by a top-level rehabilitation of the persecuted old specialists, a clamp-down on the chaotic infighting and militant cultural "hare-brained scheming" that had preoccupied the party intellectuals and students during the industrialization and collectivization drives, and a reassertion of order and hierarchy. A "struggle for quality" replaced the drive for quantity in higher education, and this soon curtailed (and by 1935 ended) the social/political promotion of "proletarian" students. University directors were given special powers to deprive students of stipends, in order to curtail the party cells and militant youth. Six universities were restored where they had existed before. "Production practice" was curtailed, and the "brigade method" condemned. Universities were now called a top priority rather than archaic.

The new course of 1932 thus relegitimized universities in the Soviet Union. Yet the imprint of the Great Break destruction would be felt in Soviet universities for the duration of the Soviet period. The provincial universities, of the twelve that existed in 1932, had been least able to weather the assault, and thus, ironically, centralization in the one showcase university (Moscow) we mentioned at the outset was in fact facilitated by

---

46. GARF f. A-2306, op. 69, ed. khr. 2114, ll. 13–16.

the assault on all universities in the previous period. Social sciences and humanities remained outside the universities until 1939, except for obligatory Marxism-Leninism and, after 1934, history. Finally, while study of the Marxist social sciences in the 1920s was highly prestigious and promising for aspirants to the "new intelligentsia" and ruling elite the regime intended to create, the period of the first Five-Year Plan firmly established technical and engineering education, often of dubious quality, as the standard training for politically mobile cadres. Higher technical education was the classic path upward for the *vydvizhentsy*, the large numbers of promoted students of humble background who formed the backbone of Stalin's new elite and the "Brezhnev generation" of party leaders.[47] In the wake of this development, both the humanities and social sciences in disciplinary terms and the universities in institutional terms lost a good deal of their importance and allure.

It was only after the violent restructuring of the 1930s—punctuated by a renewed period of radical "assault" in 1937–39, as all elites were disproportionately swept up in the Great Terror—that universities began to even approximately resemble the broad multifaculty, academically prestigious institutions that had been swept away at the outset of the 1930s. Yet once again there was no returning to a *status quo ante*. There are deficiencies to a "structural" interpretation of the Soviet system centering around the construction of the fundamental socioeconomic and institutional features of the system in the 1930s, which implies that the system was only slightly modified thereafter.[48] However, for this discussion it is well worth emphasizing the lasting legacy of the assault on the universities in the late 1920s and early 1930s, particularly since research on universities in the late Stalin and post-Stalin periods is even more sparse than for the early Soviet period. Any opposition between structural continuities versus qualitative changes in this realm is therefore not yet at a stage where it can be meaningfully debated. However, the effects of the era of assault during the first Five-Year Plan that this chapter has described are readily apparent. Despite a degree of change in

---

47. Fitzpatrick, *Education and Social Mobility*; idem, "Stalin and the Making of a New Elite, 1928–1937," *Slavic Review* 38 (1979): 377–402; Bailes, *Technology and Society Under Lenin and Stalin*; Loren R. Graham, *Ghost of the Executed Engineer: Technology and the Fall of the Soviet Union* (Cambridge: Harvard University Press, 1993).

48. See, for example, Amir Weiner's article on the historiographical neglect of World War II, "Saving Private Ivan: From What, Why, and How?" *Kritika: Explorations in Russian and Eurasian History* 1, no. 2 (spring 2000): 307–8.

the post-Stalin period, within the universities themselves natural science assumed a place of permanently greater importance and power than the humanities and social sciences. Academic rigor, prestige, and a degree of "scientific-research work," especially in the oldest and most central institutions, were increasingly reintroduced into university life after the 1932 shift, and especially in the postwar decades. But expansion and utilitarian cadre production remained paramount, and, perhaps more important, the "bolshevized" Academy of Sciences and scientific-research institutes attached to the commissariats now comprised two entirely separate sectors of advanced (fundamental and applied) research. Universities thus may have consolidated the top place in a newly reconstituted hierarchy of a vastly expanded education sector, but their role in advanced research was permanently diminished for the duration of the Soviet period.[49] If the hyperspecialization of 1930–32 was later noticeably scaled down, it nonetheless left a lasting imprint in the Soviet university system.[50]

However, the militant assaults on the privileges and participation of elites within the system had reached their apex in the early 1930s, and despite renewed outbreaks of repression during the Great Purges and the Time of Zhdanov in the late 1940s, the academic intelligentsia received lavish privileges in the decades after 1932. Never again was the university system portrayed as fundamentally old, alien, or prerevolutionary, and university elites were no longer perceived monolithically by Communist activists as dangerously autonomous rivals (as in the 1920s) or alien enemies (as in the early 1930s). Despite that most fundamental division between the periods before and after the 1930s, the politics of cadres, the acceptance of party-state definitions of institutional purpose, and the valorization of "practicality" and production in higher education persisted both during and after the universities experienced the liquidationist and monumentalist phases of Stalinism.

49. Mark Adams, "Research and the Russian University," in *The Academic Research Enterprise with the Industrialized Nations: Comparative Perspectives. Report of a Symposium*, ed. Government-University-Industry Research Rountable (Washington, D.C.: National Academy Press, 1990), 51–65. On the struggles to increase the relative importance of post-Soviet universities, see Stephen Fortescue, "The Academy versus the Rest," in David-Fox and Péteri, *Academia in Upheaval*, 225–54.
50. Thus, as Stiffler discusses in this volume, Soviet advisers in China after 1949 forcefully advocated specialized, technical institutes as opposed to comprehensive universities for the new Communist regime.

2

Italian Universities Under Fascism

RUTH BEN-GHIAT

 This chapter examines the relationship between Italian universities and Mussolini's dictatorship. What role, if any, did Italian universities play in consolidating and sustaining Fascist rule, and how successful were they as agents of Fascist elite formation? How and to what extent did the dictatorship change Italian universities and academic culture? While Italian universities operated as part of a specific regime of power during the dictatorship, they were also operated on by that regime of power, which saw them as instruments to fulfill a triple imperative: to build a mass totalitarian regime, to craft a specifically "fascist" culture to support it, and to form a new elite that would perpetuate that culture and that regime through space and time. These long-term projects, which occasioned changes in university structures, personnel, and curricula, were periodically rethought as power relations changed between the Italian state and the National Fascist Party (PNF) and as police informers and other sources communicated the potential for collective disaffection among the university students who were to form Fascism's future managerial class. Investigating the relationship of Italian universities and the dictatorship offers a means of evaluating the interactions of high culture and politics, the vicissitudes of the party-state relationship, and the formation of a generation that would furnish Italy's leadership class after 1945.

As the central component of Fascist projects of political socialization and elite formation, the university during Fascism also offers a privileged viewpoint on what Emilio Gentile calls "the Italian way to totalitarianism."[1] Although an earlier tradition of scholarship held that Italian Fascism was, at most, an "imperfect totalitarianism," incapable of penetrating Italian cultural or social life, more recent works have emphasized the repressive aspects of Mussolini's regime. Among historians of Italian universities, this has produced new interest in Fascist purge mechanisms, in the nationalizing measures imposed on borderlands universities such as Trieste, and in the impact of Italian racial theory and legislation.[2] Seen alongside those of other twentieth-century dictatorships, the university policies of Mussolini's regime share a desire to permanently alter the landscape of university life in accordance with a precise political aim. Excluding undesirables, altering curricula, and eroding university autonomy all aimed at making the university a model site for the operation of state tactics of intimidation and surveillance and for the politicization of everyday life. And as under many other regimes, the results included an eventual provincialization of intellectual and academic life, an increased reliance on familial and extramural networks for intellectual and moral sustenance, and a pervasive conformism on the part of both students and docents that suited the dictatorship's political goals but worked against its need to create quality leadership. Italian Fascist university policies did differ from those of other regimes, however, on one important point: whereas Soviet and Eastern European Communist bloc regimes used universities as avenues to promote their goals of social mobility, facilitating the education of workers and peasants, Fascist university policies aimed to forestall any social emancipation. In this they were consistent with the core ethos of Mussolini's regime, which billed itself as a "third way" to modernity that would permit economic and technological progress without disturbing social or national identities.

While the promise of a distinctively Fascist vision of modernity that accommodated both revolutionary aspirations and social conservatism

---

1. Emilio Gentile, *La "via italiana" all totalitarismo* (Rome: La Nuova Italia, 1995).
2. See, on the purges, H. Goetz, *Der freie Geist und seine Widersacher* (Frankfurt am Main: Haag-Herchen Verlag, 1993); G. Boatti, *Preferei di no: Le storie dei dodici professori che si opposero a Mussolini* (Turin: Einaudi, 2001); and Domenico Mirri and Stefano Arieti, eds., *La cattedra negata: Dal giuramento di fedelta al fascismo alle leggi razziali nell'Universita di Bologna* (Bologna: CLUEB, 2002). On the impact of the racial laws, see Roberto Finzi, *L'Università italiana e le legge antiebraiche* (Rome: Riuniti, 1997), and Giorgio Israel and Piero Nastase, *Scienza e razza nell'Italia fascista* (Bologna: Mulino, 1998). On border region universities, see Anna Maria Vinci, *Storia dell'Università di Trieste* (Trieste: Università degli studi di Trieste, 1997).

fueled much of the support university students, professors, and functionaries gave to the regime, a variety of factors tempered and complicated the "renewal" of the Italian university along the lines of Fascist ideology. At the institutional level, political factionalism and the strength of local loyalties and cliental traditions during the dictatorship meant that Fascist education reforms were often implemented unevenly.[3] The continued presence of antifascist professors (who had taken the mandatory 1931 loyalty oath imposed on docents out of economic need or to provide a counter-influence to Fascism) also checked the politicization of the classroom.[4] The exposure to new ideas and foreign culture offered by universities also vitiated the provincialization that came with Fascist policies of cultural autarchy. Foreign students (including Jewish exiles from Nazi Germany) were numerous at Italian universities until the end of the 1930s, and exchange agreements allowed Italian students to study abroad, although after 1936 this mostly meant travel to Axis-friendly countries.[5] Finally, the absence of a formal political selection of students meant that antifascists and Fascists studied together, although the presence of informers (including those from the student ranks) and the psychological inhibitions that came from years of living in a police state worked to inhibit expressions of dissent.

Yet such factors, while important, must not be overrated. As a recent study of the Fascist University Groups (hereafter GUFs) argues, the triumph of a culture of catechistic reiteration over two decades of Mussolini's rule meant that few university students possessed the critical faculties necessary to resist Fascism's "ideological and aesthetic seductions." This climate of

---

3. See Elisa Signori, "L'università in uniforme. Momenti e aspetti di vita universitaria a Pavia tra regime e guerra mondiale," *Storia in Lombardia* 1–2 (1993): 200–201. Also Maria Cristina Giuntella, *Autonomia e nazionalizzazione. Il fascismo e l'inquadramento degli atenei* (Rome: Studium, 1992).

4. There is a copious literature on antifascist mentors: on those at the University of Padova, see Angelo Venturi, ed., *L'Università dalle leggi razziali alla Resistenza* (Padova: Cleup, 1996). For others, see Franco Cambi, *Anti-fascismo e pedagogia, 1930–1945* (Florence: Vallecchi, 1980), and the recollections of former students in Ettore Albertoni et al., eds., *Generazione degli anni difficili* (Bari: Laterza, 1962).

5. On the presence and impact of foreign students, see Vito Zagarrio, "Giovani e apparati culturali a Firenze," *Studi storici*, July-September 1980, 609–35. Also Gian Paolo Brizzi, *Silence and Remembering: The Racial Laws and Foreign Jewish Students at the University of Bologna* (Bologna: CLUEB, 2002). Educational exchanges between Nazi Germany and Fascist Italy are discussed in Jens Petersen, "Vorspiel zu 'Stahlpakt' und Kriegsallianz: Das deutsch-italienische Kulturabkommen vom 23. November 1938," *Vierteljahrshefte für Zeitgeschichte* 36 (1989): 41–77.

conformism extended to professors, few of whom protested changes in university policies, even those caused by the application of racial legislation.[6] While Italian universities remained strongholds of traditional humanistic culture (which was in any case appropriated by Fascist supporters who wished to capitalize on Italy's prestigious cultural patrimony), they also served as important sites for the elaboration and divulgation of the most extremist and "revolutionary" developments within Fascism, from corporativism to racism to the New European order envisioned by the Axis.

The 1923 Gentile Reform and Transition from Liberalism to Fascism

Although the university policies of Mussolini's dictatorship clearly broke with those of the liberal era, they also represent one period in a larger continuum of governmental education interventions since the nineteenth century that had addressed the following ongoing issues: centralization versus autonomy, the university's role in professional formation, the place of Catholic education within the state, and the "intellectual unemployment" (*disoccupazione intellettuale*) caused by an overproduction of university graduates.[7] Indeed, when the Fascists took power in 1922, the Italian university system was still regulated by the 1859 Casati law, which emphasized administrative centralization and the separation of humanistic and technical education. It limited the circulation of academic power (professors were appointed by the king for life) while providing the nascent Italian state with a steady flow of uniformly trained administrators. The beginnings of industrialization in the late nineteenth century brought little change to university policies, but much debate about the inadequacies of the existing system to cope with the demands of professional formation, especially in technical and scientific fields, and about

---

6. See Luca La Rovere, *Storia dei GUF: Organizzazione, politica e miti della gioventù universitaria fascista, 1919–1943* (Turin: Bollati Boringhieri, 2003), 11.

7. Long looks at these questions and interventions are contained in Marzio Barbagli, *Disoccupazione intellettuale e sistema scolastico in Italia, 1859–1973* (Bologna: Mulino, 1974); Ilaria Porciani, ed., *L'Università tra Otto e Novecento: I modelli europei e il caso italiano* (Naples: Jovene, 1994); Francesco De Vivo and Giovanni Genovesi, eds., *Cento anni di università: L'istruzione superiore dall'unità ai nostri giorni* (Naples: Edizioni scientifiche italiane, 1986); and Antonio Santoni Rugiu, *Chiarissimi e Magnifici: Il professore nell'università italiana* (Florence: La Nuova Italia, 1991).

the need to adjust university enrollments to ease problems of postgraduate unemployment.⁸

Economic crisis and advent of mass politics following World War I (Catholic and socialist parties grew exponentially) only exacerbated the pressures on an education model that reflected the elitist and staunchly lay principles of nineteenth-century liberalism. The number of Italians receiving university degrees more than doubled between 1913 and 1923, creating problems of economic survival and a loss of status for those trained in the classic humanist tradition. The sense of crisis was palpable at the Ministry of Public Instruction, whose top post was occupied by five different men between 1919 and 1922. As one observer complained in 1921, the plethora of graduates had not only "devalued academic titles" but created the sad specter of men in their twenties and thirties "still living off of their families, disappointed by life before they have even lived it."⁹ For this cohort, the failure of the university to fulfill its traditional function as a guarantor of stable employment and social promotion symbolized the larger bankruptcy of liberal institutions. They thus gravitated in large numbers to the new Fascist Party, which received 13 percent of its votes in 1921 from secondary and university students. This last group included many demobilized young officers, who in 1919 had protested in vain to the liberal government for subsidies so that they could complete their university degrees.¹⁰

Mussolini appealed to these young Italians as a revolutionary who vowed to eliminate bourgeois decadence and the sloth of parliamentary democracy. Yet he also simultaneously promised to protect social hierarchies in the face of Communist and socialist programs of radical change. These contradictory elements within Fascist ideology, which persisted throughout the life of the regime, found expression in the university sphere.

---

8. On the educational policies of the liberal period, see Tina Tomasi and Luciana Bellatalia, *L'università italiana nell'età liberale* (Naples: Liguori, 1988); Tracey Koon, *Believe, Obey, Fight: Political Socialization of Youth in Fascist Italy, 1922–1943* (Chapel Hill: University of North Carolina Press, 1985), 35–41; and Simonetti Polenghi, *La politica universitaria nell'età della Destra storica* (Brescia: La Scuola, 1993).

9. Federico Mastrigli, "Impiegomania e Universitarismo," *Il Tempo*, 24 September 1921. On this issue, see Barbagli, *Disoccupazione intellettuale*, 170, from which these figures are drawn. In Turin, for example, graduates increased 1913–1923 from 618 to 1010, a figure that also gives a sense of the small size of the university student population in Italy. Bruno Bongiovanni and Fabio Levi, *L'Università di Torino durante il fascismo* (Turin: G. Giappichelli, 1976), 15.

10. La Rovere, *Storia dei GUF*, 18. For student participation in early fascism, see Giuntella, *Autonomia e nazionalizzazione*, 125–70, and Paolo Nello, *L'avanguardismo studentesco alle origini del fascismo* (Rome: Laterza, 1978).

Agendas of continuity prevailed at the institutional level—notably in the 1923 Gentile reform, which came less than one year after Mussolini took power—even as squadrist violence and radical populism characterized the culture of official Fascist student organizations. Indeed, in many respects the Gentile reform resembled the education reforms proposed in those years by liberals such as the philosopher Benedetto Croce (who served as minister of public instruction from June 1920 to July 1921). Responding to the problem of the overproduction of university graduates, Croce planned to limit access to university education by channeling all but the brightest students away from the prerequisite *liceo classico* (the high school that remained a legacy of the Napoleonic years).[11] Like Croce, Gentile wished to realize a model of a highly "aristocratic" university, frequented by students who had passed through tough mechanisms of selection, rather than adapt the institution to the democratic and technological imperatives of mass society. Yet the Gentile reform far surpassed Croce's plan in its rigidity and elitism and may be seen as the first of many long-term state projects by which the Fascists aimed to forestall mass social emancipation. As the historian Bruno Bongiovanni has observed, the reform intended to "block any spontaneous social mobility from above by intervening in the area of education, which was essential in a country that had traditionally lacked any alternative channels for social advancement."[12] As a creation of the transition period between democracy and dictatorship, it may be seen as the complement of the compromises the Duce made with industrialists and other interest groups that resulted in old elites retaining many privileges during the Fascist period in the private sector and in public administration.[13] The church must be included among these interest groups, and the Gentile reform's restoration of religious education in the schools (which the liberal

---

11. On Croce's tenure as minister of public instruction, see Giuseppe Tognon, *Croce alla Minerva* (Brescia: La Scuola, 1990), 318–29, and Giuseppe Ricuperati, "Per una storia dell'università italiana da Gentile a Bottai," in Porciani, *L'università italiana tra Otto e Novecento*, 318–19. For the triumph of idealism in these years, see Tina Tomasi, *Idealismo e fascismo nella scuola italiana* (Florence: La Nuova Italia, 1969), 33–39.

12. Bongiovanni and Levi, *L'Università di Torino*, 9.

13. The best studies on this topic are Adrian Lyttelton, *The Seizure of Power: Fascism in Italy, 1919–1929* (London: Weidenfeld & Nicholson, 1973); Charles Maier, *Recasting Bourgeois Europe* (Princeton: Princeton University Press, 1975); and Emilio Gentile, *Il mito dello stato nuovo dall'antigiolittismo al fascismo* (Bari: Laterza, 1982). For the revolutionary origins and rhetoric of early fascism, see Zeev Sternhell et al., *The Birth of Fascist Ideology* (Princeton: Princeton University Press, 1994).

Croce had vehemently opposed) signaled a spirit of pragmatic cooperation that would lead six years later to the signing of the Lateran Accords.

At both the institutional and curricular levels, the Gentile reform expressed Fascist concerns about elite formation and the preservation of social hierarchies. It inaugurated a three-tier system of classification that gave some campuses greater autonomy and downgraded others. Royal universities were entirely state funded; royal superior institutes, which trained for specific professions, received a combination of state and private funding; "free universities" were financially independent but subject to state intervention in all other areas. To further distinguish between universities and institutes for professional formation, Gentile created university-level schools to train Italians in technical and scientific disciplines such as pharmacology, architecture, and engineering, and added university-level teacher education faculties (the *facoltà di Magistero*). Gentile's deprofessionalization of the university and his devaluation of scientific and technical disciplines was also reflected in the demotion of medical and scientific faculties to a rank below those of letters and philosophy.[14]

The deprofessionalization of the universities also allowed the Fascists to find their own solution to the ongoing dilemma of how to address concerns about the overproduction of graduates while meeting the increased demand for higher education. Under the Gentile legislation, students were forced to decide in adolescence whether to pursue professional training or the *liceo classico*—the only secondary school that allowed students to choose from a full range of faculties for their university education. The way that the issues of democratization and overproduction of graduates were used as foils against each another can be seen by Gentile's solution to the "problem" posed by the large numbers of Italian women who wished to obtain postsecondary education: the state encouraged them early on to attend the newly instituted *liceo femminile*, which did not allow access to university education. Most women who made it to the university level were channeled to the teacher-training *facoltà di magistero*. Enrollments in this faculty counted for a good part of the increased female presence within the university during Fascism (from 6 percent in 1914 to 20 percent in 1938), although a surge in female matriculations in all faculties starting in the late 1930s and increasing further

---

14. Sternhell, *Birth of Fascist Ideology*, 321–22.

during the war further raised anxieties about job market competition and female emancipation.[15]

Gentile's pedagogical thought devolved from his conception of the state as an "ethical" entity that embodied the universality of will. Self-realization, in this scheme, was achieved by a merging of the individual with the state, and civil conscience could only be formed by an internalization of the state's ethical precepts. This attribution of a moral and spiritual value to the state had obvious implications for scholastic policy, which was seen by Gentile as a central part of an organic project of national moral and cultural reform. In appointing the philosopher as minister of public instruction in October 1922—the same month as the March on Rome—Mussolini wished to bolster the regime's intellectual integrity, even as he signaled his intent to act in a "totalitarian" manner, to use a word that Gentile appropriated from the antifascist opposition and popularized through his many activities as philosopher, public intellectual, senator, and cultural organizer.[16] Indeed, the Gentile reform asserted the state's right to interfere in internal academic affairs. Rectors and deans, as well as the members of the national Superior Council of Public Instruction, were now nominated by the king rather than elected by full professors, and professors' general assemblies were abolished. Gentile improved faculty salaries, but he also restricted their outside earnings, instituted professorial residence requirements, and gave the Ministry of Public Instruction more control over the jury and candidate pools for university chair competitions (*concorsi di cattedra*).[17]

Not surprisingly, controversy greeted the Gentile reform from the moment it appeared. Although Croce and other prominent conservatives from the worlds of philosophy and pedagogy supported it, as did Catholics who praised the restoration of religious education in the schools, its attacks on academic freedom and its elitism drew criticism from the by-then beleaguered liberal and leftist press. Nor did protests lack from the

---

15. Michel Ostenc, *L'education en Italie pendant le fascisme* (Paris: Publications de la Sorbonne, 1980); Koon, *Believe, Obey, Fight*, 49–59. For an overview of the issues relating to female education, see Victoria de Grazia, *How Fascism Ruled Women* (Berkeley and Los Angeles: University of California Press, 1992), 147–63, especially 154–55.

16. On Gentile's university reform in the context of his overall pedagogical and philosophical ideas, see Antimo Negri, *Giovanni Gentile educatore: Scuola di Stato e autonomie scolastiche* (Rome: Armando, 1996), which takes an apologist tone at times, and Piergiovanni Genovesi, *La riforma Gentile tra educazione e politica* (Ferrara: Corso, 1996).

17. Ostenc, *L'education en Italie*, 76.

universities: the rector of the University of Rome denounced the state's interference in internal academic matters as a departure from Italian university tradition, and students at the University of Turin and elsewhere protested the higher fees medical and engineering students now had to pay. Gentile was loudly booed when he spoke at the University of Turin in May 1924.[18] These initial criticisms were partly addressed by the "corrections" (*ritocchi*) made by Gentile's successors, but a general feeling remained that the reform's self-reflexive vision of culture and its devaluation of technical and scientific knowledge made it ill-adapted to the social and economic realities of interwar Italian society. Gentile's education packet may have been "the most fascist reform," as Mussolini claimed, but it hardly reflected the priorities of a "revolutionary" regime that promised to make Italy a modern power.[19]

Making Fascists: Universities, Intellectuals, and the "Regime of Youth"

Gentile left the post of minister of public instruction in July 1924, at a time of crisis and transition for the Fascists that would have far-reaching effects on Italian institutions and culture. One month earlier, the Fascists had kidnapped the popular socialist deputy Giacomo Matteotti, who had been an outspoken opponent of the regime. The discovery of his body in August of that year set off a crisis for the blackshirts that found its "resolution" in Mussolini's January 1925 declaration of dictatorship. Over the next several years, a series of laws transformed Italy into a police state with extensive powers of surveillance and detention. A series of purges of the Fascist National Party (Partito Nazionale Fascista, or PNF) sought to domesticate the party and make it subordinate to the demands of the state; and the process of disciplining and socializing students began with the creation of youth organizations.

The political crackdown drastically altered student life, which had remained pluralist through the presence of many non- and antifascist

---

18. For reactions to the Gentile reform, see Koon, *Believe, Obey, Fight*, 55–59; Bongiovanni and Levi, *L'Università di Torino*, 3–10; and Ostenc, *L'education en Italie*, 158–60.
19. Of Gentile's immediate successors, Alessandro Casati (July 1924–January 1925), Pietro Fedele (1925–28), and Giuseppe Belluzzo (1928–29), only Belluzzo, who was an engineer, instituted technical education in the secondary schools.

student organizations. These were now dissolved, to the benefit of the GUFs, which now had a virtual monopoly on student life. Only the University Federation of Italian Catholics (FUCI) survived, in part because of its willingness to collaborate with the GUFs on Fascist anti-Masonic campaigns.[20] The institutionalization of Fascist violence that was the lasting result of the Matteotti affair legitimated the consolidation of a climate of "defamation and intimidation"[21] on university campuses, where militants gave often violent lessons in "squadrist culture" that complemented the more traditional learning offered inside the lecture hall. Yet the GUFs never had the political role that official student organizations enjoyed in the early years of regimes such as Nazi Germany and Communist Czechoslovakia; rather, they were soon placed under the direct control of the PNF secretariat, depriving them of any autonomy.

While the political crackdown of the mid- and late 1920s led to no immediate purges among the professorial ranks, the threat of physical violence escalated for known antifascists, and all academics were subject to solicitations from Gentile and other functionaries who were attempting to foster the development of a recognizably "Fascist" culture. The first of these requests came in 1925 when Gentile, as the head of the newly created National Institute of Fascist Culture, asked for signatories for a "Manifesto of Fascist Intellectuals" to be published in leading newspapers. Croce quickly produced a countermanifesto, it too destined for the press, which presented antifascist academics with a quandry: should one speak out and risk being silenced? Or should one stay silent and stay at one's post to avoid leaving the field open for a Fascist colonization of culture and youth?

Such dilemmas of conscience would become common in the years to come, as the government acted to "fascisticize" Italian universities and purge all those who were not willing to serve the dictatorship. In 1925 the Fascist-dominated parliament passed a law allowing the regime to dismiss state employees who "do not give a full guarantee that they will faithfully carry out their duties or who place themselves in a situation of incompat-

---

20. La Rovere, *Storia dei GUF*, 111. On the FUCI and its relationship with the various organizations of the regime, see Richard J. Wolff, *Between Pope and Duce: Catholic Students in Fascist Italy* (New York: Peter Lang, 1990), and Renato Moro, *La formazione della class dirigente cattolica, 1929–1937* (Bologna: Mulino, 1979).

21. La Rovere, *Storia dei GUF*, 97. On the initial fascist university youth movements and their changing relationship with the PNF and the general university climate in the early period of Fascist rule, see La Rovere, *Storia dei GUF*, 15–115.

ibility with government directives." Despite the wording, no oral or written "guarantee" was asked for, and very few academics protested—one exception being the University of Turin law professor Francesco Ruffini, who had served as that institution's rector before World War I and whose open antifascism brought him threats from students and attempts by the then-current rector to remove him from examination juries.[22]

Even as Gentile and other notables painted Fascism as a regime that respected creative autonomy, measures promulgated over the next several years specifically for universities told professors that comportment counted more than culture in a totalitarian state that did not distinguish between private and professional life. As of 1926 a certificate of "good conduct" from one's mayor was required to be eligible to compete for professorial positions. One year earlier, the National Federation of Fascist Universitarians (Federazione nazionale universitaria fascisti, or FNUF), which had been created in 1922 as a student activist lobby group, was placed under the direct control of the PNF secretariat. By the end of the 1920s, its functions of patronage and punishment would parallel those of Fascist syndicates for artists and other professionals. The FNUF promised "moral and material assistance" to its members, which could include preferential treatment in job competitions. Yet it also provided a means of keeping close watch on a group that many officials considered politically unreliable. In 1931, renamed the Fascist Association of the School, it was given the task of compiling information on the political leanings of its members that was used by local PNF federations to approve or deny candidates for job competitions. With membership mandatory for PNF members, and PNF membership tacitly required for career advancement, party enrollments were high. At the University of Pavia, almost 100 percent of the teaching faculty joined.[23] In 1932, after a state investigation about the number of academics in the PNF, party membership became mandatory in order to compete for any level of academic position. Thereafter, the date of PNF enrollment became another point of government leverage over university teachers. Those who had joined before 1932 were favored in hiring and promotion decisions. Later enrollees were suspected careerists,

---

22. Bongiovanni and Levi, *L'Università di Torino*, 51; Ostenc, *L'education en Italie*, 276.
23. Signori, "L'università in uniforme," 200. On the creation of syndicates for intellectuals, see Marla Stone, *The Patron State. Culture and Politics in Fascist Italy* (Princeton: Princeton University Press, 1998); Philip Cannistraro, *La fabbrica del consenso* (Bari: Laterza, 1975); and Ruth Ben-Ghiat, *Fascist Modernities: Italy, 1922–45* (Berkeley and Los Angeles: University of California Press, 2001), 20–26.

who, the rueful joke went, had joined the PNF "for family reasons" ("per necessità famigliare") rather than faith. Rectors and deans also came under scrutiny. The Fascist Grand Council ruled that they had to be PNF members for at least five years at time of appointment and ordered them to make black shirts part of their daily uniform.[24]

By the end of the first decade of Fascist rule, the regime had thus effectively instituted its own mechanisms of selection based on politics as well as professional preparation. But the issue of purging the existing teaching corps remained open. Neither the Gentile reform nor subsequent legislation had mandated the removal of recalcitrant faculty, since the Fascists been wary of alienating the intellectual class and bourgeois opinion as they consolidated their power. By the early 1930s, though, as Fascism expanded into a mass regime, culture took on a heightened importance as an agent of collective indoctrination at home and of image rehabilitation abroad. In this scheme, academics would act as scholars whose research would bring Italy prestige and as divulgators who would bridge the gap between high and popular knowledge and form a new generation of fascisticized Italians.

The recasting of academic culture in a totalitarian light gave new urgency to the task of removing antifascist professors. In 1931, all university professors were asked to sign a loyalty oath that read:

> I swear to be loyal to the king, to his royal successors, and to the Fascist regime, to faithfully observe the statute and other state laws, to exercise the office of teacher and to carry out all my academic duties with the aim of forming productive, upstanding citizens who are devoted to the Patria and to the Fascist regime. I swear that I do not belong nor will I belong to any associations or parties those activities are not compatible with the duties of my position.[25]

Whether out of fear of reprisals, passivity, Fascist fervor, or economic need, the vast majority of academics signed. Just 12 out of 1,250 refused, out of conscience, antifascist politics, or other considerations (such as

---

24. Vinci, *Storia dell'Università di Trieste*, 266–69.
25. Koon, *Believe, Obey, Fight*, 66–67. See also Goetz, *Der freie Geist und seine Widersacher*, and Mirri and Arieti, *La cattedra negata*.

independent wealth or being close to retirement). Among these were Ruffini, the Turin law professor, who took early retirement, the art historian Lionello Venturi, the University of Bologna surgeon Bortolo Negrisoli, who was severely beaten by Fascist thugs for his action, and the literary critic and writer Giuseppe Borgese, a professor of aesthetics at the University of Milan who at the time of the oath had a visiting appointment at the University of California. Borgese resigned from his Italian position and became a permanent exile in America, teaching first at Smith College and then at the University of Chicago. In his 1937 denunciation of the dictatorship, *Goliath: The March of Fascism*, Borgese scathingly declared that the oath changed the behavior of Italian intellectuals, even those who had previously held themselves aloof from the regime: "Many of them rationalized the oath and became interested in the permanent triumph of fascism, seeking in it the justification of their behavior."[26] Drawing on this, I would argue that the oath's long-term impact lay in its performative dimension: its content was certainly important, since it committed the signer to direct his or her teaching toward a precise political goal, but so was the ritual of signing before one's rector, with two witnesses in tow. If the blackshirt-clad rector stood in for the state in this symbolic transaction, the witnesses (*testimoni*) represented the eyes and ears of the signer's peers. Such occasions bound academics together by creating a sense of collective complicity about their voluntary subjugation to the dictatorship.[27]

For the numbers of academics who believed in Fascism, such controls were a small price to pay for the transformation of Italian learning. As in most other dictatorships, purges went hand in hand with promotions for those who were specialists in areas of knowledge that had political utility (such as demography, political economy, colonialism, and anything to do with antiquity). These individuals enjoyed myriad career opportunities as the government started new institutes and journals and sponsored studies, research missions, and public works. New fields of knowledge also appeared, the most important in this period being corporativism, the regime's much-vaunted plan for reorganizing the economy. Largely due to the efforts of Giuseppe Bottai, who served as minister of corporations

---

26. Giuseppe Antonio Borgese, *Goliath: The March of Fascism* (New York: Viking, 1937), 305; also Koon, *Believe, Obey, Fight*, 66–67.

27. See Ben-Ghiat, *Fascist Modernities*, esp. chap. 1, for an analysis of the place of these rituals within fascist culture.

from 1928 to 1932 and minister of national education after 1936, corporativist studies came to constitute a sort of subculture within the academy, with its own university chairs, journals, book series, and under- and postgraduate degree offerings. Labor and legal scholars, economists, and political scientists were among those who contributed most to and benefited most from these innovations. Political science also gained autonomy and status during Fascism. In 1927 the University of Perugia inaugurated the first faculty of political science in Italy, and other universities quickly followed suit, offering courses that included the history and doctrine of Fascism and, in the 1930s, comparative studies on European fascism. This allocation of resources reflected official perceptions that political science, like corporativism, would attract the most politicized students and teachers and act as an ideological stronghold within the university. In fact, case studies of the universities of Turin, Trieste, and Pavia bear this supposition out; the senior theses (*tesi di laurea*, required for graduation) from these faculties tended to follow the flow of Fascism's ideological and diplomatic positions, as for that matter did professors' course topics.[28] Certainly, alterations to the curriculum were far from uniform. Local traditions continued to matter, as did the personality and politics of individual rectors, whose decisions about the use of campus resources (for university and external events) also set the tone of academic life.[29]

To effect these institutional and cultural changes, the regime used a combination of legislation and coercion to gain the compliance of university faculty. These instruments proved less efficacious, though, with regard to the final goal of official education reform: to socialize university students as Fascists and train them to serve as the regime's future leaders. The question of forming a new elite had preoccupied officials since the start of the regime, and the Fascist cult of youth had been an effective drawing point for the university students who were its earliest and most fervent supporters. Generational thinking formed an important characteristic of all European rightist movements, but the construct of youth

---

28. See the detailed case studies by Signori, "L'Università in uniforme"; Vinci, *Storia dell'Università di Trieste*; and Bongiovanni and Levi, *L'Università di Torino*; also Maria Cristina Giuntella, "La facoltà fascista di Scienze Politiche di Perugia e la formazione della classe dirigente," in *Politica e società in Italia dal fascismo alla Resistenza*, ed. G. Nenci (Bologna: Mulino 1978), 293–313.

29. At the University of Turin, the installation of an enthusiastically fascist rector Silvio Pivano in 1928 accelerated politicization. Pivano added courses on corporativist law and other "fascist" subjects and offered to host a "school of corporativist culture" for syndical leaders. Bongiovanni and Levi, *L'Università di Torino*, 63.

was even more central for the Italian Fascist ideological identity, though, since the blackshirts lacked mobilizing myths such as class struggle or (before 1938) race, which were so effectively utilized by the Communists and National Socialists respectively. Inside Italy, youth and education policies worked together to reinforce restrictions on opportunities for social mobility. The structure of official youth groups makes this point clearly: postsecondary school males were channeled into two distinct groups—the *fasci giovanili di combattimento*, for lower-class Italians who would not continue their education, and the GUFs, who as the future managerial class enjoyed special freedoms and privileges.[30]

In the early 1930s, paralleling the intensification of discussions about the need for a uniquely Fascist culture, the issue of elite formation occupied increasing space in the press. Mussolini had already proclaimed Fascism to be a "regime of youth," and now officials and ideologues simultaneously aired blueprints for political socialization and worried that the tepid political fervor of most university professors would limit their implementation. The sociologist Camillo Pellizzi warned that the gap between Fascism's inflammatory rhetoric and repressive reality had already begun to alienate the brightest members of the new generation. "One cannot serve the cause of revolution and reaction at the same time," he intoned in a 1932 article that perhaps necessarily remained without answer.[31] In fact, although students had provided key support for early Fascism, the generation now coming of age, those born roughly between 1905 and 1915, seemed to be more critical and disaffected. Too young to have experienced World War I or the March on Rome, many of these students felt a kind of status anxiety in a regime that made combat experience a measure of character and political faith. Excluded from Fascism's past, they claimed a starring role in the fashioning of Fascism's future, only to find themselves cast as servants, or, in the words of one young art critic, as "those who look on . . . as those who, for good or ill, merely obey."[32]

---

30. On fascist youth policies and elite formation, see Koon, *Believe, Obey, Fight*; Bruno Wanrooj, "The Rise and Fall of Italian Fascism as a Generational Revolt," *Journal of Contemporary History* 22 (1987): 401–18; Paolo Nello, "Mussolini e Bottai: Due modi diversi di concepire l'educazione fascist della gioventù," *Storia contemporanea* 1, no. 2 (June 1977): 335–66; Ben-Ghiat, *Fascist Modernities*, chap. 4; and Gino Germani, "La socializzazione politica dei giovani nei regimi fascisti: Italia e Spagna," *Quaderni di sociologia*, January-June 1966, 11–58.

31. Camillo Pellizzi, "Terza lettera," *Il Selvaggio*, 31 March 1932; also Massimo Bontempelli, "Scuola dell'ottimismo," *Occidente*, November-December 1932.

32. Nino Bertocchi, "Imposizione della sobrietà," *L'Orto*, April 1932.

Judging from police reports and youth journals, this sense of failed expectations became more widespread at Italian universities in the early 1930s. Informers related that in Turin, Rome, Naples, and other cities "antagonism, diffidence, and demoralization" reigned among university students, who were disappointed at the disjunction between the regime's youth-promoting propaganda and the limitations imposed by political controls and a depression-era job market. "This regime, which claims it wants to valorize youth, is actually trying to clip their wings and protect the old guard," reported one Neapolitan spy in summing up their feelings.[33] Independent youth journals run by university students confirm these sentiments, as do the reviews of local GUF organizations. The reviews *Saggiatore* and *Orpheus*, run by philosophy students at the Universities of Rome and Milan, respectively, stand out in the first category. Both enthusiastically Fascist publications blamed the hegemony of "old men and old ideas" for the slow pace of change in Italy, and Gentile was a favorite target. Both reviews lambasted Idealism for its preoccupation with obsolete "metaphysical concerns" and championed doctrines that would reflect the "anti-ideological" nature of Fascism—namely, pragmatism and phenomenology. *Saggiatore* also advocated the inclusion of science in school curricula, whereas the more modernist-inflected *Orpheus*, which had many female contributors, complained of gender discrimination in the universities and the lack of sex education in the lower schools.[34] Attacks on the education establishment also came from the more independed-minded reviews of the GUF. In *Vent'anni*, the journal of the University of Turin GUF, Alberto Bairati complained that the Gentile reform had allowed liberalism's "decrepit and moldy atmosphere" to continue well into the dictatorship. He argued for a renewal of the

---

33. Quotations from 30 May 1931, report from Turin, in Archivio Centrale dello Stato (ACS), Ministero dell'Interno (MI), Division Generale Pubblica Sicurezza (DGPS), Affari Generali e Riservati (AGR) (1927–33), Cat. C2, b.1; and 20 April 1931, report from Naples, in ACS, MI, Divisione Polizia Politica (DPP), Affari per materia, pacco 149, ff. 21, K112 (1929–31). This last file also contains reports from Parma, Modena, Milan, and Bologna, and the original order from the Fascist police chief, who asked informers to find out "what [university] students are doing and if bad feelings are brewing."

34. Quotations from Mario Pannunzio, "Contributo all'inchiesta sulla nuova cultura," *Saggiatore*, August-October 1933. On these independent youth journals and their attacks against idealism, see Ben-Ghiat, *Fascist Modernities*, chap. 4, and Mario Sechi, *Il mito della nuova cultura* (Manduria: Lacaita, 1984).

professorial ranks through earlier retirements and the promotion of younger scholars who shared his generation's worldview.[35]

The regime responded to this situation of collective disaffection with a new set of policies meant to convince university students that Fascism was going to "make way for youth" (*far largo ai giovani*). These measures favored Italians under thirty for civil service posts (including in academia), spawned new postgraduate professional schools to stave off intellectual unemployment, afforded students more freedom of discussion, and established patronage programs for young intellectuals. For most university students, this new largesse was experienced most directly through the GUFs, which underwent a massive expansion of their programs and resources in the 1930s. GUF chapters appeared in every Italian university town, and membership was extended to students of military academies, who, like university students, could participate in GUF activities even after graduation, up to age twenty-eight. GUF budgets increased almost tenfold between 1930 and 1937, and sevenfold more between 1937 and 1943. By 1941, funding for GUF activities amounted to 54 percent of the budget of PNF youth programs. This enormous figure communicates the importance the party gave them as a means of training a new elite.[36]

Like the Sindicato Español Universitario (SEU) of Franco's Spain, for which they served as a model, the GUFs engaged university students in many ways, and it is no exaggeration to say that most of postwar Italy's political and cultural elite participated in their activities, even though membership was voluntary until 1939.[37] As was the case in Spain and in Nazi Germany, students became active for pragmatic as well as political reasons. The GUFs offered low-cost meals and medical care, as well as the use of an on-campus Student House (Casa dello Studente) with lodging and recreational spaces. The GUFs were also essential cultural resources: they gave young men and women access to cultural events and fields of endeavor that might have normally been closed to them, and public

---

35. Alberto Bairati, "La missione educativa ai giovani," *Vent'anni* 3 (1933), cited in Bongiovanni and Levi, *L'Università di Torino*, 97.
36. On the GUFs, see Koon, *Believe, Obey, Fight*, 196–216; La Rovere, *Storia dei GUF*; and Benedetta Garzarelli, "Un aspetto della politica totalitaria del PNF: I Gruppi universitari fascisti," *Studi storici*, October-December 1997, 1121–61.
37. GUF enrollments rose from 55,000 in 1931 to 75,000 in 1936 and reached 164,000 by end of the regime. Figures from Koon, *Believe, Obey, Fight*, 190.

recognition to those with talent. The GUFs' Experimental Theatre companies, many of which went on tour, attracted budding actors and directors, and the "Cineguf" cinema groups, of which fifty-four existed by 1939, allowed Italians to learn 16mm film production. With government permission, the Cinegufs also sponsored film series of uncensored, undubbed movies; Pier Paolo Pasolini was among those who attended the Bologna GUF's showings of foreign films. Finally, dozens of GUF journals offered writers, journalists, cartoonists, and photographers hands-on experience. "I took advantage of the GUF to change my status in life, to pass from a simple office worker to the creative and independent work of the intellectual," recalled the journalist Antonio Ghirelli, who got his start writing for his local GUF journal during the war.[38]

In this panorama of GUF activities the Littoriali della cultura e dell'arte competitions merit particular attention. The relaxed censorship, special mentoring, and other privileges afforded to university youth were all operative in these events, which gave students national exposure for their intellectual and creative abilities. Designed to stimulate competition among the very best youth and bring them to the attention of Fascist officials, the Littoriali consisted of debates on written and oral presentations in areas that ranged from film criticism to racial doctrine. Topics changed each year, making the Littoriali a yardstick of the changing priorities of the regime from the first competition in 1934 to the last meeting in 1940. Female students had their own Littoriali, which were held from 1939 to 1941. While the press gave much more attention to the male competitions, winners of both sexes received money, a gold M, and a chance to meet Mussolini and jurors such as Ottorino Respighi and Giuseppe Ungaretti. As a mechanism for identifying future leaders, the Littoriali functioned rather efficiently: the list of winners includes the designer Ettore Sottsass, the politicians Mario Alicata and Aldo Moro, and the director Giuseppe De Santis.[39] By the end of the 1930s, the competitions had a reputation for tolerating nonconformist thinking and behavior, both of the type that Fascist officials had probably anticipated (irreverent pranks, riotous

---

38. Antonio Ghirelli, "Il GUF di Largo Ferrandina," in *La Campania dal fascismo alla repubblica*, ed. Giovanna Percopo and Sergio Riccio (Naples: Storia, 1977), 2:142. The Cinegufs are analyzed in Elena Banfi, "Attività del Cineguf-Milano," *Communicazioni sociali*, July-December 1988, 304–29, and Gian Piero Brunetta, *Storia del cinema italiano, 1896–1945* (Rome: Laterza, 1993), 76–97.

39. Marina Addis Saba and Ugoberto Alfassio Grimaldi, *Cultura a passo romano* (Milan: Feltrinelli, 1983), give a complete chronicle of each Littoriali with themes and winners.

discussions) and of the type that they had not (booing officials, open criticism of foreign policy decisions such as the alliance with Hitler). Indeed, the Littoriali have been remembered as an important stop on the "long voyage" that took young Italians from Fascism to antifascism. Antifascists did come to the Littoriali in search of converts: the University of Padova student Eugenio Curiel covered the competitions simultaneously for the Padova GUF review *Il Bò* and the Italian Communist Party exile paper *Lo stato operaio*. It is more accurate, however, to say that for most participants the Littoriali, like other GUF activities, functioned as a space of education about the range of opinions their peers held about Fascism rather than as any catalyst to active dissent.[40]

Italian Universities Between Empire and War

In 1935–36, Italy invaded and conquered Ethiopia, setting in motion a chain of events that brought Italy into an alliance with Nazi Germany and ultimately into World War II. Domestically, the declaration of empire produced paroxysms of patriotic rhetoric and fueled protectionist and autarchic measures that had an impact on Italian cultural and university life. Most immediately, it strengthened the hand of those in and out of government who believed that Italy's future as a leader of rightist Europe required a total fascisticization of the school. The pedagogue Luigi Volpicelli argued that Italian schools needed "four or five years of really tough dictatorship" to effect change at the human as well as institutional level. The students of *Vent'anni* echoed this sentiment in terms that convey the militarized climate that took hold in the universities: "The Gentile reform is outdated . . . because it had as its goal the free spiritual, moral, cultural and civic formation of youth . . . but today the common

---

40. On the Littoriali as an antifascist recruiting site, see Ruggero Zangrandi, *Il lungo viaggio attraverso il fascismo: Contributo alla storia di una generazione* (Turin: Einaudi, 1948); Ettore Albertoni et al., eds., *La generazione degli anni difficili* (Bari: Laterza, 1962); Alessandro Bonsanti, "La cultura degli anni trenta: Dai Littoriali all'anti-fascismo," *Terzo programma* 4 (1963): 183–219; and Paolo Alatri, "Cultura e politica: Gli studenti romani dal 1936 al 1943," *Incontri meridionali* 3–4 (1979): 7–17. These works, which are authored by or include interviews with men who had grown up under the regime, tend to exaggerate the degree of antifascist feeling among university youth. La Rovere, *Storia dei GUF*, provides a corrective to such views. On the GUF journal *Il Bò* and Curiel's uncover operations, see Ivano Paccagnella, "Stampa di fronda: 'Il Bò' tra Guf e Curiel," in *Credere, obbedire, combattere: Il regime linguistico nel Ventennio*, ed. F. Foresti (Bologna: Pendragon, 2003), 129–54.

denominator of all scholastic policy must be the task of forming the Fascist citizen-soldier . . . the school must not be afraid of forcing, with a violently educative intervention if necessary, the individual formation of every single youth."[41] Indeed, after 1935, war provided a new context for Fascist social engineering projects. It was no longer enough for the regime to create Italians who could "believe, obey, and fight"; now they must prepare to conquer and rule. Over the next several years, Mussolini undertook a "reform of custom" in Italy that imposed the goosestep and other practices designed to inculcate a command mentality. Within this scheme, university students would serve as a new class of colonial experts, from administrators to specialists in tropical medicine, and as the creators and propagators of a new Fascist imperial culture to be diffused throughout the world.[42]

Without a doubt, the conquest of Ethiopia marked the height of popular and intellectual enthusiasm for the regime. For students, the war offered a chance to finally translate their political faith into concrete action. So many university students volunteered for combat that Mussolini had to authorize additional "Universitarian's Battalions," and special honors were accorded to those who fell on the battlefield. The University of Pavia gave honorary degrees to students who were killed in action, and commemorated them with marble placards in its "courtyard of the martyrs." The climate of excitement spurred political activism, and the GUFs surged in popularity at this time: enrollments at the University of Trieste chapter doubled between 1936 and 1937.[43]

The appointment in 1935 of Cesare Maria De Vecchi as the new minister of national education suggests that Mussolini, too, was ready to embrace a harder pedagogical line. De Vecchi was in many ways an unlikely education bureaucrat; although his Catholic and monarchist sentiments placed him on good terms with Italian conservatives, his shaved head and mustache bespoke a past history of head-busting. Inaugurating a course on Fascist culture two years earlier, he had referred to himself as "mountain warrior," and he now declared war on the "individualistic and

---

41. Luigi Volpicelli, quoted in Rino Gentili, *Giuseppe Bottai e la riforma fascista della scuola* (Florence: La Nuova Italia, 1979), 26; also Alberto Bairati, "De Vecchi e l'educazione fascista," *Vent'anni*, 1935. Luigi Volpicelli, quoted in Gentili, *Giuseppe Bottai*, 26.

42. On this nascent colonial culture and the shift in cultural climate after 1936, see Ben-Ghiat, *Fascist Modernities*, chap. 5.

43. Signori, "L'Università in uniforme," 193; Vinci, *Storia dell'Università di Trieste*, 347; Zangrandi, *Il lungo viaggio*, 66; La Rovere, *Storia dei GUF*, 255–64.

decentralized spirit" that still reigned in the schools thanks to the Gentile reform. The universities were his particular target, and he used his brief tenure to eliminate much institutional and academic autonomy by arrogating responsibility for professorial hires and transfers (which gave the government the power to threaten academics with transfers to remote areas); by requiring academic institutes to be affiliated with the nearest university; and above all by establishing set curricula for each course of study. Although professors could petition to deviate from this norm, few exceptions were granted. Border region universities were hardest hit by this centralizing measure, as were universities with strong specialized programs that attracted students from throughout the country. At the University of Trieste, central European languages were downgraded to electives in a move that asserted the nationalizing agendas of the state.[44] De Vecchi's emphasis on centralization and uniformity mirrored contemporary trends within cultural policy and party structures. Yet his anti-intellectual bent and rude manner evoked the squadrist heritage that the Fascists wished to bury, especially at a time when Italy was the target of foreign observations and League of Nations sanctions for invading Ethiopia. Thus in late 1936 Bottai took over the post of minister of national education, where he would remain until he helped to remove Mussolini from office in July 1943.

Bottai's curriculum vitae made him well suited for the job. Although he was an ex-squadrist who had recently won medals for his volunteer service in Ethiopia at the age of forty, he was also the darling of the intelligentsia for his campaigns for a Fascist culture, his influential journal *Critica fascista*, and his position as the preeminent official patron of the intellectual class. He enjoyed a particular popularity among youth for championing all things modern: corporativism, some forms of artistic modernism, and later, anti-Semitism, which he understood as a salutary cure of degenerate influences on the national body. He presided over the expansion of the education establishment at a time when university enrollments had increased, and worked together with the Ministry of Popular Culture (MCP, established in 1937) to alleviate intellectual unemployment. The MCP also expanded to encompass five general directorates (press, propaganda, cinema, tourism, and theater), and assumed management of important cultural bodies such as the Society of Italian Authors and Editors.

---

44. On De Vecchi's tenure as minister of national education, see Koon, *Believe, Obey, Fight*, 68–70; Ricuperati, "Per una storia dell'università italiana," 340–43, from which the quotations are taken; and Vinci, *Storia dell'Università di Trieste*, 256.

These innovations were welcome news to the legions of under- and unemployed university graduates, many of whom found freelance or permanent work at the MCP.⁴⁵ Under Bottai's leadership, the Ministry of National Education also increased its staff and its connections with academics as it undertook ambitious efforts to protect Italy's cultural patrimony, and to promote the work of living Italian artists through a law that set aside 2 percent of public works project budgets for public art.⁴⁶

Bottai's activism and his totalizing and totalitarian worldview affected the Italian universities in three major ways: through the implementation of anti-Jewish laws in the schools, through initiatives that fostered Italian-German exchanges in line with the new Cultural Accord; and through the 1939 School Charter, which constituted the first thoroughgoing revision of the scholastic system since the Gentile reform. The question of why a country and a regime without a history of anti-Jewish violence adopted racial laws in 1938 is too complex to be fully addressed here. While the 1936 alliance with Nazi Germany clearly played a part, since Fascist anti-Semitic laws were modeled on the Nuremberg laws, racism also built on and responded to national issues and traditions. Aside from the contributions made by a history of Catholic anti-Judaism, anti-Semitic sentiments and legislation built on demographic measures that aimed to remold the Italian population; articulated fears about threats to Italy's autochtonous traditions at a time of rapid modernization; displaced onto the Jews older discourses about national groups (previously Southerners) who supposedly hindered the achievement of modernity and nationhood; and galvanized those who saw Fascism as a means of fighting bourgeois capitalism.⁴⁷ It is to such concerns, rather than to any desire to "imitate" Nazi Germany, that we must look in order to explain the support given to the racial laws by intellectuals in and out of the academy. Indeed, racism became for some intellectuals a means of differentiating Fascist from

---

45. The Ministry of Popular Culture had almost two hundred employees at its inception, and the minister, Dino Alfieri, aimed to expand it to eight hundred. On the MCP, see Philip Cannistraro, "Burocrazia e politica culturale nello Stato fascista: Il Ministero della Cultura Popolare," *Storia contemporanea* 1, no. 2 (June 1970): 273–98.

46. A good discussion of these projects is Alessandra Masi's introduction to Giuseppe Bottai, *La politica degli arti* (Rome: Editalia, 1992).

47. I have sketched out here arguments about the national appeal of racism that I develop in *Fascist Modernities*, 148–57; see also Carl Ipsen, *Dictating Demography* (Cambridge: Cambridge University Press), 184–94, and Gabriele Turi, "Ruolo e destino degli intellettuali nella politica razziale del fascismo," in *La legislazione antiebraica in Italia e in Europa* (Rome: Camera dei Deputati, 1989), 95–121.

National Socialist ideology, especially as worries about Italian subjugation within the Axis alliance set in.[48]

The changing climate of Italian culture was in fact first felt in the schools and universities, since Fascist ideologues and policymakers had labeled education an area of pronounced Jewish influence. "Our universities are invaded by Jewish professors. Here we need a true clean cut," wrote one polemicist on 4 August 1938.[49] In fact, the cutting process had already begun; one day earlier, foreign Jewish students had been removed from all universities, followed by textbooks by Jewish authors.[50]

The central role that Italian academics played in launching the racial campaign also made universities an immediate target. The July 1938 "Manifesto of Racial Scientists," which had signaled the start of state anti-Semitism, was authored by men who all held full-time positions within the Italian university system. These same individuals also served as editors of the notorious periodical *Difesa della razza*, which had started as an antimiscegenationist journal during the colonial war and now extended its prohibitions to include Jews.[51] It is no exaggeration to state that from 1938 to the end of the regime, anti-Semitism was a normal component of Italian Fascist culture and ideology and a routine category in the curriculum vitae of many Italian academics and intellectuals.

A "racial census" later that month prepared the way for more expulsions, which came in September with a decree that forbad Jews to teach or attend schools and universities (students currently matriculated were allowed to finish their degrees) and banned them from academies and cultural institutions. Commenting on these developments, the antifascist exile paper *Giustizia e Libertà* observed that recourse to purges of the

---

48. On this subject, see Ruth Ben-Ghiat, "Italian Fascists and National Socialists: The Dyamics of an Uneasy Relationship," in *Art, Culture, and Media*, ed. Richard Etlin (Chicago: University of Chicago Press, 2002), 255–84; Aaron Gillette, *Racial Theories in Fascist Italy* (London: Routledge, 2002); and Reiner Pommerin, "Rassenpolitische Differenzen im Verhältnis der Achse Berlin-Rom, 1938–43," *Vierteljahrshefte für Zeitgeschichte* 27 (1979): 646–60.

49. Giorgio Pini, "Difesa della razza," *Popolo d'Italia*, 4 August 1938.

50. See Giorgio Fabre, *L'elenco: Censura fascista, editoria e autori ebrei* (Torino: Zamorani, 1998); and Brizzi, *Silence and Remembering*.

51. The manifesto's authors were Guido Landra, research assistant at the Institute of Anthropology of the University of Rome and head of the Racial Studies Office at the Ministry of Popular Culture, as primary author; Lidio Cipriani, director of National Museum of Anthropology and Ethnology in Florence; Leone Franzi, assistant in pediatric medicine at the University of Milan; Marcello Ricci, assistant in zoology at the University of Rome; and Lino Businco, assistant in general pathology at the University of Rome, with input from Mussolini himself. *Difesa della razza*'s chief editor was Telesio Interlandi.

existing academy was a measure of the regime's failure to realize a viable culture of its own after sixteen years of Fascist rule. The government and its supporters saw it differently. In October, the ministerial bulletin *Vita universitaria* expressed its "unconditional admiration" for a measure that would "liberate us from a treacherous people, rejuvenate the University, and purify the race." A few weeks later the rector of the University of Palermo lauded the racial campaign and linked it to a larger attempt to discipline Italian universities, which had become through their own tolerance "a sort of asylum for the most undesirable people . . . Italians and foreigners, believers and unbelievers, faithful subjects and dangerous anarchists."[52]

The racial laws changed the composition of the Italian academy. A total of two hundred professors lost their positions, about 7–8 percent of the total national faculty. At the University of Trieste, for example, four of thirteen full professors, three of fifteen associates, and two of sixteen assistants left the academy.[53] The laws came as a particular shock to Jewish academics of Fascist leanings, such as the corporativist expert Gino Arias and the statistician Pier Paolo Luzzatto Fegiz, a PNF member from 1923, who had that year given talks at the request of the MCP while on a state-funded research trip to America. Medical and science faculties were especially hard hit, and the expulsion of Jews from these fields, which were seen as Jewish strongholds, was seen as a particular cause for celebration. The rector of Pavia declared that the racial laws would allow Italian science to become Italian and recommended continued vigilance against the "Jewish and Masonic conceptions that still pollute our intellectual life"[54]

Among non-Jewish Italian academics, the racial laws inspired no overt opposition — only one intellectual, the writer Massimo Bontempelli, refused to occupy a forcibly vacated chair — but only "a tired and passive acceptance."[55] Rather, as in Nazi Germany, state anti-Jewish provisions

---

52. "Come coprire i vuoti," *Vita universitaria*, 5 October 1938; Giuseppe Maggiore, "La scuola agli italiani," *Critica fascista*, 1 October 1938; "Neorazzismo," *Giustizia e Liberta*, 2 September 1938. See Finzi, *L'Università italiana*, for a full discussion of this measure. Also valuable case studies: Angelo Ventura, "Le leggi razziali all'Università di Padova," in *L'università dalle leggi razziali alla Resistenza*, ed. Ventura (Padua: CLEUP, 1996); F. Cavarocchi and A. Minerva, "La persecuzione razziale nell'ateneo fiorentino," in *Razza e fascismo: La persecuzione degli ebrei in Toscana, 1938–1943*, 2 vols., ed. Enzo Collotti (Roma: Carocci, 1999), 1:467–510, and Mirri and Arieti, *La cattedra negata*.

53. Vinci, *Storia dell'Università di Trieste*, 299.

54. "Come coprire i vuoti," in Signori, "L'università in uniforme," 209. On scientific culture and the racial laws, see Israel and Nastasi, *Scienza e razza*.

55. Turi, "Ruolo e destino," 104.

offered professional opportunities for academics, who disseminated the new ideology in academic and popular publications, on the radio, and in public lectures funded by cultural institutions. Ultimately, the career advancement possibilities created by the posts vacated by Jews and the formation of new or additional chairs in disciplines such as demography, biology, and anthropology proved more convincing than any pangs of conscience.[56] University students in this case took their cues from their teachers: the GUFs became important centers of racial propaganda, and every GUF headquarters had an office of demography and race. Although informers encountered occasional "hostility to the Rome-Berlin Axis" on university campuses, and Italian students sometimes booed newsreels on Nazism, such sentiments reflected opposition to Hitler's aggrandizing tendencies in the wake of the Anschluss rather than to the Italian racial laws.[57] The example of racism shows the extent to which Fascist ideology transformed the academy, despite the claims made by some that "autonomy of research" was respected and that neither racism nor other Fascist themes affected the substance of university life.[58]

The 1938 Cultural Accord between Italy and Germany also affected Italian university life. As Jens Petersen has written, for both German and Italian intellectuals, the Axis "opened the doors to a flood of desires to make contact, plan visits, and project long-term studies and collaborations." Education exchange agreements were just one aspect of a host of scientific, medical, legal, cultural, and youth group collaborations that began even before the formal signing of the accord in November 1938.[59] The Cultural Accord offered each regime the potential of new markets and audiences for its intellectual and artistic production and the chance to communicate its own history and vision of Europe's future. New university chairs and other teaching positions in German and Italian culture

---

56. On the formation of a culture of racism, see Renzo De Felice, *Storia degli ebrei sotto il fascismo* (Turin: Einaudi, 1993), 379–401, and Ben-Ghiat, *Fascist Modernities*, 148–57.

57. Reports from Milan, 12 January, and from ten other cities, 7 April 1938; reports from 9 April, 8 May, and 31 May 1938, all in ACS, MI, DGPS, DPP, b.132, F.K11. On changing youth attitudes in the late 1930s, see Ben-Ghiat, *Fascist Modernities*, 157–70; Koon, *Believe, Obey, Fight*, 237–46; and Zagarrio, "Giovani e apparati culturali."

58. Enrico Opocher, "L'università dalle leggi razziali alla resistenza," in Ventura, *L'Università dalle leggi razziali alla Resistenza*, 38–41.

59. On the Cultural Accord, see Petersen, "Vorspiel zu 'Stahlpakt'"; Andrea Hoffend, *Zwischen Kultur-Achse und Kulturkampf: Die Beziehungen zwischen "Drittem Reich" und faschistischem Italien in den Bereichen: Medien, Kunst, Wissenschaft und Rassenfragen* (Frankfurt am Main: P. Lang, 1998); and Ben-Ghiat, "Italian Fascists and National Socialists."

and literature appeared in both countries, Italian became an approved subject for state examinations in Germany, and innumerable conferences and exchanges brought together university students and academics in every field.

Pragmatism as well as ideology inspired these German-Italian intellectual collaborations. Hoping to advance their knowledge in medicine, biology, and the natural sciences, the Italians gave Germans access to their rich cultural patrimony. Job possibilities opened up in Germany for the underemployed Italian intellectual class, paralleling an Axis-produced flow of Italian manual laborers to Nazi factories; German art historians and classicists benefited from improved access to Italian sites and sources. These joint endeavors compensated for both regimes' exclusions from League of Nations–sponsored cultural-exchange networks. With the imposition of League sanctions on Italy, for example, the Fascists were shut out of the International Committees on Popular Arts and Traditions and lost their leadership of the League-affiliated International Institute for Educational Cinematography. The Italian-German Cultural Accord was merely the first of a series of agreements among authoritarian powers (such as those struck separately by Italy and Germany with Spain and with Japan) designed to establish a counter-web of cultural relations that would further anticommunist and imperialist political agendas.

In 1939, in the midst of these developments in racial and cultural politics, Bottai unveiled his School Charter as a means of finally realizing a truly Fascist education system. In 1935, as he was being considered for his future post as minister of national education, Bottai had attacked the Gentile reform as having worsened the problem of intellectual unemployment and perpetuated bourgeois solipsism with its protection of humanistic studies for their own sake.[60] Now, four years later, he had prepared his own reform designed to shift the emphasis within the school system from humanistic studies to fields associated with technology and labor. As Bottai argued in the 1939 Charter, the state was acting against its own interests in continuing to form a type of subject that could not meet its exigencies. "Although the country needs engineers, it makes lawyers . . . although it needs men in step with modern life, it remains guided by the ideas of a humanism that is outdated (and thus not humanistic) even

---

60. "La libertà degli studi e l'esame di Stato," *Critica fascista*, 1–15 June 1935; also Luigi Volpicelli, "Problemi della scuola," *Critica fascista*, 1 July 1935.

though it continues to profess its Fascist faith."[61] Bottai wished instead to produce a new knowledge and labor base that could sustain Italian Fascist projects of modernization and conquest. To this end, he engineered a complete revision of the school system that integrated labor service into the school and university curricula (following the example of the National Socialist Arbeitsdienst) and discouraged students from taking the path of classical education. Bottai's Charter otherwise affected universities only tangentially; *liceo classico* students no longer had the privilege of enrolling in any faculty they pleased, whereas choices expanded for graduates of the *liceo scientifico*. The Charter also attempted to discourage overall university attendance at a time when university enrollments were increasing by establishing a host of professional high-school level institutes to accelerate the production of trained technicians as Italy prepared for war.[62]

Although Bottai felt he was giving Italy a school system that finally took into account the realities of contemporary existence, the Charter's labor requirement caused much controversy and confusion among lower- and high-school teachers and parents. Lack of funds, the war, and obstructionism from these groups prevented it from ever being fully implemented. At the university level, too, Bottai clearly wished to engineer a radical shift in academic mentalities and culture. The expulsion of Jews from the system can be seen as a means to that end, even though the racial laws cost the Italians the most in fields of science, since distinguished physicists such as Enrico Fermi (whose wife was Jewish) emigrated. As a contribution toward this transformation, Bottai organized a 1941 debate on the topic "The Universities and Culture" in his review *Primato* that became a sort of referendum on the success of twenty years of Fascist cultural and education policies. University students, writing individually and as part of GUF journal collectives, gave the regime a failing vote. They observed that the academic establishment had never abandoned its liberal mindset, and placed the blame on a government that had been too respectful of democratic canons of academic freedom to force through changes befitting a dictatorial state. Even the loyalty oath had accomplished little in their

---

61. Giuseppe Bottai, "Carta della Scuola," in Gentili, *Giuseppe Bottai*, 96. Alexander De Grand, in *Bottai e la cultura fascista* (Rome: Laterza, 1978), 175–216, places the School Charter in the context of Bottai's long interest in education and elite formation.

62. See Barbagli, *Disoccupazione intellettuale*, 289–305, for a discussion of how Bottai's charter aimed to solve job-market problems; also see Gentili, *Giuseppe Bottai*, 65–150, and Ricuperati, "Per una storia dell'università italiana," 351–61.

estimation: "The Italian is much too shaped by the Catholic experience not to know intimately the tactic of the 'mental reservation,'" one young contributor concluded provocatively.[63]

At the other end of the spectrum lay the opinions of Gentile. The Idealist philosopher acknowledged the limitations of Fascist education reform, but concluded that the fault lay with those who had transformed his 1923 master plan beyond all recognition. Leveling a thinly veiled critique at Bottai's School Charter in particular, Gentile upheld the cause of limited academic autonomy and diagnosed the Italian university's ailment as a lack of liberty: "And I don't mean political liberty. That is a liberty quite difficult to define. It too is necessary; but impossible without the good will of individuals . . . I wish rather to speak of scientific, didactic liberty; that liberty proper to the life of the university and which subsists on thought. This [liberty] is always suffocated by laws and rules that are alien to its own nature: by uniform and rigid scholastic structures and by preestablished programs."[64] Although Gentile's viewpoint reflected sentiments shared by many academics, by 1941 it seemed almost anachronistic as a statement of Fascist education policy. It bespoke a bourgeois sense of cultural propriety that was totally absent from the totalitarian mentalities evinced in the student contributions.

Ultimately, it is to these students we must look to evaluate the consequences of Fascist education policies for Italian culture and the effects of twenty years of dictatorship on younger Italians. As in Nazi Germany, the political socialization of students was complicated by the impact of consumerism and mass culture on collective leisure practices and individual fantasies,[65] as well as by unresolved contradictions between nationalism and internationalism, revolution and reaction, tradition and modernity. Yet the Italian regime's longevity meant that an entire generation of youth developed from birth through university with a very limited

---

63. Pompeo Biondi, "Le università e la cultura," *Primato*, 1 April 1941; also Rivoluzione, "Le università e la cultura," ibid, and Il Bò, "Le università e la cultura," *Primato*, 1 March 1941.

64. Giovanni Gentile, "Le università e la cultura," *Primato*, 15 May 1941.

65. For insight into the way these contradictions operated in different spheres of Fascist policy, see Emilio Gentile, "La Nazione del fascismo: Alle origini del declino dello Stato nazionale," in *Nazione e nazionalità in Italia*, ed. Giovanni Spadolini (Bari: Laterza, 1994), 95–100; Victoria de Grazia, "Nationalizing Women: Competition between Fascist and Commercial Models in Mussolini's Italy," in *The Sex of Things*, ed. de Grazia (Berkeley and Los Angeles: University of California Press, 1996), 337–58; Ben-Ghiat, *Fascist Modernities*; and Alexander De Grand, "Cracks in the Façade: The Failure of Fascist Totalitarianism in Italy, 1935–39," *European History Quarterly* 4 (October 1991): 515–35.

political reference point: Mussolini and Fascism. Indeed, to those who did not travel abroad and received no conflicting messages from family, mentors, or peers, all of Fascism's causes and campaigns might have appeared perfectly normal and natural. In the recollection of the director Renato Castellani, whose interest in filmmaking had been jump-started by participating in his GUF, "we were like canaries born in a cage with no idea of what existed outside . . . one lived in a world organized in a certain manner, and one went ahead agreeing more or less with what this world did."[66] After the fall of Fascism, this generation became "a generation without a past":[67] entire subjects that had occupied student energies for years (such as corporativism, colonialism, or racism) vanished from the universities in 1945, even as the professorial corps responsible for those areas of study remained intact. What was the afterlife of this suddenly discredited knowledge base, and what kind of intellectual unemployment did graduates in these fields face after 1945? Answering these questions can clarify the consequences of the changes wrought to Italian universities as institutions and as networks of social and cultural life by twenty years of engagement with Mussolini's regime.

---

66. Renato Castellani, interview in *Nuovi materiali sul cinema italiano, 1929–1943* 2 vols. (Ancona: Mostra del nuovo cinema, 1976), 2:110.

67. The phrase "generation without a past" is from Luisa Mangoni, "Civiltà della crisi. Gli intellettuali fra fascismo e anti-fascismo," *Storia dell'Italia repubblicana*, 3 vols. (Turin: Einaudi, 1994), 1:617.

3

German Universities Under the Swastika

MICHAEL GRÜTTNER

For many decades, German universities were among the most prestigious institutions of the German Reich and served as a model for similar institutions in other countries. Most professors believed that universities and politics were, and ought to be, two fundamentally separate spheres. This meant that higher learning had to preserve its independence against politics, especially party politics, if it wanted to be credible and successful. And yet the universities made no serious effort in 1933–34 to resist the inroads of the Nazi state, and in the years that followed many professors deeply compromised themselves.

The following chapter attempts to explain this paradox and concentrates upon three main points: *First*, the capitulation of the universities without a fight in 1933. This discussion includes an analysis of the crisis of the universities at the end of the Weimar Republic, which was above all a crisis of the younger generation of academics. *Second*, the aims and structures of Nazi policy concerning the universities and its effect on the institutions of higher learning. Special attention will be given to personnel policy. *Third*, the reaction of faculty and students to the new reality in politics and university policy and their attitudes toward National Socialism.

Scholarly literature has offered extremely diverse, often contradictory judgments on the role of universities in Nazi Germany. While the older literature tended to portray universities in the Third Reich as basically healthy institutions, only marginally touched by politics, newer studies frequently represent teaching faculty as completely integrated in the Nazi system, fully devoted to its political goals. Neither interpretation does justice to historical reality, and should be replaced by a more differentiated view.

The following analysis is limited to the twenty-three universities that existed on German soil in 1933. Universities that were absorbed into the German Reich in the wake of the Nazi policy of expansion[1] or were under German occupation are not included. Their history differed significantly from that of traditional German universities and is best recounted within the context of Nazi occupation policy.[2]

The Universities in the Final Phase of the Weimar Republic

Traditionally, German universities were state institutions, but until 1933 they enjoyed a high degree of autonomy. University professors formed a relatively small group, all told about five thousand individuals. They were recruited chiefly from the educated and propertied middle class and were almost without exception men.[3]

By and large the structure of the universities had changed little since the nineteenth century.[4] The most important requirement for making an academic career was the *Habilitation*, a second, larger work of research or scholarship (after the doctoral dissertation) meant to demonstrate a person's qualification for a professorship. A successful *Habilitation* resulted in the appointment as a *Privatdozent*. *Privatdozenten*, a peculiarity of the German university system, had the right and obligation to offer regular courses, though this did not bring with it a fixed and regular income. As a rule, about five or six years after the *Habilitation*, a *Privatdozent* could expect to receive an appointment as an associate professor without civil-

---

1. These were the universities in Graz, Innsbruck, Poznań, Prague, Strasbourg, and Vienna.
2. On this topic, see "Universitäten im nationalsozialistisch beherrschten Europa," ed. Dieter Langewiesche, special issue, *Geschichte und Gesellschaft* 23, no. 4 (1997).
3. On the social structure of university professors, see Christian von Ferber, *Die Entwicklung des Lehrkörpers der deutschen Universitäten und Hochschulen, 1964–1954* (Göttingen: Vandenhoeck & Ruprecht, 1956), 163ff. On the number of university professors and the gender distribution, see *Statistisches Jahrbuch für das Deutsche Reich* (Berlin: Reimar Hobbing, 1932), 428.
4. On the structure of the universities prior to 1933, see Abraham Flexner, *Universities: American, English, German* (New York: Oxford University Press, 1930), 305ff., and Arnold Köttgen, *Deutsches Universitätsrecht* (Tübingen: Mohr, 1933).

Table 1   Religious affiliation of university professors at Prussian universities by status group, 1924

	Protestant		Catholic		Jewish		other		total	
		(%)		(%)		(%)		(%)		(%)
Tenured professors	770	78.0	168	17.0	39	4.0	10	1.0	987	100
Professors without civil-servant status	350	68.1	63	12.3	97	18.9	4	0.8	514	100
Privatdozenten	379	70.1	110	20.3	43	7.9	9	1.7	541	100
Total	1499	73.4	341	16.7	179	8.8	23	1.1	2042	100

SOURCE: Geheimes Staatsarchiv Preussischer Kulturbesitz (GStAPK) I Rep. 76 Va Sekt. 1 Tit. IV Nr. 28 Bd. II. folio 156f.; author's calculations.

servant status (*nichtbeamteter ausserordentlicher Professor*). This did not change his insecure position. *Privatdozenten* and professors without civil-servant status formed the pool of candidates for full professorships or professorial chairs (*Ordinariat*). Full professors or holders of chairs formed the core of the faculty. They dominated the most important university committees, the departmental faculties, as well as the university senates, which put them into a position to decide appointments or *Habilitationen*. Moreover, the deans and rectors were drawn exclusively from their ranks. In 1919, Carl Heinrich Becker, the most influential figure in education policy in the Weimar Republic, described the power of full professors with good reason as "nearly absolute."[5] Next to the full professors there existed a second, smaller group of regular professors, the so-called *planmässige ausserordentliche Professoren* (regular associate professors). Unlike the *Privatdozenten* and associate professors without civil-servant status, their jobs and incomes were guaranteed for life, but they earned substantially less than full professors and had much less influence on university politics.

When it comes to the denominational structure of the professoriate, the only detailed data we have at this time pertains to Prussia (Table 1). Yet these numbers are likely to be fairly representative, especially since more than half of German universities were on Prussian soil. According to this data, in the 1920s nearly three-quarters of all professors were Protestant (percentage of Protestants within the overall population: 64.1 percent). By comparison, Catholic professors, who made up 16.7 percent of university faculty, were clearly underrepresented (percentage of Catholics within the overall population: 32.4 percent).

5. Carl Heinrich Becker, *Gedanken zur Hochschulreform* (Leipzig: Quelle & Meyer, 1919), 55.

We know that the stance taken by the majority of German university professors toward the project of a democratic republic was from the outset one of rejection or at least pronounced distance. Most mourned the demise of the Bismarckian empire and saw the Weimar Republic primarily as "the shameful result of a lost war," as Wolfgang Kunkel put it in retrospect.[6] But nostalgia for Imperial Germany was not the only reason for rejection of Weimar. As early as the summer of 1918, Max Weber noted that behind all the "clamor" against democracy lay another, weightier cause: anxiety over the leveling consequences of democratization.[7]

The antirepublican stance was interlaced with anti-Semitic resentments, though these were rarely articulated openly and aggressively. University professors disapproved of "rowdy anti-Semitism." The prevailing prejudice was a "quiet anti-Semitism," which "one could feel more than see," as one contemporary noted.[8] In practice this led to open discrimination against Jewish candidates for professorial chairs.[9] To be sure, until 1933 Jews did play a significant role in higher education. As Table 1 shows, in 1924 nearly 9 percent of all Prussian university teachers were members of the Jewish religious community (percentage of Jews within the overall population: 0.9 percent), among them numerous important scientists and several Nobel laureates.[10] But as a result of discrimination, very few Jewish scholars were given regular professorships. In 1924, 4 percent of tenured professors were Jews, but among professors without civil-servant status the figure was 18.9 percent, and among *Privatdozenten* 7.9 percent (Table 1).

Universities defined themselves as apolitical institutions which sought to preserve their autonomy vis-à-vis the political parties: "Parties and party politics stand in contradiction to the nature of the university," Rudolf Smend, a well-known professor of law, stated at the time.[11] To be sure,

---

6. Wolfgang Kunkel, "Der Professor im Dritten Reich," in *Die deutsche Universität im Dritten Reich: Eine Vortragsreihe der Universität München* (Munich: Piper, 1966), 107.

7. Max Weber, "Parlament und Regierung im neugeordneten Deutschland," in Max Weber, *Gesamtausgabe* (Tübingen: Mohr, 1984), sec. 1, vol. 15, p. 593.

8. Kunkel, "Der Professor im Dritten Reich," 109.

9. Notker Hammerstein, *Antisemitismus und deutsche Universitäten, 1871–1933* (Frankfurt am Main: Campus, 1995), 68ff.

10. Shulamit Volkov, "Soziale Ursachen des Erfolgs in der Wissenschaft—Juden im Kaiserreich," *Historische Zeitschrift* 245 (1987): 315–42; idem, "Juden als wissenschaftliche 'Mandarine' im Kaiserreich und in der Weimarer Republik: Neue Überlegungen zu den sozialen Ursachen des jüdischen Erfolgs in den Naturwissenschaften," *Archiv für Sozialgeschichte* 37 (1997): 1–18.

11. Rudolf Smend, "Hochschule und Parteien," in *Das Akademische Deutschland*, ed. Michael Doeberl et al. (Berlin: Weller, 1930–31), 3:153.

this attitude was not free of hostility toward the multiparty Weimar state.[12] But it was also directed against the political right if it threatened university autonomy. When the nazified government of Thuringia procured a chair for racial scientist Hans F. K. Günther in 1930 against the will of the university, the Association of German Universities decried this "politicization of the universities."[13]

And yet a surprisingly large number of university professors were involved in party politics between 1919 and 1932. Recent local studies have consistently shown that about 20–30 percent of all university faculty were politically active,[14] chiefly in the nationalist conservative German National People's Party (Deutschnationale Volkspartei, DNVP). Alongside nationalist strongholds such as Tübingen, Göttingen, or Bonn, there were universities, for example Hamburg, where the more moderate German People's Party (Deutsche Volkspartei, DVP) attracted professors' allegiance. Heidelberg University, where for a time the supporters of the democratic parties—especially the German Democratic Party (Deutsche Demokratische Partei, DDP)—were in the majority, was a singular case.[15]

It is probably safe to say that members of the NSDAP did not play a numerically important role at any university prior to 1933. Moreover, the vast majority of party members were assistants, *Privatdozenten*, and associate professors; that is, not part of the core faculty.[16] The petit bourgeois and plebeian social profile of the NSDAP, the demagogic style of its propaganda,

---

12. Christian Jansen, *Professoren und Politik: Politisches Denken und Handeln der Heidelberger Hochschullehrer, 1914–1935* (Göttingen: Vandenhoeck & Ruprecht, 1992), 92ff., 215ff.

13. On the appointment of Günther, see Universitätsarchiv Jena D 1010 und N 46/1 folio 126–224. See also "Der Hochschulverband zum Fall Günther," *Karlsruher Tageblatt*, 8 November 1930.

14. On this and the discussion that follows, see Rainer Hering, "Der 'unpolitische' Professor? Parteimitgliedschaften Hamburger Hochschullehrer in der Weimarer Republik und im 'Dritten Reich,'" in *Hochschulalltag im "Dritten Reich." Die Hamburger Universität, 1933–1945*, ed. Eckart Krause et al. (Berlin: Dietrich Reimer, 1991), 1:88ff.; "... *treu und fest hinter dem Führer": Die Anfänge des Nationalsozialismus an der Universität Tübingen, 1926–1934* (Tübingen: Universitätsarchiv, 1983), 22; Barbara Marshall, "Der Einfluss der Universität auf die politische Entwicklung der Stadt Göttingen, 1918–1933," *Niedersächsisches Jahrbuch für Landesgeschichte* 49 (1977): 271; Hans-Paul Höpfner, *Die Universität Bonn im Dritten Reich* (Bonn: Bouvier, 1999), 7f.

15. Jansen, *Professoren und Politik*, 298ff.

16. Hering, "Der unpolitische Professor?" 92f.; Michael H. Kater, "Die nationalsozialistische Machtergreifung an den deutschen Hochschulen," in *Die Freiheit des Anderen: Festschrift für Martin Hirsch*, ed. Manfred Degen et al. (Baden-Baden: Nomos, 1981), 62f.; H. W. Niemann, "Die TH im Spannungsfeld von Hochschulreform und Politisierung," in *Universität Hannover, 1831–1981* (Stuttgart: Kohlhammer, 1981), 1:84.

and the fear that it would restrict intellectual freedom all ensured that few full professors joined the party. Fear of career disadvantages also kept some otherwise sympathetic professors from joining.[17] University teachers figured among the traditional elites who contributed significantly to Weimar's unraveling, but they did not participate in any meaningful way in the rise of National Socialism as a mass movement.

By contrast, students embraced National Socialism very early and with particular enthusiasm. In 1931 the National Socialist German Student League (Nationalsozialistischer Deutscher Studentenbund, NSDStB) emerged as the strongest political force at most German universities. Over 44.6 percent of all student voters cast their ballots for the National Socialists; the following year, that number rose to 49.1 percent.[18] Since voter participation ranged between 60 percent and 80 percent, these results are clear evidence of the political attitudes of a large portion of the student body. The story was not new: students had been highly receptive to *völkisch* ideologies long before the rise of the NSDAP. In the 1880s significant numbers of students embraced an aggressive nationalism, and with it anti-Semitism.[19] After 1919 this trend spread and became increasingly radical.[20]

At the beginning of the 1930s German universities faced a multifaceted crisis. It was above all financial. In Prussia, funding for the universities was slashed by more than one-third during the Depression, dropping from 70.8 million Reichsmark (1929) to 43.2 million Reichsmark (1932).[21] But the crisis was also one of legitimacy, caused by growing criticism of overspecialization and the "estrangement of higher learning from real life." This criticism was strongly shared by the Nazi students, who charged that universities had nothing to say about contemporary problems.[22] Most

---

17. In Prussia, membership in the NSDAP was prohibited for civil servants after 1930. See Hans-Peter Ehni, *Bollwerk Preussen? Preussen-Regierung, Reich-Länder-Problem und Sozialdemokratie, 1928–1932* (Bonn: Neue Gesellschaft, 1975), 56.

18. Michael Grüttner, *Studenten im Dritten Reich* (Paderborn: Schöningh, 1995), 53ff. See also Anselm Faust, *Der Nationalsozialistische Studentenbund*, 2 vols. (Düsseldorf: Schwann, 1973).

19. See Konrad H. Jarausch, *Students, Society, and Politics in Imperial Germany* (Princeton: Princeton University Press, 1982), 333ff.

20. Jürgen Schwarz, *Studenten in der Weimarer Republik: Die deutsche Studentenschaft in der Zeit von 1918 bis 1923 und ihre Stellung zur Politik* (Berlin: Duncker & Humblot, 1970).

21. Frank R. Pfetsch, *Datenhandbuch zur Wissenschaftsentwicklung, 1850–1975* (Köln: Zentrum für Historische Sozialforschung, 1985), 120.

22. See, for example, Andreas Feickert, *Studenten greifen an: Nationalsozialistische Hochschulrevolution* (Hamburg: Hanseatische Verlagsanstalt, 1934), 15–19.

visibly perhaps, the crisis involved recruitment into the academic profession. For some years, the proportion of full professors within university faculties had been in steady decline, while the number of young academics living without tenure and often in very meager circumstances had risen substantially. In 1931 there were 1,721 full professors as compared with 2,665 *Privatdozenten* and associate professors without civil-servant status.[23] For every two full professors there were therefore three young scholars and scientists with the *Habilitation*, all of whom hoped to receive tenure, even though the statistical likelihood of reaching that goal was low.[24] Moreover, students' prospects were severely impaired by what contemporaries regarded as a disastrous crisis of oversupply of academics. The number of university graduates around 1930 was allegedly about two to three times the number of academic job openings.[25] The resulting sense of hopelessness among the up-and-coming generation of academics created an explosive mood, the full force of which did not emerge until 1933.

The Nazi Seizure of Power at Universities

The *Gleichschaltung* (coordination) of German universities gained momentum from two sources: first, from the workings of the cultural bureaucracy; second, from the energies of Nazi students, who felt called upon to push forward the nazification of the universities on their own. The Nazi ministers of culture appointed in the spring of 1933 were mostly former school teachers with little knowledge of the inner life of universities. They therefore needed politically reliable advisers at the institutions of higher learning, and they took these mostly from the NSDStB, the only organization available for this purpose. Nazi students thus assumed unusual powers.[26] There was probably no university where they did not participate actively in the dismissal of university teachers, and the book

---

23. Michael Grüttner, "Machtergreifung als Generationskonflikt: Die Krise der Hochschulen und der Aufstieg des Nationalsozialismus," in *Wissenschaften und Wissenschaftspolitik: Bestandsaufnahme zu Formationen, Brüchen und Kontinuitäten im Deutschland des 20. Jahrhunderts*, ed. Rüdiger vom Bruch and Brigitte Kaderas (Stuttgart: Franz Steiner, 2002), 339–53.

24. F. Solger, "Die Statistik des Hochschulverbandes über den akademischen Nachwuchs," *Mitteilungen des Hochschulverbandes* 11 (1931): 2ff.

25. Hartmut Titze, *Der Akademikerzyklus* (Göttingen: Vandenhoeck & Ruprecht, 1990), 263ff.

26. See Grüttner, *Studenten im Dritten Reich*, 63ff.

burnings of May 1933 resulted principally from student initiatives.[27] Sharp criticism of the reserve that "ossified professors" had displayed toward the Nazis until 1933 was on the agenda of all student events. Some university teachers felt that Nazi student leaders had become the real power centers at the universities. "What has become of proud Heidelberg University," lamented the historian Otto Brandt in 1934 in a letter to his colleague Hermann Oncken: "It is not the rector who is in charge but a wild student leader, in whose antechamber professors wait for more than an hour until they are generously admitted."[28]

Following the elections of March 1933, hundreds of university teachers also stood in line at party offices to apply for membership in the NSDAP. By the summer of 1933, 20–25 percent of all teachers at some universities had joined.[29] At the same time, numerous scholars openly declared their approval of the goals of the Nazis.[30] The mass dismissals that began as early as the summer of 1933 were generally accepted without protest. Only sporadically did scholars threatened by dismissal receive support from their colleagues.[31]

A large proportion of university teachers welcomed the collapse of Weimar, which was discredited even among its early supporters, and allowed themselves to be swept along by the "myth of national awakening" (Hans Mommsen). However, one must not conclude from this that most turned into enthusiastic Nazis. As the art historian Werner Weisbach, expelled from Berlin University in 1933 as a "non-Aryan," noted, there "was quite a number of scholars" who regarded the National Socialist coordination of the universities as "pernicious." But almost nobody had the courage to protest openly. Instead, Weisbach continued, "people confined themselves to grumbling in private. To the outside

---

27. Gerhard Sauder, ed., *Die Bücherverbrennung: Zum 10. Mai 1933* (Munich: Hanser, 1983).
28. Quoted in Helmut Heiber, *Universität unterm Hakenkreuz*, 2 vols. (Munich: Saur, 1994), part 2, vol. 2, p. 82f.
29. Hering, "Der unpolitische Professor?" 92f.; Höpfner, *Die Universität Bonn*, 14.
30. Even at a relatively liberal university like Heidelberg, there were numerous declarations of this kind. Jansen, *Professoren und Politik*, 276ff.; Steven P. Remy, *The Heidelberg Myth: The Nazification and Denazification of a German University* (Cambridge: Harvard University Press, 2002), 12ff.
31. Examples in Rudolf Schottländer, *Verfolgte Berliner Wissenschaft: Ein Gedenkwerk* (Berlin: Edition Hentrich, 1988), 85ff.

world it seemed as though . . . the entire world of academia—save for a few scattered exceptions—was entering into good terms with the new government."[32]

A rare document in which reservations were publicly articulated was the declaration of the executive board of the Association of German Universities from April 1933. It began with an emphatic affirmation of support for the "national awakening," but avoided a clear position on National Socialism: "For the universities of our fatherland the rebirth of the German people and the rise of the new German Reich mean the fulfillment of their yearnings and the confirmation of their ardent hopes. Just as they cofounded the Bismarckian Reich in the intellectual sense, defended it in the World War and against un-German threats in the post-war period, their professors and students now follow, with trust and enthusiasm, the leaders appointed by the Honorable Reich President."

The declaration went on to emphasize the university teachers' determination to carry out reforms and their willingness to support "new forms of national education" such as labor service or military sport. Following this principled approval of the "national awakening," various concerns and reservations were voiced, some openly, some not. While the declaration affirmed a "politicization that strengthens the common national will," it rejected "the *kind* of politicization that amounts to a restriction to special viewpoints." In this way the Association cautiously reaffirmed a principle it once repeated incessantly, namely that higher learning had to remain free from the influence of party politics. The declaration further emphasized the need to preserve the "diversity of ways of life and convictions." There was, however, a significant qualification: "We will continue to stand firmly for the freedom of conviction, provided it arises from German nature." The Association also affirmed the principle of university autonomy: "We defend our old venerable structures: self-government through a rector, senate, and departments . . . [and] the self-replenishment of the faculty." Last, the text contained a passage which was generally interpreted as critical of the Nazi students: "Sustained by the inner powers of our bond to the people we will . . . take up the battle not only against

---

32. Werner Weisbach, *Geist und Gewalt* (Vienna: Anton Schroll, 1956), 344. Similarly: David Baumgardt, "Looking Back on a German University Career," *Leo Baeck Institute Year Book* 10 (1965): 261 and passim; Werner Krauss, "Marburg unter dem Naziregime," *Sinn und Form* 35 (1983): 941ff.

oppression from outside, but also against harm to our people from lies, pressures upon conscience, and anti-intellectualism."[33]

This ambivalent declaration mirrored both the widespread feeling that change was in the air and the fear that academic traditions would be destroyed. What was more important—the desire for self-coordination or the fear of destructive Nazi university policies—often depended in these early years on the status of individual university teachers, or on the generation to which they belonged. To be sure, eminent figures such as Martin Heidegger or Carl Schmitt publicly embraced the Nazi regime in 1933, but the majority of the regime's proponents were drawn from younger cohorts.[34] "Active Nazis are confined almost entirely to the younger lecturers," wrote the freshly converted Carl Schmitt in an unpublished report of 1934. Although Schmitt attested that the older professors were struggling for "intellectual clarification," his assessment of their readiness for political action was decidedly negative:

> With few exceptions, one should not expect older professors to decisively promote National Socialism in the field of law. Rare in their number are the vigor and determination required to tear oneself loose of the accustomed ideas of previous science and scholarship, and to become champions of National Socialism in higher learning. Even among those with positive attitudes the vast majority have maintained the reserve typical of the German scholar; they are devoid of any spirit of struggle. The number of National Socialists truly ready for action is therefore still relatively small.[35]

Functionaries in charge of university policy were likewise recruited chiefly from the ranks of the rising generation of academics. This is made

---

33. Quotations from the declaration dated 22 April 1933, taken from a copy at the Bundesarchiv (BA) Berlin R 43 II 936 Folio 109. On the background to how this declaration came about and the conflicts it spawned, see Eduard Spranger, "Mein Konflikt mit der nationalsozialistischen Regierung, 1933," *Universitas* 10 (1955): 457–73, and Heiber, *Universität unterm Hakenkreuz*, part 2, vol. 1, pp. 110ff.

34. Grüttner, "Machtergreifung als Generationskonflikt"; Hering, "Der unpolitische Professor?" 96f. and 100; Höpfner, *Die Universität Bonn*, 14ff.; Ute Deichmann, *Biologists Under Hitler* (Cambridge: Harvard University Press, 1996), 67; Jansen, *Professoren und Politik*, 243.

35. Carl Schmitt, "Bericht über die Entwicklung der Reichsfachgruppe Hochschullehrer im BNSDJ und die Verhältnisse an den rechts- und wirtschaftswissenschaftlichen Fakultäten während des Wintersemesters, 1933/34," manuscript, 2f., in Staatsarchiv Hamburg Hochschulwesen II Aa 38/2.

clear by a glance through the biographies of local and regional leaders of the National Socialist German League of Lecturers (Nationalsozialistischer Deutscher Dozentenbund, NSDDB), the *Dozentenbundführer* and *Gaudozentenbundführer*.³⁶ To summarize: active Nazi professors were not identical with the National-Conservative spokesmen of the professoriate in the Weimar Republic. But neither were they academic outsiders, as the older literature claimed. Instead, the vast majority were academics who had been active prior to 1933 as assistants or *Privatdozenten*. An analysis of the biographical material shows that only three of ninety-one *Gaudozentenbundführer* and *Dozentenbundführer* at all twenty-three universities were full professors prior to 1933.

Nazi university politicians promoted the embrace of the NSDAP by a considerable proportion of the younger generation; in 1933–34 they quite consciously acted as representatives of younger academics against the full professors.³⁷ Another factor was perhaps more important still: precisely nontenured professors and lecturers profited substantially from the Nazi seizure of power, because the mass dismissals in 1933–34 fundamentally improved their previously dismal career prospects.

By contrast, for established academics the Nazi takeover ushered in a considerable weakening of their traditional powers. The essential measures of Nazi university policy—the erosion of competences held by the faculties and the university senates, the introduction of the *Führer* principle,³⁸ the shift of the decision-making authority from the universities to the state and party bureaucracy—amounted to a partial disempowerment of the full professors. Beside the dismissed teachers, they were the true losers of the Nazi takeover of power at the universities.

National Socialist University Policy

Four institutions were created between 1934 and 1936 to realize the essentials of Nazi university policy: the Reich Ministry of Education (Reichserziehungsministerium, REM), the University Commission of the NSDAP, the National Socialist German League of Lecturers (Nationalsozialistischer

---

36. Michael Grüttner, *Biographisches Lexikon zur nationalsozialistischen Wissenschaftspolitik* (Heidelberg: Synchron, 2004).
37. "Kampfansage an Liberalismus und Reaktion," *Deutsches Ärzteblatt* 64 (1934): 62f.
38. Hellmut Seier, "Der Rektor als Führer: Zur Hochschulpolitik des Reichserziehungsministeriums, 1934–1945," *Vierteljahrshefte für Zeitgeschichte* 12 (1964): 105–46.

Deutscher Dozentenbund, NSDDB), and the Office on Scholarship in the Rosenberg Department. The REM was entrusted to the former secondary school teacher Bernhard Rust, who paid little attention to university policy and enjoyed a low status within the NSDAP. In 1940 Alfred Rosenberg described him as "unstable, old, and sick,"[39] while the propaganda minister Joseph Goebbels portrayed him as "not entirely sane" and a "bull in a china shop."[40] The Office on Scholarship in the REM tried to compensate by seeking optimal relations with the armed forces (the ministry was soon considered *"militärfromm,"* devoted to the military), and with the SS.[41]

Initially the University Commission of the NSDAP competed with the REM for influence. Because Nazi physicians ran the commission, it concentrated heavily on medical schools, where it controlled a network of confidence men and at times gained considerable influence on appointments.[42] However, the commission declined quickly in importance, and in 1936 suspended most of its activities. Into its place stepped the NSDDB under Walter Schultze. Within the party hierarchy and at the university, Schultze and his league had little standing. They were often seen as incompetent academics who tried to compensate for their lack of professional achievement with excessive political zeal.[43] However, NSDDB functionaries carried considerable weight in personnel policy, and could delay or destroy academic careers through negative political evaluations. Some NSDDB leaders, such as Robert Wetzel in Tübingen and Arthur Schürmann in Göttingen, carved out dominant positions for themselves at their universities.[44]

Despite fierce rivalry, neither the REM nor the NSDDB nor any of the other governmental and party offices active in university policy figured among the influential players of the Nazi state. Their clashes gave rise

---

39. Alfred Rosenberg, *Das politische Tagebuch Alfred Rosenbergs aus den Jahren 1934/35 und 1939/40*, ed. Hans-Günther Seraphim (Göttingen: Musterschmidt, 1956), 95.

40. *Die Tagebücher von Joseph Goebbels*, ed. Elke Fröhlich (Munich: Saur, 2000), part 1, vol. 4, p. 32 (3 March 1937), p. 340 (3 October 1937).

41. Helmut Heiber, *Walter Frank und sein Reichsinstitut für Geschichte des neuen Deutschlands* (Stuttgart: Deutsche Verlags-Anstalt, 1966), 641ff., 815ff.

42. Hendrik van den Bussche, ed., *Medizinische Wissenschaft im "Dritten Reich": Kontinuität, Anpassung und Opposition an der Hamburger Medizinischen Fakultät* (Berlin: Dietrich Reimer, 1989), 65ff.

43. This view was widespread even in party circles. Alfred Rosenberg to Rudolf Hess, 8 March 1941, 4f., in BA Berlin NS 8/185 folio 148f.

44. On Wetzel, see Uwe Dietrich Adam, *Hochschule und Nationalsozialismus* (Tübingen: Mohr, 1977), 70f., 145ff. On Schürmann, see Heinrich Becker et al., eds., *Die Universität Göttingen unter dem Nationalsozialismus*, 2d expanded edition (Munich: Saur, 1998), 643ff.

to mutual obstructionism, in which many of the Nazi initiatives for reshaping the universities became mired. That in turn encouraged other agencies—such as the Propaganda Ministry or various offices of the SS— to involve themselves in university policy. Hitler himself mostly stayed out of these conflicts, since he took no interest in university policy.[45] His indifference only exacerbated the chaos. In 1939, Ernst Krieck, one of the leading Nazi professors, complained in a confidential letter to the leader of the Student League: "Nineteen thirty-three offered the unprecedented opportunity . . . for creative and path-breaking leadership. By now this has been thoroughly botched across the board, by *everyone* involved in cultural policy. One could write a book about it, probably with the result that the author would be locked up for saying the truth. Leadership in the area of scholarship and literature is virtual anarchy."[46]

With higher education policy fragmented, the various power centers of the Nazi state sought to erect empires independent of and in competition with one another. The Office on Scholarship of the REM was dominant in research funding; in 1936 it took control of the German Research Association (Deutsche Forschungsgemeinschaft, DFG) and also played a central role in the Reich Research Council (Reichsforschungsrat) set up in 1937.[47] Alfred Rosenberg focused his energy on founding a party university, the Hohe Schule (Higher School). In spite of official support from Hitler, it never went beyond the initial establishment of institutes.[48] Furthermore, the Rosenberg Department attained a dominant role at the University of Halle, which appointed Rosenberg its "patron" in 1938 to avoid being shut down.[49]

More successful, in contrast, were the efforts by the SS to set up its own research society, Ahnenerbe (Ancestral Heritage).[50] Other SS institutes with special tasks were established alongside the Ahnenerbe, such

---

45. Michael Grüttner, "Wissenschaftspolitik im Nationalsozialismus," in *Geschichte der Kaiser-Wilhelm-Gesellschaft im Nationalsozialismus*, 2 vols., ed. Doris Kaufmann (Göttingen: Wallstein, 2000), 2:557f.

46. Ernst Krieck to Reichsstudentenführer G. A. Scheel, 8 May 1939, Staatsarchiv Würzburg RSF/NSDStB I* 06 Φ 123.

47. Notker Hammerstein, *Die Deutsche Forschungsgemeinschaft in der Weimarer Republik und im Dritten Reich* (Munich: Beck, 1999).

48. Reinhard Bollmus, "Zum Projekt einer nationalsozialistischen Alternativ-Universität: Alfred Rosenbergs 'Hohe Schule,'" in *Erziehung und Schulung im Dritten Reich*, ed. Manfred Heinemann (Stuttgart: Klett-Cotta, 1980), part 2, pp. 125–52.

49. Heiber, *Universität unterm Hakenkreuz*, part 2, vol. 2, pp. 470ff.

50. Michael H. Kater, *Das "Ahnenerbe" der SS, 1935–1945: Ein Beitrag zur Kulturpolitik des Dritten Reiches* (Stuttgart, Deutsche Verlags-Anstalt, 1974).

as the Wannsee Institute charged with "Eastern research" (*Ostforschung*).[51] Various university institutes also transformed themselves into de facto SS installations, for example the Institute for Research on the State at the University of Berlin headed by Reinhard Höhn or the Institute of German Law at the University of Bonn headed by Karl August Eckhardt.[52] Individual *Gauleiter* of the NSDAP—for example Fritz Sauckel in Thuringia—occasionally behaved as though the universities in their *Gau* were their private property.[53]

Some historians have concluded from the analysis of these structures that there was no such thing as a Nazi university policy.[54] This argument does not strike me as convincing. Even if there was no central control of universities and scholarship, it is undeniable that after 1933 the face of German universities was changed more profoundly than it had been for a century by measures of university policy that were guided by the basic principles of Nazi ideology. Nazi university policy can be encapsulated in six points, on which all the governmental and party offices active in this area agreed:

1. The expulsion of Jews and politically disagreeable university teachers or students. While the number of students driven from the universities was relatively small, the faculty of the universities experienced a substantial bloodletting in both qualitative and quantitative terms. According to the figures of Edward Hartshorne (probably somewhat high), 16.3 percent of university teachers were expelled in the first four years alone. All told, nearly one-fifth of the faculty was dismissed at the universities.[55] Various case studies have convincingly shown that the vast majority of dismissed

---

51. Gideon Botsch, "'Geheime Ostforschung' im SD. Zur Entstehungsgeschichte und Tätigkeit des 'Wannsee-Instituts,' 1935–1945," *Zeitschrift für Geschichtswissenschaft* 48 (2000): 509–24. Other research institutes of the SS are listed in Michael Fahlbusch, *Wissenschaft im Dienst der nationalsozialistischen Politik?* (Baden-Baden: Nomos, 1999), 741ff.

52. On Höhn and Eckardt, see Heiber, *Walter Frank*, 88iff., 931ff., and Grüttner, *Biographisches Lexikon*, 42, 76.

53. Uwe Hossfeld et al., eds., *"Kämpferische Wissenschaft": Studien zur Geschichte der Universität Jena im Nationalsozialismus* (Cologne: Böhlau, 2003).

54. Notker Hammerstein, *Die Johann Wolfgang Goethe-Universität Frankfurt am Main*, vol. 1 (Neuwied: Metzner, 1989), 174, 187ff.

55. On Hartshorne's numbers, see Table 2 (p. 00). See also E. Y. Hartshorne, "The German Universities and the Government," *The Annals of the American Academy of Political and Social Science* 200 (1938): 222, and Klaus Fischer, "Die Emigration von Wissenschaftlern nach 1933," *Vierteljahrshefte für Zeitgeschichte* 39 (1991): 537. On the repercussions of the dismissals, see Mitchell Ash, "Emigration und Wissenschaftswandel als Folgen der nationalsozialistischen Wissenschaftspolitik," in Kaufmann, *Geschichte*, 2:610–31.

university teachers—more than two-thirds, perhaps even more than three-quarters—were victims of the regime's anti-Semitic ideology.[56] Only a small percentage of dismissals occurred exclusively because of an individual's political beliefs.

2. The elimination of democratic structures, to the extent that such structures can be said to have existed at the universities prior to 1933.[57]

3. The implementation of personnel policies in which "race" and reliability played a role alongside professional achievement. While the various institutions of the Nazi state involved in university policy agreed on the necessity of a "political selection" among university teachers, they disagreed on the question of who should carry it out. Moreover, the question of whether professional or political criteria should be given precedence remained contested.

4. The strengthening of those segments of the faculty previously underprivileged. The position of nontenured professors within the universities was noticeably enhanced in 1933–34: by the increased presence of *Privatdozenten* and associate professors in the governing bodies of the universities (faculties and university senates),[58] by the establishment of *Dozentenschaften* (to represent the interests of nontenured professors and to act as an agency of political control), and by the staffing of new positions of leadership in university policy (heads of the *Dozentenschaften*, leaders of the NSDDB, etc.) with academics who were drawn chiefly from the ranks of the new generation.

5. The establishment of new chairs in fields that seemed highly relevant politically. Between 1933 and 1939, the following fields, in particular, were expanded and institutionalized: racial science (*Rassenkunde*) and racial hygiene (*Rassenhygiene*),[59] military science (*Wehrwissenschaft*) and

---

56. Hammerstein, *Die Johann Wolfgang Goethe-Universität*, 1:220; Birgit Vézina, "Die Gleichschaltung" der Universität Heidelberg im Zuge der nationalsozialistischen Machtergreifung (Heidelberg: Winter, 1982), 170ff.

57. The "Führer principle," which was supposed to take the place of traditional university self-government, existed essentially only on paper, since the position of the rectors, who officially advanced to become the "führers" of the universities, was undermined by a diversity of secondary governments. Seier, "Der Rektor als Führer." As a case study, see also Anne Chr. Nagel, ed., *Die Philipps-Universität Marburg im Nationalsozialismus. Dokumente zu ihrer Geschichte* (Stuttgart: Franz Steiner, 2000).

58. Adam, *Hochschule und Nationalsozialismus*, 54ff. and 65; Helmut Böhm, *Von der Selbstverwaltung zum Führerprinzip* (Berlin: Duncker & Humblot, 1995), 161ff.

59. Paul Weindling, *Health, Race and German Politics Between National Unification and Nazism, 1870–1945* (Cambridge: Cambridge University Press, 1989), 511ff.; Robert N. Proctor, *Racial Hygiene: Medicine Under the Nazis* (Cambridge: Harvard University Press, 1988), 327ff.

military history,[60] as well as folklore (*Volkskunde*)[61] and prehistory (a hobby of Rosenberg's and Himmler's).[62]

6. And, after 1938, the dissolution of departments of theology. However, this plan was only partly implemented because the regime shied away from a head-on confrontation with the churches after the outbreak of the war.[63]

Given the multitude of competing institutions active in university policy during the Third Reich, it is not all that easy to clearly delineate various periods of Nazi university policy. Still, it is possible to distinguish at least four phases:

1. The years 1933 to 1936 were characterized by mass dismissals of Jewish and politically unwanted university teachers, and by numerous measures that restricted the autonomy of universities. Nazi students initially took a leading role, and the traditional rights of the full professors were curtailed. Some segments of the party took a fundamentally critical stance toward the universities and university teachers.

2. A second period stretches from 1937 to 1939. A change of course in university policy became apparent around 1936–37. The shortage of young scholars and scientists in many disciplines showed that academic professions had lost much of their attractiveness, a development that could also be attributed to the contempt that many National Socialists had for higher learning. In October 1936 the party's leading players in university policy met in Frankfurt and decided that the situation of university teachers had to be improved. What was needed was an "intellectual pacification" of university teachers, since "many German academics, who are indispensable because they are irreplaceable, feel downtrodden and oppressed."[64] And in fact, after 1937 university teachers were once again granted greater latitude.

---

60. For a contemporary overview of military science in the Third Reich, see Hermann Franke, ed., *Handbuch der neuzeitlichen Wehrwissenschaften*, 3 vols. (Leipzig: de Gruyter, 1936–39).

61. Wolfgang Jacobeit et al., eds., *Völkische Wissenschaft: Gestalten und Tendenzen der deutschen und österreichischen Volkskunde in der ersten Hälfte des 20. Jahrhunderts* (Vienna: Böhlau, 1994).

62. Achim Leube, ed., *Prähistorie und Nationalsozialismus: Die mittel- und osteuropäische Ur- und Frühgeschichtsforschung in den Jahren, 1933–1945* (Heidelberg: Synchron, 2001).

63. See the material in BA Berlin R 4901/12909.

64. Walter Gross, "Betrifft: 'Entpolitisierung' von Wissenschaft und Hochschule (MS), 20.10. 1936, p.1," Staatsarchiv Würzburg RSF/NSDStB II* 91 α 32. The participants included, among others, the head of the NSDAP's Office of Race Policy, Walter Gross; Rudolf Hess's commissioner on university issues and the head of the Nazi Physicians' League, Gerhard Wagner; and the head of the NSDAP's University Commission, Franz Wirz.

3. From 1939 to 1941 many younger academics were drafted into the armed forces, a development that seriously impaired research and teaching. The composition of the student body also changed fundamentally, since many male students were sent to the front lines while the number of female students increased noticeably. In the occupied territories, the Nazi regime established new universities or took over existing ones (Strasbourg, Prague, and Poznań). These universities were much more strongly nazified than their established German counterparts.

4. The fourth period between 1942 and 1945 was characterized by multifarious efforts to use science and scholarship for the purposes of war. Attempts to infuse individual disciplines with Nazi ideology took a back seat to efforts at placing traditional research and science in the service of the regime.[65] At the same time, Allied bombing raids destroyed many university facilities. Increasingly, university policy had to confine itself to maintaining basic university functions.

Personnel Policy

Personnel policies at universities of the Third Reich aimed at driving out real or presumed enemies, pushing for accelerated generational change, and "politically selecting" scientists and scholars active in the Nazi state.

Mass dismissals began in the summer semester of 1933 and, for the most part, were not completed until 1938. There were significant differences from one university to the next. While some institutions of higher learning, such as those in Frankfurt or Berlin, lost about a third of their faculty, other universities (Rostock, Tübingen) were virtually untouched by the dismissals (Table 2). Such differences reflect the varying willingness of universities during the Weimar Republic to admit Jews, Social Democrats, or left liberals into their faculties. As a rule of thumb, the more open universities were prior to 1933, the more profoundly they were affected by the dismissals after 1933.

Those scholars who were not affected by the dismissals and who did not hold tenured positions faced a new situation after 1933. In purely statistical terms their career prospects improved noticeably. However, beginning in

---

65. Perhaps the clearest symptom of this development was the decline of "German physics" after 1939. On this, see Alan D. Beyerchen, *Scientists Under Hitler: Politics and the Physics Community in the Third Reich* (New Haven: Yale University Press, 1977), 188.

Table 2 Dismissals at German universities, 1933–36

University	Faculty (winter of 1932/33)	Dismissals, 1933–36 number	(%)
Berlin	746	242	32.4
Frankfurt/M.	334	108	32.3
Heidelberg	247	60	24.3
Breslau	311	68	21.9
Göttingen	238	45	18.9
Freiburg	202	38	18.8
Hamburg	302	56	18.5
Cologne	241	43	17.4
Kiel	207	25	12.1
Giessen	180	21	11.7
Leipzig	369	43	11.6
Königsberg	203	23	11.3
Halle	220	22	10.0
Greifswald	144	14	9.7
Bonn	277	24	8.7
Münster	207	18	8.7
Marburg	172	15	8.7
Jena	199	17	8.5
Munich	387	32	8.3
Erlangen	115	8	7.0
Würzburg	146	9	6.2
Rostock	120	5	4.2
Tübingen	185	3	1.6
Total	5752	939	16.3

SOURCE: Edward Yarnall Hartshorne, *The German Universities and National Socialism* (Cambridge: Harvard University Press, 1937), 94, and corrigenda.

1933, all personnel decisions, whether tenure appointments or the hiring of assistant professors, as well as permission for trips abroad, depended not only on the professional qualifications of candidates, but also on their political evaluation. Anyone who did not appear "politically reliable" had no chance of a permanent academic position. This aspect of personnel policy created massive pressure to conform, and most young scholars became members of the NSDAP or one of its affiliates.[66] From 1939, such

66. Accordingly, the proportion of party members among academics was higher the younger they were. See Deichmann, *Biologists Under Hitler*, 61ff.; Geoffrey J. Giles, "Professor und Partei: Der Hamburger Lehrkörper und der Nationalsozialismus," in Krause et al., *Hochschulalltag im "Dritten Reich,"* part 1, 116ff.; and Höpfner, *Die Universität Bonn*, 17.

membership was a condition for entering the civil service.⁶⁷ Not surprisingly then, by the end of the Third Reich, about two-thirds of university teachers belonged to the NSDAP.

Such personnel policies produced tensions between political and professional selection criteria. In the first years after the Nazi seizure of power offices charged with higher education policy strove to staff as many influential positions as possible with reliable National Socialists. They often passed over departments when making appointments, and in some cases filled professorial chairs with party faithful lacking all professional qualifications. Certain party circles celebrated such appointments as a veritable triumph over the "liberal" university of the past.⁶⁸

However, this policy proved problematic even in the eyes of leading National Socialists. It was soon discovered that outsiders without professional qualifications were generally avoided by students, often becoming the butt of popular jokes.⁶⁹ Moreover, politicians increasingly realized that personnel policies guided by political criteria damaged the productive capacities of science and thus also its usefulness to the political system. In October 1936, Walter Gross, head of the NSDAP's Office of Race Policy, noted in an unpublished memorandum that the party had hitherto "chosen an unsuitable path." A "ministerial decree" could not possibly "turn a good old fighter, who was an academic nobody for external and internal reasons, into a pillar of German higher learning." Under no circumstances could "political reliability make up for poor achievement"; if his advice was disregarded, he feared that "the overall performance of the National Socialist regime in this field will suffer."⁷⁰

Though Gross's view was not universally endorsed, from about 1936–37 professional criteria took on increasing weight against political considerations. In 1937, this approach was advocated by the new department chief of the Reich Ministry of Education, Otto Wacker. In April 1937, a functionary of the Reich Student Leadership noted: "The current appointment policy of the REM is based on the notion that professional achievement is

---

67. Decree on the educational background and the careers of German civil servants of 28 February 1939, in Reichsgesetzblatt 1939, vol. 1., 371.
68. Report on the month of May by the NSDStB in the *Gau* Cologne-Aachen, Staatsarchiv Würzburg RSF/NSDStB II* 109 α 53.
69. Several examples appear in Böhm, *Von der Selbstverwaltung zum Führerprinzip*, 506ff.
70. Gross, "Betrifft 'Entpolitisierung,'" 4ff.

the first consideration, and that an appointment merely on the basis of political reliability is out of the question."⁷¹ Accordingly, recommendations from university departments were given greater weight than had been the case in the first years of Nazi rule.⁷²

However, the party was unwilling to dispense completely with political evaluations in personnel decisions, especially when tenure was involved. Lengthy negotiations between the REM and the staff of Rudolf Hess, "Deputy Leader of the Party," produced a compromise on new procedures for appointments. It stipulated that departmental recommendations, which were put forth as lists of three candidates, would form the basis of the procedure, as had been the case prior to 1933. Departmental lists would then be passed on to the REM through the rector. Once the REM had decided to accept one of the candidates, it was obligated to procure a statement from Hess's staff—a general requirement for civil service appointments. Hess's staff in turn solicited political evaluations from the NSDDB, the Security Service of the SS, the Rosenberg Department, and from the respective *Gau* leadership of the party. The party then expressed its official judgment on the proposed candidates. The critical question of who would have the last word if there were differences of opinion was not resolved by the official decree,⁷³ and was hotly debated for some time. In the end, however, the REM had to yield to the demands from Hess and his associate Martin Bormann. Department chief Wacker announced the Ministry's capitulation in December 1937: "We are not entitled to take a position on a decision of the Deputy Leader of the Party."⁷⁴

The party thus had de facto veto power over personnel decisions in higher education, but the outcome was still a compromise. On the one hand, the new appointment procedures answered the party's wish for more political control in forming future generations of academics, but on the other, in the REM's scheme of things, the right of departments to put forth recommendations supposedly ensured that individuals without professional qualifications would not be considered in the first place. In fact appointments against the wishes of departments were relatively rare after

---

71. Fritz Kubach to the Reich Student Leader, 12 April 1937 (carbon copy), in Staatsarchiv Würzburg RSF/NSDStB 175 α 103.

72. Hammerstein, *Die Johann Wolfgang Goethe-Universität*, 420.

73. Decree on the participation of the deputy of the Führer in the appointment of civil servants, 24 September 1935, in Reichsgesetzblatt 1935, vol. 1, 1203.

74. Minutes of the Rectors' Conference on 15 December 1937, in BA Berlin R 49.01 Nr. 708 folio 125.

1937, except at universities where party potentates had carved out positions of dominance. Such was the case at Königsberg and Jena, where the respective *Gauleiter* carried out personnel policies independent of the Ministry, and at the University of Halle, which for a while was under the thumb of Alfred Rosenberg.

By 1936, the basic conditions for personnel policy had changed. For the first time, shortages of qualified young academics were becoming apparent. National Socialist Ernst Krieck asserted that "the weakness of the younger generation of academics, whether in qualitative or in quantitative terms, constitutes the main threat to the future of the German university."[75] Problems seemed greatest in the departments of law and economics, whereas medical schools continued to have an oversupply of nontenured professors.[76] The situation grew considerably worse during the war when young academics were sent to fight. Yet the Security Service of the SS also noted emphatically that the lack of lecturers and assistants was not due primarily to the war, "but much more to the *younger generation's reluctance to pursue the profession of university teacher*, a reluctance which has become increasingly visible during recent years. This reluctance is fed by the perception that academic professions have been devalued in terms of status and financial compensation, and it is no longer worth the risk or the trouble of a *Habilitation*."[77]

A few months later the Security Service of the SS even spoke of a veritable "flight from academia."[78] Especially in the natural sciences and in technical fields, many talented scientists went into industry, enticed by significantly higher pay and better working conditions. They were also escaping heightened political control and surveillance at the universities.[79] The growing shortage of young academics made a rigorously political personnel policy practically impossible—unless of course universities completely dispensed with professional criteria in making appointments. This constellation also improved the career prospects of scholars considered

---

75. Ernst Krieck, "Der Nachwuchs der Hochschullehrer," *Volk im Werden* 4 (1936): 111.

76. See the statistical overview "Die unbesetzten und überaltert besetzten ... Lehrstühle der wissenschaftlichen Hochschulen Grossdeutschlands nach dem Stande vom 15.3.1943," Archiv der Humboldt-Universität Berlin Rektor und Senat, 155.

77. *Meldungen aus dem Reich*, vol. 10, 3960 (16 July 1942), emphasis in the original. In a similar vein, see vol. 11, 4141ff. (27 August 1942).

78. *Meldungen aus dem Reich*, vol. 12, 4494ff. (23 November 1942).

79. See, for example, the comments by the Marburg chemist Alfred Thiel, "Denkschrift über Fragen des akademischen Nachwuchses, 10.8.1936," copy in Hessisches Hauptstaatsarchiv Wiesbaden 483/4648a.

"politically unreliable," provided they did not act publicly as opponents of National Socialism.[80] Beginning about 1936 no less a figure than Ernst Krieck spoke up for undesirables even when there were "strong political reservations" about them, provided they were specialists for whom there was no replacement of equal qualification.[81]

University Teachers and National Socialism

In the years after 1933 a significant portion of professors who were initially skeptical drew closer to the regime. In particular, the regime's foreign policy successes prompted academics who had once felt alienated to change their position. University teachers of every stripe welcomed the introduction of universal compulsory military service in 1935, like other measures aimed at overturning the Versailles Treaty.[82] A conservative skeptic like the Göttingen professor Siegfried A. Kaehler had no problem thanking the Führer in a public speech for "restoring military sovereignty."[83] By 1938, after the annexation of Austria and the successful resolution of the "Sudeten crisis," the Nazis had achieved almost everything the nationalistic middle class had dreamed of. Even a critic like Gerhard Ritter, who was later imprisoned for his contacts with the conservative resistance, praised the annexation of Austria as "the boldest and most felicitous foreign policy feat of our new government."[84] Formerly liberal university teacher Percy Ernst Schramm concurred: "Eighty million— without the shedding of blood. Neither Bismarck nor the Maid of Orleans could accomplish that, only somebody who combined the abilities of both. One is too thrilled to go back to work. . . . And so 1938 is after all the great year of our life, and no other year can elevate us above it."[85]

80. Examples in Heiber, *Universität unterm Hakenkreuz*, part 1, pp. 238, 282ff., and Mark Walker, *German National Socialism and the Quest for Nuclear Power, 1939–1949* (Cambridge: Cambridge University Press, 1989), 86ff.

81. Vézina, "Gleichschaltung," 172.

82. *Deutschland-Berichte der Sozialdemokratischen Partei Deutschlands (Sopade)* 2 (1935) (Salzhausen: Zweitausendeins, 1980), 706. See also Gerd Tellenbach, *Aus erinnerter Zeitgeschichte* (Freiburg: Wagner, 1981), 44.

83. Siegfried A. Kaehler, *Briefe, 1900–1963* (Boppard am Rhein: Boldt, 1993), 71.

84. Quoted in Gerhard Ritter, *Ein politischer Historiker in seinen Briefen* (Boppard am Rhein: Boldt, 1984), 81.

85. Personal note of 16 October 1938, quoted in Joist Grolle, *Der Hamburger Percy Ernst Schramm—ein Historiker auf der Suche nach der Wirklichkeit* (Hamburg: Verein für Hamburgische Geschichte, 1989), 33.

The previous year Schramm had attempted to explain his contradictory impressions of National Socialism to the archbishop of Canterbury. Asked whether he was a Nazi, Schramm, according to his own testimony, responded as follows:

> With respect to rearmament (balance of power)—a two-hundred percent Nazi; to "labor peace," fortifying the farmers, "Strength through Joy,"—a one hundred percent Nazi; to racial theory, the cult of the Germanic peoples, educational policy, Nazi worldview—a one hundred percent opponent. Every night . . . I have to ask myself to what extent I agree with the party's goals and to what extent I reject them. The answer is different every night. This is not only my fate, but that of the German intelligentsia as such.[86]

When World War II broke out, the response of the universities, and of the German population as a whole, was at first restrained. All the greater, however, was the enthusiasm following the first victorious campaigns of the Wehrmacht. The defeat of France seems to have had an effect on skeptical university professors that was like the effect the establishment of the Reich in 1871 had had on the liberal generation of 1848. Even a man like the historian Hermann Oncken, who had been forced into retirement in 1935 for political reasons, joined in the general jubilation in 1940 and did not hesitate to publicly justify the National Socialist policy of conquest.[87] His colleague Friedrich Meinecke, a leading liberal who had been forced out of the editorship of the *Historische Zeitschrift* for political reasons, had much the same reaction. In a letter of July 1940, he wrote: "What I feel now above all else: joy, admiration, and pride in this army. And the recovery of Strasbourg! How could this not make one's heart quicken. The most remarkable, and greatest positive accomplishment of the Third Reich was to build a million-strong army in only four years and make it capable of such achievements . . . I wish . . . to change my views on many things, but not on everything."[88]

---

86. Quoted in Grolle, *Der Hamburger Percy Ernst Schramm*, 33ff.
87. Karen Schönwälder, *Historiker und Politik: Geschichtswissenschaft im Nationalsozialismus* (Frankfurt am Main: Campus, 1992), 179ff. Schönwälder gives many other examples of this kind.
88. Friedrich Meinecke to Siegfried A. Kaehler, 7 April 1940, in Friedrich Meinecke, *Ausgewählter Briefwechsel*, edited with an introduction by Ludwig Dehio and Peter Classen (Stuttgart: Koehler, 1962), 364.

There is much to indicate that a considerable number of initially critical university teachers had drawn very close to the regime by 1939–40. Yet chiefly because of the Nazi regime's demonstrative disdain for intellectuals, we cannot speak of an unconditional identification with National Socialism. Hitler practically breathed contempt for intellectuals, who invariably appear in his public and private utterances as lacking backbone. In a secret speech to the press in 1938, he declared: "If I look at the intellectual classes among us—unfortunately, we need them, after all, otherwise one could one day, well, I don't know, exterminate them or something like that—but, unfortunately, we need them."[89] Such anti-intellectualism was often linked to a rhetoric of social leveling, for example in the speeches of Robert Ley, the head of the German Labor Front, who cultivated a populist tone: "One of these professors sits in a lab for years to discover a bacterium. I'll take a street sweeper any day. He takes his broom and with a single flick of his hand sweeps thousands of bacteria into the gutter."[90]

This undisguised contempt for their work was a special blow to university teachers, who had once fondly thought of themselves as the political-moral teachers of the nation. In the end even a fanatical Nazi like the Germanist Franz Koch could not close his eyes to the professoriate's drastic decline in social status. In November 1939 he expressed deep disappointment in a confidential memorandum titled "Keeping silent would be tantamount to betrayal," which he sent to various party offices. "The authority of the university, and in the broader sense of *higher* learning, has been destroyed," he wrote, "scientists and professors, are written off as 'intellectuals,' as people whose opinions are not worthy of respect, who should be challenged whenever possible." The professor, Koch went on, "is looked upon with contempt and mistrust, is repeatedly attacked in public, is rarely protected and defended . . . [and] never appreciated."[91]

Disappointment over lack of recognition did not necessarily impel academics to reject the regime. To the contrary, it caused some to try even more vigorously to convince the leadership of their usefulness.[92]

---

89. Speech given on 10 November 1938. Excerpts in Max Domarus, *Hitler: Reden und Proklamationen, 1932–1945* (Munich: Süddeutscher Verlag, 1965), here 1:975ff.

90. Quote in Helmut Joachim Fischer, *Erinnerungen* (Ingolstadt: Zeitgeschichtliche Forschungsstelle, 1984), 1:178.

91. There is one copy of this memorandum in BA Berlin R 43 II 940b folio 28ff.

92. See, for example, Max Steenbeck, *Impulse und Wirkungen: Schritte auf meinem Lebensweg* (Berlin: Verlag der Nation, 1977), 104.

Notable, however, were the efforts of many university teachers to frustrate party intrusions into university life and preserve the autonomy of higher education.[93] Several studies show that a large majority of professors continued to insist that primary consideration be given to a candidate's professional accomplishments and not to his political activities.[94] Those who tried to obtain a professorship through party favoritism usually encountered opposition at the universities, as the Security Service of the SS noted: "In general, when it comes to personnel policy and *Habilitation*, there is opposition to those candidates who are promoted by the party. This opposition is justified on the grounds that the party overemphasizes positive traits of a person's character without allowing for an evaluation of professional accomplishments."[95] On this issue even some National Socialists agreed with the majority of their colleagues. This unanimity resulted not only from what might seem self-evident preconditions for successful scholarship, but was also a question of preserving traditional structures of power. By insisting so tenaciously on the primacy of professional qualifications, most established university teachers were also expressing their determination to have the decisive say in matters of professorial appointments.

Student Life

In the first years following the Nazi seizure of power the student body became a favorite area of experimentation for Nazi policies. Various Nazi organizations—the NSDStB, the German Student Association (Deutsche Studentenschaft), and SA university offices—endeavored, independently of one another, to align the students with the spirit of the regime through training courses, marches, and military sports. But many ambitious plans of 1933 were off the table within a few short months. For example, the plan to house all freshmen in barracks-like "comradeship houses" was

---

93. Beyerchen, *Scientists Under Hitler*, 198f.
94. Reece Conn Kelly, "National Socialism and German University Teachers: The NSDAP's Efforts to Create a National Socialist Professoriate and Scholarship" (Ph.D. diss., University of Washington 1973), 360ff., 373ff.; Adam, *Hochschule und Nationalsozialismus*, 120ff., and summary, 210; Volker Losemann, *Nationalsozialismus und Antike* (Hamburg: Hoffmann und Campe, 1977), 176; Van den Bussche, *Medizinische Wissenschaft im "Dritten Reich,"* 107; Böhm, *Von der Selbstverwaltung zum Führerprinzip*, 424ff.; Höpfner, *Die Universität Bonn*, 524.
95. Report of the SD section Frankfurt auf Main, "Stimmung und Haltung der Hochschullehrer, 3.8.1944," 9, Hessisches Hauptstaatsarchiv Wiesbaden 483/11269.

scrapped by the end of 1934.⁹⁶ The SA university offices, which placed demands on students that often cost more time than did their academic work, disappeared in the fall of 1934, a few months after the "Röhm putsch."⁹⁷ More stable structures began gradually to emerge in 1936.

The impact of Nazi university policy on students can be summarized, slightly simplified, in six points:

1. Between "high school" (*Gymnasium*) and university lay a transition phase of up to thirty months which was filled by the obligatory labor service and, in the case of male students, a two-year stint in the military. In 1933, Konstantin Hierl, the head of the Labor Service, described the goals of his organization: "There is no better way to overcome social fragmentation, class hatred, and class arrogance, than by having the son of a factory owner, the young factory worker, the young academic, and the farm hand perform the same service, dressed in the same uniform and eating the same food."⁹⁸ In fact, the Labor Service was probably the most consistent attempt by the Nazis to put into practice the ideology of the people's community (*Volksgemeinschaft*) with its pseudosocialist elements.⁹⁹

2. Membership in the party or one of its associated organizations was not obligatory for the mass of students. Still, at many universities a good deal of pressure was exerted on students to join. Moreover, many students felt that political abstinence could someday have negative repercussions, and therefore most became members of at least one of the Nazi organizations.¹⁰⁰

3. By 1937, all student organizations—with the exception of the NSDStB and its female counterpart, the Working Community of National Socialist Women Students (Arbeitsgemeinschaft Nationalsozialistischer Studentinnen, ANSt)—had been forced to dissolve. In most cases this took place quietly and inconspicuously. Only the disbanding of the student fraternities, to which more than half of all male students belonged in 1930, provoked intense conflicts. The university city Marburg, where the vast majority of male students were members of fraternities, found itself for a time thrown into "a kind of civil war," as a contemporary observer, the

---

96. Grüttner, *Studenten im Dritten Reich*, 260ff.; Geoffrey J. Giles, *Students and National Socialism* (Princeton: Princeton University Press, 1985), 136ff., 173ff.

97. Grüttner, *Studenten im Dritten Reich*, 245ff.

98. Konstantin Hierl, "Der Arbeitsdienst, die Erziehungsschule zum deutschen Sozialismus," *Ausgewählte Schriften und Reden* (Munich: Eher, 1943), 2:96. On the student labor service, see Grüttner, *Studenten im Dritten Reich*, 227ff.

99. Grüttner, *Studenten im Dritten Reich*, 230f.

100. Staatsarchiv Würzburg RSF/NSDStB II* 450 α 353. See also Grüttner, *Studenten im Dritten Reich*, 324ff., 503.

Marxist scholar of Romance languages Werner Krauss, noted.[101] The action taken against fraternities was so unpopular that the leadership of the NSDStB eventually felt compelled to strike a compromise with the Associations of Fraternity Alumni, which led to a de facto revival of the fraternities during the war.[102]

4. Initial plans aiming at a drastic cutback in numbers of women students were not realized. A decree of 1934 stipulating that the number of female students was to be limited henceforth to 10 percent of all newly enrolling students was suspended after only two semesters. Although the proportion of women students declined from 18 percent in 1933 to 14 percent in 1939, during the war numbers of women at university surged. In 1944, for the first time in the history of German universities, parity between the sexes was achieved in the student body.[103]

5. Beginning in 1933 students were burdened with nonacademic obligations on top of their professional training. These included obligatory sports, labor assignments on farms and in factories, so-called women's service (a special program to prepare women students for war), and political training. The question of how to balance professional training, on the one hand, and the students' political education, on the other, was a source of constant conflict. New National Socialist students were supposed to make sacrifices willingly, learn ideological precepts without becoming bookish, and excel in athletics. But the regime also needed qualified doctors, scientists, teachers, and technicians, without whom an industrial state is not viable in the long run. While the Reich Ministry of Education tended to emphasize professional training, the party for the most part highlighted ideological indoctrination. As a result the level of professional training in all departments suffered a noticeable decline. This was a diagnosis on which contemporary experts were in remarkable agreement.[104]

6. The core vocabulary of Nazi ideology included the concept of "selection," and it went without saying that the education system was to

101. Krauss, "Marburg unter dem Naziregime," 942.
102. Michael Grüttner, "Die Korporationen und der Nationalsozialismus," in *"Der Burschen Herrlichkeit": Geschichte und Gegenwart des studentischen Korporationswesens*, ed. Harm-Hinrich Brandt and Matthias Stickler (Würzburg: Schöningh, 1998), 125–43.
103. On women students, see Claudia Huerkamp, *Bildungsbürgerinnen: Frauen im Studium und in akademischen Berufen, 1900–1945* (Göttingen: Vandenhoeck & Ruprecht, 1996), 80ff., 157ff.; Grüttner, *Studenten im Dritten Reich*, 109ff.; and Jacques R. Pauwels, *Women, Nazis, and Universities: Female University Students in the Third Reich, 1933–1945* (Westport, Conn.: Greenwood Press, 1984).
104. Hellmut Seier, "Niveaukritik und partielle Opposition: Zur Lage an den deutschen Hochschulen, 1939/40," *Archiv für Kulturgeschichte* 58 (1976): 227–46.

serve the selection of an elite defined by racial-ideological and political criteria. In practice this policy was essentially confined to the dismissal and expulsion of both Jews and leftist students, principally Communists. About 5 percent of the student body was affected.[105] More far-reaching plans to make university admission dependent on a political evaluation were thwarted by Martin Bormann in 1940, who evidently feared that such a policy would further exacerbate the shortage of up-and-coming academics.[106] In the conflict between the ideological and the professional goals of the education system, even a man like Bormann could not simply come down on the side of the former.

As early as 1934 the enthusiasm with which the majority of students had welcomed the Nazis gave way to increasing criticism. The motives for this reversal in sentiment were many. The attacks by the NSDStB against the fraternities played a role, as did the burden placed on students by political commitments and the increasing attacks by the party on the Christian churches. In May 1935, Reich Education Minister Rust confessed in an internal speech to student leaders: "National Socialism is not as strong at the universities today as it was in 1933. I have the gravest, most profound, and most serious concerns about the spirit at the universities. It cannot go on like this."[107] From about 1937 a generation of students entered the universities that had already belonged to the Hitler Youth in school, and had completed both labor service and military service. The result of these experiences, as we learn from a report by a student functionary in Würzburg, was "a very radical antipathy toward anything having to do with service, uniforms, lining up in formation and the like."[108] In almost every case these students had no interest in political activity but wanted to enjoy the "freedom of student life" (or rather, what was left of it).[109]

This does not mean that students turned into opponents of National Socialism. While it is true that student resistance groups emerged at a number of universities, sources do not indicate that the majority of the student body supported these groups. Even the best-known resistance group, the "White Rose" in Munich, remained isolated from the mass of

105. Grüttner, *Studenten im Dritten Reich*, 206ff.
106. BA Berlin NS 6/466.
107. "Konferenz der Leiter der Studentenschaften an den deutschen Hochschulen im REM, 26 May 1935," stenographic protocol, in BA Berlin R 4901/708 folio 209.
108. Quoted in Friedhelm Golücke, "Das Kameradschaftswesen in Würzburg von 1936 bis 1945," in *Korporationen und Nationalsozialismus*, ed. Friedhelm Golücke (Schernfeld: SH-Verlag 1989), 201.
109. Grüttner, *Studenten im Dritten Reich*, 242, 389ff.

students.[110] Though a large segment of the student body maintained a certain distance toward National Socialism, there was still a basic nationalistic consensus which left no room for active resistance to one's own government in time of war.

Scholarship and Science

Nazi higher education functionaries left no doubt that scholarship of the future would have to be National Socialist. However, the party officials had great difficulty defining what the new National Socialist world of higher learning would look like.[111] The official texts of the NSDAP—Hitler's *Mein Kampf* and the party program—provided no guidance. As a result, a few National Socialist professors quickly tried to furnish the missing blueprints after the takeover of power. Their writings can be summarized in six major points:

1. They vehemently rejected the idea of "objective scholarship" (*voraussetzungslose Wissenschaft*), such as Theodor Mommsen had once advocated in his protest against professorial appointments linked to specific denominations.[112] The claim that science and scholarship are never free of prior preconditions or ties—a claim that is worth discussing as such—led the academic pioneers of Nazism to the conclusion that the Nazi state had the right to determine, in a binding manner, what these preconditions and ties ought to be. From this argument it was but a small step to the demand that higher learning "must of necessity be in service to National Socialism."[113]

---

110. Christiane Moll, "Die Weisse Rose," in *Widerstand gegen den Nationalsozialismus*, ed. Peter Steinbach and Johannes Tuchel (Berlin: Akademie, 1994), 443–67; Grüttner, *Studenten im Dritten Reich*, 457ff.

111. For more recent, concise overviews on the history of science and scholarship in the Third Reich, see Margit Szöllösi-Janze, "National Socialism and the Sciences: Reflections, Conclusions and Historical Perspectives," in *Science in the Third Reich*, ed. Szöllösi-Janze (Oxford: Berg, 2001), 1–35; Ulrich Sieg, "Strukturwandel der Wissenschaft im Nationalsozialismus," *Berichte zur Wissenschaftsgeschichte* 24 (2001): 255–70; Klaus Fischer, "Repression und Privilegierung: Wissenschaftspolitik im Dritten Reich," in *Im Dschungel der Macht: Intellektuelle Professionen unter Stalin und Hitler*, ed. Dietrich Beyrau (Göttingen: Vandenhoeck & Ruprecht, 2000); and Jonathan Harwood, "German Science and Technology under National Socialism," *Perspectives on Science* 5 (1997): 128–51.

112. Jürgen von Kempski, "'Voraussetzungslosigkeit': Eine Studie zur Geschichte eines Wortes," *Archiv für Philosophie* 4 (1952): 157–74.

113. Hans Frank, "Der Nationalsozialismus und die Wissenschaft der Wirtschaftslehre," *Schmollers Jahrbuch* 58, no. 2 (1934): 646.

2. Henceforth, higher learning could no longer be an end in itself: "From now on we will no longer recognize any spirit, any culture, any education which does not serve the self-perfection of the German people and derives its meaning from this," Ernst Krieck proclaimed in 1933.[114] This placed pressure on scholars to demonstrate their usefulness to the state. Such a demand embodied a clear break with the traditional self-conception of the German universities, which had always emphasized that their task was the "disinterested search for pure knowledge."[115]

3. The notion of race as the core element of Nazi ideology was supposed to move into the center of scholarly research: "For us the ordering principle for all areas of intellectual life arises from biology, from the understanding of race," Reich Education Minister Rust declared in 1940. "The discovery of race . . . also imparts to higher learning its decisive revolutionary impulse."[116]

4. In opposition to the growing specialization within science and scholarship stood the Nazis' call for higher learning that was "holistic" (*ganzheitlich*) and overcame the boundaries between the disciplines. As Walter Schultze, the head of the NSDDB, put it, overcoming these boundaries was "the most radical means in the fight against the Jewish spirit and for German nature."[117] Apart from the anti-Semitic flavor of this concept, this was not an original Nazi idea. "Wholeness" had already been a key concept in discussions among intellectuals during the Weimar Republic; it uniquely captured the widespread discomfort with a world that was increasingly and impenetrably complex.[118]

5. Leading Nazis fundamentally challenged the international character of science and scholarship. In 1934 Alfred Rosenberg declared that there never had been international science and scholarship.[119] Higher learning had its roots in the folk, in the race. Behind such assertions stood the belief that only members of the "Nordic" or "Aryan race" were capable of productive scholarly work.

114. Ernst Krieck, *Die Erneuerung der Universität* (Frankfurt am Main: Bechhold, 1933), 8.
115. Carl Heinrich Becker, *Vom Wesen der deutschen Universität* (Leipzig: Quelle und Meyer, 1925), 8ff.
116. Bernhard Rust, *Reichsuniversität und Wissenschaft* (Berlin: Deutsche Forschungsgemeinschaft, 1940), 9.
117. Quoted in *Frankfurter Zeitung*, 5 November 1940.
118. Fritz K. Ringer, *The Decline of the German Mandarins: The German Academic Community, 1890–1933* (Cambridge: Harvard University Press, 1969), 344ff.; Jansen, *Professoren und Politik*, 83.
119. A. Rosenberg, "Freiheit der Wissenschaft," in Rosenberg, *Gestaltung der Idee: Reden und Aufsätze von 1933–1935* (Munich: Eher, 1936), 203.

6. The "people" was to be become a more pronounced object of scholarly research. *Volksforschung* (people's research) was to strengthen the ties with "Germans in the border regions and abroad" politically and scientifically, thereby reinforcing the claim to territories inhabited by Germans outside the boundaries of the Reich."[120]

To be sure, these ideas were never officially sanctioned. Nor were they sufficient to provide precise guidance on what Nazi literary studies, Nazi historiography, or Nazi physics should be.[121] This lack of clarity encouraged a host of Nazi scholars to make names for themselves as champions of Nazi scholarship. Especially in disciplines closely related to politics, these professors were soon confronted with bitter competition from others pursuing similar ambitions.[122] Thus, "the period after 1933 spawned a hundred-headed professorial National Socialism that devoured itself," as *Das Schwarze Korps*, the paper of the SS, commented sarcastically in July 1941.[123] These sorts of complaints reflected the lack of a central authority that might have declared certain positions binding, or given guidance to professors willing to accommodate themselves. The frustration over this state of affairs was still evident in the 1984 memoirs of a former functionary of the Security Service of the SS who had been in charge of supervising science and higher learning:

> In fields that were of particular importance to the worldview of National Socialism, such as German folk studies, prehistory, or racial science, contending parties had formed, each of which wanted to be the appointed guardian of National Socialist thinking. In order to acquire backing they approached various subdivisions of the party, and the latter therefore became actively involved in the quarrels. For public consumption this was all about the one true worldview; in reality it was more about egotism,

---

120. Willi Oberkrome, *Volksgeschichte: Methodische Innovation und völkische Ideologisierung in der deutschen Geschichtswissenschaft, 1918–1945* (Göttingen: Vandenhoeck & Ruprecht, 1993), 111ff.

121. This has been shown in the case of physics by the pioneering study of Beyerchen, *Scientists Under Hitler.*

122. Several examples in Michael Stolleis, *Geschichte des öffentlichen Rechts in Deutschland*, 3 vols. (Munich: Beck, 1999), 3:316; Hannjost Lixfeld, "Nationalsozialistische Volkskunde und Volkserneuerung," in Jacobeit, *Völkische Wissenschaft*, 255ff.; Michael Grüttner, "Das Scheitern der Vordenker: Deutsche Hochschullehrer und der Nationalsozialismus," in *Geschichte und Emanzipation: Festschrift für Reinhard Rürup*, ed. Michael Grüttner, Rüdiger Hachtmann, and Heinz-Gerhard Haupt (Frankfurt: Campus, 1999), 458–81.

123. "Politik den Berufenen," *Das Schwarze Korps*, 31 July 1941, 4.

a struggle for power, and key posts. And there was no one who put his foot down and ended this vile squabbling.[124]

Thus, on the one hand, university teachers were under considerable pressure to adopt the National Socialist worldview in their scholarly work, with up-and-coming academics, in particular, facing little chance of advancement without political concessions. But on the other hand these scholars remained part of an academic community, with its own rules and criteria of relevance, which had always opposed the use of scholarship for politics. For the younger generation it was not advisable to ignore these rules and criteria, because the departments played a significant role in making decisions on hiring. That was especially true after 1937.[125]

This helps explain why the political accommodation of scholars clearly fell below the expectations of Nazi functionaries. In 1938, Gustav Adolf Scheel, the Reich Student Leader, publicly decried that "science and scholarship . . . are not yet National Socialist."[126] And Heinrich Härtle from the Office on Scholarship in the Rosenberg Department noted in 1941: "So far we have been able to cleanse universities only of Jews and enemies of the state, but a real infusion of our universities with National Socialism has not been accomplished."[127] As late as March 1944 participants at a "meeting on higher learning" at the party chancellery concluded "that the ideological renewal of the university can be achieved only through a lengthy process of inner transformation and the inner ideological pervasion of individual fields."[128] At a time when National Socialism was very close to its end, the party politicians in charge of university policy felt that they were almost at the beginning.

Analyses of contemporary journals have indeed revealed that it was quite possible to publish professional journals in the humanities without

---

124. Fischer, *Erinnerungen*, 1:74ff.
125. A report of SS-Sturmbannführer Hans Schick of 24 July 1942 discusses this problem from the viewpoint of the regime. See Joachim Lerchenmueller, *Die Geschichtswissenschaft in den Planungen des Sicherheitsdienstes der SS* (Bonn: Dietz, 2001), 262ff.
126. "Dr. Scheel über die Zukunft der Hochschule," *Frankfurter Zeitung*, 1 May 1938.
127. Heinrich Härtle, "Entwurf einer Denkschrift an den Reichsmarschall, 17 June 1941," in BA Berlin NS 15/297 folio 172.
128. "Bericht über die Wissenschaftsbesprechung in der Parteikanzlei am 17. März 1944," 3, in BA Berlin NS 8/241 folio 167. Similar statements are quoted in Gerd Simon, ed., *Germanistik in den Planspielen des Sicherheitsdienstes der SS* (Tübingen: GIFT, 1998), 1:9ff.; Lerchenmueller, *Die Geschichtswissenschaft*, 193, 217, 266.

making substantial concessions to National Socialism.[129] Frank-Rutger Hausmann has argued that even in the "war service of the humanities" (*Kriegseinsatz der Geisteswissenschaften*), "with a few exceptions, flagrant breaches of the precepts of objectivity and neutrality were avoided."[130] Especially those scholars who felt part of an international scientific community were generally at pains to avoid concessions to Nazi ideology in academic publications, since these would invariably diminish their reputations among foreign colleagues.[131]

Still, we must be careful not to generalize such case studies too readily. Recent research has shown that scholars collaborated more closely with the Nazi regime than had previously been imagined possible.[132] In its mildest form, accommodation was limited to avoiding certain delicate topics, ceasing to mention the names of émigrés and other unpersons, and citing Jewish colleagues very rarely if at all.[133] In extreme cases, university professors became the intellectual pioneers and even planners and perpetrators of the National Socialist policy of extermination. Included here are professors of psychiatry like Carl Schneider (Heidelberg) or Max de Crinis (Berlin), who were involved in preparing the euthanasia policy and later, as experts, decided over life or death for many psychiatric patients.[134] Also included are physicians who abused camp inmates as subjects in scientific experiments.[135]

---

129. Holger Dainat, "'Wir müssen ja trotzdem weiter arbeiten.' Die Deutsche Vierteljahrsschrift vor und nach 1945," *Deutsche Vierteljahrsschrift für Literaturwissenschaft und Geistesgeschichte* 68 (1994): 562ff.; Frank-Rutger Hausmann, "Aus dem Reich der seelischen Hungersnot": *Briefe und Dokumente zur Fachgeschichte der Romanistik im Dritten Reich* (Würzburg: Königshausen & Neumann, 1993), 71ff.

130. Frank-Rutger Hausmann, *"Deutsche Geisteswissenschaft" im Zweiten Weltkrieg: Die "Aktion Ritterbusch" (1940–1945)* (Dresden: Dresden University Press, 1998), 275.

131. Dainat, "'Wir müssen ja trotzdem weiter arbeiten,'" 565ff.

132. See, for example, Remy, *Heidelberg Myth*, 50ff.; Ingo Haar, *Historiker im Nationalsozialismus: Deutsche Geschichtswissenschaft und der "Volkstumskampf" im Osten* (Göttingen: Vandenhoeck & Ruprecht, 2000).

133. On the change of the citation practice, see M. Stadler, "Das Schicksal der nichtemigrierten Gestaltpsychologen im Nationalsozialismus," in *Psychologie im Nationalsozialismus*, ed. C. F. Graumann (Berlin: Springer, 1985), 150ff.

134. See especially Hans-Walter Schmuhl, *Rassenhygiene, Nationalsozialismus, Euthanasie: Von der Verhütung zur "Vernichtung lebensunwerten Lebens," 1890–1945* (Göttingen: Vandenhoeck & Ruprecht, 1992), 190ff.

135. Although much has been written on this topic, there is no recent standard work. Still valuable is the classic study of Alexander Mitscherlich and Fred Mielke, *Doctors of Infamy: The Story of the Nazi Medical Crimes* (New York: Henry Schuman, 1949). See also Angelika

These experiments have long been labeled "pseudo-science," but most "pseudo-scientists" had all the conventional academic qualifications (Ph.D., *Habilitation*), and some went on to respectable careers after 1945. In fact, some human experiments reflected a genuine scientific curiosity, because certain problems of research—for example, the efficacy of drugs—could be resolved with the greatest degree of precision in this way. What set those who carried out these experiments apart from other scientists was not their scientific qualification, but their willingness to ignore ethical precepts. In this respect, these experiments were the logical result of an ideology that ignored the needs of the individual in favor of the interests of "community," "folk," and "race."

While only a minority of university teachers were directly implicated in the crimes of the regime, a considerable number served the Nazi policy of conquest. Especially in the area of weapons research many scientists willingly supported the regime's expansionist policies. Even for scholars outside the NSDAP service in war-related research hardly posed a problem. It was regarded as an unquestioned "patriotic duty," but also as an opportunity to be exempted from military service and to obtain additional resources for one's own work. In contrast, ideological projects like "German physics," "German chemistry," or "German mathematics" met with little resonance among natural scientists.[136]

However, it would be incorrect to claim that the natural and technical sciences were made to serve the war in their entirety.[137] This had less to do with unwilling scientists, and more with the regime's inability to use science efficiently as a factor that might decide the war. During the first years, many younger scientists and technicians were drafted into the armed forces with no concern for their professional qualifications.[138] As late as February 1943, an internal study found that about 50–80 percent of war-relevant research potential at universities lay idle.[139] Not until 1942–43

Ebbinghaus and Klaus Dörner, eds., *Vernichten und Heilen: Der Nürnberger Ärzteprozeß und seine Folgen* (Berlin: Aufbau, 2001).

136. Grüttner, *Studenten im Dritten Reich*, 193ff.

137. On the organization of armaments research, see the standard work of Karl-Heinz Ludwig, *Technik und Ingenieure im Dritten Reich* (Düsseldorf: Droste, 1974), 210ff., 403ff. See also Helmut Maier, ed., *Rüstungsforschung im Nationalsozialismus* (Göttingen: Wallstein, 2002). In his introduction the editor tends to overrate the efficiency of armaments research.

138. Walker, *German National Socialism*, 42.

139. See the secret letter from Hermann Göring to the members of the supervising board (Präsidialrat) of the Reich Research Council (Reichsforschungsrat) on 29 June 1943, in BA Berlin R 26 III 185a.

did leading representatives of the regime, like Albert Speer and Joseph Goebbels, recognize the importance of science in determining the outcome of the war. In May 1943, Goebbels recorded in his diary: "Our weapons technology in both submarine and air warfare is far inferior to that of the English and the Americans. We failed to muster the initiative to harness the willingness that undoubtedly existed among scientists, and that is coming back to haunt us."[140]

Goebbels was also critical of university policies that placed greater stress on political attitude than professional competence: "The student league or the league of university teachers usually exerted significant influence on the appointment to professorships. Personnel policy was pursued less on the basis of professional accomplishments than on a National Socialist mindset. The consequences are easy to calculate. [Education Minister] Rust should have opposed these trends much more strenuously."[141]

Influenced by this new assessment of the situation, the regime began frantic efforts in 1942–43 to make better use of the country's scientific potential. Funding for "war-related" research was increased considerably after 1942. Between December 1943 and July 1944, the Wehrmacht discharged two thousand scientists and technicians to their institutes and laboratories. To motivate scientists to do their very best, the regime's propaganda apparatus under Goebbels sought to wipe away the anti-intellectual resentments of the early years. Highly confidential communiqués from the propaganda ministry instructed the German press in June of 1943 "to think about the important role of the German scientist as researchers and technician. His efforts should be repeatedly presented to the reader in a positive light."[142]

These measures did not have any real influence on the further course of the war. They came too late, and their effects were thwarted by the growing devastations of war—which did not spare university buildings—and the ubiquitous shortage of vehicles, chemicals, and fuel.

Conclusion

Though few German professors were Nazi Party members in early 1933, the regime's first encroachments on academic freedom elicited hardly a

---

140. *Die Tagebücher von Joseph Goebbels*, part 2, vol. 8, p. 295.
141. Ibid., p. 413 (3 June 1943).
142. *Deutscher Wochendienst*, 18 June 1943.

murmur of protest from their number. Universities were divided into those who actively supported National Socialism (a substantial part of the students and some of the younger scholars); those who hoped for personal advantages from the Nazi seizure of power (especially younger, non-tenured scholars); those who bided their time because they longed for a "national rebirth," but at the same time rejected intrusions into the inner life of the universities (a majority of the tenured professors); and finally a fifth or so of the teaching faculty who had every reason to expect the worst from the National Socialists (Jews, Socialists, pacifists, etc.).

Members of the last group were mostly gone by 1934, and Nazi higher education policy focused on conformists among the younger scholars, for whom astonishing new career opportunities opened. The initially severe policies of the new rulers toward universities, whose faculties were forcibly nazified through politically guided personnel policies, were somewhat relaxed beginning in 1937. Both the state and party bureaucracy came to believe that universities mattered not only as manufacturers of ideology but also as producers of expert knowledge. At the same time an increasing shortage of qualified young academics gave evidence that Germany did not possess inexhaustible scholarly resources. In order to make effective use of these resources authorities had to take better account of the interests of university faculty. That helps explain the greater freedoms accorded to professors in the late 1930s.

These years witnessed a string of domestic and foreign policy successes for the Nazis, for example, the apparent stabilization of the economy and the practical annulment of the Versailles Treaty, and professors who had been skeptical now drew closer to the regime. By contrast many students lost their earlier enthusiasm as they watched the National Socialist German Student League grow from a radical opposition movement to an integral part of the ruling order, with the task of supervising and disciplining students. Nevertheless, student opposition movements like the "White Rose" were exceptional.

The penetration of individual disciplines with National Socialist ideology was left in the hands of willing scholars who formed competing circles on their own initiative yet claimed to speak for the regime. From our present perspective, the ideologization of research and teaching that resulted appears considerable, but for the National Socialists it was entirely inadequate. Precise assessment of these matters is difficult, however: on the one hand, there were significant differences between the various disciplines; on the other, the question of what kind of scholarship was desired by the regime remained unclear. Take the case of "German physics," which initially acted as a group bearing the imprimatur of the Party, but during the war faded into insignificance. Its development exemplifies the gradual shift in emphasis from a propaganda of ideologically correct scholarship to a promotion of conventional science that promised usefulness for the goals of the regime (armaments, Four-Year Plan). The war thus promoted a de-ideologization of the universities, while at the same time a radicalization occurred that demolished previously existing moral boundaries and caused an unknown number of professors to take an active part in Nazi crimes (euthanasia, lethal experiments on humans, and so on).

Translation: Thomas Dunlap

4

Spanish Universities Under Franco

MIGUEL ÁNGEL RUIZ CARNICER

 In a comparative overview of European universities that were subject to fascist or fascist-like regimes, two things stand out about the Spanish experience. First, Franco retained power for nearly four decades, making him the most tenacious of the right-wing dictators of twentieth-century Europe. His rule lasted through the 1960s, a time in which Spanish universities, like universities all over the world, were experiencing the tensions of growth and massive entry of new students. Second, Franco's regime was the product of a civil war that lasted for almost three years, from July 1936 to April 1939, following a coup against a young democratic republic, which had lasted only five years, and which had tried to reform paralyzed political and social structures.

The civil war and its conclusion always figured as the ultimate self-justification of Francoism. The war is also the starting point for understanding how Spanish universities evolved; they, like all of Spanish society, had been subjected to a tremendous schism. And they were not gradually introduced to the rules of the new game, as in other fascist regimes but rather suffered the brutal shock of radical and summary purging, executions, and the mass exile of distinguished names in Spanish culture.[1] The process

---

1. An example of the extent of this rupture can be found in the works of Juan Jose Carreras Ares and Miguel Angel Ruiz Carnicer, eds., *La Universidad Española bajo el régimen de Franco (1939–1975)* (Zaragoza: Institución Fernando el Católico, 1991), and with greater application to the historiographical field, in Gonzalo Pasamar, *Historiografía e ideología en la postguerra española: La ruptura de la tradición liberal* (Zaragoza: Prensas Universitarias de Zaragoza, 1991).

of adaptation by the Italian or German university systems was much smoother. Although they experienced the brutality of their respective regimes, their transformation proceeded more "legally."[2]

But the long civil war not only conditioned the process of regimentation and control of universities; it also turned them into active agents in the inculcation of the new regime's values, since the gaps left by the exiled, the dead, and the purged were filled by teachers whose credentials were based more on political than academic merit.[3] Universities were to be transformed into an elite training system for adherents of the regime, by means of mechanisms directly controlled by the government or under the influence of groups that had thrown their lot in with the winning side, especially the Falangists and conservative Catholics.

However, this university system, so steeped in the spirit of the victorious side, failed to produce new generations of loyal Francoist students. From the 1960, students, along with many of their teachers combined with the labor movement as the driving force in the struggle against the regime.

The Franco Regime

On 18 July 1936, the Africa Army rose up against the legitimate republican government, supported by the Falange Española and other fascist and fascist-sympathizing sectors, as well as by the Catholic Church. The long, harsh civil war split society at all levels, including, of course, the intellectual and cultural planes and the field of teaching and education, ensuring that the political and social segmentation of Spain followed a course different from comparable processes in other European countries.[4] The new regime lasted to the dictator's death in November 1975. Various stages may be discerned in this long rule, although the common objective in all was the

---

2. See the contributions in this volume of Ruth Ben-Ghiat and Michael Grüttner.

3. For further reading on purging as a global phenomenon linked to repression, see Santos Julia et al., eds., *Víctimas de la guerra civil* (Madrid: Temas de Hoy, 1999). See also the memoirs of Pedro Lain Entralgo, *Descargo de conciencia* (Madrid: Alianza, 1989). This process resembles that of German universities in the years immediately after the Nazi seizure of power. See the contribution of Michael Grüttner to this volume.

4. José Castillejo, *Guerra de ideas en España: Filosofía, política y educación* (1937; Madrid: Ediciones de la Revista de Occidente, 1976). On the subject of contemporary Spain, two summaries stand out: Raymond Carr, *Spain, 1808–1975* (Oxford: Oxford University Press, 1982), and Walther L. Bernecker, *España entre tradición y modernidad: Politica, economia, sociedad (siglos XIX–XX)* (Madrid: Siglo XXI, 1999).

survival of the regime. This was achieved by adopting varying political postures and, depending on the circumstances, giving greater or lesser weight to the various political sensibilities of the winners of the civil war (Falangists, conservative Catholics of Asociación Católica Nacional de Propagandistas [ACNP],[5] Carlists, authoritarian monarchists, and later the technocrats linked to Opus Dei, a religious organization whose influence was on the increase), but always keeping faith with the reactionary values of those who took part in the coup of 18 July, with General Francisco Franco ultimately deciding who would suit his political needs.[6]

The pillars for the new regime were to be the army, which had risen against the Republic, hardened by its North African experience; a church hostile to social reform and harassed by left-wing anticlericalism; agrarian landholders; and groups of the conservative right hostile to democracy. But it was to be a relatively small party, the Falange Española de las Juntas de Ofensiva Nacional-Sindicalista, one of the many imitations of the Italian fascist model in Europe, which was to embody for a good part of the world the shape of the new regime. Given the important role played by the Nazis and Fascists in aiding the winning side in the war, it was the Falangists, having merged with the Carlists at the behest of Franco in the middle of the war, who were to appear as the face of the regime. Indeed, the blue shirt, the omnipresent symbol of the yoke and arrows, and the personality cult of José Antonio Primo de Rivera, the son of the dictator of the 1920s, were to be the clearest signs of the new order. In addition, the Falangists appeared as the equivalent of the Nazis and Fascists on Spanish soil, and therefore might ensure good political relations with those who, once the Second World War was under way, seemed likely to emerge as winners.

---

5. The ACNP (Catholic National Association of Propagandists), established in 1911, had always been a Catholic, conservative, and elitist association, whose aim was to recruit those who were best prepared and catapult them into important state positions. For more information on the *propagandistas*, see Mercedes Montero, *Historia de la Asociación Católica Nacional de Propagandistas: La construcción del Estado confesional, 1936–1945* (Pamplona: EUNSA, 1993), and above all, the splendid work by Javier Tusell, *Franco y los católicos: La política interior española entre 1945 y 1957* (Madrid: Alianza editorial, 1984).

6. Opus Dei (God's Work) was founded in 1928 by an Aragonese Catholic priest, José María Escrivá de Balaguer, now beatified by the church. Much has been written about the Opus Dei, almost all of it influenced by the controversy surrounding this movement in Spain. Worth mentioning are Joan Estruch, *Santos y pillos, El Opus Dei y sus paradojas* (Barcelona: Herder, 1994), and Alberto Moncada, *Historia oral del Opus Dei* (Barcelona: Plaza & Janés, 1987).

It was said that in Spain a "National-Syndicalist regime" was being established, and fascist institutions linked to the ruling party and largely copied from Berlin and Rome were swiftly set up with the aim of encompassing workers, young people, and women. Its ideology was similar to that of any fascist movement of the time, and its "twenty-six clauses" were a compendium of nationalism, anticommunism, anticapitalism, and antiliberalism, while acknowledging the central role of the worker in the new age of the masses.[7] It was called "National-Syndicalism" because the role granted to the Organización Sindical included the power of economic and political leadership. However, the weakness of the Falange Española Tradicionalista y de las JONS, the definitive name of the unified party, was soon apparent, since it never had the popular support that its European counterparts enjoyed; in addition, the civil war itself made any attempts at mobilization and recruitment, such as those carried out in Germany or Italy, unnecessary. All this explains why the Falangists, although on paper extremely influential, carried relatively little political weight. And this weight was to decrease with the decline in fortunes of the Axis. Nevertheless, the party as such survived 1945 and kept going, ever more bureaucratized and with ever decreasing force, until 1975.

It is precisely this weakness, together with the force of the Catholic Church and the army, which has made it difficult for many people to perceive the Franco regime as fascist. Indeed, its nature has always been, and still is, one of the great debating points of Spanish historians.[8] In any event, the type of label one attaches to a phenomenon depends on comparison with other cases. In the case of Spain, this is very difficult, in

---

7. There have been extensive writings on the Falange. Worthy of note are Stanley G. Payne, *Fascism in Spain, 1923–1977* (Madison: University of Wisconsin Press, 1999); Ricardo L. Chueca, *El fascismo en los comienzos del régimen de Franco: Un estudio sobre FET-JONS* (Madrid: Centro de Investigaciones Sociológicas, 1983); Sheelagh M. Ellwood, *Spanish Fascism in the Franco Era: Falange Espanola de las JONS, 1936–1986* (New York: St. Martin's Press, 1987); Joan María Thomas, *Lo que fue la Falange: La Falange y los falangistas de José Antonio, Hedilla y la Unificación. Franco y el fin de la Falange Española y de las JONS* (Barcelona: Plaza & Janés, 1999); and José Luis Rodríguez Jiménez, *Historia de Falange Española de las JONS* (Madrid: Alianza Editorial, 2000).

8. It lies outside the scope of this work to reproduce the entire debate, but two points of view stand out: first, those who see Francoism as an authoritarian regime, for example, Juan Linz, "An Authoritarian Regime: Spain," in *Cleavages, Ideologies and Party Systems: Contributions to Comparative Political Sociology*, ed. Erik Allardt and Yrjö Littunen (Helsinki: The Academic Book Stores, 1964); and those who characterize it as fascist in terms of the regime's social effects, which evoke parallels to Italian or German models. A good summary of this long polemic can be found in Manuel Perez Ledesma, "Una dictadura 'por la gracia de Dios,'" *Historia Social* 20 (autumn 1994): 173–93.

part because of the peculiarity of the civil war, but above all because the regime, having survived 1945 and finding itself in an atmosphere of democracy in Europe, had to adapt its institutions and thinking to this context if it wanted to survive. The Franco regime had other elements that differentiated it from the Italian or German cases: state leadership was not in the hands of the fascist leader; the Catholic Church wielded considerable influence in all political and social fields.

However, in my opinion, the Francoist regime was more than a reactionary clerical dictatorship. To see this, one need only look at the way the civil war was used to physically eliminate workers' leaders and left-wing and liberal politicians; or at how political institutions and recruitment of the postwar years were copied from fascist models; or at the totalitarian desire to reshape the entire nation around the ideology of the victors of the war. Naturally, in this process the conservatives and reactionaries (with the church at their head) were a very important ingredient, but they were also present in the German or Italian cases.[9]

After 1945, the Cold War helped a regime survive that was characterized by anticommunism; and the West began to tolerate it as the lesser of two evils, although Spain was still understood to be under a "totalitarian government."[10] The 1950s witnessed the persistence of economic problems, especially early in the decade,[11] but this period also witnessed a growing regularization of diplomatic relations, exemplified by the agreements of 1953 to construct U.S. bases on Spanish soil. In this year Spain also signed a concordat with the Holy See. As a result of economic liberalization the 1960s were characterized by *"desarrollismo"* — a major economic and social transformation of the country — in which the agricultural sector declined while manufacturing and service industries took off. The result of this process was stable economic growth, which helped the country shake off depression and come closer, in all respects, to the European capitalist democracies.

The society that emerged was very different from the society of the 1930s. Its political class consisted of pragmatic Francoists of various political

9. On this subject, see the major work by Martin Blinkhorn, ed., *Fascists and Conservatives: The Radical Right and the Establishment in Twentieth-Century Europe* (London: Unwin Hyman, 1990).

10. This term was used by the British Foreign Office in its reports. "Internal situation in Spain, 12 March 1951," FO 371/96156 WS 1016/16.

11. One only has to look at the British Foreign Office reports on the Spanish economy and the country's internal situation for the late 1940s and early 1950s. See *Annual Review* for 1949, 30 January 1950, FO371/89479 WS 1011/1.

leanings and included members of the religious organization Opus Dei, which acted as a springboard for political promotion and social and economic influence. Franco finally died in November 1975, leaving behind a society apprehensive about freedom and with an authoritarian political culture, but a vigorous and growing economy. As whole Spain can be characterized as unbalanced and largely marginalized from the cultural, political, and social reality of a Europe it had always wanted to be a part of.

The Spanish University System and the Origins of the Franco Regime

The university system in the 1930s was still characterized by structures inherited from the French system at the beginning of the nineteenth century. It was highly centralized, as is shown by the academic predominance of Madrid, whose university was called the Central University. The curriculum was identical for the whole country and strongly weighted toward the humanities rather than technical or scientific studies, and there was a great gap between teaching staff, erudite and elitist, usually inaccessible, and a small student body that was, with a few exceptions, drawn from the upper classes. This old nineteenth-century university system was to become increasingly involved in the political radicalization of the period.

Although the hierarchical structures of the university system and its teaching seemed unchanging, it is worth pointing to a marked process of modernization which took place during the first third of the twentieth century, not only in the area of research, especially through specialized organizations such as the Junta para la Ampliación de Estudios (the Committee for the Extension of the Syllabus), but also, albeit at a slower rate, in the area of teaching. There were also tentative efforts to increase university autonomy, such as those proposed by Minister César Silió in 1919. The student environment was also subject to upheaval in this period, and for the first time in Spanish history there appeared a student movement, which was increasingly organized into ideologically based groups: the sizable Federación de Estudiantes Católicos and the secular progressive Federación Universitaria Escolar (FUE). The students had already manifested their critical stand against the dictatorship of Primo de Rivera and played an important role in the public call for the abdication of King Alfonso XIII in 1931. The FUE was openly republican and firmly entrenched—from before the Republic until the early stages of the clandestine struggle against the dictatorship.

However, in spite of the FUE's fervor and the existence of influential groups with liberal and progressive attitudes, the student body was also a framework in which a minority of radical students displayed an openly antirepublican stance. Just as in other European states, it was young people who were the first to be mobilized by fascist movements;[12] thus the Falange Española y de las JONS, an organization financed in part by Mussolini, was very soon to have its own university youth movement, the Sindicato Español Universitario (SEU), which included both high school and university students. Although they were in a minority, they published their own newspapers, used violent methods, and even carried arms, which gave rise to confrontation and violence in Spanish universities. There were also uniformed, at times armed, groups belonging to the Young Socialists and the Communist Party. Thus, even during peacetime one could witness the confrontation that would evolve within the universities after 1936. The teaching staff was little affected by this political mobilization before the outbreak of fighting.

During the civil war, universities near the various fronts were of course closed; however, the call to arms meant that students manned the trenches and temporarily abandoned political activism, with the exception of publishing weekly magazines dealing with war matters. On the republican side some universities, such as Valencia, *de facto* capital of the Republic since the end of 1936, became a focus of alternative culture, but at the same time it also purged itself of teachers who sympathized with the rebel side.[13] On the Francoist side, the universities concentrated all their efforts on the struggle.

The war period served to initiate a profound and radical purging, not only of the teaching staff, but also all the administrative and service staff in the university system. Some teachers were shot, others were expelled from the university system, and many others fled. Teachers supporting the Francoist side actively collaborated with the rebels by providing their skills: in censorship, propaganda writing, translation, chemical warfare,

---

12. See the rapid growth of the NSDStB in Germany and the support of students in Fascist Italy as portrayed in the contributions of Grüttner and Ben-Ghiat in this volume.
13. José Manuel Fernandez Soria, *Educación y Cultura en la Guerra Civil (España, 1936–1939)* (Valencia: Nau Llibres, 1984); María Fernanda Mancebo, *La Universidad de Valencia en Guerra: La FUE (1936–1939)* (Valencia: Ayuntamiento de Valencia, Universidad de Valencia, 1988).

international relations, or the supply of political and legal doctrines for the construction of the "New State" (translating and publishing Italian and German theorists, for example). Among students, a certain mythology grew up around their fight against the Republican regime: students at the front were often commissioned as officers, and this was used as an argument for student influence in universities but also in the design of the New State. Heroic deeds of the past (such as the student Literary Battalions who fought against the Napoleonic forces in 1810) were cited as precedents. By war's conclusion in 1939, students were accorded a central role in the generation that "had saved Spain." Organizations such as the SEU came to see themselves as responsible for ensuring that the ideas of José Antonio Primo de Rivera took pride of place in the design of the new regime. In some aspects, the first steps of SEU remind us of the Nazi League of Students and its vision as the avant-garde of the new university regime, as described by Michael Grüttner in this volume.

Yet universities as a whole played a passive role in this period. They suffered a severe blow with respect to traditional activity. Attempts at renovation and improvement dating from the early decades of the century were now frustrated, and the system experienced a brutal politicization. Universities did not, however, resist: although culture was mostly on the side of the Republic, most of the teaching staff were closer to conservative Catholicism or a nonpolitical right wing. There were some distinguished left-wingers, but these were a small minority. Thus, a large proportion of teachers happily accepted the new political and institutional system.[14]

The Bases of the Francoist University System in the Postwar Years: The Break with Liberalism

Fascism aims to eliminate autonomy, especially scientific and academic autonomy. The various fascist movements were quick to appreciate this and act accordingly.[15] However, this does not mean that fascism did not need universities or that it did not grant some individuals a measure of autonomy in certain subjects, according to the needs of the moment. The fascist movements viewed the indoctrination of youth as critical,

---

14. See Antonio Fontan, *Los católicos en la Universidad española actual* (Madrid: Rialp, 1961), and Carreras Ares and Ruiz Carnicer, *La Universidad Española*. This finding is also based on careful reading of the journals of Sindicato Español Universitario and on interviews with scholars who experienced this period.

including the marginalization of alternatives to the dominant doctrine. In all this Spain was no exception to the fascist rule.

As in the case of primary and secondary schools, the Spanish university system became a faithful agent of the new system's essential purpose: the consolidation of the social order existing before the Republic and the war, and the maintenance of a basic consensus among young people about the mechanisms of political power. In view of the circumstances of the birth of the regime, one can hardly avoid talking about breaks, especially in the continuity of personnel. Those who succeeded the purged, executed, and exiled were selected through a political filter, so that war service and ideological merits counted for more than academic merit. This led to a thorough pedagogical and intellectual break, which was reflected in almost all specialties, not only because of the departure of distinguished scholars or the cessation of innovative research, but also because of the imposition of political and religious criteria upon intellectual qualification.[16] Higher education took a step backward, in research as well as in teaching. Old methods were resurrected whereby students were restricted to merely repeating their lessons—lessons now taught by teachers who had poor training and often little interest in their subject. Absenteeism increased because of the multiplicity of duties. The minister of education, José Ibáñez Martín, supplanted university autonomy with the hierarchical-authoritarian and religious criteria that were present in all areas of Spanish life, at an administrative as well as academic level. The result was a frosty climate for study and research, and a sharp fall in the academic standards of universities, thus putting an end to the positive evolution of academic endeavor.[17]

Despite this obvious break in universities' previous academic and political evolution, we nevertheless still find great respect for the traditional idea of the university, the academic status of the teaching staff, former university rituals (which were revived), and the pomp and solemnity of stately university ceremonies. In this regard, Spanish officials did not

---

15. See the contributions of Ruth Ben-Ghiat and Michael Grüttner to this volume.

16. Pasamar, *Historiografía e ideología*, esp. chap. 1. See also the memoirs of Carlos Castilla del Pino, *Pretérito Imperfecto* (Barcelona: Tusquets Editores, 1997).

17. There is much testimony about sinking academic standards. Worthy of mention are Pedro Laín Entralgo, *Descargo de conciencia (1930–1960)* (Madrid: Alianza Editorial, 1989); Elías Diaz, *Pensamiento español en la era de Franco (1939–1975)* (Madrid: Tecnos, 1983); and Elena Hernandez Sandoica, "Reforma desde el sistema y protagonismo estudiantil: La Universidad de Madrid en los años cincuenta," in Carreras Ares and Ruiz Carnicer, *La Universidad Española*.

mirror the contempt Michael Grüttner describes of top Nazis for professors, nor were university faculty publicly humiliated in speeches by the Falangist ruling class. Still, one should not overrate these exceptions to the rule, for the Spanish regime did attempt to instrumentalize tradition. Radical fascists tried to steer higher education in a national-syndicalist direction, against the resistance of moderate sectors of the teaching staff. Thus, in the years immediately following the war, we find criticism, sarcasm, and veiled threats in SEU magazines directed against teachers who were known to have monarchist sympathies or who were simply lukewarm toward the regime. This was to give rise to tension and episodes of violence against these teachers, especially on key occasions such as the fall of the Duce in 1943 or the defeat of Germany in 1945, but always outside the classroom, slyly and anonymously.

The regime equipped itself with the legal instruments to carry out its aims while making use of organizations such as the SEU or the Servicio Español del Profesorado de Enseñanza Superior (SEPES), as well as the cooperation of the academic authorities. This early stage, which has been dubbed by Salvador Giner (among others) as the "Fascist University" or the fascisticization of the university system,[18] should really be called "clerical fascism." Clearly there was an attempt to fascisticize the university system in the strict sense of the word, led by the Falange in the pattern of Italian or German regimes. Thanks to constant pressure, the ministry once again became the fiefdom of the Catholics, and the entire university system approximated a giant mechanism to reproduce conservative and elitist values. But the very weakness of the dictatorial party, its scant power in the university environment, precisely because of the predominance of Catholic-based teaching staff, and later university growth meant that the university system escaped the direct influence of the Falange, in spite of its nominal control of the system.

This final result was far from apparent in the 1940s. Particularly worthy of note was the purging of academic personnel, which began during the civil war. Trusted professors reviewed the teaching staff one by one. Foremost among their targets were colleagues who had fled the rebel zone, not reported for duty, or were actively involved in the defense of the Republic. The purge looked not only for political evidence, but also

---

18. Cf. Salvador Giner, "Power, Freedom and Social Change in the Spanish University, 1939–75," in *Spain in Crisis: The Evolution and Decline of the Franco Regime*, ed. Paul Preston (New York: Barnes & Noble, 1976), 183–211.

delved into private lives, focusing on religion and morality, on friendships, and the books scholars kept in their homes. Over half of all professors were forced out of their jobs: of 278 university professors teaching in 1944, 155 (55.75 percent) had been hired after 1939 to fill the spaces opened by the war and the purge.[19] In addition, many teachers were forcibly transferred to universities of a lower category or away from their homes and suffered other restrictions of an institutional nature, for example, debarment from posts of academic authority, sometimes temporarily, sometimes permanently. Those who emerged unscathed kept their posts, including a few liberals who were not politically significant, but who now owed favors to colleagues who had supported them and worried about official surveillance. These factors more or less spontaneously cemented their conformity to the new state of affairs. In 1951, three-quarters of all professors of the time had been appointed in the first twelve years of the regime, with all that that implies for adherence to new principles, since the professorship appointment system guaranteed that those who filled the gaps left by exile, purging, and repression would be ideologically safe elements for the regime.

As to students, after the civil war there was a steady, though not dramatic, growth in the number of university admissions.[20] The only exception was the 1939–40 academic year, when universities reopened after the war, and many entered wishing to make up for the lost years. Special examinations and intensive courses explain a huge increase in graduations. From 1940–41, the first "normal" academic year, figures were much more in line with the logical increase in student numbers, indeed echoing trends from the Republic. In that year 33,763 students studied at the twelve Spanish universities. Ten years later, in the 1950–51 academic year, this figure had risen to 51,633. Numbers of female students in the student population rose in this period from 13.2 percent to 14.8 percent. The Franco regime resembled its Fascist and Nazi counterparts in its hostility to female university enrollment.

---

19. Antonio Fontan, *Los Católicos en la Universidad Española Actual* (Madrid: Rialp, 1961). There is also data in Josep María Colomer i Calsina, *Els Estudiants de Barcelona sota el Franquisme* (Barcelona: Curial, 1978), 1:21.

20. The figures that follow are taken from the Instituto Nacional de Estadística, *Anuario Estadístico de España*, various years, and from Ricardo Montoro Romero, *La Universidad en la España de Franco (1939–1970) (Un análisis sociológico)* (Madrid: Centro de Investigaciones Sociológicas, 1981), 141, 143–45, 148–49.

Clearly, there was a predominance of enrollment in fields of study linked to the traditional bourgeoisie—like medicine and law—although enrollment figures for other university disciplines less linked to popular careers, such as philosophy and the sciences, were also high. New faculties were established in political science and economics, and quickly found their niche in the overall picture. Faculties that experienced limited, or even negative growth in enrollments were pharmacology, which increasingly became a course almost solely for women, and veterinary medicine, because of harsh working conditions and the low esteem accorded it as a career. By the late 1950s, law and medicine evened out, while the sciences began to gain ground.

Students were also regimented in their daily lives, and for this purpose, the Ministry of National Education restored what was considered an "imperial" tradition of the Spanish university system: the *colegios mayores universitarios* (university residences). Primo de Rivera had already resurrected them during his dictatorship, but now they were to be more than student housing, they were to be sites for political, religious, and moral instruction, since all students had to enroll with a *colegio mayor*. As the relevant decree of September 1942 put it, their purpose was to forge the students' "integral personality." However, these proposals could not be fully implemented; there were simply too many university students to house and instruct individually. Nevertheless, the *colegios mayores* did play a significant role, as shown by the fact that the party and the church competed in setting them up. One example was the "Jiménez de Cisneros" *colegio mayor* whose first director was the Falangist Pedro Laín Entralgo. Mention should also be made of the "César Carlos" *colegio mayor* for graduates, run by the SEU, whose role was to prepare young sympathizers of the Falange for competitive exams, and especially for professorships. This *colegio mayor* became a de facto "nursery of high-ranking officials" for the different branches of the regime.

From 1943, a single compulsory union attempted to control students politically. This was the historic SEU, which, through its activities at all Spanish universities, became the reference point for the Falange's objective of control of the university system.[21] Its monopoly over student activities—such as sports, the arts, theater, and cinema—resembled that of the GUF in Italy. In the postwar years, the SEU saw itself as the essence of the "national revolution," with a mission to remind the authorities of

---

21. Carreras Ares and Ruiz Carnicer, *La Universidad Española*.

their obligations to those who had died in battle, but it came to play an increasingly bureaucratic role in organizing university activities. Gradually, this function outweighed political control, and students demanded not only military but also political demobilization, in order to reconstruct lives that had, one way or another, been irreversibly affected by the war.

Although in some places, such as in Barcelona, the SEU played a repressive role, in most cases its activity was syndicalist in nature[22] and limited to the internal workings of each university, thereby upsetting a good number of conservative lecturers (namely, those who were unwilling to give up their traditional right to run their departments as they pleased). These teachers opposed SEU aspirations to act as the vanguard of the political, aesthetic, and intellectual construction of the New State. Such aspirations were first given in the national journal *Haz*, which was started before the war, and resurrected at the end of 1938, lasting until the middle of the next decade. A new journal, *Juventud*, first published in 1942, maintained this combative tone, reporting on the Second World War and Spain's participation through the División Azul. Many other journals, each linked to the SEU, were to follow. Other cultural initiatives of the SEU were the groups devoted to theater, the TEU (Teatro Español Universitario); the SEU Cine-Club, under various names depending on district; academic discussion seminars; and the organization of debates and conference cycles, using the refectories, libraries, and other infrastructure at its disposal in the twelve university districts. All these activities were strongly influenced by the Italian Littoriali della cultura e dell'arte.[23]

These initiatives help explain the long-lasting importance of the SEU in university life, and why it was the first victim of student disaffection with the regime in the late 1950s, although within the party itself its attitudes were unorthodox. The SEU had demanded that the Francoist state implement the "National Syndicalist Revolution" in full, by for example "giving the Falange total power in the university system." Their models were the League of National Socialist Students in Germany and Italy's Gruppi Universitaria Fascista. This attitude made the SEU an irritation to the authorities, who eventually chose stable conservatism over fascist

22. The activities of the SEU were broad-ranging, but centered around the representation of students, who from 1944 were able to elect class delegates from a single list approved by the head of the Sindicato's University District. All student activities depended on the SEU. See Carreras Ares and Ruiz Carnicer, *La Universidad Española*, esp. part 2, which is devoted to these activities.

23. The major work on Littoriali is Ugoberto Alfassio Grimaldi and Marina Addis Abba, *Cultura a passo romano: Storia e strategie dei Littorili della cultura e dell'arte* (Milan: Feltrinelli, 1983).

radicalization. Various authors have applied the epithet "heterodox" to the SEU, not only because of its revolutionary stance versus a reluctant state, but also because it was close to the lively student world, and often defended positions that contradicted the inertia of an increasingly bureaucratized Falange.[24] Beginning in the late 1950s the SEU found itself yielding to demands for direct elections of student delegates for the university district, something that completely opposed the *Führerprinzip*, which the SEU and the Falange both espoused. The SEU, both for its regimented origins as well as its evolution, may therefore be classified as somewhat unorthodox within the gloomy context of the Francoist dictatorship.

Our picture of the regime's attempts to control students is rounded out by mention of the complementary subjects sanctioned by the Ley de Ordenación Universitaria (University Planning Act): political training, religious training, and physical education. Although soon considered *marías* (second-rate subjects, soft options), these courses reflect the seriousness of the state's intent to socialize university students. To these must be added what was known as premilitary education (*instrucción premilitar superior*), the successor to the Milicia Universitaria of the immediate postwar years, designed as a party police force in the universities. From the mid-1940s, however, this course evolved into a convenient way for university students to fulfill their military obligations, albeit in isolation from the rest of the male population. One way or another, then, an elitism attached to university studies until the 1960s, not only because of students' class background and low numbers, but also because such traditions were regarded by the regime as a guarantee of its political continuation.

The fundamental legal document governing the university system under Franco was the Ley de Ordenación Universitaria (University Planning Act) of July 1943. However, this text cannot be analyzed without taking into account the Consejo Superior de Investigaciones Científicas (CSIC), a body created in 1939 that advanced the radical separation of research and teaching. The LOU highlighted universities' teaching and political indoctrination functions, while the responsibility for research was handed over to the CSIC. In this way, a separation was established in which institutions close to CSIC were endowed with research resources and tasks, while universities were reduced to ideological training grounds, with moderate attention to professional training.[25]

---

24. For example, see Chueca, *El fascismo*, 32–518.
25. Pasamar, *Historiografía e ideología*, 4–7.

The LOU contained a good many clearly totalitarian aspects: the rector was "leader" of the university; students were placed under rigid control of the SEU; and physical, religious, and above all, political instruction were made obligatory.[26] These complemented such initiatives as Compulsory Labor Service, which directly imitated the Nazi counterpart (and was introduced at the request of the SEU) and the strict political surveillance of universities, which turned deans into mere delegates of the rector, who was supposed to be a party militant.

However, as Carlos París has stated, "Anyone who experienced the Spanish university system when the LOU was in force can appreciate the distance between a programmed university system in line with a totalitarian model and reality, although naturally this distance grew over time."[27] The fact is that the LOU was never fully implemented. This was because, among other things, many of its precepts—such as the dependence of political bodies on the party—became meaningless, or simply obsolete, after World War II. Relationships within an ideologically homogeneous conservative teaching staff also softened the highly autocratic governing of the university system legislated by the LOU. With regard to the SEU, its decline within the university ran parallel to the political crisis of the Falange, and its ineffectiveness as a student control mechanism soon became apparent.

Although there was formal equilibrium among the forces of 18 July (the date of the military uprising), the spirit of strict Catholicism gained ground at universities to the detriment of a hypothetical national-syndicalist order. Of course, this does not mean that there was no political control over teachers and students. Naturally, some control did exist, but not so much because of the dictates of LOU, but rather, as París rightly notes, because of everything that had occurred up to that time: the purging of the teaching staff and their replacement with highly ideologized personnel; the military and hierarchic atmosphere of academic life; and the role played by the Falange, through the SEU and SEPES, in the university system during the preceding years.

Though the legislation's success was relative, Spanish higher education took a giant step backward within the European context. Universities were stripped of their most notable researchers, and students in uniform

---

26. Manuel Puelles Benitez, *Educación e Ideología en la España Contemporánea* (Madrid: EDICUSA, 1980), 374–78. See also Mariano Peset Reig, "La Ley de Ordenación Universitaria de 1943," in Carreras Ares and Ruiz Carnicer, *La Universidad Española*, 125–57.

27. Carlos Paris, *La Universidad Española Actual: Posibilidades y Frustraciones* (Madrid: EDICUSA, 1974), 57.

filled lecture halls and corridors, and the brutal nature of the Francoist victory was manifest in thousands of ways. Especially harsh was the climate of the University of Barcelona, where the awful atmosphere resulting from the purges and a pitiful lack of resources combined with the repression of anyone who spoke Catalan or came from a politically suspect family. Here the SEU was much more aggressive than in any other part of Spain.[28]

Although it might seem that this regimented university system was a successful tool for socially implanting the regime in the university elite, in fact the Francoist university system was little more than the old "restorationist" system, if much more reactionary and corporative, amidst a poverty of human, moral, and material resources and agitated by the hatreds arising from the civil war. Attempts to make universities fascist, based on the 1943 law on universities, were actually a smokescreen, behind which old vices were maintained and amplified. This crisis situation was not clearly seen until Minister Joaquín Ruíz-Giménez Cortés (1951–56) made a general examination of higher education. From 1956 onward, a structural crisis began to manifest itself and finally broke out in full force with the massification of the 1960s, when the technical and scientific requirements of the *desarrollismo* made expansion of higher education essential. It was then that society began to put the role of the university system under a microscope.

Teaching and Research in the University System Under Franco

With regard to teaching, we have already mentioned the purging of the teaching staff and its scope, which in just a few years changed the face of the Spanish university system, thus ensuring that its teachers were in tune with the political regime. This was achieved by organizational changes that guaranteed the Ministry of Education control over professorial appointments. Candidates for professorships took a competitive examination before a board appointed by the ministry, in which they were supposed to show their merits, as well as prove their "firm adherence to the fundamental principles of the State, certified by the Secretary General of the Movement" (from article 58 of the Ley de Ordenación Universitaria). In short, candidates did not prepare slowly and gradually for professorships by gaining experience first as instructors. Rather, a

28. Colomer i Calsina, *Els Estudiants de Barcelona*.

tribunal either thrust them into positions for which they were not prepared or barred them from university teaching altogether. This situation lasted until the 1960s.

The chair was the basic unit of teaching, and chairs were held by professors. No data exist concerning the dedication of professors to their chairs, but in many cases this was certainly minimal. Auxiliaries, who received all but symbolic salaries, did the bulk of professors' teaching. Professorial predominance took on a stifling force throughout higher education, making impossible any thought of "team work"; only a new generation will be able to modify the conservative thought that dominated Spanish universities for decades.

Teachers who had been purged and desired reinstatement had above all to adopt the norms of Catholic morality and defend the principles of the regime, and only secondarily comply with academic standards. The result was not so much a change in the content of teaching as an intensification of the highly conservative values that had existed previously, and were now given new life by a state intent upon rewarding the least modernized sectors of Spanish higher education. Repetitive syllabi and poorly prepared teachers were the indelible features of the university under Franco. One did occasionally encounter highly skilled intellectuals, but in a European context they tended to be extremely dated in their approach. The few "liberals" who managed to emerge unscathed from the purging worked alone behind the scenes, or in parallel activities outside the universities. The standard of teaching of that time was extremely low, as historians of the subject and contemporary student accounts both attest.[29]

Surprisingly, the Falangist leaders of the SEU were aware of this mediocrity and lack of "vigor" in university teaching and political life and hoped to activate universities in line with Nazi or Fascist models. They proposed setting up a "national-syndicalist" university system that would be steeped in Falangist ideology and made up of young Falangist teachers, with skills and inclinations that would distinguish them from the majority of conservative and Catholic teachers who swam with the tide, failing to comprehend the "revolutionary" needs of these young followers of Primo de Rivera. Thus the immediate postwar years saw such initiatives as the "Joven Academia,," which aimed to have pro-Falange professors hold lectures and seminars. There were also requests from party figures that

---

29. The most satisfying treatment of this issue is Pasamar, *Historiografía e ideología*, esp. chap. 1.

Falangist university graduates take part in selection exams for professorial chairs. The latter aim was not realized, however, since chairs tended to be occupied by traditional sectors with Catholic links, especially to the ACNP and Opus Dei.

Likewise the sphere of university research registered a great step backward. Spain, which had never been a leading force in the field of research in the nineteenth century, be it scientific, technical, or humanistic, had made considerable progress in the first third of the twentieth century as a result of backing from successive governments as well as stimulation given by progressive groups such as the Institución Libre de Enseñanza and Ateneos and a growing openness to cultural and scientific influences from outside the country. The Junta para la Ampliación de Estudios e Investigaciones Científicas, set up in 1907 as an autonomous institution, although dependent on the Ministry of Public Instruction and Fine Arts, was inspired by the Institución Libre de Enseñanza, and its personnel and management committee were made up of illustrious figures such as Santiago Ramón y Cajal, José Echegaray, Marcelino Menéndez y Pelayo, Ramón Menéndez Pidal, and Leopoldo Torres Quevedo.[30] The new body had guided and supported this renaissance in research by means of scholarships and grants for visits abroad but also by setting up an important center for the promotion of research in Spain; as a result several Spanish faculties experienced major developments in research. These activities were looked on with mistrust by the more traditional sectors of the Spanish university establishment, partly because of suspected connections with secular and progressive values foreign to Catholic tradition; this explains the hostility that greeted the Junta para la Ampliación de Estudios and its offshoot, the Residencia de Estudiantes, which managed to brew up a very special atmosphere in the late 1920s and 1930s, when it gathered together under its roof figures of the caliber of Salvador Dalí, Luis Buñuel, and Federico García Lorca.

This modest yet clear progress in the international standing of Spanish higher education was cut short by civil and world war, as well as by the vehemence with which the new rulers swept away the remains of the Junta para la Ampliación de Estudios and the staff of the Institución Libre de Enseñanza. Their ashes gave birth to a new body, the Consejo

---

30. S. Ramón y Cajal was an important researcher of the human nervous system; José Echegaray was a playwright; M. Menéndez y Pelayo, was a writer and publicist; Ramón Menéndez Pidal was a historian; and L. Torres Quevedo a pioneer engineer. The first two won the Nobel Prize.

Superior de Investigaciones Científicas (CSIC) in November 1939, presided over by the minister of national education, José Ibáñez Martín. Its aim was to foster academic research, and it set up an oligarchic scholarly network parallel to the university system that favored conservative sectors linked to Catholicism.[31] Theoretically as well as in practice—it used the same offices—the Consejo was a continuation of the Junta de Ampliación de Estudios e Investigaciones Científicas (JAE). However, this formal continuity contradicted the intent of the CSIC to efface the traditions of the JAE, accused as it was of links to Freemasonry.[32] According to its main promoter, Minister Ibáñez Martín, the CSIC would ground research in church doctrine, an intention symbolized well in its official seal, which depicts the Tree of Knowledge as rooted in knowledge of God. In this vision theology was the mother of all sciences. This explicit national-Catholicism was to shape the evolution of the Consejo to the end of the regime. Ibáñez Martín's men in the Consejo were members of Opus Dei, and thus this Catholic organization became the overseer of research in postwar Spain. Furthermore, the Consejo became the springboard for the promotion of its men in the competitive examinations for professorships in the Spanish university system, and for the development of the Opus Dei's work both in and out of Spain. José María de Albareda Herrera, a member of Opus Dei and chemistry professor since 1940, was its supreme head and remained a confidant of Ibáñez Martín until the former's death in 1966, with great power in the formulating of academic policy in Spain. Until the 1960s, the CSIC was heavily weighed down by this concept of science as subject to church doctrine, and this acted as a brake on scientific progress. It also meant a predominance of theological studies and in biology the favoring of pre-evolutionary concepts.

The Consejo was an alternative to the world of the university, a means of promotion, a way to collect funds that universities could not dream of, and for this reason, the Consejo served as a model in which research was separated from teaching. Albareda's idea was not to engage in *forward-looking* research or to send students abroad like the JAE, but to establish an organization that would cover the whole academic spectrum, creating institutes that dealt with widely varying subjects, all subject to a Catholic theology based on neoscholasticism.[33] It became a body capable of

31. See Pasamar, *Historiografía e ideología*, esp. chap. 1.
32. José Manuel Sánchez Ron, *Cincel, martillo y piedra, Historia de la ciencia en España (siglos XIX y XX)* (Madrid: Taurus, 1999).
33. Pasamar, *Historiografía e ideología*, 310.

hierarchizing research but also of exerting influence on the university job ladder and controlling research and funds through the institutes into which the Consejo was divided, and subsequently through the provincial institutes under the "José María Cuadrado" Trust which appeared throughout Spain, most of them being financed by, and under the auspices of, the local powers.

These establishments, both central and local, evolved into a parallel university system, in which the ideological and political aspects of directing research became even more patent. The heads of institutes and trusts were senior professors, most of whom held professorships from before the civil war. They were all supporters of the Catholic right, and some leaned toward Falangism or a vehemently anti-institutionist cultural right wing. All the institutes received names linked to Spanish intellectual tradition, such as Francisco Suárez, Benito Arias Montano, Luis Vives, and Jerónimo Zurita, and though pride of place was accorded theology, the Trust aimed to include all branches of knowledge: philosophy, law, economics, Arabic and Hebrew Studies, history, art, archaeology, and geography. To these others were added in anthropology, sociology, pedagogy, and musicology. Growth was extremely rapid under ministerial control and funding. Gonzalo Pasamar describes this situation as an oligarchy, since the CSIC of the first half of the Franco regime was a tool of powerful professors of the central university system, who used it to distribute academic sinecures. In contrast to university posts, these had "absolute budgetary security."[34]

Political interests determined the shape of Spanish research, and it suffered accordingly: from the precariousness of resources as far as universities were concerned, since the bulk of the scant investment went to the CSIC; from a lack of native roots for much research, since some former teachers and their able pupils had either died, been sent into exile, purged, or banished to universities with very few resources; and from international isolation, except for contacts that were maintained with Germany and Italy during World War II. A step backward was taken across academia, further than dictated by scarce resources alone.

Despite the ruptures caused by political intervention, certain ideas and persons from the past remained influential, and in some cases even attracted adherents. Certain continuities ensured that the deficiencies generated in the 1940s were overcome two decades later. The fate of scholarship varied by discipline. From an ideological point of view, it was

34. Ibid., 46.

the humanities, so beloved by the Minister Ibáñez Martín, that were predominant in research work in postwar Spain. A leading role was reserved for theology and a dogmatically driven philosophy, characterized by the prevalence of scholasticism and an extreme Thomism. While the religious orders (especially the Dominicans and Augustinians) had great force in the Consejo and at Spanish universities, names such as Ortega y Gasset and Zubiri were partially forgotten, as part of a hateful past that was never to return. On the other hand, experimental sciences, though also subject to politicization, escaped such extremism by virtue of their relative political neutrality.

When discussing medicine or biology one should mention the "eugenics debate" which also took place in other European countries and merged with racial theories in Nazi Germany. In Spain this was limited to an intellectual debate in some journals, such as the *Revista Internacional de Sociología*, published by the CSIC, and always within the context of Catholic thought and directed mainly against abortion or contraception, with the goal of controlling women's bodies, although the notion of a "Spanish race" did appear in the work of some authors.[35]

The University's Role in Structure of the Elite Under the Franco Regime

The Franco regime, like all fascist regimes, sought to create an elite that could carry out important duties, help draw up new laws, influence coming generations, and create institutions supporting the regime and its values. The Spanish university was one of the few environments in which such an elite could be educated; a country with Spain's low socioeconomic development, and lacking strong organizations of civil society (chambers of commerce, lobbies, trade unions, association or syndicate) could hardly generate alternatives.

There were, however, militant Catholic pressure groups active at universities from the early days of the regime that were ready to intervene in public life. Let us briefly turn our attention to them. From the beginning of the century, as Spanish society became more complex, resolute Spanish

---

35. For a good summary of the eugenics controversy in Spain, see Marie-Aline Barrachina, *Propagande et culture dans l'Espagne franquiste, 1936–1945* (Grenoble: ELLUG/Université Stendhal, 1998), 61–318.

Catholics felt the need to mobilize to defend the values of the Catholic faith in public as well as private; they noted how forces of a secular nature, such as the trade unions or progressive intellectuals, as well as republicanism and socialism, were slowly but inexorably gaining ground. To stop this decline of moral, religious, and political values groups such as the ACNP were set up. Founded in 1911 by the Jesuit Ayala and patronized by later Cardinal Ángel Herrera Oria, it showed strength in the 1930s through ownership of influential newspapers, such as *El Debate*, and the presence of its members in the parliamentary group of the right-wing coalition CEDA (Confederación Española de Derechas Autónomas).[36] Its critical stance toward the Republic, although initially benign, would later lead to support for the military uprising of 18 July 1936. The ACNP was active in the upper levels of government, especially after the defeat of fascism elsewhere, when its contacts within European Catholicism made it most useful for ensuring the regime's survival. From its ranks were to emerge key figures in the dictatorship such as Alberto Martín-Artajo, Joaquín Ruiz-Giménez, and Fernando María Castiella, who followed evolutionary paths, seeking to transform the dictatorship into a monarchical regime of a more moderate and accommodating nature. Although they never really made headway in this direction, this did not stop them from actively collaborating with the system.

Cardinal Herrera Oria gave clear instructions at the beginning of the postwar period: university chairs had to be conquered for the church. The *propagandistas* launched the attack, outflanking Falangist sectors outside the church in education and related fields. Other groups were to act in the same way, such as the Opus Dei. This latter group also had a proselytizing mission directed initially at university students that then evolved into a powerful confessional association, which, while not independent of the church, did enjoy autonomy. Although it had little impact during the Republic, it grew under the Franco regime, especially in the 1950s, until it finally managed to incorporate key members into the government in the decisive governmental changes of 1957 and throughout the 1960s. From 1959 members of Opus Dei, avowedly nonpolitical and more open to international capitalism and economic liberalization, figured among the influential elites of Franco's Spain, aspiring, in the same way as the *propagandistas* in the early 1940s, to the occupation of

---

36. The CEDA was the right-wing coalition winner of the general elections of 1933, and was in government with the centrist Radical Party until February 1936.

university chairs as a first step to power. Mention should be made here of the official recognition, in 1962, of a university run by this group, the University of Navarre.

The Falangists had similar aspirations: the conquest of university professorships as a means of proselytizing university youth, strengthening a party with a weak framework and thereby acquiring weight in the shaping of dictatorship. Many Falangists indeed occupied important posts in the government, and in local and provincial administration, but their influence shrank because of insufficient preparation and planning, especially in areas that had traditionally spawned the governing elite, like the universities. The years 1941 and 1942 saw many calls by Pedro Laín Entralgo, professor of medicine and an early Falangist, to build a national-syndicalist state starting with universities, by acquiring professorships at the expense of confessional sectors that lacked the Falange's "revolutionary" aspirations. But the Falangists' lack of support in the university system and the cultural area in general doomed them to defeat against confessional candidates, and in the end they secured only a few professorial chairs.

The Spanish University System in Franco's Dictatorship: A Risk or a Support for the Regime?

As we have seen, the university system was indisputably a prop for the dictatorship during its first fifteen years; but during the Republic it had not been a promoter of fascism; indeed often the reverse was the case, as was shown in the civil war. It was only after the war and extremely harsh purging and repression that universities and their more conservative and stagnant elements embraced the new regime and began to inculcate young people in its values.

But this regimented university system, subject to fascist mechanisms, also became an extreme risk for the regime from the mid-1950s on. The reason for this was the failure of Spanish youth—like their Italian counterparts—to internalize conservative and reactionary values. The mid-1950s saw the entry into Spanish universities of a generation that had not directly participated in the civil war and had no first-hand awareness of it; except for those coming from families that had directly suffered Francoist repression, they mostly accepted the regime as an indisputable framework that "had always been there," and therefore lacked the fanaticism of war veterans or those who remembered that struggle's cruelty. Thus their approach to the sociopolitical situation was different. As Ruth Ben-Ghiat shows in this volume, a similar situation obtained in Italy in the 1930s.

The regime, which initially encouraged fascist mobilization and celebrated Axis victories, had also changed. Indeed, by the mid-1950s, an apparent social consensus had been achieved, but this produced a restlessness in young people's minds. They started to contrast the ideas that had been transmitted to them from a very early age in the Frente de Juventudes (Youth) Camps—the imminence of the national-syndicalist revolution, the principles of the historic leader of the Falange, José Antonio Primo de Rivera, and the important role to be played by youth—with a reality that was mediocre, apathetic, featureless, and in their eyes, riddled with social injustice. These young people began investigating social reality for themselves—on the one hand, dire working-class conditions and miserable suburban slums, populated with recent arrivals from the countryside, and on the other, a regime that could not care less. Their growing awareness of hypocrisy and injustice triggered a gradual release of pent-up anger that by the 1960s would grow into full-scale rejection of the regime. Yet the first such emotion was not openly political.

Young people from the universities were foremost in expressing frustration, angst, and a groping desire for social change, and they did so mainly in magazines linked to the SEU of the 1950s and 1960s. Magazines such as *La Hora, Alcalá, Acento, Presencia,* and *Marzo,* as well as smaller local magazines, expressed students' aspirations to broaden their horizons, to change an offensive reality, to learn about new cultural trends, especially in the cinema, the theater, art, and literature, and to know more about Europe. The pages of these magazines, although strictly *"joseantonianas"* and formally loyal to the spirit of 18 July, were to provide an outlet for students linked to Communist positions and critical of the regime.

Two well-known events precipitated the rupture between students and regime which previous events had foreshadowed: a student demonstration in 1954 for the return of Gibraltar to Spain, which, though backed by the SEU, ended with a violent police charge; and, more important, a confrontation of February 1956 in which Falangists clashed with students defending their right to freely elect delegates. The intransigence of the regime became clear for all to see, and the discrepancy between its fascistoid "revolutionary" discourse, which promised power to the young, and a reality that was ultraconservative drove students ever further away from the regime. Some chose Communist militancy (the epitome of opposition in view of the smear campaign the Francoists had launched against the Communists), while others focused on their profession, creating a "position" for themselves, as people said at the time, and distancing themselves from political commitment. Still others reasserted a Falangist discourse, but even these relatively few students took a purist stance critical of the governing political structures. This generation's repudiation of official values attests to the complexities of political socialization. This process has been analyzed for the Italian case by Koon and Zangrandi,[37] but comparisons to the Communist world appear more difficult.

From the late 1950s, large numbers of students took part in the struggle against the SEU and academic authorities. They began by infiltrating the SEU in order to gather evidence of that organization's mendacity, but later founded their own clandestine unions such as the Federación Universitaria Democrática de Estudiantes (FUDE) or the Sindicatos Democráticos de Estudiantes (SDE). Only later would such secret structures be coordinated at a national level. Debates, mass assemblies, sit-ins (such as the *caputxinada* in Barcelona in 1966), and open confrontation with the police (the "grays") characterized the 1960s in Spanish universities. This growing student movement also established links with labor movements, especially in the north of Spain (the Basque Country and Asturias), where steelworkers traditionally opposed the regime.

At the end of the 1960s, influenced by May 1968 in France, and to a lesser extent, the riots in U.S. universities, students formed radical left-wing, Marxist-Leninist, and Maoist groups, some of which were inspired by Fidel Castro's Cuban model, although the Partido Comunista de España continued to be the basic rallying post in the struggle against the dictatorship on the university front. Christian Democrat and socialist groups also emerged. Universities were transformed into oases of freedom, because people could speak a different language on the campus, one that was more open and more hostile to the regime. Clandestine publications circulated, and taboos were shattered. Sometimes the campus became a veritable battlefield on which "subversive" students faced a government that wanted to repress revolt with police violence, and academic authorities who used disciplinary measures in order to keep the university from "slipping out of their hands." There is no doubt, then, that the university

---

37. Tracy H. Koon, *Believe, Obey, Fight: Political Socialization of Youth in Fascist Italy, 1922–1943* (Chapel Hill: University of North Carolina Press, 1985); Ruggero Zangrandi, *Il lungo viaggio attraverso il fascismo: Contributo alla storia di una generazione* (Milan: Feltrinelli, 1962). See also Michael A. Ledeen, "Italian Fascism and Youth," *Journal of Contemporary History* 3, no. 4 (1969): 137–54.

system in the later years of the regime was an active element of the struggle against the dictatorship, although most teachers remained faithful to their original principles.

But even among teachers, critical attitudes could be registered. This was a result of the so-called massification, that is, the significant increase in numbers of students from the 1960s until the 1980s, which gave rise to changes in the old structure of the teaching staff and necessitated the hiring of more assistant lecturers. These new lecturers were employed under precarious conditions, and most of them expressed their commitment to the student struggle and became heavily involved in the defense of their employment rights and criticism of the dictatorship. A large proportion of these young teachers were to become linked to ideas contrary to the regime; a good number of them were Marxist in their teaching as well as in their politics, and this was another major element in spreading democratic values among the students of that time.

To sum up, the discrepancies between the Francoist discourse and the reality created by the regime, and the desire of a growing sector of the population for social change caused the university system to be transformed into one of the main hubs of the struggle against the dictatorship from the end of the 1950s up to the storm-tossed final years of the Franco regime.

5

The Communist Idea of the University:
An Essay Inspired by the Hungarian Experience

GYÖRGY PÉTERI

The postcommunist era has witnessed a desperate struggle for institutional survival, including a scramble for fiscal resources as well as the spoils of privatization and reprivatization, and an intense competition to maximize the reputation of the martyrs of Communist oppression. In all of this effort, so vital to the symbolic economy of both organizations and individuals in East Central Europe after 1989, universities appeared to be just as eager as the churches to assert themselves.

Mythologies have emerged feeding on misconceptions about higher education before and under Communist rule. The dominant genre is martyrology. From these narratives we learn what the Communist dictatorship did to the university: how university autonomy was destroyed and the freedoms of teaching and learning (*Lehrfreiheit* and *Lernfreiheit*) demolished; how old regime scholars and scientists, especially if they failed to conform to the requirements of political and ideological correctness, were victimized and forced to leave their jobs; how recruitment policies and student admissions were thoroughly politicized and subjected to the

This paper was written for the conference "Universities in Twentieth-Century Dictatorships," Berkeley, 13–14 May 2000. I closely followed the questions posed by the organizers of the conference, John Connelly and Michael Grüttner. My thanks are due to the organizers and participants of the conference for an inspiring meeting and discussion. I am especially indebted to John Connelly for his extremely useful comments and suggestions. I have also had the privilege and advantage of receiving comments from three anonymous readers. As always, the author alone bears responsibility for errors of fact and thinking that have remained in the paper.

criteria of social promotion; how, as part of a vicious plan to minimize its critical potential, the university was depleted of its research talents, of the right to educate graduate students, and of the most elementary prerequisites for up-to-date research activity; how it was transformed into a politically controlled institution of mass professional education and vocational training.[1]

The martyrology of the university has been nourished by institutional hagiography and institutional demonology. On the one hand, idyllic images have been evoked for the precommunist era, and on the other, these have been complemented by the vilification of the Communist party's central apparatus, its university committees, the government ministry of higher education, and last but not least, the Academy of Sciences, which was the institutional locus of the Communist academic elite, and the main beneficiary of the university's misery. These institutions have been accused of conspiring to deprive the university of its most essential features, to erode "Humboldtian ideals," to arrest the development of the modern research university, and so on and so forth.[2]

My greatest problem with these accounts is one of a methodological nature. I am perplexed by the apparent ease with which they take for granted what "the university" and, indeed, what "the dictatorship" are. Concern with method and conceptualization is the predominant theme of this chapter, while the various moments and episodes taken from the history of Hungarian universities and academic life constitute my source of inspiration. My intention in the latter respect has been to exemplify or illustrate rather than to "reconstruct" or provide a survey, with a good "balance" between various disciplinary sectors and organizations.

I am not looking for a static, universally valid definition of "university" or "dictatorship"; on the contrary, I find important a dynamic, historical view of these entities. Much of what is problematic in these narratives has been informed by an essentialist understanding of "the university"—as if this "venerable institution" had some constitutive thing or things at

---

1. For more detail and discussion of the postcommunist struggle between institutions of learning and the mythologies originating in this struggle, see Michael David-Fox and György Péteri, "On the Origins and Demise of the Soviet Academic Regime," in *Academia in Upheaval: Origins, Transfers and Transformations of the Communist Academic Regime in Russia and East Central Europe*, ed. David-Fox and Péteri (Westport, Conn.: Bergin & Garvey, 2000), 15–18.

2. An example illustrative of this tendency is the offensive in the early 1990s against the Hungarian Academy of Sciences reaching even the pages of *Nature* (see György Péteri, "On the Legacy of State Socialism in Academia," in David-Fox and Péteri, *Academia in Upheaval*, 287–89).

its core; as if there were some universally valid "idea of the university."³ If the criteria stemming from this "idea" apply, then the university exists and may even flourish; but if they don't, because some evil (most often external) power destroyed them, then it is too bad for the university.

To my mind, there exists no eternal truth about the university, no "idea" or "core" that underlies the self-identity of this institution irrespective of time and place. The university is but an institutionalized field of human activity: what it actually contains and how it is institutionalized are historically contingent, and it will, therefore, exhibit considerable variation. The university is not only a socially embedded institution; it is also part of the broader world of learning comprising a number of other institutions—and this is important, even if the university is restricted to the function of professional education.

Thus, there is only one feature that I believe eternal about universities: the never-ceasing contestation about what the "idea of the university" should be, what "in fact" the defining, essential characteristics of the university are. Seen in this way, we could conceptualize the university as a dynamic social field (à la Bourdieu), which is inhabited by various agents of academic and scientific-political activity and where various ("orthodox" and "heterodox") positions on the idea of the university confront one another and attempt to assert their particularistic ambitions as essential, universal truths.⁴

The Interwar Legacy

On the basis of the foregoing discussion, it seems that the assessment of the role of the university in the foundation period of the Communist dictatorship in Hungary (1945–49) has to start from a historical analysis of the field of "the idea of the university," of the conflicting positions, and their relative power and dynamics, constituting this field.

---

3. The sources of inspiration for this discussion of the idea of the university are Sheldon Rothblatt and Björn Wittrock, eds., *The European and American University Since 1800: Historical and Sociological Essays* (Cambridge: Cambridge University Press, 1993), and Sheldon Rothblatt, *The Modern University and Its Discontents: The Fate of Newman's Legacies in Britain and America* (Cambridge: Cambridge University Press, 1997).

4. For a concise exposition of Bourdieu's theory of social/cultural fields, see "Some Properties of Fields," in Pierre Bourdieu, *Sociology in Question* (London: Sage Publications, 1993), 72–77.

The legacy of postwar Hungary was anything but conducive for liberal-democratic development or modernization in higher education. Hungary's interwar political, cultural, and academic regimes were formed under the combined impact of (1) a counterrevolutionary reaction that put an end to the radical liberal and socialist tendencies of 1918–19, and (2) the traumatic shock caused by the Trianon peace settlement leaving but a third of the country's prewar territory and population under Hungarian control. Interwar Hungarian politics took place on a scale stretching, in domestic politics, from conservative nationalist authoritarianism to fascist totalitarianism; and in international politics, from peaceful revisionism, to be pursued through economic and cultural superiority, to "immediate" territorial revisionism, resorting to pro-Axis policies and war.

This strong rightist bias in Hungary's interwar politics did not, however, exclude major modernization efforts in higher education and science. Count Kuno Klebelsberg, minister of education and religion in István Bethlen's government (1921–31), is the most important person to be named in this respect.[5] His ministry secured perhaps the highest relative budgetary share for education, science, and the universities that has been seen in twentieth-century Hungary. His determination to promote modern scientific research persuaded the Rockefeller Foundation to invest considerable sums into major scientific establishments like the University of Szeged and the Institute of Fresh Water Biology in Tihany on Lake Balaton.[6] The establishment of the National Scholarships Council, which provided generous funding for Hungarian scholars to carry out study trips abroad, and the development of a network of Hungarian Institutes (Collegium Hungaricum) in the major Western European capitals opened Hungarian academic life to international influences. Klebelsberg felt that science and higher education should play a central role in modern societal development and that the state should assume increased responsibility for developing science and for securing proper conditions for the advancement of the nation's research endeavors.

5. For a recent, informative discussion of Klebelsberg's ministry, see Andor Ladányi, *Klebelsberg felsöoktatási politikája* (Budapest: Argumentum Kiadó, 2000).
6. See Erik Ingebrigtsen, "Ungarsk nasjonalisme og amerikansk filantropi: Rockefeller Foundations støtte til modernisering av ungarsk vitenskap og helsevesen, 1920–1941" [Hungarian Nationalism and U.S. Philantropy: The Support Lent by the Rockefeller Foundation Toward the Modernization of Hungarian Science and Public Health, 1920–1941] (master's thesis in history, Institutt for historie og klassiske fag, Norwegian University of Science & Technology, Trondheim, Norway, Spring 2000).

While Klebelsberg achieved a great deal by getting his colleagues in government and parliament to accept his modernizing agenda, he proved less effective in overcoming the resistance of the conservative academic establishment. His suggestions for national planning and coordination *for* science through new types of organizations bringing together high-level governmental administrators and the scientific elite fell mostly on deaf ears or were received with hostility within academia. While his "neo-nationalist" conservatism brought with it a new, higher level of ambition on the part of the state vis-à-vis academic life, it is also important to see that it articulated and posed, in a more resolute and explicit manner than ever before, not only professional but also political and ideological demands and expectations against the public universities. The dominant discourse of the interwar era concerning the idea of the university was conservative, nationalist, and authoritarian. Its ideal was a "service university," higher education geared to serving the national interest as understood by the ruling political class: a university which retained its formal autonomy but which, at the same time, was controlled by a professoriate politically and ideologically loyal to those in power. "Our universities cannot be said to have disregarded the national interest," said philosopher Gyula Kornis, interwar Hungary's leading conservative ideologue of science, "all the less so as the final decision over appointments, approvals, and consent lies with the governing power. If the activities of a faculty member of the university are harmful to the interests of the nation, the university would remove him on its own initiative, as has been confirmed by the history of our universities after the revolutions. The spirit of university autonomy and state power can collaborate with each other as both are motivated solely by the interests of the immortal Hungarian nation."[7]

While the formal, institutional autonomy of the universities remained intact throughout, this was an autonomy which shielded a politically correct, conformist, and professionally largely mediocre professoriate; an autonomy which reproduced rigid, status- and seniority-related hierarchies in academia. This was a world of learning and education within which autonomy promoted "the dominance of [status-related] privileges instead of excellence [*kiválóságok helyett kiváltságok*], and where the lack of talent is granted prominence."[8] Because of conservative, nationalist,

---

7. Kornis's opening address in Károly Mártonffy, ed., *Magyar felsőoktatás. Az 1936. évi december hó 10-től December hó 16-ig tartott országos felsőoktatási kongresszus munkálatai* (Budapest: Vallás és Közoktatásügyi Minisztérium, 1937), 1:23.

anti-Semitic, and in the 1930s, increasingly fascist policies and practices, interwar Hungary's academia not only lost some of its best talents in the human and natural sciences, but it also tended to keep a great deal of modern research and thought, especially in the social sciences and humanities, outside the official walls of its universities and academy of sciences. In this environment, rarely did the aspirations of the political elite and of scientists oriented toward modern international standards of scholarship coincide, as had been the case with the conservative "neonationalist" modernizer Kuno Klebelsberg and the biochemist Albert Szent-Györgyi.[9]

Even though they were fueled by his neonationalist ambitions to assert "Hungarian cultural superiority" over neighboring nations (the beneficiaries of Trianon), Klebelsberg's modernization efforts did to some extent promote the beginnings of a new, modern organization of research and teaching in interwar Hungary. These beginnings, however, remained restricted and affected only a few universities and almost exclusively the natural sciences (especially at the University of Szeged). Klebelsberg was mostly concerned with rebuilding and extending the physical infrastructure of higher education, replacing, among other things, the two universities lost to Czechoslovakia (Pozsony) and Romania (Kolozsvár) by "moving them" to Pécs and Szeged respectively. He seemed less keen on reforming and modernizing the organization of research and higher education.

During the 1930s even the achievements and improvements of the Klebelsberg era came into question. Discussions continued on reforms that might cope with massive enrollments, the "overproduction" of university graduates, and the increasing conflict between the needs of scientific education on the one hand and professional training on the other.[10] But

---

8. This was Gábor Kemény's way of describing the state of Hungarian public education (applicable, in my opinion, to university education as well) in his "A tehetségek érvényesülése és a demokrácia," *Szocializmus*, 1929, 246, quoted in Miklós Lackó, "Az ellenforradalmi rendszer művelödéspolitikája" [The Cultural Policies of the Counterrevolutionary Regime], in *Magyarország története*, ed. György Ránki (Budapest: Akadémiai Kiadó, 1976), 8:868. The present section of my chapter is greatly indebted to this and other essays of Miklós Lackó on Hungary's interwar cultural and academic life: see the relevant parts of his *Szerep és mü: Kultúrtörténeti tanulmányok* (Budapest: Gondolat Könyvkiadó, 1981); *Korszellem és tudomány, 1910–1945* (Budapest: Gondolat Könyvkiadó, 1988); and *Sziget és külvilág: Válogatott tanulmányok* (Budapest: MTA Történettudományi Intézete, 1996).

9. On the improbable or, rather, paradoxical alliance between Kuno Klebelsberg, Albert Szent-Györgyi, and the Rockefeller Foundation, see Ingebrigtsen, "Hungarian Nationalism."

10. See, inter alia, the talks delivered by Zoltán Magyary and Albert Szent-Györgyi to the 1936 Congress on Higher Education, in Mártonffy, *Magyar felsöoktatás*, 1:205–12 and 3:63–72.

political developments, the growth of rightist radicalism outside as well as within the university squeezed modernizing reforms entirely out of the university's agenda.

Forces Shaping the University of the Postwar Era

The end of World War II found Hungary's official academic establishment, including the university professoriate, paralyzed. Like everybody else in the country, they were affected by the destruction of the war, both as private persons as well as in their work. More important, however, they emerged from the war as a group that had lost control over their own destiny and the destiny of the institutions in their hands, *because* they had lost legitimacy as an elite. For the second time in a quarter of a century, Hungary and its social and political elites came out of a war with a devastating defeat—this time, however, the defeat was not mainly military and there were no scapegoats, such as the Jews, Communists, and liberals whom the counterrevolutionary regime had victimized after August 1919. Seen from the perspective of 1945, theirs had been a regime of stupid aristocratic and "gentry" amateurs and vicious, often pathological, criminals; who without scruples could aid a foreign power in the slaughter of half a million Hungarian citizens who were Jews; and who in addition gave away the lives of hundreds of thousands of young men for a military enterprise in which Hungary had no interest or any real say. And, last but not least, they were to be held responsible for the country's liberation and occupation by—and defenseless exposure to—the Soviet Red Army.

Considering their pathetic and sometimes criminal record from the interwar and war years, the predominantly rightist and nationalist academic establishment could hardly act as an authentic representative of the best interests of the university or of science. Instead, they either withdrew with a well-deserved sense of guilt or waited silently for pardon and reconfirmation from the emerging political elite. Those few who had nothing to fear on account of their past and whose integrity and authority in academic matters were intact, acted along two main lines:[11]

---

11. For a detailed analysis of the postwar policies and politics of Hungarian academic elite, see my *Academia and State Socialism: Essays on the Political History of Academic Life in Post-1945 Hungary and Eastern Europe* (Boulder, Colo.: East European Monographs & Atlantic Research & Publications, 1998), chaps. 1–4.

1. Some tried to assert institutional autonomies and defend the values of intellectual freedom.[12] They did so by countering the demands of leftist and progressive radical reform politicians and academics for increased social accountability, macrocoordination of higher education and research, and in general, what the latter presented as a thorough modernization of academic activity. The voices of academic freedom went unheeded as they had no convincing political force behind them and failed to defuse the leftist charge that academic freedom and autonomy "objectively served the interests of reactionary forces" hiding behind the walls of the universities and the Academy of Sciences. In 1947 historian István Hajnal demanded respect for the autonomy of scientific life and protested György Lukács's lists which forced Communist-sponsored members upon the Academy of Sciences. He was ignored. In vain he argued that

> the greatest mistake has been trying to coerce the election of the whole list by threatening the Academy with withdrawal of state support. What Hungarian public life needs is a self-conscious, professionally oriented, independent institution of learning whose words carry weight not only within domestic but also in international public opinion. Not even the political leadership [*államvezetés*] can find much use for the Academy unless it is beyond all doubt an objective forum, free of interference from all other criteria, which the state tries to maintain, under difficult circumstances, at the level of world science.[13]

In January 1947 political scientist István Bibó gave an inaugural lecture on the separation of powers. He could hardly have chosen a more timely topic. Bibó, newly elected a corresponding member of the Hungarian Academy of Sciences and a centrist in the National Peasant Party's leadership, was a scholar deeply involved in the political debates of the early postwar coalition period. His lecture was neither the first nor the only of his works from this period reflecting increasing apprehension as to the fate of institutions of democratic polity and society. He urged

---

12. For example, the legal scholar Gyula Moór, the political scientist István Bibó, the historian István Hajnal, and the literary scholar Dezsö Keresztury. Keresztury was the minister of culture and education of the coalition government in 1945–47.

13. Documents pertaining to István Hajnal's activities as secretary of the academy's second section include this note titled "Az Akadémia ügye," dated 2 July 1947, *Manuscripts Department of the Library of the Hungarian Academy of Sciences*, Budapest, Ms 5348/398.

adherence to the old European tradition of separation of powers, for he regarded it as supremely relevant for the present as well as future. From the rich content of this principle Bibó gave special emphasis to the idea that "technically, power can most effectively be made morally legitimate by disrupting the concentration of power, separating functions from one another, and establishing power centers opposing one another and generating particular identities."[14] One field of social activity where, in his view, "the demoralizing impact of power concentration" was most dangerous was that of "intellectual life and culture." He reiterated the increasing practical and ideological significance of sciences for the state. This, in combination with the technological revolution of mass media, had created a major arena for political propaganda, and exerted a mighty push toward concentration of power beyond all previously known proportions. From the viewpoint of democracy this trend implied grave dangers, for it "brought mass culture into a relation of dependence to the objectives of state power and made state power a prisoner of its own propaganda."[15] As a signal warning of this universal tendency, Bibó referred to German National Socialism "which, if it did not want to lose its momentum, had to follow its own propaganda and, exactly by following its own propaganda, ran directly into its own great historical catastrophe." Bibó therefore urged an improved defense of democracy by measures taken to "make the scientific, artistic, and educational professions, like the judiciary, autonomous." He believed "state power and science have to be separated from one another lest their fusion lead to the complete corruption of intellectual life."[16] On the basis of these general considerations Bibó took up the debate on university and academic autonomy in Hungary:

> In connection with this question, quite a few people mention universities and the Academy which more or less defend their historical autonomy. These [institutions] are exposed to assaults on the grounds that their autonomies are merely crystallization points of certain personal and social power relations. However, this only means that the Academy or universities provide frameworks that are too narrow. This recognition justifies not the

---

14. István Bibó, "Az államhatalmak elválasztása egykor és most," in *Összegyüjtött munkái* (Bern: EPMSZ, 1982), 2:555.
15. Ibid., 557.
16. Ibid.

destruction of autonomy but on the contrary, its organization on an even larger scale. It confirms that intellectual life, cultural production, and the consumption of mass culture necessitate the establishment of autonomy. . . . The contours, again, of some kind of scientific or cultural "state power" are taking shape, [a scientific "state power"] which, just like the judiciary, will have to gain, by struggle, its independence, its autonomy, and its constitutionally guaranteed separation from the concentration of power.[17]

However, Hajnal's and Bibó's arguments for autonomy evoked little resonance in a world haunted by the fresh memories of war and fascism and by the fear of a reactionary backlash. Indeed, in the dominant (and not only Communist!) discourse of the short "popular democratic" period (1945–48), an overwhelming anxiety over a possible repetition of the blunder of Weimar (allowing fascists to turn democracy and liberalism to their own advantage)[18] went hand in hand with the new totalitarian-democratic wisdom that separated the causes of social progress and democracy, demanding and claiming that the former should be paramount: "The meaning of every step, procedure, and reform is determined not by the extent to which it is in accordance with democratic rules crystallized in the past but by the extent to which it serves the fundamental political ambition of our age, the liberation of the people."[19]

2. Others,[20] often at the instigation and always with backing of leftist politicians, were so eager to improve the social-political status of science and to attract large portions of public funding, that they were ready to actively undermine the unity of the academic elite, to initiate what contemporaries called "the war of academicians," and to accept and even invite external political intervention in academic life. Nobel Laureate biochemist Albert Szent-Györgyi is not merely a case in point—he was

17. Ibid., 557–58.
18. "One of the greatest threats Hungarian democracy is exposed to today is that the poison of reaction infiltrates into its veins by using its own laws and exploiting, from the inside, the opportunities offered by it to destroy all chances of the young popular forces and of a democratic restoration of the Hungarian nation." Mátyás Rákosi, "A magyar demokrácia kérdései" [The Questions of Hungarian Democracy], speech delivered as part of a series of lectures at the Budapest Pázmány Péter University, 26 June–6 July 1945," in *Demokrácia*, ed. Ferenc Erdei et al. (Budapest: Pázmány Péter Tudományegyetem Bölcsészettudományi Kara, n.d.), 152.
19. Erdei et al., *Demokrácia*, 11.
20. Progressivist radical reformers and communists, most of whom came from among the country's leading scientists, such as Albert Szent-Györgyi, Zoltán Bay, István Rusznyák, and others.

also the leading personality of the radical reformers. This group distinguished itself (a) by emphasizing the need to separate scientific research and professional higher education either within universities, or to remove research from universities altogether; (b) by claiming generous public funding for research in exchange for social accountability in the production of knowledge; (c) by offering social and political engagement on the part of scientists in exchange for the integration of academic elites in the social matrix of policymaking processes; and (d) by insisting less on autonomy and freedom than on the social and political relevance and power of academic elites.

As the post-1989 assault on the academies of sciences in East Central Europe and, after 1991, in Russia, focused to a great extent on the *separation of research and higher education*, and also in order to keep this chapter within some limits, I will provide more detail on this particular issue. After 1945, most leading scientists readily renounced the ideal of the unity of teaching and research—the ideal that is often seen as the *sine qua non* of the "Humboldtian university." Indeed, the suggestion that a separation was desirable had been sympathetically discussed in the 1920s. After 1945, among the practitioners of the humanities and social sciences, only the historian Gyula Szekfü raised his voice against resurfacing demands for freeing research from teaching. The necessity of the separation for "obvious" reasons was widely taken for granted—a fact clearly reflected in the minutes of the discussion "University, Science, and Academy," arranged by the Free Trade Union of the Hungarian Teachers. The meeting was attended by the country's academic elite, old and young, including Albert Szent-Györgyi, Gyula Szekfü, Domokos Kosáry, László Mátrai, István Hajnal, and Tibor Erdey-Grúz, and the introductory talk was delivered by the young Communist historian, Károly Vígh.[21] Natural scientists, like Tibor Erdey-Grúz and Albert Szent-Györgyi, argued forcefully for separation. They maintained that universities should concentrate on specialized education for the professions, and thereby raised the question of where to locate the functions of initiating, managing, coordinating, and conducting scientific research. The answer, in view of the large amount of resources requested for research in the natural sciences, seemed self-evident. In agreement with J. D. Bernal and with what was understood to be Soviet experience, both Erdey-Grúz and Szent-Györgyi

---

21. The discussion took place on 5 September 1945. The minutes were published in *Embernevelés* 1 (November-December 1945).

believed that the Academy of Sciences should combine the functions "of a general staff of scientific advance with the active pursuit of fundamental research under its immediate direction."[22] Szent-Györgyi maintained, that

> the trouble with our old university system has been that nothing was defined clearly by it. Professors claimed to be scientists and were engaged in specialized higher education, but actually they did neither science nor education. A sharp line should be drawn. Today we can no longer force everything into the old forms. They worked quite well some fifty years ago. The university still has the tasks of scientific research and specialized education, but they ought to be sharply distinguished from one another. . . . I believe the academy has to be the organization that looks after scientific research. The academy should have nothing to do with education and specialized professional training. The university concerns itself with science, but its foremost duty should be to concentrate on higher education and specialized professional training.[23]

The pharmacologist Erdey-Grúz put the new suggestions less ambivalently: "This problem should clearly be split into two questions, the question of scientific research on the one hand, and the question of university education, on the other. Even initiative and management should be separated. In the field of scientific research, a properly [re]constructed Academy should be entrusted with the role of leadership."[24]

Well before these leading Hungarian natural scientists sought to turn the Academy of Sciences into an institution responsible for national science policy, similar suggestions had been made in Western Europe, especially in Britain.[25] Although Szent-Györgyi and his friends did not

---

22. John D. Bernal, *The Social Function of Science* (London: Routledge, 1939), 280.
23. *Embernevelés* 1 (November-December 1945): 136.
24. Ibid., 133.
25. The British interwar debate on the planning and the organization of science was probably a major source of inspiration for Albert Szent-Györgyi's postwar ideas and proposals. On various aspects of the debate in Great Britain, see Gary Werskey, "British Scientists and 'Outsider' Politics, 1931–1945," *Science Studies*, vol. 1 (1971), and *The Visible College: A Collective Biography of British Scientists and Socialists of the 1930s* (London: Free Association Books, 1988); Philip J. Gummett, and Geoffrey L. Price, "An Approach to the Central Planning of British Science: The Formation of the Advisory Council on Scientific Policy," *Minerva* 15 (summer 1977): 119–43; and William McGucken, *Scientists, Society, and State: The Social*

propose introducing "Soviet Science" to Hungary, they contributed to and gained momentum from a tendency of the Communist-dominated coalition to broaden the range of institutions brought under central planning. The radical scientists' critique of the university as a research organization was quite akin to the Communist point of view, which was spelled out at an early stage by Károly Vígh. In his introduction to the debate of September 1945, Vígh noted that

> our scientific life, with its old spirit and framework, cannot answer the demands of democratic Hungary. What is least tolerable is the disorganized shape of Hungarian scientific life. Comprehensive management with a wide horizon is needed. The individual universities, with their modest facilities, are unable and ill-equipped to organize and administer science. Our scientific life can only be managed and organized by a small collegial body of genuine scientists. Therefore, it is necessary to distinguish very sharply between scientists and professors, as there are quite a few professors who believe themselves to be scientists, although few of them deserve the name.[26]

In György Lukács's notion of "plebeian democracy" a distinction is drawn between "formal democracy" and "substantive democracy." In the agenda of the new societal order the latter was placed at the top. In a similar way academic freedom and modernizing reforms of universities were separated and turned against each other, with the former held suspect and relegated to an inferior position. University autonomy had thus lost out *before* the Communists secured a monopoly over politics in 1948. It was not the dictatorship of the proletariat that caused its defeat. Rather, it was the postwar antireactionary and modernizing agendas, pursued by a much broader grouping of social forces than just the Communists, which turned them into untimely objectives of little relevance, indeed suspicious hide-outs for the compromised elites of pre-1945 Hungary. In the field of "the idea of the university" the causes of academic autonomy and freedom failed to receive effective representation because, whatever their merits, their protagonists had lost authenticity and credibility.

Relations of Science Movement in Great Britain, 1931–1947 (Columbus: Ohio State University Press, 1984).
   26. *Embernevelés* 1 (November-December 1945): 131.

But it would also be false to describe the new university, the university of "people's democracy" and later, of "proletarian dictatorship" as merely a result of Communist designs. Rather, it resulted from and was nourished by distinct discursive tendencies dating back at least to the 1920s. These tendencies were given rise to by various reformist ideas and movements among scientists as well as administrators of science.[27] Suggestions for the macrocoordination of public provision for scientific research and higher education; for the utilization of scientific knowledge production toward objectives of public utility ("national interests"); for the separation of professional training from scientific research—these had all been present in Hungarian discourse at least since the ministry of Count Kuno Klebelsberg, when the Communist movement in Hungary was still underground and its members would not have filled the classrooms of a high school in Budapest.

These ideas and tendencies had as their broader background the breakdown of the post–World War I liberal economic order and the increasing acceptance, especially from the late 1920s, of the need for active public involvement in steering economic and technological-scientific development. How robust was the pull of an activist state is exemplified by Hungary's regent, Admiral Miklós Horthy, who figured among the admirers of Soviet central planning, himself suggesting in 1931 the introduction of central economic planning based on "expert knowledge."[28]

Indeed, "the university of the dictatorship" was the joint baby of the radical progressive reformers within academia, adopting, reinforcing, and to some extent radicalizing the Klebelsbergian tradition, and of leftist and Communist politicians. The former, similar to one of their sources of inspiration, the British "social relations of science movement,"[29] contended that scientists could claim a share of the country's economic resources only if they made an unqualified acknowledgement of their responsibility to society. Generous funding and a radical improvement in the social status of science and the scientist would be, in their eyes, compensation enough for having to accept demands for greater social

---

27. Like Zoltán Magyary, the right hand of Count Kuno Klebelsberg in science and university-political matters.

28. Cf. György Péteri, *Revolutionary Twenties: Essays on International Monetary and Financial Relations After World War I* (Trondheim: Department of History, University of Trondheim, 1995), 115–17.

29. The single most important work on this movement is McGucken, *Scientists, Society, and State*.

utility or the political coordination and planning of the development of the nation's academic endeavor.[30] All of these were important components of the Communist agenda for science and higher education and, indeed, until about 1947–48, Communist spokesmen in science policy did not articulate more radical demands.

Surely, the "university reform" of 1948 confirms a situation, deadly for university autonomy, emerging not simply from the contest over "the idea of university" but also, and more important, from the establishment of the Communist monopoly in politics. The university ceased being an institution of self-governance and had to accept central planning not only *for* but also *of* science. From this point, "class affiliation" became a legitimate criterion for selecting students and faculty, and fields of scholarship of high ideological significance were purged and populated with new, politically reliable, but often intellectually inferior personnel. Policies forcing social promotion transformed the student body, turning the university even more into an institution of mass education, and a large number of working-class students were rushed through crash courses and began studies ill-prepared for independent work at a level "worthy of a university." Many of these features proved to be the excesses of high Stalinism and disappeared or faded away either with the Thaw or by János Kádár's counterrevolutionary restoration of the late 1950s and early 1960s. Only for a very limited period (1949–53) did militant revolutionist oppression have exclusive say in determining what the idea of the university was.

The period of Thaw and the revolution of 1956 brought new groups onto the field while changing the attitudes of older ones. Most important, even among the party-soldiers who advanced into academic positions during Stalinism *a new Communist academic intelligentsia emerged with a professional consciousness and identity, and with aspirations to assert professional interests.* They lent authenticity, legitimacy, and social and political energy to the demands for academic freedom that surfaced in the summer and autumn of 1956 and early 1957.[31] Though these demands

---

30. As if he had wished to invert Bibó's principle of separation of powers, Albert Szent-Györgyi emphasized repeatedly during the coalition years the Saint-Simonian idea that "in fact, the task of the politician in the modern state is nothing else than the transplantation of the results of science into life. Therefore, science and politics have to go hand in hand, and the proper place of the workshop of science is beside the workshop of politics." Albert Szent-Györgyi, "Az Akadémia válsága," *Szabad Nép*, 12 December 1945.

31. For the transition from the ethos of party-soldier to a professional-academic identity among economists, see chaps. 5 and 6 in Péteri, *Academia and State Socialism*.

yielded no results that were formalized by legislation or officially sanctioned, they did result in an archipelago of informal autonomies and freedoms acquired, enjoyed, and repeatedly lost and regained by various sectors of academia—an archipelago, that is, that throughout the Kádár era constantly changed borders and dimensions depending on losses and gains in the contest among a multitude of positions about "the Communist idea of the university."

Ruptures, Continuities, Influences

To the extent that there were ruptures in personnel and in "university tradition" they were a matter of redefining the idea of the university brought about in the interactions between various groupings in dictatorship and academia. In this, "university tradition" itself was but one position on the political-scientific field where the meanings and functions of the university were contested.

The bulk of the ruptures were suffered by the social sciences and some of the humanities. After the Communist takeover in 1948, economics lost most of its old regime practitioners and sociology ceased to exist altogether as a university subject or research area.[32] But modern social science research had not had a secure place in the official academe of interwar Hungary either. Sociology was an extramural enterprise, stuck in the documentary genre of belles-lettres called rural and urban sociography, with mostly amateur practitioners from leftist *and* rightist student movements. Some of the greatest talents in economics left the country in the late 1920s and early 1930s, and the field lagged, conceptually as well as methodologically, behind the international frontline, except for the empirical research conducted in the Hungarian Institute of Economic Research (an independent nonuniversity institution of *Konjunkturforschung*). Underlying these phenomena were the conservatism, nationalism, and anti-Semitism of the interwar university establishment. Why should a talented Jewish pupil of the renowned "Model Gimnazium" of Budapest, like Nicholas

32. For the changes taking place in economics in 1948–51, consult my "A fordulat a magyar közgazdaságtudományban," in *A fordulat évei 1947–1949. Politika, ideológia és müvészet a pártállam születésének idöszakában*, ed. Éva Standeisky (Budapest: 1956-os Intézet, 1998), 185–201. As to the end of sociology in Hungary in 1948–49, see Pál Péter Tóth's series of interviews on Sándor Szalai's Department of Sociology in the Budapest journal *Mozgó Világ*, 1987, nos. 8–11.

Káldor, have attempted to go on with university studies in Hungary in 1924, when *numerus clausus* restrictions on Jewish access to higher education had been in force for three years? Why should Thomas Balogh, or Tibor Scitovsky, have conceived of academic careers for themselves in a country whose political elite, especially during the 1930s, was increasingly occupied with the introduction of new measures of racial discrimination and the revision of the post–World War I peace treaties? What was there in Hungary and its university system during the interwar years that could have made Arnold Hauser, Oscar Jászi, Karl Mannheim, Karl and Michael Polányi, or indeed, György Lukács consider a return to Budapest? Sadly and revealingly enough for "people's democracy," the "ruptures" seem to have perpetuated rather than destroyed certain features of the old regime university.

On the other hand, new subjects were introduced after 1948 into the university curriculum designed to bring the main ideological doctrines of Marxism-Leninism to the new educated class: the political economy of capitalism and socialism, historical and dialectical materialism, scientific socialism, the history of the workers' movement. This brought a whole network of new university departments into existence with considerable resources and personnel. And even though the primary function allotted to these departments was to produce and reproduce ideological legitimation for the ruling regime, once established, the social, political, and intellectual processes in these departments were never and could never be controlled *fully and exclusively* by the needs of the agitprop apparatus of the party.[33] For example, those teaching Marxist-Leninist political economy could not remain totally unaffected by the norms and standards set by the economics profession in the country. Some of them wished to share the high status and prestige yielded by relevant contributions to a better understanding of major economic-political issues, especially issues of the so-called economic mechanism. Some departments of political economy gave shelter to professional and methodologically quite sophisticated research in agrarian economics, history, and sociology, while the ideas and ethos of "reform economics" "contaminated" a number of political economy departments in the capital. The origins of the revival in Marxian critical social theory by Ágnes Heller, Ferenc Fehér, György Márkus, and others can be traced back to departments of (Marxist-Leninist) philosophy. The department of Marxism-Leninism at the law school of

---

33. Cf. chaps. 5 and 6 in my *Academia and State Socialism*.

the Loránd Eötvös University in Budapest emerged from the late 1970s as a major center of political science research; a decade earlier the department of (Marxist-Leninist) economic history at the Karl Marx University of Economics was putting out works on Hungarian and East Central European economic and social history that attracted international attention and recognition. The list of examples could easily be extended.

"Ruptures" therefore did not always mean discontinuity, nor did they bring with them, inevitably and finally, the end of all professionalism, the *sortie* for decent academic standards from the university, and the unconditional triumph of political-ideological controls.

Any assessment of the *influences* of the political system upon the content of teaching and research at the university should take its starting point in a dynamic understanding of the dictatorship. The most important development in this respect is the break with the *revolutionist political style* that had characterized the Stalin era. In Hungary, this break secured important positions for a new pragmatist style of policymaking, but took almost a whole decade to consummate (1953–61). Not until the 1980s did Hungarian Communists finally abandon Marxist-Leninist utopianism to legitimize their absolute rule. The revolutionist style is best described according to the principle: "The more harm and pain it causes to the class enemy, the better a policy measure is." The political culture of the era was militarized, not only in terms of the political significance accorded to the armed forces and political police, but also in the clothing of the party apparatus and, more important, in the vocabulary of the prevailing political discourse. Various spheres of societal life were presented as "fronts" ("the cultural front," "the economic front," "the front of international relations"). Communists working in various walks of life were presented as "soldiers of the party"; ministries and governmental authorities were "headquarters" of their respective branches; and political projects were launched and pursued as "the Battle for Bridges," "the Battle for Coal," "the Corn Battle." If policies proved successful, they were said to have delivered "fatal blows to the (class) enemy," even if this meant but a three percent drop in wasted corn during a harvest. If policies failed—as, in fact, they tended to—then failure was ascribed to the subversive work of international imperialism and its internal allies and described as a first step toward open war. Ordinary societal life was a prelude to another form of (class) warfare.

After Stalin's death and in the wake of the general crisis of state socialism in the USSR and in East Central Europe, a new attitude asserted itself in

Hungarian Communist politics which I call, following Sidney Verba, *pragmatic* or, even, *scientistic political style*.[34] To a great extent, this is what the "New Course" in Hungary was about. Policies tended to be judged by the pragmatic results they yielded in terms of improved supplies, balances on various markets, economic growth, improved social welfare, improved quality, and in general, advances that could be made in the solution of various social, economic, and cultural problems. No doubt, the political system remained a dictatorship, suffering a chronic shortage of democratic feedback. That is why, in my view, the transition from the early years' revolutionism to more pragmatically oriented policymaking went hand in hand with the advances of scientistic attitudes and positions within Communist political thinking and discourse. The predicted benefit of a policy was no longer measured by the expected harm to the (class) enemy, but by the solid scientific expertise upon which the making of policy relied.

However gradual and uneven, this shift from revolutionism to a pragmatism in various sectors of Hungarian Communist politics gave rise to enormous opportunities in university teaching and research.[35] Because scholars seized these opportunities, they benefited from new structures and the potential to pursue new directions, for example policy-oriented empirical social research, "reform economics," and sociology, all of which were reborn and grew. Mighty transinstitutional coalitions developed between groups in the Communist political elite and groups in the academic community, and this period witnessed a radical upgrading of the social and political status of social science knowledge and its producers. I have spelled out in greater detail elsewhere the far-reaching implications of these developments for Hungarian economic thought and research.[36]

A Note on 1956 and the University

The year 1956 was not a "revolt of the mind"; it was a revolution against the Stalinist regime that encompassed all social strata. But intellectuals—and

---

34. Cf. Lucian Pye and Sidney Verba, *Political Culture and Political Development* (Princeton: Princeton University Press, 1965), 544–60.

35. On the emergence and history of pragmatically oriented Hungarian reform communism the two most informative books are still Iván Petö and Sándor Szakács, *A hazai gazdaság négy évtizedének története, 1945–1985*, vol. 1, *Az újjáépítés és a tervutasításos irányítás idöszaka* (Budapest: Közgazdasági és Jogi Könyvkiadó, 1985), and Iván T. Berend, *The Hungarian Economic Reforms, 1953–1988* (Cambridge: Cambridge University Press, 1990).

36. Péteri, *Academia and State Socialism*, chaps. 5–7.

mostly Communist intellectuals—had a major role in the process of delegitimizing Rákosi's regime. University students and young university faculty had a decisive role in organizing various discussion circles (the most famous of which was the Petőfi Circle), and publicly articulated a thorough critique of Soviet-type socialism as it was known in Hungary. As noted above, the (re-) emergence of professional consciousness among scientific and scholarly groups predates the revolution of October 1956, as well as the Twentieth Congress of the Communist Party of the Soviet Union.[37] This tendency applies as much or even more to fields dominated by the new Communist intelligentsia as it does to fields where many old regime scholars were allowed to stay. Professional associations had been (re-) established, and discussions were afoot about restoring considerable autonomy to universities and the Academy of Sciences. New academic periodicals were started and old ones reinstated, thus providing professionally oriented forums for discussion.[38]

What lent explosive character to the situation after February 1956 was the relentless fight put up by the conservative Stalinist left in the party to fend off "rightist deviationism," preserve its power, and continue its disastrous policies. The wrangling of the revisionist right wing with the conservative Stalinist left between the change of government in June 1953 and the revolution of October 1956 increased people's inclination to take to the streets. In the light of the 1956 experience in Hungary, there is reason to doubt whether policies of social promotion (resulting in the massive enrollment as university students of working class and "poor peasant" youth) produce loyal and easily manipulable subjects for the dictatorship. To the contrary, the universities and their student communities were among the initiators of the anti-Stalinist revolt. Students coming from peasant and working-class environments knew better than the urban intelligentsia what the brave new world really meant for peasants and workers: they had firsthand knowledge of the ruthless collectivization, the senseless extortion of all surpluses, the recurring drives of terror against "kulaks," the mismanagement of industries (the low esteem of skills, the irrational preoccupation with quantity rather than quality), endless queues

---

37. Cf. chaps. 5–6 in my *Academia and State Socialism*.
38. Probably the most important single periodical of this sort was *Közgazdasági Szemle* (*Economic Review*), relaunched in October-November 1954, and soon to become a major forum for the country's economists.

for the most elementary necessities, and deteriorating living standards.[39] And the university was a ready infrastructure to serve the growing needs of a relatively independent public sphere.

Indeed, students turned it into a major venue of an otherwise extinct public life: it was in university corridors, canteens, and seminar rooms that they discussed Stalinist rule, and it was at the university that they articulated their demands, often for a reformed and more democratic, more just, more effective, and more humane socialism.[40] The anti-Stalinist revolt reached and made a modest breakthrough even at the reddest of all universities, the Karl Marx University of Economics (established by the Communist regime in 1948). Students meeting there on 22 October not only welcomed the fifteen points articulated three days before by the students of the Budapest University of Technology—demanding, among other things, the improvement of the economic situation of students, the reduction of compulsory ideological education, autonomy for universities, and democratic self-government for students—but also added to and radicalized them: they demanded (1) the withdrawal of the Soviet troops from Hungary, (2) the release of Hungarian prisoners of war still held captive in the Soviet Union, many of whom had not even been soldiers when they were abducted by the occupying Soviet army, (3) increased salaries for those who had just completed their university education, and also for all workers in the country, (4) access to information about the lawless terror of Rákosi's rule and, in general, improved public information, and (5) the cessation of Soviet exploitation of Hungarian mineral resources (especially bauxite and uranium). Iván Berend talked to the meeting on behalf of all the teachers at the university. He reassured the students that the teachers supported their demands and expressed the latter's hope that through a change in the leadership of the party (removing such ardent Stalinists as István Kovács, Béla Szalai, Erzsébet Andics, and Ander Berei, and adding reformist personalities such as Imre Nagy, György Lukács, and Ferenc Donáth) it would become unnecessary to escalate

---

39. For illuminating details about the sentiments and politics of working-class and peasant students in the 1950s at the universities of economics and technology in Budapest, I am indebted to Professor Antal Máriás, who shared his experience with me in a series of interviews in the autumn of 1986.

40. For an informative catalog of data related to revolts at universities in 1956, see András B. Hegedüs, Péter Kende, György Litván, and János M. Rainer, eds., *1956 kézikönyve*, vol. 1, *Kronológia* (Budapest: 1956-os Intézet, 1996).

student manifestations to demonstrations and strikes, which he considered dangerous.[41]

The university, students and teachers alike, thus came to play a central role in the political process leading up to and culminating in the revolutionary uprising of 23 October 1956. But 1956 was also a year when the Communist idea of the university was intensely discussed, interpreted, and reinterpreted. At a debate on education arranged by the Petőfi Circle on 28 September 1956, Imre Lakatos delivered a devastating critique of Stalinist higher education and its destructive effects on new scientists and scholars, and declared that renewal required the assertion of talent, independence, curiosity, respect for facts, and exact thinking as decisive criteria in the education of scholars and scientists.[42]

During the summer of 1956, members of the Karl Marx University of Economics had discussed the necessity of improving methods of education. Their deliberations exposed the Communist university's inability to harbor creative scientific work and at the same time to train large masses of professionals. Leading professors and officials concluded that—in terms of standards, teaching practices, and low scientific performance—the

---

41. "Jegyzőkönyv a Marx Károly Közgazdaságtudományi Egyetemen 1956. október 22-én tartott diák-nagygyűlésről" [Protocol of the General Student Meeting Held at the Karl Marx University of Economics, 22 October 1956], *Papers of the Rector's Office, Archives of the Budapest University of Economics and Public Administration*, box 8 (1956/57). I would like to add two comments regarding this meeting: First, the demand regarding the withdrawal of Soviet troops from Hungary was dropped in the course of the discussion; however, it was among the demands accepted as one of sixteen points at the joint 22 October meeting of the students of the Budapest University of Technology, the University of Construction and Transportation, the University Colleges of Agricultural Engineering, Sports, Gardening and Wine Production, and three military institutions. Second, it is much in harmony with the cautious formulae used by Berend at this meeting, that most of the teachers at the Karl Marx University assumed a passive wait-and-see position vis-à-vis developments in October and that they still expected a solution to the political crisis from the "processes started by the July 1956 Central Committee resolutions" (i.e., from a central committee meeting that left most of the Stalinist leadership, except Rákosi, in power). Those who had more courage to demand and to fight for genuine change and who saw October 1956 as a popular uprising against an illegitimate oppressing power, had to face disciplinary procedures, loss of their jobs, or prison terms. Iván Berend himself was among the silent majority who would soon join the Communist party "renewed" by János Kádár (the Hungarian Socialist Workers' Party), and who, in accordance with a Politburo decision of 2 July 1957, and in accordance with detailed central instructions, would lecture and lead seminars about "the October *counter-revolutionary* uprising" early in the autumn term of 1957. *Papers of the Rector's Office, Archives of the Budapest University of Economics*, box 10 (1957/58), and box 1 (Protocols and documents of the University Council meetings).

42. András B. Hegedüs et al., eds., *A Petőfi Kör vitái*, vol. 6, *Pedagógus vita* (Budapest: Múzsák Kiadó and 1956-os Intézet, 1992).

institution worked like a secondary school rather than a university.[43] The question was how to elevate university education to the standards worthy of a university. Pál Sándor, associate professor of economic history, condemned the intellectually dubious practice of requiring students to learn centrally approved textbooks by heart (*jegyzet*), instead of permitting—let alone encouraging—them to read whole works independently. He recommended ending the obligatory seminars at which students did little more than regurgitate material from such centrally ordained texts.[44]

The notion of students motivated by intellectual curiosity, working independently in a problem-oriented manner, reading, debating, and assessing a broad range of literature pertinent to the field they studied was closely related to renewed discussions about the need for increased autonomy of the university. The issue of autonomy came up *not* as part of the general demand for democratization and for a relaxation of central political control, but rather as a pragmatic method of improving higher education and research at the universities. The discussion about increased autonomy and "decentralization" had been afoot already in July 1956. A letter from the vice rector of the Karl Marx University of Economics suggested to the Ministry of Education that the latter should content itself with approving the longer-term plans for education of the universities—instead of the prevailing order whereby the ministry annually approved plans covering even the theses according to which lecturers were supposed to teach. Furthermore, it was suggested that examinations as well as short-term plans for teaching and faculty hiring should be taken care of within the university.[45] As to professors' demands for autonomy, allow me to quote a contemporary document from Karl Marx University: "[We suggest] introducing autonomy in such a way that the only remaining

43. Árpád Orosz, "Javaslatok a Marx Károly Közgazdasági Egyetemen folyó oktatás módszereinek továbbfejlesztéséről," 2 July 1956, *Papers of the Rector's Office, Archives of the Budapest University of Economics and Public Administration*, box 8 (1956/57).

44. Pál Sándor, "Néhány szempont az egyetemi oktatás megjavítása érdekében," attached to his letter to Vice Rector Imre László, 24 August 1956, *Papers of the Rector's Office, Archives of the Budapest University of Economics and Public Administration*, box 8 (1956/57). Having proved politically unreliable—because, among other things, he explicitly refused to subscribe to the official view on the "counterrevolution" of October 1956 and because he was one of five professors at the university who opted not to join Kádár's new party—associate professor Pál Sándor lost his job at the Department of Economic History in 1958, upon the initiative of the head of his department.

45. Imre László to Aladár Sipos of the Department for Universities at the Ministry of Education, "Suggestions for the development of university autonomy," 10 July 1956, *Papers of the Rector's Office, Archives of the Budapest University of Economics and Public Administration*, box 6 (1955/56).

contact with higher authorities should be our reception of the funding required for the maintenance of the university. Intervention by higher authorities in university affairs is permissible only if the activities of the university violate the constitution."[46]

By December 1956 a draft for a new university law was circulated and discussed. It defined the university as an institution of self-government, whose objective it was to cultivate science and perform scientific education.[47] Although the protocols of Karl Marx University record discussions about autonomy, decentralization, and other necessary reforms well into mid-1957, little or no actual results were possible under Kádár's counter-revolutionary terror and consolidation. Yet by the mid-1960s the close, detailed controls of education and research at universities, characterizing the first decade of Communist rule, had been left behind. Of course, political interference in academic matters remained an ever-present threat—and has been a feature of the new order emerging after 1989. However, the Jinni of professionalism had replaced the party soldier ethos and could not be forced back into the bottle. The Kádárist political and social order was more complex than that of the early years of Stalinist rule. While in terms of the prevailing attitudes, values, and norms a considerable and ever increasing part of academia was already a product of the Communist era, it consisted of relatively independent, self-conscious, and professionally oriented scientists and scholars. The relationship between them and the Communist rulers was more and more one of negotiating, bargaining, and compromises rather than a relationship between officers and soldiers or oppressors and oppressed.

The Academic Elites

The creation of a new academic elite, whatever the intentions of the Communist dictatorship in 1948–49, could not be accomplished in a

---

46. "Javaslat az új felépítésü Közgazdasági Egyetemre vonatkozóan," undated, probably October or November, 1956, *Papers of the Rector's Office, Archives of the Budapest University of Economics and Public Administration*, box 8 (1956/57).

47. Cf. attachment to State Secretary Albert Kónya, Ministry of Education, to the rector of Karl Marx University of Economics, 14 December 1956, *Papers of the Rector's Office, Archives of the Budapest University of Economics and Public Administration*, box 7 (1955/56). The draft bill was elaborated by Miklós Világh, rector of the Loránd Eötvös University.

single blow. Certainly, an intense wish that this elite identify with the interests of the regime was always there. More important, however, both the regime—in its ambitions and expectations—and the academic elite—in its composition, ethos, and self-understanding and relation to politics—were undergoing constant change in the forty years of Communist rule. Indeed, Communist regimes could hardly feel safe even when they managed to create basically loyal elites in academia: neither the political loyalty nor the professional attitudes of newly recruited scholars and scientists (or pseudo-scholars and pseudo-scientists) could be taken for granted indefinitely. On the contrary, in all these respects we are talking of people whose path was characterized by dynamic processes of change. A *static view* of elite formation which assumes that a politically controlled elite will always be pro-regime cannot account for the many professors who had been thoroughly "sovietized" in 1948–49 but nevertheless turned against the Stalinist dictatorship in Hungary in 1956.[48] Nor can it convincingly explain that the major input in the demonstration of 23 October 1956 came from the university that benefited most from the Communist modernization drive in higher education: the University of Technology.

We should not forget that both "the regime" and "the university" were inhabited by knowledgeable agents with experience and ability to learn. A regime may try to affect the formation of various elites in order to secure their loyalty. But elites never depend entirely on the goodwill of those in power—if they are to be effective, they also need the acceptance and acknowledgement as an elite from their own professional, artistic, or academic peers. And that acceptance and acknowledgement has to be earned by asserting, exemplifying, guarding, and promoting professional, artistic, or academic values, attitudes, and norms. As the academic elite, by necessity, has to cultivate and harmonize conflicting loyalties, "the regime" can never take the loyalty of this elite for granted—indeed, "the regime's" room of maneuver in restricting its academic elite is limited: the higher its ambitions for control, the greater are the chances it will undermine the elite positions of the target group. A group of academics

---

48. Indeed, revolutionary ferment affected the Academy of Sciences to the extent that Kádár's counterrevolutionary regime had no confidence in them at all and established, as the new "headquarters" for science-political management, the Scientific and Higher Education Council (Tudományos és Felsőoktatási Tanács, TFT). TFT had ministerial authority and exercised the central administrative mandates over the scientific field that had been the prerogative of the Academy before the revolution of 1956.

that is too tightly controlled will hardly be able to assert and maintain its authority as elite in relation to the rest of the academic society.[49]

These tensions and contradictions, together with the regime's genuine interest in the knowledge and the competent professionals produced by the academic sphere, provided scholars and scientists with a certain amount of leverage in their negotiations with the Communist political elites.

The foregoing also makes clear that universities, like other institutions, were both a support for and a danger to the Communist political regime. Academia constituted one of the societal dimensions within which the tragedy of the state socialist modernization project unfolded: to the extent that Communist elites acted as modernizing elites they worked toward their own undoing. They were incapable of managing modern, complex societies, and when they tried to block modern development with all its complexities and professional orientation, they only signed their own death warrants well before outside observers began to register the final agony of the Communist system.

In Place of a Conclusion

The study of "universities under dictatorships" cannot fruitfully proceed from an axiomatic understanding of what the university and dictatorship are. On the contrary, its foremost task should be to question the emergence

---

49. The relative position within their disciplinary field of a great majority of the practitioners of various "Marxism-Leninism subjects" (political economy of capitalism and socialism, historical and dialectical materialism, scientific socialism, history of the workers' movement) at institutions of higher education in Hungary constitutes a case in point here: political economists, Marxist-Leninist philosophers, historians, and political scientists teaching and writing in these subjects tended to become marginalized intellectually, professionally, and socially in their respective disciplinary communities. The background to this phenomenon was the fact that university departments of Marxism-Leninism were controlled by a specialized ministerial and party hierarchy in Hungary (headed by the Main Department of Marxism-Leninism in the Ministry of Education and the agitprop apparatus in the Central Committee). Thus, for example, while matters of employment and advancement at a department of (Marxist-Leninist) political economy belonged, normally and according to the nomenklatura, to various levels of the agitprop management (within the party as well as in the state), the same questions in other departments of economics (and research institutes in economics) were decided upon by other agencies (the Department of Higher Education at the Ministry of Education or one of the economic ministries or, as the final and highest instance, by the Department of Economic Policy in the Central Committee apparatus). In the two lines of command, both the mix of criteria applying and the level of ambitions in ideological control tended to be rather different, which led to a far-reaching compartmentalization (or partitioning) of the field of economics as a whole. See Péteri, *Academia and State Socialism*, chap. 7.

and development of the idea of the university and the changing ways in which dictatorship is exercised, depending on time and place. In Hungary, the idea of the university underwent a number of changes in the Communist era, as did the style of Communist policymaking and, in general, the ways in which Communist power was exercised. I have not ventured to make comparisons in this essay, but we know enough about Eastern Europe's experience to be sure that the Communist idea of the university exhibited considerable variation in the area that used be the Soviet bloc.[50] This was true of Communist power practices in other fields as well. A similar variation was manifest in each country within the region across time—even in the Soviet Union, which was seen as the "model" for organizing science and higher education in the rest of the "socialist camp." For universities "'serving the state' meant many different things in the very different subperiods of Soviet history."[51] The postwar positions of academic intelligentsia and university autonomy were certainly much stronger in Poland than in Hungary; in the former the legitimacy of scholars' elite position could not be questioned as easily as that of the latter.[52] This explains the conspicuous fact that the Polish professoriate could wield informal power through informal networks—the *srodowisko*—and that even in times of the worst oppression, like the early 1950s or the early 1960s, they could sustain a high degree of *de facto* autonomy, as is well shown in John Connelly's contribution to this volume.

In the early years of Communist rule universities in Poland could not be turned into institutions of specialized vocational training as readily as in Hungary. The first crisis of state socialism in East Central Europe yielded great variation in political and social change because, among other things, the options of exit, voice, and loyalty differed greatly by country.[53] In Hungary, as opposed to the GDR, cultural and administrative constraints upon emigration, the trauma of 1956, the shift in a number of

---

50. The most important single work in this respect is John Connelly's *Captive University: The Sovietization of East German, Czech, and Polish Higher Education, 1945–1956* (Chapel Hill: University of North Carolina Press, 2000).

51. See the contribution of Michael David-Fox to this volume.

52. Cf. John Connelly's most instructive essay on the Polish "sovietization" efforts in the social sciences, "Internal Bolshevisation? Elite Social Science Training in Stalinist Poland," in "Social Science under State Socialism," special issue, *Minerva* 34, no. 4 (winter 1996): 323–46.

53. See the contributions to György Péteri, ed., *Intellectual Life and the First Crisis of State Socialism in East Central Europe, 1953–1956* (Trondheim: Programme on East European Cultures and Societies, 2001), originally published as a special issue of *Contemporary European History* 6, no. 3 (November 1997).

policy areas from revolutionist to pragmatic political style—all of these created favorable conditions for the cultivation of professional norms and practices, and for the establishment of islands of semiformal professional-academic autonomy. Even if this autonomy was fragile and easy prey to arbitrary political intervention, there can be no doubt that certified academic knowledge became a source of power. Advocacy coalitions between practitioners of various policy areas, state-socialist managers in economic and other sectors of public administration, and practitioners (at the university and at the academy) of technological, scientific, and social-scientific research proliferated and crisscrossed the formal lines of command in the Communist party-state.[54] Top university leaders, as representatives of knowledge production, were co-opted into state and party political organs at various levels and were thus enabled to compete with other sectors and institutions of society for scarce resources.

There remains a great deal to do in the study of universities of the Communist era. But we already know enough to be able to claim that the impositionist-totalitarian narratives, with their dualistic frameworks of perpetrators and victims, oppressors and oppressed, villains and martyrs, provide little help in understanding the early years of high Stalinism. Even Creation became a field of contestation after Eve accepted the apple—why should fallible dictators, Communists or fascists, with their own ambiguities, have been superior to God when it came to imposing their vision of the university?

---

54. In this respect I can only mention such highly important lobby-like formations as the coalition organized around the so-called OLEFIN program, headed by Deputy Prime Minister Gyula Szekér, which secured a concentrated breakthrough for petrochemical industries in the late 1960s and early 1970s, or the "agrarian lobby," that is, the food-industrial (*élemisz-ergazdasági*) coalition under the leadership of Politburo member and deputy prime minister Lajos Fehér. Both of these coalitions included important allies from the academic sector.

6

Czech Universities Under Communism

JAN HAVRÁNEK

During the nineteenth and the first decades of the twentieth century, universities in Central Europe played a double role expressed in the words: "Forschung und Lehre" (research and teaching). Yet while universities won broad autonomy in their research activities and full freedom of expression in their scholarly opinions, their teaching had to respect the demands of the state, which employed most of their graduates—as lawyers, teachers, technicians, doctors, and priests. Occasionally the old monarchies, with their stable, conservative regimes, directed moderate forms of repression against proponents of democratic and oppositional nationalist ideas, who were quite numerous among university intellectuals. During the interwar period many small states emerged in this area, and despite democratic constitutions, most of them witnessed different forms of authoritarian regimes. Yet these too more or less respected academic liberties even when they regulated student admissions ("numerus clausus").

In Czechoslovakia, much as in the Austrian Republic, liberal traditions continued, although adherents of the extreme right and to lesser degree extreme left could be found among students and professors. Four universities, five technical universities, a university of commerce, and several less important agrarian and artistic institutions of higher education existed in the Czechoslovakia of 1938. One university and two technical universities had German as the language of instruction, and the others were Czech or Czechoslovak. At the university at Bratislava most teachers were Czechs, and they used their language, fully understandable to the Slovak students, in their lectures. Czech universities supported the democratic republic of Masaryk, despite demonstrations expressing rightist nationalism with anti-Semitic accents that took place between 1929 and 1934. At the Prague German university liberal ideas prevailed among the professors, but among students the position of the Nazis had been strong since 1922 when a strike was organized against the election of a professor of Jewish origin as rector.[1]

In March 1939 the Nazis occupied the Czech lands, and on 17 November 1939 Nazi authorities closed Czech universities in reprisal for patriotic demonstrations Czech students had staged some three weeks earlier.[2] They executed nine student leaders and sent twelve hundred Czech students to the concentration camp in Sachsenhausen. During the remainder of the occupation the Germans arrested over a thousand more Czech students because of activities in the anti-Nazi underground, partisan activities, or Jewish origin. Czech professors were pensioned, and later many of them were arrested, and some executed. The character of the Prague German University changed too, as it became a "Reichs-Universität," and one of the "brownest" of German universities. Some of its liberal or Catholic professors were replaced by Nazi adherents from Germany. This university ceased to exist in May 1945.

Slovakia became a satellite of Nazi Germany under the control of the Hlinka Party, and its universities took a different course. Slovak authorities expelled most of the Czech professors from Bratislava University during the last months of 1938, and after the declaration of the Slovak Republic on 14 March 1939 fascist prime minister Vojtech Tuka became the university rector. The university was active up to the summer of 1944 and was reopened the following year after a few of the most active supporters of the Tiso Regime were removed from office.[3]

---

1. František Kavka and Josef Petráň, eds., *Dějiny Univerzity Karlovy, 1348–1990*, 4 vols. (Prague: Univerzita Karlova–Karolinum, 1995–98); Jan Havránek and Zdeněk Pousta, eds., *History of Charles University*, vol. 2, *1802–1990* (Prague: Univerzita Karlova–Karolinum, 2001); František Jordán, ed., *Dějiny Univerzity v Brně* (Brno: Universita J. E. Purkyne, 1969); František Jílek, Václav Lomic, and Pavla Horská, eds., *Dějiny Českého vysokého ucení technického*, 2 vols. (Prague: České vysoké učení technické, 1973–78).

2. František Buriánek, *Akce 17. listopad — svědectví českých studentů ze Sachsenhausenu* (Prague: Naše vojsko, 1974); Jozef Leikert, *Čierny piatok sedmnáctého novembra* (Bratislava: Veda, 2000).

3. Júlia Hautová, ed., *Univerzita Komenského, 1919–1994* (Bratislava: Univerzita Komenského, 1994); Lubor Cibulka, ed., *Právníci na Univerzite Komenského v Bratislavé 80 rokov*

The Early Postwar Years

Czech universities were reopened in May and June 1945 and enrolled twice as many students as in the 1930s. The full professors who had been executed or had died during the six years of war were replaced by prewar associate and assistant professors who were nominated by their faculties according to the old laws and customs. The Communist Party obtained the Ministry of Education in the first postwar government, and it appointed as minister its supporter Zdeněk Nejedlý, a professor of musicology at Charles University who had spent the war years in Moscow. Generous state support for student veterans, anti-German nationalism, and postwar enthusiasm for socialist reforms (nationalization, health service, pensions, full employment) overshadowed interference in university matters by the Fierlinger government. Its Košice Program of 5 April 1945 resolved to create new chairs for Soviet Law, Soviet History, and Soviet Literature at all Czechoslovak universities. These chairs were unofficially reserved for active members of the Communist Party.

In 1945, the prestige of students in Czech society was very high, and their organizations were influential. Among their leaders a dominant position was held by those who had survived German prisons and concentration camps. Former servicemen from the Czechoslovak army units fighting in Great Britain and in the Soviet Union also played important roles among the students. Faculty-level and central city branches of the student organization elected their leaderships each year by proportional representation of the political parties. The first postwar chairman of the Students' Central Organization in Prague (svs) was the Communist Jan Kazimour, and his party claimed the strongest position in the svs executive committee during the academic year 1945–46. At that time the Communist Party proclaimed adherence to Masaryk's ideas of democracy and favored the Czech anti-German nationalism that was supported by nearly all Czech students. Yet the Communist Party gradually declined in power, with its opponents (the "democrats") taking the svs chair in 1946 and winning a two-thirds' majority in its executive committee in January 1948. In May 1946 student adherents of the democratic parties—the Nationalsocialists (left liberal) and People's (Christian)—organized traditional student May Celebrations ("Majales") separately from the left-leaning

---

činnosti Právnickej fakulty UK (1921–2001) (Bratislava: Vydavatelské oddelenie Právnickej fakulty UK, 2001).

united youth organization SČM. In 1947 democratic students in Prague and Brno organized street demonstrations against the press policies of the Communist information minister Václav Kopecký. Still, more than a quarter of the Prague university students supported the Communist Party, which was dominant in the art schools, the Higher Political School, and the philosophy faculty at Charles University. The political discipline of Communist students was incomparably more severe than that of their opponents.[4]

The crucial moment for the democrats came in February 1948 when the KSČ (Communist Party of Czechoslovakia) enforced its dictatorship through a combination of street demonstrations, control of the Ministry of Interior, and massive intimidation of its opponents, but without open use of armed force. When tens of thousands of Communist supporters took part in the manifestations of revolutionary power in the streets of Prague, among them were at least one thousand disciplined Communist students. One student of history who belonged to the Communist Party told the head of his party group that he could not go onto the streets because he was finishing his thesis; for this he was marked as politically unreliable for the next twenty years. On the democratic side some three to five thousand students had courage enough to organize two protest marches to the Prague Castle (Hradčany) on 23 and 25 February, in order to encourage President Edvard Beneš to resist Communist pressure. This constituted the sole manifestation in favor of the democratic parties on the streets of Prague. On 25 February, the day the president accepted the Communist dictat, the SNB (Communist Police) fired on students near the Castle, wounding one. It also arrested some fifty more.[5]

Beginning on 25 February 1948, when the Communists took full power in Czechoslovakia, "action committees" led by Communist students (and with support of the Ministry of Education) took full control of faculty administration and the old academic institutions; henceforth, the Academic Senate and faculty staffs would play subordinate roles. Contemporaries coined the term "studentocracy" to describe the regime that governed

---

4. Hana Kráčmarová, *Vysokoškoláci v revolučních letech, 1945–1948* (Prague: Oddělení vysokoškolských organizací ÚV SSM v nakl. Mladá fronta, 1976); Antonín Kratochvíl, *Die kommunistische Hochschulpolitik in der Tschechoslowakei: Geschichte und Analyse der Entwicklung bis zur Gegenwart* (Munich: Fides-Verlagsgesellschaft, 1968).

5. Zdeněk Pousta, "Smuteční pochod za demokracii," in *Stránkami soudobých dějin: Sborník statí k pětašedesátinám historika Karla Kaplana*, ed. Karel Jech (Prague: Ústav pro soudobé dějiny AV ČR, 1993), 98–207.

Czech universities in the years 1948–50. A university law of 1950 abolished traditional academic liberties, but also constrained the influence of the students. From that point party apparatchiks played a decisive role in nominating teachers and intervened in such matters as student admissions.

The most memorable expression of student power was the purges of early 1948, when student-led action committees removed all anticommunists from leading positions at the universities. Similar processes of purging took place at the same time in state service, nationalized enterprises, and the institutions of the local government. The most spectacular of these removals was the deposition of Charles University rector Karel Engliš. This famous professor of the faculty of law, an economist, and minister of finance during the First Republic, was forced by the action committee of his faculty to resign. Because of the irritation this produced at Western universities, many of whom canceled plans to participate in celebrations of the six-hundredth anniversary of Charles University that April, the Gottwald government tried to persuade Engliš to rescind his resignation. He refused.

Deans of the faculties and the faculty councils obediently accepted the dictates of the Communist-led committees, but there were a number of individual protests. Růžena Vacková, professor of classical archeology in the philosophy faculty, spoke out at a faculty meeting against the expulsions of students who had been arrested at the Hradčany demonstration, and as a result was herself dismissed from the faculty. Subsequently, she was arrested and spent sixteen years in prison. In the first days and weeks after the "February Victory" expulsions were limited to professors and students who had been active opponents of the new regime. Fourteen students were expelled from the University of Economics, where most of the five hundred students had supported the democratic parties. The action committee of the law faculty expelled twelve students and barred seven professors from further teaching.

Dictatorship and Universities

Because of the April 1948 anniversary celebrations, the most important measures that instituted the dictatorial regime were introduced with a slight delay at Charles University. The Communist regime paid closer attention to the legality of its interventions in the face of a still significant turnout at the event of West European university representatives and scholars, for example attempting to portray its coup d'état of February as a legal action, fully respecting the constitution. In his last public appearance, President Edvard Beneš took part in the anniversary celebrations on 7 April, and appealed to spiritual and human liberty as necessary conditions for scholarly life and intellectual activities.

After this ceremony the Communist Party line through the spring of 1948 read as follows: "Complete destruction of political positions held by reactionaries in higher education." The ambitions suggested by these words were fully realized. During the first months of 1948 the KSČ founded organizations at each faculty: for teachers, employees, and students. These organizations swelled after a campaign to attract new members (in July 1948 the KSČ had 2 million members in a state of 12 million inhabitants). As is suggested by the term "studentocracy," students seized leading positions, but clerical staff also played an important role, whereas teachers, because of their relative numerical weakness, were reduced to a subordinate role. Numbers of academics in the Communist organizations did rise somewhat, however, after the dismissal of those assistant professors who were not in the party and their replacement by young people who were. The demand for—and numbers of—assistant professors increased rapidly as a result of reforms which added many examinations and "practical" activities to the curriculum in the years 1949–53.

Students who began their studies in October 1948 or later were organized into relatively small (ten-to-twenty-member) study groups within which the party could easily monitor their learning and political behavior. Study programs were officially codified in the university law of 1950. The idea of curricular reform was not entirely new: it had been popular among the students of 1945 who desired shorter and more effective studies. But for these students academic freedom and financial support had been much more important demands. Professors, especially at the law faculties, had mostly opposed reform ideas before 1948, at a time when Communist students were making reform of legal studies one of their central planks. The reforms introduced after 1948 included some reasonable measures, but they also served to strengthen Communist control of the teaching process. This was true at all faculties, but especially at the law faculty. Only after 1953 were scholars who were not party members considered for positions as assistant professors. That was due not to any great liberality on the part of the Communist apparatus, but rather to the fact that university graduates in possession of "red booklets" could look forward to more attractive career opportunities than academia.

After the election of a Communist as rector of Charles University on 31 May 1948 a new period commenced in the subordination of the Czech universities to the policies of the Communist Party. Freshmen of the winter semester 1948–49, most of whom completed high school (gymnasium) in June 1948, were forced to undergo an "admissions colloquium" before they were registered. Their academic qualifications for studies were examined only superficially, but detailed questions were asked on their political opinions and much attention was paid to references about them obtained from Communist organizations at their high schools and places of residence. In subsequent years admissions examinations demanded ever more from a political and professional point of view, and the proportion of those admitted to the most popular faculties grew smaller and smaller. The system was continually perfected and eventually became one of the most effective means of political supervision, not only of potential students, but also of parents concerned for the professional futures of their children, and so to a high degree of Czechoslovak society as a whole.

Those beginning studies in 1948 were carefully segregated from their older colleagues, with the exception of the instructors of their study groups, who were drawn from Communist students active in the upper classes. During the first months of 1949 the Ministry of Education organized for all students, except these newcomers, a "screening" that was supposed to gauge suitability for continued attendance at the university. The public was told that many had enrolled as students in order to take advantage of student privileges (food rations, spots in student dormitories, reduced fare in public transport). In reality those studying under false pretense had mostly been expelled by their schools or student organizations in 1946 and 1947. The screening was organized by the Communist-controlled Ministry of Education and students' faculty organizations. Faculty action committees appointed three-person screening commissions and subcommissions, which consisted entirely of students. Rectors, deans, and faculty staffs had no role in this process. Each subcommission was supposed to screen about fifty students. The criteria—from most to least important—included political orientation, class origin, and the number and results of exams passed. These commissions expelled 42 percent of the students from the Prague, and 46 percent from the Brno law faculty. Another 10 percent of the students of these faculties did not bother to appear before the screening subcommissions. At the Prague philosophy faculty 21 percent of the students were eliminated, and 9 percent refused to take part. Though the purging was less severe in the faculties of medicine and science, in the end approximately one-quarter of the students of Charles University had been refused permission to continue their studies.[6]

The reconfiguration of the student body also had a social dimension: during the 1950s (except in 1956) universities nearly fully closed their doors to applicants whose families were identified as "bourgeois," and limited access for students of middle-class and intelligentsia backgrounds. At the same time "courses" were organized which prepared workers for admission to universities in the space of a year. Nearly all of the participants in such courses were party members, and they went on to form the hard core of the party organizations at their respective faculties. The party's ambitions were not fully realized, however: on the one hand, not all of these worker students were successful at the universities, and on the other, some of those who succeeded recognized early the character of the regime they served, especially those who were sent as graduate students to the Soviet Union and became active in the reform movement of 1968.[7] After 1952 the one-year courses could not fill their quotas because the salaries in white-collar professions—with the exception of leading positions—were not much higher than workers' wages.

The purges of Stalinism affected relatively few full professors, except those teaching ideological subjects—law, history, philosophy, economics, and biology (the last was influenced by the Lysenko campaign). The law faculty at Brno University was closed and all its professors—with one exception—were dismissed; at the Prague law faculty and the School of Economics about one-third of the professors were dismissed and replaced by the Marxists. The regime frequently arrested citizens for political reasons or sent them to labor camps in the years 1949–53; university teachers and students were no exceptions. Several professors spent between four and eight years in prison. Among the 233 persons sentenced to death in political trials in Czechoslovakia between 1948 and 1954 six were active students. The only executed university teacher was Otto Fischl, professor of financial law, a Communist who had replaced his politically unreliable predecessor in 1949. He was sentenced in the trial of Rudolf Slánský.

---

6. Zdeněk Pousta, "Persekuce studentů Univerzity Karlovy," *Škola a město: Sborník příspěvků z konference "Škola a město," konané ve dnech 5.-6. října 1992, Documenta Pragensia* 11 (1993): 237–42.

7. John Connelly, "Students, Workers and Social Change: The Limits of Czech Stalinism," *Slavic Review* 56 (1997): 307–35.

According to the university law introduced in 1950, all university teachers of a single subject or those sharing similar specializations were incorporated into newly formed "departments" (called *katedry*). These were led by professors who belonged to the party, and were supposed to oversee teaching and scholarship as well as assure loyalty to the Communist regime. Increasingly, pedagogical burdens were shifted to assistant professors, who took on a far greater share of the teaching than had been the case in the interwar period. The result in many faculties was an intensification of studies.

As a result of the reforms, students were obliged to study according to a rigorous and detailed schedule of lectures and seminars. In great contrast to the relatively liberal Central European system in place up to that point, the new regime required students to sit for examinations at the end of every semester.[8] Courses in the history of Communist parties, Marxist-Leninist philosophy, and Marxist economics and politics (later called "Scientific Communism") became obligatory from the first to the fourth year of studies, with two hours of lectures and two hours of seminar every week. These ideological subjects were used as a means of political persecution—for example, a student might be expelled from the university for requesting more clarification during seminar on why the Americans had been the aggressors in Korea. Later the character of ideological courses became quite formal and superficial, and students' attitudes toward them were mostly modeled on the example of "the Good Soldier Švejk." During the 1960s some of the lecturers even discussed their doubts about some of the tenets of Marxism-Leninism.

These strict plans of study, examinations at the end of every semester, and political screenings for all students represented important successes for the political system in its efforts to revolutionize university studies. It also changed the life of university students in what one might call "extracurricular" ways. One remarkable innovation in students' lives was the obligatory "brigade," that is four weeks of labor during the holidays in construction or agriculture (later mostly hop-picking), that were supposed to bring future white-collar employees closer to the working class.

---

8. Previously, students had far fewer examinations. Law students, for example, had been obliged to take three state examinations in over four years of study. Students at the philosophy and science faculties who wished to teach in high schools had been required to take four obligatory examinations during their studies. Students of medicine and engineering needed to take more examinations, but even in those fields the number of required examinations doubled or tripled after 1950.

Actually, especially from the 1960s, brigades proved counterproductive for the regime, because students were witnessing the socialist economy's weaknesses first-hand.

Beyond the new courses in Marxism-Leninism and "scientific socialism" mentioned above, political indoctrination of students also included new views on the history of Charles University, and was realized both at university ceremonies and in lectures featuring a Marxist interpretation of history. The university's medieval roots were highly regarded because of the role played by one-time rector Jan Hus in the Hussite Revolution, an event interpreted by Nejedlý and his followers as the most glorious page in Czech history. University authorities likewise deemed the "Students' Revolution" of 1848 an important revolutionary tradition, and celebrated such important nineteenth-century scholars as B. Bolzano, J. E. Purkyně, and B. Brauner. The official attitude to the most important Czech professor as well as founder of Czechoslovakia, T. G. Masaryk, was very positive up to 1950, but in 1951 the party launched a campaign branding him as the "ideological representative of the Czech bourgeoisie." Beginning in 1960 Masaryk's scholarly and political activities were again appreciated to a limited degree, but party ideological leaders decreed important restrictions on how he might be honored. The interwar period was mostly interpreted by the former leftist student leaders, who wrote proudly of their struggle against the fascists and with hatred about rightist, nationalist leaders like former rector Karel Domin.

One consequence of the regime's interventions that was visible only in the long term was to isolate Czech universities from international scholarship. Between 1948 and 1956 contacts were reduced to a minimum even with the universities in the other countries of the Soviet bloc. The first individual exchanges of scholars started in 1955, and the following year student groups traveled on exchange to Poland, Hungary, and the GDR. Individuals were not permitted to study in the West until the 1960s, but even then such cases remained rare, and the lucky few had to subject themselves to political screening. From this resulted a relatively poor familiarity with foreign languages, though according to the curriculum from 1950 one Western language (mostly German or English) was an obligatory subject for all university students. Graduate students ("aspirants") had to pass quite severe exams in at least one of these languages.

With the foundation of the Czechoslovak Academy of Sciences (ČSAV) new institutes emerged, both in sciences and humanities. Political demands were not as strict as those made on university teachers, and a number of scholars who were primarily interested in research sought refuge here. Research did not entirely disappear from universities, but working conditions at the academy institutes were superior.

Continuity, Reform, and Repression

The most important parts of university tradition—the freedom of learning, the right to appoint new professors, and to evaluate scholars according to their knowledge or scholarly production—these were not respected, although during the 1960s some improvements could be observed. The establishment of the Communist dictatorship in Czechoslovakia in February 1948 did not cause a full personal and structural rupture with tradition, however. The formal sides of university tradition—graduation ceremonies, reconstruction of historical buildings, the use of professors' gowns at solemn occasions—were observed very carefully. The old professors who supported, at least formally, the Communist regime—mostly noncommunists—were highly valued, and a number of them obtained the prestigious titles and lucrative salaries of members of the Czechoslovak Academy of Sciences, which was founded in 1952. To give some examples—Bohumil Němec, a great biologist and the nationalist candidate for president of Czechoslovakia in 1935, was among the first Academy members, as were the ghost writer of nationalist politician Karel Kramář, historian Václav Vojtíšek, and the conservative lawyers Antonín Hora and Václav Hobza. On the other hand, those who expressed an oppositional attitude to the regime might be sentenced to many years in prison, for example, professor of classical philology Bohumil Ryba, historian Zdeněk Kalista, and the professors of Catholic theology Karel Kadlec and Jan K. Vyskočil.

Despite all that has been described, the events of the years 1948–55 did not have quite the negative effects one might have expected. The scholarly standards of the medical, science, and technical faculties were mostly retained, though doubtless the severed personal contacts with the West and limitations for the younger staff members had their harmful consequences, despite continued availability of Western scholarly journals. At the faculties of philosophy, pedagogy, law, and economics many of the assistant professors appointed in the early 1950s became critical of Marxism-Leninism as a foundation of social sciences and practical politics and attempted to reestablish contact with Western currents of learning, especially after the crisis of 1956. Books such as Karel Kosík's *Dialektika konrétního* (The dialectics of the concrete, 1963) and Milan Machovec's biography of T. G. Masaryk (1967) reflected this tendency, and became quite popular because they were critical and open-minded.

Czech journals of the late 1940s and early 1950s had regularly featured pictures of thousands of Czech students celebrating such events as May Day, but this practice ceased after 1956. Official youth organizations at universities still existed, and were still capable of rounding up enough students and younger teachers for "brigades" of "voluntary" labor, but party apparatchiks grew ever more disappointed with the political atmosphere at universities. During the 1960s the youth organizations and their journals at Prague's technical faculties, and later also at Charles University, gave voice to the disillusionment of young people with "really existing socialism." Though critics focused mostly on the problems of students' daily life, they were unwittingly preparing the atmosphere for the revolutionary activities that was sparked by the students' demonstration from Strahov dormitories on 31 October 1967.

The often heated discussions that took place at universities after Khrushchev's denunciation of Stalin at the Twentieth Party Congress of the CPSU in 1956 had demonstrated the existence of an oppositional mood at Czech universities. Hundreds of teachers and students took part in demonstrations, though many more potential supporters remained passive. By contrast, the overwhelming majority of the academic community became active in the democratic movement of the Prague Spring in 1968.[9] After the Soviet invasion in August 1968 students, supported by the majority of their teachers, protested against the reintroduction of dictatorship with occupation strikes, and the suicide of student Jan Palach on 16 January 1969 inaugurated the last great series of anti-Soviet demonstrations.

Repression of reformist sentiments commenced in a serious way in the fall of 1969 and reached their highpoint in the spring of the following year. The new minister of education, Communist hard-liner Jaroslav Hrbek, did not confirm the rectors and deans who had been elected in the democratic atmosphere of the years 1968–69. The first to be dismissed were the teachers of Marxism because most had supported Dubček's

---

9. Michal Svatoš, "Studentské majáles 60. let," in *Zlatá šedesátá, česká literatura a společnost v letech tání, kolotání a . . . zklamání*, ed. Radka Denemarková (Prague: Ústav pro českou literaturu AV ČR, 2000), 92–102.

reforms. Up to the end of the year 1969 faculty staffs resisted pressures to purge teachers who had taken an active part in the democratic reforms and occupied leading positions. But with the help of replenished faculty organizations of the Communist Party, consisting only of those who approved the Soviet occupation of Czechoslovakia, the Ministry of Education succeeded in 1970 in dismissing a great number of professors, especially social scientists. At Charles University alone ninety-two professors were fired; a further thirty-nine were fired because they had left the country. More than one hundred other professors were barred from teaching and transferred to positions as researchers. These measures clearly contributed to the lowering of standards of university education after 1970. New appointments to the vacated posts had to be approved by the city party committees.

The new Communist authoritarian regime abstained from persecuting students who had taken part in democratic life in 1968, yet it summarily expelled those who were arrested for participating in the demonstrations of 21 August 1969, the first anniversary of the Soviet invasion. Party apparatchiks again interfered in the daily life of universities. Institutes of Marxism were renewed, but centralized in a single institute for the whole university, and their lectures had only a very limited influence on students. These new attempts to subordinate universities fully to party and state control were codified in a law of 10 April 1980, which established full ministerial control of the universities, including the right to appoint rectors and deans.

Despite the purges that took place after the defeat of the Prague Spring in 1968, a full restoration of party discipline and Marxist orthodoxy was not possible. Those who stayed in Czechoslovakia and retained party membership were often very critical in daily conversations with the students and sometimes even in their lectures. Much information seeped in from the West by other channels, in part because of liberal atmosphere in two neighboring "socialist countries," Poland and Hungary, but also because the oppressors feared going too far, especially after the ascent of Mikhail Gorbachev in the Soviet Union. For example instructors of political economy had to respect the acquaintance students had gained with living standards in West Germany and Austria from television.

The party leadership during the Husák period faced a dilemma: it needed tens of thousands of specialists with university qualifications but was not able to inspire more than political passivity among most students and teachers. The fact that students, with individual exceptions, did not take part in Charter 77 and other oppositional activities, was taken by party authorities as a sign of the success of their policies.

This passive behavior began to change in 1987, when students in several faculties published journals criticizing the situation at their schools and to some degree Czech society as a whole. Beginning in 1989 a number of students took part in street demonstrations against the Communist regime. The first demonstrations at Prague's Wenceslaus Square started in January 1989 with a commemoration of the twentieth anniversary of the suicide of Jan Palach in so-called Palach-week at Wenceslaus Square, and changed the students' attitudes toward political affairs. A group of teachers at Charles University founded the oppositional platform "The Club of the Independent Intelligentsia."

Some students took part in demonstrations on 1 May, 21 August, and 28 October 1989, but they were not the leading element of those protests. The oppositional mood among students rose in proportion to the severity of crisis in other East bloc states. At some faculties unofficial student representations emerged which chastised fellow students for their passivity. Gradually the official student organizations became involved in criticizing political conditions, and the fiftieth anniversary of the closing of Czech higher schools by the Nazis gave both groups an opportunity to stage a demonstration that could hardly be forbidden by the authorities. On 17 November 1989 the students gathered at the place in Prague-Albertov where a previous generation had once buried the medical student Jan Opletal, shot by the Nazis in October 1939. That earlier funeral had itself grown into the final public manifestation against the Nazis for the duration of the war. Four spokespersons—two older students and two organizers—called for greater political involvement on the part of the students. Then the assembled marched to the cemetery in Vyšehrad and finally—despite a clear prohibition by the state security police—to Wenceslaus Square. Before they could reach this central point, the demonstrators were intercepted by armed police contingents and dispersed by force. The response of students at practically all higher schools to reports of brutality was to stage occupation strikes, at which demands were made for the punishment of police and their stage managers. The Czech public massively supported these demands by attending demonstrations called by the strike committee that numbered in the hundreds of thousands. Within a week the Communist regime had fallen, and student leaders transferred leadership of the movement for democracy to the civic forum, headed by Václav Havel. On 10 December the Communist president Gustav Husák resigned, and Václav Havel was elected as his successor.[10]

The role of students—and also many of their teachers—in rejecting "really existing socialism" in the crucial years 1968 and 1989 can be explained by the fact that this social group—young, enthusiastic, and not yet subordinated to the discipline of the professions—had courage enough to express publicly the critical attitude of most of Czech society. From their own experience, especially in the late 1980s, most Czechs recognized the defeat suffered by the authoritarian regime in economic competition with the West.

Conclusion

In conclusion I would like to consider how the experience of Czech higher education differed from that of other countries which experienced Communist dictatorship in the second half of the twentieth century. One important distinction was the situation of the academic elites in Czechoslovakia. Not only did the overwhelming majority of intellectuals welcome the soldiers of the Red Army as liberators, but also very many of them joined the Communist Party. Some of the leading scholars were prewar Communists, for example, the outstanding mathematician Eduard Čech and the pedagogue Otakar Chlup. Others were very close to the Communist Party, like Zdeněk Nejedlý. Some prewar leftists joined the KSČ in 1945 after establishing contacts with Communists in underground anti-Nazi activities. There were also prewar nationalists who accepted friendship with the USSR as a continuation of their old Panslavic orientation. Last but not least one must mention the prewar liberals and conservatives who were influenced by their Communist sons and daughters.

Thus the KSČ could nominate outstanding scholars from its own ranks for the important posts of rector and dean of the philosophy faculty at Charles University once seizing power in 1948: Jan Mukařovský and Bohuslav Havránek, both of whom had been leading members of the prewar Prague Linguistics Circle. Even among the teachers of the conservative law school (Václav Vaněček) or school of economics (Jan Janáček)

10. Milan Otáhal and Miroslav Vaněk, eds., *Sto studentských revolucí* (Prague: Lidové noviny, 1999); Marek Benda et al., eds., *Studenti psali revoluci* (Prague: Univerzum, 1990).

there were respected specialists who became Communists in 1945. The Secretariat of the Central Committee of KSČ was later disappointed with some of them, as they did not wish to accept passively all party instructions. One of them, professor of Polish literature Karel Krejčí, was forbidden to teach at any university because of the wrath his activities as Charles University prorector in 1956 had engendered among party functionaries.

In part because of such independence older professors were later replaced in their academic functions by young Communists who had started their scholarly careers after 1948. But these people too (for example, mathematician and Charles University rector from 1954 to 1958, Miroslav Katětov, or philosopher Karel Kosík), after a short period of obedience, became members of the "academic elite," and as such, not only undisciplined Communists, but also openly critical of the party leadership. It was characteristic for the subsequent development of such scholars that Miroslav Katětov would address a student meeting of 17 November 1989 as a representative of "independent intellectuals."

Although the Communist dictatorship developed a relatively sophisticated system to supervise university students and teachers, higher education continued to be one of the politically weakest links of the system of dictatorship. From the political point of view universities were always a potential danger for the regime. During the early period the enthusiasm of young Czech and Slovak teachers achieved some success in the sciences and in technical studies, and even later these schools continued to prepare good specialists. These facts were advantageous for the regime, but it neglected the necessary contacts with the scientific development in the world.[11] Such contacts were limited for mainly political reasons, although later the state's economic weakness also became an important obstacle to research, and as a consequence Czechoslovak universities

---

11. Since 1997 Charles University and the Academy of Sciences of the Czech Republic have sponsored five conferences on the development of Czech scholarship. See Hana Barvíková, *Věda v českých zemích (1939–1945)* (Prague: Archiv Akademie věd České republiky, 1998); Blanka Zilynská and Petr Svobodný, eds., *Věda v Československu, 1945–1953* (Prague: Univerzita Karlova, 1999); and Hana Barvíková, Marek Ďurčanský, and Petr Koderaj, eds., *Věda v Československu, 1953–1963* (Prague: Archiv Akademie věd České republiky, 2000). On the 1960s, see Antonín Kostlán and Markéta Devátá, eds., *Věda v Československu v období normalizace (1970–1975): Sborník z conference (Praha,21.–22. listopadu 2001)* (Prague: Výzkumné centrum pro dějiny vědy, 2002). All these collections have chapter summaries in English. See also *Vývojová ročenka školství v České republice, 1989–97* [Retrospective Yearbook of Education in the Czech Republic, 1989–97] (Prague: Ústav pro informace ve vzdělávání,1997), and *Reviews of National Politics for Education: Czech Republic* (Paris: OECD, 1996).

fell behind the times in many respects. Yet on the other hand the active resistance of the universities, both of their teachers and students, in 1956 and 1968, created an inspiring tradition for the following years which led to the students' revolution of 17 November 1989, which opened the doors for the end of the Communist regime in this country.

7

Polish Universities and State Socialism, 1944–1968

JOHN CONNELLY

 Did Poles willingly submit to the Communist regime introduced after 1945, or were they united against it in courageous resistance? Debates on this issue have been simmering through Polish journals since the emergence of underground media in the 1970s, but consensus remains elusive. Proponents of the former view note the millions of Poles who joined the Polish United Workers' Party (PZPR), the successful transplantation to Poland of Soviet-type command structures, Stalinist-era show trials, and the Polish army's assistance in the crushing of the Prague Spring in 1968. Their opponents point to deeper currents of opposition, such as a vibrant underground press, resolutely defiant church leaders, and a private peasantry, as well as periodic, indeed almost regular outbursts of dissent.[1]

The student of intellectual life in Communist Poland similarly encounters discordant opinions, although in recent years the more critical approach has been favored among analysts, whether of left or right. Former

---

1. The "resistance of its cultural fabric against a foreign implant was so strong that instead of a communization of the nation Poland witnessed a nationalization of Communism." Krystyna Kersten, "Bilans zamknięcia," in *Spór o PRL* (Kraków: Znak, 1994), 24. This collection also contains a range of opposing perspectives. Błażej Brzostek, "Contrasts and Grayness: Looking at the First Decade of Postwar Poland," *Journal of Modern European History* 2, no. 1 (2004): 110–33, and Krzysztof Ruchniewicz, "Zeitgeschichte in Polen nach 1989: Forschungsschwerpunkte, 'weisse Flecken' und historische Kontroversen," *Jahrbuch für europäische Geschichte* 4 (2004): 39–69, both provide excellent overviews of the literature and its basic dichotomy between the critical/martyrological and the "objective"/apologetic approaches.

dissident Jacek Kuroń—himself a former Communist—has wondered "how was it possible that the Polish intelligentsia, especially young people, so massively joined the system?"[2] Even when intellectuals were leading forces in opposition—as in 1968, for example—they seem guilty of attempting to realize socialism, and thereby prolonging the bondage of the Polish people.[3] Conservatives in academia have organized such conferences as "Failure of the Clerks" and seek "the roots of evil" in the behavior of intellectuals.[4]

These views find backing in the best-known works on intellectuals under Communism, especially Czesław Miłosz's *Captive Mind*, which depicts writers succumbing wholesale to the allures of Stalinism. Though written half a century ago, the book's central theses have not been seriously questioned. At best conservative critics such as Jacek Trznadel or Zbigniew Herbert have wondered whether Miłosz's invocation of the "Hegelian sting," "Ketman," or "the pill of Murti-Bing" might not rest in a circuitous and indirectly exculpatory logic. They instead stress more mundane inducements for conformity, such as vacation homes, exalted positions, guaranteed print runs.[5]

Polish sociologists have confirmed a classic interpretation in their own field, namely George Konrad and Ivan Szelenyi's *Intellectuals on the Road to Class Power*, which drew upon Milovan Djilas's conception of a "new class": the managers, functionaries, and technicians who reaped the benefits of the socialist economy in return for loyal service to the

2. Jacek Kuroń and Jacek Żakowski, *PRL dla początkujących* (Wrocław: Wydawnictwo Dolnosląskie, 1996), 42. See also Jacek Kuroń, *Wiara i wina: Do i od komunizmu* (London: Aneks, 1989). For further references and discussion, see Krystyna Kersten, *Między wyzwoleniem a zniewoleniem, Polska, 1944–1956* (London: Aneks, 1993), 100–162; and Henryk Słabek, *Intelektualistów obraz własny, 1944–1989* (Warsaw: Książka i wiedza, 1997). For a recent overview by a Western scholar assuming the success of Stalinist-era intelligentsia policies in Poland, see A. Kemp-Welch, "Introduction: Reconstructing the Past," in *Stalinism in Poland, 1944–56*, ed. A. Kemp-Welch (New York: St. Martin's, 1999), 1–19.

3. For a critical discussion of such views, see Andrzej Friszke, *Opozycja polityczna w PRL, 1945–1980* (London: Aneks, 1994), 583–91.

4. Thus the title of a symposium that took place in Warsaw on 7 November 1998 under the auspices of Towarzystwo im. Stanisława ze Skarbimierza with the participation of professors Piotr Hübner, Janusz Gaćkowski, Wiesław Karel Szymański, Jarosław Marek Rymkiewicz, and Jacek Trznadel. For references on this sort of portrayal of the Polish past, see Andrzej Friszke, "Epilogue: Polish Communism in Contemporary Debates," in Kemp-Welch, *Stalinism in Poland*, 146.

5. See Jacek Trznadel, *Hańba domowa: Rozmowy z pisarzami* (Lublin: Wydawnictwo Paweł Skokowski, 1993), and "An Interview with Zbigniew Herbert," *Partisan Review* 54, no. 4 (1987): 557–75.

socialist state. This group emerged at the dawn of People's Poland, and grew steadily thereafter. In the crisis of 1956 the technical intelligentsia demanded, and was granted, higher pay, and increasingly the gap between its wages and those of manual workers widened. This new class enjoyed access to a broad range of privileges, especially scarce goods and services, unobtainable by ordinary workers.[6] From the late 1950s leading positions in party and state were filled by cadres with higher education, and by 1973 virtually all major executive positions required "more than secondary" education.[7] The number of professionals holding the party card grew nearly fourfold between 1960 and 1973, while party membership as a whole only doubled. Among engineers the number of party members went from 32 to 40 percent between 1963 and 1967; yet, by contrast, only 9 percent of skilled and 4 percent of unskilled manual workers belonged to the party. Because of the intelligentsia's previous reluctance to acquire party cards, sociologist Maria Hirszowicz has called this intellectualization of the party a "quiet revolution."[8]

Against this weight of anecdote, analysis, and theoretical elaboration stand several histories which highlight the role of the intellectuals in political opposition. Writers and students spearheaded resistance to Stalinism during the Polish thaw (1954–55), wrote, spoke and demonstrated against the increasingly sclerotic Gomułka regime (1962–68), founded the Committee for the Protection of Workers (KOR) in 1976, and engaged fully and enthusiastically in the Solidarity revolution of 1980–81, electing colleagues who supported democratic reforms and rehabilitating victims of state persecution. Despite the constraints of martial law (1981–83) the underground press continued to grow. Historians, writers, journalists, and

---

6. The intelligentsia tended to live far better than workers, as measured in average number of rooms per apartment, presence or absence of central heating, and so on. For example, over half the intelligentsia had apartments with central heating in Łódź in 1971, whereas in other social groups no more than a fifth enjoyed this privilege. Members of the intelligentsia had an average of 2.90 rooms per apartment, while skilled workers had only 1.85 rooms. Maria Hirszowicz, *The Bureaucratic Leviathan* (Oxford: Martin Robinson, 1980), 186–90.

7. Ibid., 185–87. Between 1956 and 1958 the number of plant directors with higher education increased from 38.0 to 52.5 percent. David Lane and George Kolankiewicz, *Social Groups in Polish Society* (London: Macmillan, 1973), 195, 197, 200.

8. In Albert Szymanski, *Class Struggle in Socialist Poland: With Comparisons to Yugoslavia* (New York: Praeger, 1984), 82–83. According to Lane and Kolankiewicz, *Social Groups in Polish Society*, 206–7, engineers joined the Party not out of political loyalty, but in order to increase their professional independence. This judgment is based upon the findings of Polish sociologists in the 1960s.

economists figured prominently among those who negotiated the transfer to democracy in Poland in 1989.

In what follows I examine the question of intellectual complicity in the Communist regime from the perspective of universities, the institutions charged with reproducing the "new class." The source base includes reports written by state and party functionaries, but also memoirs and letters of scholars who lived in Stalinist Poland. One indeed finds much apparent acceptance of the "New Faith" in journal articles or speeches at scholarly conferences, as well as in a general structural transformation causing Polish universities to visually resemble Soviet counterparts. More important, however, for understanding the role of the universities in socialism are deeper currents of continuity in the student body and professoriate. Because of massive anticommunist agitation at universities in the early postwar period, the regime hesitated to move forcefully against either students or professors in the Stalinist period (1948–55) that followed. Unlike their counterparts in the Soviet Union or in Czechoslovakia and East Germany, Polish Communists did not purge the professoriate, even in subjects like law and history. Even new worker and peasant students were taught by an old, mostly conservative professoriate. In what follows I trace the consequences of this signal failure of Polish Communists to emulate Soviet examples.

Opposition to the Creation of a New Academic Regime

The early postwar years were a time of relative openness in Poland, and students as well as professors could speak their minds with little fear of political repercussions. They used available arenas to protest the gradual imposition of dictatorship both within academia and throughout the country. When the political climate chilled in 1948, university communities sought shelter in heretofore-private spaces. Opposition was now expressed in "structural" and "cultural" terms: in the refusal, for example, of academics and students to involve themselves in official life by remaining outside mass organizations, especially the party, or by engaging in activities organized by the Catholic Church.

The best-known manifestations of political dissent occurred on Constitution Day (3 May) of 1946. The Communist-led regime had defined this event out of existence by making 1 May the sole national holiday. A "first confrontation" (Wojciech Mazowiecki) of the new Polish regime with Polish society resulted, centered in conservative Kraków. After morning mass, thousands of young people streamed out onto the historic central square, chanting, "Long live [opposition politician Stanisław] Mikołajczyk!" and "No more propaganda!" Onlookers cheered. Security police pressed the multitude back onto the square, scuffling ensued, and one student was shot in the face. Demonstrators eventually did escape the square and rallied at several other points in the city. In the course of the day's events police arrested several hundred, mostly young people.[9]

The protests were not limited to Kraków; high school and university students as well as boy and girl scouts staged marches in cities and towns all over Poland that day.[10] In subsequent weeks students in all major university towns struck for the sake of arrested colleagues. At issue was "solidarity."[11] These actions led to new arrests, for example, of 633 students in Poznań.[12] Most of the students were released in the course of the year, but the regime had learned a lesson. Student organizations came under increasing political pressure, so that by 1950 traditionally independent student clubs of "fraternal assistance" had disappeared, and the final "enemies" were being eliminated from the leadership of the student "academic clubs" (*koła naukowe*). No further street demonstrations occurred for ten years.[13]

Polish professors not only tolerated, but encouraged, the striking, for example by canceling classes. Yet the student strikes exposed them, and the university community as a whole, to intensified repression, because the regime made the strikes an excuse for curbing university autonomy. It claimed that universities were harboring "reactionary forces." In 1947 plans

---

9. Estimates range from five hundred to fourteen hundred. Wojciech Mazowiecki, *Pierwsze starcie* (Warsaw: PWN, 1998), 87–110.

10. A complete list of the over fifty demonstrations is in ibid., 154. Demonstrations also occurred in Gliwice, Łódz, Warsaw, Toruń, and Gdańsk. Jan Walczak, *Ruch studencki w Polsce, 1944–1984* (Wrocław: Ossolineum, 1990), 34–35.

11. For use of this word by students in Chrzanów, Poznań, Gdańsk, Gdynia, and Toruń, see Mazowiecki, *Pierwsze starcie*, 173, 179–80, 190, 192.

12. Ibid., 184.

13. Some 250 such clubs existed throughout Poland in 1950. Yet little had been done to influence their activities, which included running departmental libraries, organizing after-hours instruction, and publishing lecture notes. Some larger clubs were still in possession of property, and could thus aid students materially. "Tezy do projektu nowej organizacji Kół Naukowych na Prezydium Rady Głównej," 2 December 1950, Archive of the Polish Academy of Sciences, Warsaw (APAN-W), III-192 74, k. 20; Walczak, *Ruch studencki*, 62.

emerged for a "Main Council" in Warsaw which would usurp the self-governing functions of the universities, for example, the admission of students, the drafting of curricula, and the granting of the *Habilitacja*.[14] Each university was to receive a "director of administrative matters" who would watch over the work of the rector. The qualifications of those sitting on the Main Council were not made clear. Only the Sejm would have the power to alter its decisions. The public was told that universities were "medieval relics," and that state-driven reforms would make them "modern."[15]

Unlike counterparts in Hungary, however, Polish professors mobilized, seeing in the regime's plans not so much reform as revolution, not so much the desire to improve universities institutionally as to control them politically. Like intellectuals in China, they felt driven by considerations of patriotism; but unlike their Chinese counterparts, they contested the regime's right to speak for the nation. They felt their role in wartime resistance gave them a special right to contest infringements—a rhetorical choice denied the politically compromised professoriates in Germany or Hungary. Jagiellonian University in Kraków, for example, questioned the rationale for "incapacitating the professorial world, given its honest services for the Fatherland."[16] Professors in Warsaw also laid claim to special rights to speak for "Poland," not the Poland of a shallow historical present, but for a Poland of deep historical resonance: they condemned the government proposal as "not Polish in spirit, for in Poland the university has enjoyed autonomy since the end of the fourteenth century,"[17] implicitly condemning the state's distinctions between modern or pre-modern as secondary, indeed traitorous.

The academic community was thick with patriotism, and exerted a kind of gravitational pull upon those of its number who dared to stray from accepted norms of behavior. On 8 March 1947 Polish rectors called a meeting; state representatives were invited. The group conceded that

---

14. *Habilitation* (German), *habilitacja* (Polish), *habilitace* (Czech): A second dissertation required to attain teaching credentials at universities. The word "habilitation" is also understood to imply the process of having the second dissertation approved, often including a public defense (there is a corresponding verb: *habilitieren, habilitować*); it can also imply the credential, as in "he 'has' the Habilitation."

15. See, for example, W. Sokorski, "Organizacja nauki i szkół wyższych," *Odrodzenie*, 18 May 1947.

16. This response was drafted by the law faculty and bears the date 1 March 1947. Archive of Jagiellonian University (AUJ), S III/18.

17. Memorial of Warsaw University (undated). The professors of Toruń university compared the new proposals to the German higher education law of January 1935. AUJ, S III/18.

reform was necessary, but it rejected the government proposal. Every rector, except Władysław Kuczewski of the Silesian Polytechnic, the sole Communist in the group, signed the protest. But soon he changed his mind. On 11 March 1947 he wrote to Stefan Pieńkowski, rector of Warsaw University: "Since, besides me, every rector without exception decidedly condemned [the government's] preliminary project, I have revised my position and in the end signed the resolution passed in this matter by the rector's council."[18]

The government did pass a higher education decree on 28 October 1947, but as a result of these protests it was a measure of compromise and indecision and was valid only to 1951, one year less than planned, and did not significantly limit the power of universities to promote new teachers. A "Main Council" was created, but its powers were decidedly negative, for example, to deny *habilitacjas* already awarded by the faculty councils. These councils as well as university senates remained, but were expanded to embrace assistant professors. A new general university council came into existence that included six students but could only "advise" the rector. The rector likewise was not bound by the decisions of new administrative directors.[19] The decree had the unintended consequence of dividing power in the administration of higher education because the minister had to ask the approval of the Main Council before creating new higher schools, faculties, and chairs. Higher schools, wanting to be left alone, benefited from this institutionalized rivalry above them.[20]

Neither the Ministry nor the Main Council ever felt strong enough to carry out a major purge of the tenured professors, and therefore had to make use of them even within the new structures of Stalinism. Thus a "rupture" in the basic repository of university tradition, the professoriate, never occurred. A professorial community that had repulsed Communist encroachments in the early postwar years remained intact. So did its rejection of the new regime.

---

18. Bolesław Krasiewicz, *Odbudowa szkolnictwa wyższego w Polsce Ludowej w latach, 1944–1948* (Wrocław: Ossolineum, 1976), 329–30.

19. This provision was diluted by an emergency regulation toward the end of the decree which took away from the university the right to name candidates for a period of five years. Instead, the Main Council, in consultation with local agencies of the party, nominated rectors, deans, and their deputies. Piotr Hübner, *Nauka polska po II wojnie światowej — idee i instytucje* (Warsaw: Centralny Ośrodek Metodyczny Studiów Nauk Politycznych, 1987), 54.

20. Krasiewicz has written that "the creation of a Main Council for Science and Higher Education limited more the Ministry of Education than it did the prerogatives of world of science." Krasiewicz, *Odbudowa*, 332.

Increasingly, in the years following the new decree, rectors and deans were selected who seemed likely to loyally execute the state's wishes. In Kraków, the rector in the late 1940s and early 1950s was the agronomist Teodor Marchlewski, who had joined the PZPR in 1945 and was nephew to the famous Polish socialist Julian Marchlewski; in these years the socialist Konstanty Grzybowski acted as dean in the law faculty. Unlike Marchlewski he did not join the PZPR, however. Rectors' councils stopped meeting, and with the import of Soviet models for the organization of higher education, the university increasingly became part of state administration.

Administered Changes in Polish Higher Education

The main features of the Soviet system of higher education were central direction, subordination to state planning for the needs of cadre training, thorough politicization, the introduction of Marxist-Leninist indoctrination into the standard curriculum, and promotion of upward social mobility (*vydvizhenie*) for people of underprivileged background (the "worker-peasants").[21] All of these features were visible in Poland by the 1952–53 academic year just as they were in China and the other states of the Soviet bloc: the rectors and deans, no longer "first among equals," were state-appointed managers responsible for fulfilling all aspects of centrally determined plans. Every operation of the university was subordinated to planning: numbers of students accepted and graduated, research and teaching, the day-to-day workings of all university offices. Students, who had previously enrolled in courses according to personal desire, now received schedules regulating practically every moment of the week. Even summer vacations came under the purview of the state, as students were sent to gain experience in their branches of "production." Students were enrolled in two hours of lecture and two hours of seminar in Marxist-Leninist ideology each week. Increasingly, they came from new social groups: between 1946 and 1952, the numbers of students from "working-class and peasant background" grew from less than 20

---

21. This summary derives from categories identified by Russian historian A. P. Nikitin, "Die sowjetische Militäradministration und die Sowjetisierung des Bildungssystems in Ostdeutschland, 1945–1949," *Bildung und Erziehung* 45, no. 4 (1992): 406–7.

percent to over 60 percent of the total student body. At the university, party cells were established to "supervise" the fulfillment of state directives.

If one looks beyond the university to the landscape of higher education as a whole, one sees the sort of deprofessionalization that Ruth Ben-Ghiat discerns under Italian Fascism, or the dismemberment that Michael David-Fox describes in the Soviet Union during the socialist offensive in the early 1930s. Universities were stripped of medical and veterinary medical and later theological faculties, and new institutions of higher education emerged to provide specialists for the socialist economy in a supposedly more efficient way: pedagogical academies would churn out teachers, higher schools of economics would churn out managers for the socialist economy.

But if one returns to what remained of the traditional university, with its intact law and philosophy faculties, and looks behind the facade of banners, party pins, and plan targets, one sees that at the core relatively little had changed, because the old conservative, and largely anticommunist professoriate remained in place and still controlled the teaching process, even in sensitive fields like law. Professors' activities could not be subjected to "party discipline" because very few of them were party members. Aware of its weakness in the intelligentsia and in Polish society as a whole, the party had decided upon a course of gradual transformation in academia, a "mild revolution" that dispensed with radical purging of professors. Instead, the party placed its faith in young people: if they were taken from the proper class background, they could exert ideological pressures on the old professoriate and "use" them for their valuable expertise. New students would supposedly invest their subjects with new content derived from their "healthy" class consciousness.

The party leadership did not forsake all administrative methods of disciplining university teaching staffs, however. A number of politically troublesome professors, like the former National Democratic Sejm deputy, historian Władysław Konopczyński, were forced into retirement, and several others, like Konopczyński mostly historians from conservative Kraków, were transferred to western universities in Wrocław and Poznań between 1947 and 1949. This shift supposedly eroded one "reactionary" milieu while strengthening Poland's claims to the new western territories; several of these conservative historians indeed worked on the history of Silesia. Since their families tended to remain in Kraków, they endured half-day commutes twice weekly into the late 1950s, when these penalties were reversed, usually after years of appeals, by both the scholars themselves and their colleagues. Existing correspondence suggests that these appeals were often supported by the local party apparatus, thus testifying to continued strength of local academic milieus.[22] Annoying as they were to the scholars involved, these transfers were a relatively mild form of restricting their influence: they could after all go on forming young minds in their new university environments.

With the advance of central planning and Marxist-Leninist ideology a number of departments, indeed entire fields, were closed down, for example, sociology, classical economics, and most branches of philosophy (save logic). Scholars in these fields were forced to limit themselves to research. This fate befell a number of Poland's leading social scientists and philosophers in the early 1950s, including Stanisław and Maria Ossowski, Władysław Tatarkiewicz, and Roman Ingarden. In the wake of central planning, resources were frequently concentrated in Warsaw, thus necessitating the closing of departments in provincial universities. For example, after the early 1950s one could no longer study law or most fields of philology in Toruń. As far as can be ascertained, no professors were denied their titles, however, and the ostracized continued to enjoy the salaries and benefits associated with their positions. Several, like the Ossowskis and Tatarkiewicz, continued teaching graduate students in private.

A more serious challenge to the ability of the universities to reproduce themselves intellectually was the so-called Action N (N = *nauka*, "science"), an offensive launched by the party in 1949 in order to weaken "reactionary" influence among the junior faculty. The 1947 decree still permitted professors to recommend assistant professors, and faculties to conduct *habilitacja*s, but actual appointments depended on recommendations of local Communist Party organizations, and professional advancement on approval of tiny handfuls of professors in the "Central Qualification Commission for Scientific Workers" in Warsaw. The party required two years to assemble this commission, as well as the personnel dossiers necessary for assessing scholars' past lives, and for the next six years, until the de-Stalinization of 1955–56, it performed its task with great effectiveness. Only then could "politically hostile" professors, like the Catholic scholars Stanisław Stomma (law) and Irena Sławińska (dramatic arts) finally get the titles they deserved.

---

22. Affected by these measures were historians Henryk Barycz, Henryk Wereszycki, and Kazimierz Piwarski and legal scholars Jan Gwiazdomorski and Marian Zygmunt Jedlicki.

Defense of Academic Standards in Stalinist Poland

The old professoriate often managed to protect its protégés in the now vulnerable junior ranks. In 1949 the Warsaw education bureaucracy required the dismissal of eleven assistant professors in Toruń, thought to be a repository of anti-Soviet sentiment because of the presence of students and teachers from Wilno, a city absorbed by the Soviet Union in 1940. Yet almost immediately senior professors in Toruń began contacting colleagues elsewhere, and in the short run secured teaching positions for six of the eleven. In the end, nine of the eleven went on to make academic careers. In 1949 an ambitious five-year plan for removing junior and senior faculty in Polish studies emerged in the Central Committee of the PZPR, with a precise schedule by name and university. In all some ten professors were to be released for their ideological "hostility." In fact, only one was released, and then not until 1954.

This plan went unfulfilled in part because of the dire need for teachers, but also because top functionaries required the support of "progressive" professors in order to reach the over 90 percent of teachers who did not belong to the party. These "middlemen" were loath to cooperate in the removal of their own colleagues, and in fact attempted to assist them where possible. Such collusion between politically "loyal" and conservative scholars had a deadening effect on the party's attempts to advance its own candidates into the professoriate. It could not simply dictate its choices for scholarly appointments, but rather had to achieve majorities in the subcommissions that judged qualifications for the individual disciplines. Professors in and outside the party cooperated in gate-keeping through work in these subcommissions, because, as a Central Committee reporter ruefully noted, party members "did not wish to incur the disfavor" of their colleagues. The subcommissions became a form of "quality control" for Polish academia as a whole, limiting the ability of those departments with high political profiles to push their candidates through to professorship. PZPR members therefore entered academia at a leisurely pace: of 302 promotions to university docent or professor approved by the Central Commission between 1951 and 1954, 42 were party members.[23] In the end, a number of underqualified scholars entered universities, but because of the insistence on academic standards by certain

---

23. Archive of Modern Documents, Warsaw (AAN), KC PZPR 237/XVI/186, k. 5–6. Stomma is a legal scholar associated with the Kraków Catholic weekly *Tygodnik Powszechny*.

old professors, the party was forced to push its candidates, for example in Marxism-Leninism, onto less respected sidetracks, especially the less prestigious position of "acting professor" (*zastępca profesora*).

The pervasive presence of old professors also jeopardized the party's attempts to train new cadres for socialism. Even under the new study plans, old professors could continue directing students' work much as they always had, even in discontinued fields, like sociology. In the early 1950s sociologists, anthropologists, and legal scholars, such as J. Chałasiński, K. Dobrowolski, T. Szczurkiewicz, and J. Lande, were able to discuss the work of sociologists in courses on related subjects. In the lecture course "History of Pre-capitalist Formations" at Łódź University Chałasiński introduced students to the work of Montesquieu, Locke, and Malinowski.[24] In 1950–51 Lande still taught and examined in sociology, including the works of Vico, Durkheim, G. Tarde, Simmel, Guizot, Comte, P. Lilienfeld, and Spencer; and though he taught Marx he advised his students not to treat Marxism as a "dogma." In a seminar on legal philosophy offered in 1951–52, Lande contrasted Marxist approaches to those of his teacher Leon Petrażycki, for example, on the origins of law. Not a single work of Marx, Engels, or Lenin figured on the reading list, and there was no mention whatsoever of Soviet authors.[25]

Various standard courses on the law in Kraków were equally traditional. Lande's colleague Ludwik Ehrlich gave a two-semester course on the history of international law in the academic year 1951–52, and mentioned Soviet approaches only in lecture no. 28 of 13 November, which he introduced as follows: "Today, in keeping with a decision of the law faculty council I will discuss Soviet scholarship on international law." The following day he returned to his schedule, and for the rest of the year neither Marxist nor Soviet theories were a subject of discussion; the October Revolution was not mentioned, let alone accorded special relevance to human history. Ehrlich had identified his preferred methodology at the

---

24. Antonina Kłoskowska, "Bunty i służebności uczonego," in *Bunty i służebności uczonego: Profesor Józef Chałasiński*, ed. Leszek Wojtczak et al. (Łódź: Wydawnictwo Uniwersytetu Łódzkiego, 1992), 14–15. In 1953–54, T. Szczurkiewicz, sociologist of Poznań University, was giving lectures on "selected questions of philosophy" to students of archeology, psychology, and musicology. *Spis wykładów na rok akademicki, 1953/54* (Poznań, 1953).

25. Rather, the seminar list includes works of H. Kelsen, E. Bierling, F.-S. Somlo, E. Westermarck, G. S. Seidler, L. Duguit, and G. Gurvitch. The third week considered the concept of "freedom" based on writings of C. Znamierowski and L. Petrażycki. APAN-W, III-47, j. 35/98; j. 30, 37.

outset: "neopositivism."[26] Tadeusz Silnicki taught canon law at Jagiellonian University in the early 1950s. He dwelt at length on the threats to "freedom of conscience" in the new constitution and concluded, "When the state did battle with the church, it usually came to regret it."[27] Typed lecture notes on West European law still in use in Kraków in 1949 included the following passage: "In 1923 Soviet Russia attempted to create a federal state of Soviet Socialist republics united by a common constitution. Yet because of Soviet terror this constitution remains an illusion."[28]

In the lectures and evaluations of many old professors Marxist methodology seems a thin veneer overlying rather straightforward social and political history. Ironically, it was those who took Marx most seriously, like historians Witold Kula, Marian Małowist, and Stefan Kieniewicz, who proved most resistant to treating Marxism as orthodoxy. Evaluations of students' work by "progressive" scholars such as Kazimierz Wyka, Kazimierz Lepszy, and the "loyal" nonparty historian Tadeusz Manteuffel show the barest traces of official doctrine. In judgments of master's theses there is no mention of Soviet literature, and only very rarely of Marxist "classics." In one case Lepszy recommended the work of Karl Kautsky. He did not discriminate against more traditional history-writing, for example, of Anna Owsińska, whom he praised for "source-based, independent, and creative" discussions of German policies in Poland during World War I and the Polish question at Versailles.[29]

---

26. The course was based on the work of Lassa Oppenheim and made reference to the thought of Augustine, Gracian, Thomas Aquinas, Innocence IV, Paweł Włodkowic, Jan Długosz, Andrzej Frycz Modrzewski, Piotr Skarga, Achilleis, Livius, F. de Vitoria, and F. Suarez. In a treatment of the question of just wars, Ehrlich cited the Polish thinker Konstanty Święcicki, who in 1763 had opposed alliances with "tyrants" as "collusion with injustice." Manuscript Collections, Jagiellonian University Library, Kraków (Rkp BJ) Przyb. 93/73.

27. Report from 1951. AAN, KC PZPR 237/XVI/80, k. 36.

28. The author was Stanisław Estreicher. This was one of many examples of teaching at law faculties mentioned at a central PZPR meeting on higher education of 7 May 1949. AAN, KC BO tom 8, k. 143.

29. Of Owsińska's inability to become passionate about the project of the institute to which she was attached—the socioeconomic history of the Polish Enlightenment—Lepszy wrote, "I am of the conviction that one has to take account of the individual interests of every historian." Letter to Ziembiński, 4 September 1955, Rkp BJ Przyb. 785/73. Evaluations of doctoral dissertations and master's theses are in Rkp BJ Przyb. 781–84/73. Lepszy's letter of recommendation for Adam Przyboś for a professorship at the Higher Pedagogical School in Kraków, dated 3 December 1951, praises his "mastery of historical method, precision . . . Benedictine working habits, and intimate knowledge of the epoch." Unlike evaluations for such an advanced position in Czechoslovakia or the German Democratic Republic, this letter contains

Students had simple choices when looking for role models; they could identify with scholars of outstanding erudition and professional and personal self-confidence, like legal historian Adam Vetulani or Polonist Stanisław Pigoń, or with the half-educated and outnumbered representatives of Marxist-Leninist scholarship. To give some sense of the continued numerical dominance of the old professoriate: in 1953 law students in Kraków had eighteen hours of lecture in their first semester, of which thirteen were with nonparty professors Vetulani (history of Polish state and law), Lande (theory of state and law), Patkaniowski (general history of state and law), and Władysław Wolter (logic). The five remaining hours were in Marxism-Leninism and political economy, and taught by individuals holding only master's degrees or doctorates. In the course of their studies, these law students had 60 percent of their lectures with full and associate professors.[30] In history, a faculty that had lost five major figures to emigration, death, and retirement, the total was 35.8 percent.[31]

Communist academics lived ghettoized existences in institutes of political economy or Marxism-Leninism, invariably places where the teaching staff did not have full academic qualifications. All too frequently, prominent party academics in the social sciences and humanities lost their positions because of allegations of plagiarism. The most sensational case was that of prewar Communist and historian Leon Grosfeld, who acted as prorector at the Institute of Social Sciences and deputy director of the institute of history at the Polish Academy of Sciences, until in 1956 extensive excerpts without attribution were found in his work from J. Ryng (Z dziejów kapitalizmu w Polsce, 1948).[32] The major Communist representative at Lublin University, Witold Reiss, was removed after professors there discovered his plagiarisms of work by R. Taubenszlag. A leading figure in the Poznań university PZPR organization, historian Władysław Rogala, was to conclude work on a doctorate in 1951, but the

---

no mention of historical materialism, "social work," or the results of Soviet scholarship. Rkp BJ Przyb. 784/73.

30. If one excludes Marxism-Leninism and political economy, that figure rises to 75.3 percent. *Spis wykładów na rok akademicki, 1953–54* (Kraków, 1953). Law students in Poznań had 58.8 percent of their lectures with associate and full professors (73.2 percent when one excludes Marxism-Leninism and political economy). *Spis wykładów na rok akademicki, 1953–54* (Poznań, 1953).

31. These were J. Feldman, W. Konopczyński, W. Sobieski, S. Kutrzeba, and S. Kot. *Spis wykładów na rok akademicki, 1953–54* (Kraków, 1953). The total in Poznań was 37.3 percent. *Spis wykładów na rok akademicki, 1953–54* (Poznań, 1953).

32. *Słownik historyków polskich* (Warsaw: Wiedza Powszechna, 1994), 165.

date of his defense had to be postponed indefinitely, because the dean's office began to suspect that his master's diploma was a forgery.[33]

Again and again, the party's candidates for professorship proved to be academically inadequate. PZPR historians Józef Sieradzki and Celina Bobińska were imposed on Jagiellonian University despite doubts of the faculty council; neither could compete with older professors when it came to attracting students for thesis seminars. S. Rogowski, the major party figure in Polish studies at Toruń university, did not complete a doctorate until 1961 and never wrote a *habilitacja*. Likewise Jerzy Ziomek, the leading party representative in Polish studies at Wrocław University until his transfer to Poznań, did not have a doctorate. Shortage of cadres made it difficult even to get competent figures to manage basic organizations. The head of the university committee of the official youth organization (ZMP) in Wrocław had to be released in 1952 after declaring at an open party meeting that "we will win the elections, because there has never been a case in history when a government in power suffered an electoral defeat."[34]

A basic index of the party's failure to win the younger generation was the relatively low membership of students in the party. By 1953 barely 9 percent of Polish students were PZPR members, and by 1958 that total declined to 2.5 percent.[35] They proved even more "conservative" than their professors, among whom party membership in the same period had increased from 10.7 to 11.4 percent.[36] By way of contrast, in the same period party membership among Czech professors exceeded one-half, and among students one-third.

Academia During and After the Polish October

The events of autumn 1956 (the "Polish October"), in particular the accession to power of Władysław Gomułka, are taken by historians to be

---

33. Letter of 8 July 1951 by Kazimierz Piwarski, APAN-K, KIII-24, j. 109. The party's personnel officer at the Silesian Medical Academy had forged his high school diploma. AAN, KC PZPR 237/XVI/77, k. 12.

34. AAN, KC PZPR 237/XVI/25, k. 98. In early 1956 the party's two leading assistant professors at Toruń University's Faculty of Fine Arts had to be fired because of incompetence. Both had been party secretaries of the faculty and had been political appointees. "Błędy, ktore się mszczą," *Trybuna Ludu*, 5 May 1956.

35. Ibid., 134, 173; Barbara Fijałkowska, *Polityka i twórcy (1948–1959)* (Warsaw: PWN, 1985), 464.

36. Hübner, *Nauka polska*, 174, 210.

a major shift in the political constellation of postwar Poland. Professors who had lost the right to teach were reinstated, discontinued fields blossomed anew, and in general, the party retreated from the campus, recognizing significant autonomy. In September the Polish parliament passed legislation that returned to universities the right to elect rectors, deans, prorectors, and assistant deans, who during Stalinism had been nominated by the minister. Now the minister had to consult with universities before introducing changes in higher education, and the rector was obliged to consult with university senates before important decisions.[37] Yet universities were not only beneficiaries of this process, they also actively contributed to it, especially through the activities of students. The crisis of confidence that became apparent in the course changes and reversals after Stalin's death three years earlier had encouraged discussions of reform among young intellectuals, which grew into a broad movement, whose center of gravity was the student magazine *Po prostu* (Frankly speaking). Yugoslavia, with its model of worker self-management, seemed to demonstrate that a more humane socialism was feasible.

The major organization through which university students attempted to realize their demands was the Union of Polish Youth (ZMP), whose Warsaw University organization had fallen into the hands of later famous party dissidents including Jacek Kuroń, Karol Modzelewski, and Krzysztof Pomian.[38] They demanded the publication of inner-party discussions, justice for perpetrators of Stalinism, precise regulation of censorship, and decriminalization of "hostile propaganda." From July 1956 these "revolutionary students" sustained close contacts with workers at the automotive factory FSO Żerań.[39] In September they created the first organization uniting students of Warsaw with those of other cities. At the same time students elsewhere began establishing liasons with workers.[40]

Perhaps the most radical students were to be found in conservative Kraków, where a semi-clandestine "Club of the Burning Tomato" had emerged in January 1956. In the fall, members in this group attempted to wrest control of the city administration from the authorities through various maneuvers, such as setting up, for example, their own militia and

---

37. Jakub Karpiński, *Countdown: The Polish Upheavals of 1956, 1968, 1970, 1976, 1980* (New York: Karz-Cohl, 1980), 80.
38. This had occurred in April 1956. Andrzej Friszke, *Opozycja polityczna w PRL, 1945–1980* (London: Aneks, 1994), 73.
39. Ibid., 75, 78.
40. Ibid., 78.

housing committees. Yet by early 1957, enjoying wide support in a population that had been deeply impressed by the Hungarian Revolution, Gomułka began to immobilize the independent factory and university committees. Pro-Gomułka "normalizers" now gained prominence within a new all-Polish youth organization, the Union of Socialist Youth (ZMS), and with police pressure, including arrests, managed to marginalize prodemocracy forces by the end of the year.[41] Concluding acts from this time of crushed hopes are well known: *Po prostu* was forced to cease publication in October 1957, and the following year a general party purge removed "revisionists"; gradually popular reformers in the party leadership, like W. Bieńkowski and J. Morawski, were shunted aside; and in a final scene, the intelligentsia discussion group the "Crooked Circle" was closed following a police provocation in 1962. Several of its prominent members had been university professors.

Yet new life was already visible in the ruins of October. The universities, especially in Warsaw, remained relatively independent of party interference until 1968, and thick networks of professional friendships, extending deep into the milieus of the artistic and literary intelligentsia, made for a rather cohesive intellectual elite. Meetings were less formal than in the time of the Crooked Circle, and took place in cafes, clubs, editorial boards, and even "salons."[42] Professors remained professionally interested in maintaining high levels of research and teaching, and as a partial consequence, broad spheres of free discussion remained intact. As Andrzej Friszke argues, it was impossible, especially in the social sciences, to fully separate academic and public freedoms of expression. Academics' support for the latter may not have derived from general sympathies for the opposition, but rather sprang from "a defense of the code of values of the scholar and the autonomy of the university."[43]

Academic staff were at the center of political confrontation in the early 1960s. In 1961 university researcher Henryk Holland plunged to his death from his Warsaw apartment, perhaps in an attempt to escape the secret police, perhaps at their hands. His funeral attracted several dozen party intellectuals united by an increasing sense of alienation from the Gomułka leadership—which duly punished them for their attendance. This event is often seen as the crystallization of a new left intellectual

---

41. Ibid., 90–91.
42. Ibid., 130.
43. Ibid., 159.

opposition.⁴⁴ The following year Anna Rudzińska of the university's philosophical faculty was arrested and tried for translating Feliks Gross's *The Seizure of Political Power in a Century of Revolutions*. In 1964 the historians Ludwik Hass and Romuald Śmiech were imprisoned as Trotskyites,⁴⁵ and thirty-four professors and writers drafted a letter protesting censorship and defending "culture." In 1965 the young lecturers J. Kuroń and K. Modzelewski were convicted of having criticized the party leadership in an "open letter" for its bureaucratism, which "robbed the working class of any organization, program, or means of self-defense."⁴⁶

Much of the university community manifested solidarity with the persecuted dissenters. On 15 April 1964 some two thousand students attended a rally in front of the library at Warsaw University to express support for the authors of the letter of thirty-four, many of whom had come under massive pressure to withdraw their signatures.⁴⁷ In July 1965 a number of students expressed solidarity with Kuroń by striking up the "International" outside the courthouse where he was sentenced. Horrified over this expropriation of a sacred hymn, Central Committee functionaries demanded that six of the students involved be expelled from the university. First, however, the university disciplinary commission had to be consulted, and here a number of well-known professors (M. Ossowska, W. Kula, J. Zakrzewska, Z. Bauman) defended the accused. Several others scholars attended the proceedings as "observers" (T. Kotarbiński, W. Brus, B. Baczko, A. Mączak). Three of the students were suspended for a year, but the other three were only censured. As a result party authorities directed the Ministry to alter regulations in order to permit the university rector to dismiss students without consulting university organs of self-governance.⁴⁸ In this sense, the state assured itself of greater repressive force than it had possessed in the Stalinist era.

The persecuted students belonged to a group at Warsaw University known as the "commandos," which had about thirty core members and

---

44. Witold Jedlicki, *Klub Krzywego Koła* (Paris: Instytut Literacki, 1963).

45. Peter K. Raina, *Political Opposition in Poland, 1954–1977* (London: Poets' and Painters' Press, 1978), 95.

46. The letter called for the introduction of workers' councils as well as "full freedom of the press, of scientific and cultural activity, of formulating and propagating various trends of social thinking." Modzelewski received three and a half and Kuroń three years in prison. Raina, *Political Opposition in Poland*, 82–87; Friszke, *Opozycja polityczna*, 156–59. The letter is reproduced in Jacek Kuroń, *Revolutionary Marxist Students in Poland Speak Out, 1964–1968* (New York: Merit Publishers, 1969).

47. Friszke, *Opozycja polityczna*, 152–53.

48. Ibid., 228–29.

several dozen sympathizers. The group had roots in a "Club of Seekers of Contradictions" founded in April 1962 by the high school students Jan T. Gross and Adam Michnik and the university student Jan Kofman. They and their friends tended to come from old communist families, and read widely, especially in Marxist revisionist literature. Warsaw philosophy professor Leszek Kołakowski made space available to them at the university, but under pressure of the top party leadership the Club had to dissolve in the summer of 1963. Yet its members continued to meet informally, and by the fall of 1964 had enrolled at the university. They became known as "commandos" because of their assault on taboos: in a meeting on foreign affairs in 1967 Michnik, for example, embarrassed Gomułka's secretary Walery Namiotkiewicz with a question about the Molotov-Ribbentrop pact.[49]

Michnik dared speak these words though he had been threatened several times before with expulsion, most recently in October 1966, after a lecture the commandos held with Leszek Kołakowski "commemorating" the tenth anniversary of Gomułka's accession to power. Kołakowski delivered a withering critique of the de facto lawlessness of People's Poland, for which he was expelled from the party. The PZPR Central Committee then directed the Ministry of Higher Education to demand the expulsion of eight students most active in the critical discussion accompanying this lecture, as well as disciplinary measures against eight more. History professors S. Herbst, H. Samsonowicz, and A. Garlicki defended the endangered students by testifying that their behavior did not "go beyond accepted norms." In all, 1,036 students and 150 academics signed a petition urging the rector to drop the proceedings. Impressed more by pressure from below than above, the rector reinstated all students save Michnik, who was suspended for a year.[50] The university entered the year 1968 a relatively cohesive body.

March 1968

Because of the shift they initiated away from Marxist "revisionism" and toward the noncommunist dissidence of the 1970s, the events of March 1968 have come to be seen as a turning point in the history of the Polish

---

49. Other leading "commandos" included Seweryn Blumsztajn, Jan Lityński, and Barbara Toruńczyk. Ibid., 229, 233.

50. Ibid., 233–34.

intelligentsia, but central questions remain unanswered. Early in the month, Warsaw's students mobilized against the cancellation of Adam Mickiewicz's *Forefather's Eve*, whose anti-Russian accents had been applauded by standing-room-only audiences.[51] The play, written by Poland's leading poet in an earlier time of national oppression, had near mythic quality for many Poles, as it seemed to give meaning to current plight, and the closing outraged national sensibilities. Given the dimensions of the ensuing confrontation, and the evidence it gave of Gomułka's weakening grip on power, historians have wondered about the degree to which the March events were provoked by his nationalistic opponents, specifically the interior minister Mieczysław Moczar. Were they actually a spontaneous outburst of dissent or were they a sequence of events staged by one faction in the party leadership?[52]

What is indisputable is that the March Events displayed the solidarity of university communities throughout Poland and that they triggered the severest repression of these communities in the postwar era. Several "commandos" had attended the final performance of *Forefathers' Eve*, and with some five hundred others demonstrated against its cancellation (a poster demanded "further performances!").[53] Protest resolutions circulated among Warsaw students and accumulated 3,145 signatures before submission to the Sejm. In addition, almost one thousand signatures were collected in Wrocław.[54] The Union of Polish Writers (ZLP) held a heated meeting condemning the cultural policies of the government, but student leaders hesitated in calling for a demonstration of their own, fearing repercussions—several were out of prison on parole. But the expulsion from the university of Adam Michnik and Henryk Szlajfer on 3 March moved them to action. Karol Modzelewski later explained: "We

---

51. The play was closed on order of the Ministry of Culture and Art. Andrzej Paczkowski, *Pół wieku dziejów Polski* (Warsaw: PWN, 1995), 364. The play included lines such as "Am I to be free? Yes! Where this news came from I do not know, but I am alive to what it means to be free under the hands of a Moscovite. These scoundrels? They only take the fetters off my hands and feet, but crush my soul" and "Moscow sends only rogues to Poland." Raina, *Political Opposition in Poland*, 113–14.

52. For a discussion of competing arguments about March, see Marcin Kula, Piotr Osęka, and Marcin Zaremba, eds., *Marzec 1968: Trzydzieści lat później* (Warsaw, PWN: 1998). Soon after the events of March 1968, Zygmunt Bauman maintained that the Moczar group had staged the provocation in order to cause a growing student movement to exhaust itself before it had reached full strength. They may have feared that, as in Czechoslovakia, students would activate the liberal wing of the party. Friszke, *Opozycja polityczna*, 239.

53. Ibid., 240–41.

54. Ibid.; Raina, *Political Opposition in Poland*, 115.

had been active as a group, but only two of us were singled out for punishment. Under those circumstances we could not remain silent."[55]

Several thousand students gathered for a protest demonstration on 8 March. Now for the first time in memory, police encroached upon university premises and indiscriminately punished those in attendance with their truncheons. This had the effect of mobilizing even more students to protest. The following day a large meeting was held at Warsaw Polytechnic, after which a column of students advanced upon central Warsaw to protest anti-Semitism in the newspaper *Życie Warszawy*. But police intercepted the demonstrators and beat them with even greater zeal than on the previous day. Over a hundred students had to be hospitalized. Two days later over three thousand students demonstrated at Warsaw University against the arrests of Jacek Kuroń and leading commandos; they passed a resolution condemning the "violation of constitutional rights [and] interference by security services in academic life." Once again police provoked a violent confrontation, and students responded by torching police wagons. Scores were injured on both sides, and over seven hundred students were arrested. The party pressed forward its media campaign of hatred, explicitly identifying those among the commandos' leadership who were of Jewish background, and alluding to the high positions in the state and party apparatus supposedly held by their parents.[56]

Security forces instituted checks at train stations to seal off Warsaw from the outside. Nevertheless, between 11 and 14 March students clashed with the police across Poland, in old university milieus like Kraków, Poznań, and Wrocław, but also in the newer centers of higher education of Gdańsk, Katowice, Szczecin, and Łódź.[57] The most impressive mass protest was perhaps the sit-down strike held in Wrocław on 15–16 March, yet the greatest number of arrests, surpassing even those of Warsaw, took place in Gdańsk. In each place, students were drawn to action by news of the events of 8 March, somewhat embellished by an erroneous report that one student had been killed.

The sudden emergence of massive support for Warsaw's students came as a surprise, on the one hand because everyone knew that the regime was prepared to crush dissent with force, but on the other hand because students had been socialized in People's Poland, and presumably

55. Friszke, *Opozycja polityczna*, 243.
56. Raina, *Political Opposition in Poland*, 131.
57. Jerzy Eisler, *Marzec 1968: Geneza, przebieg, konsekwencje* (Warsaw: PWN, 1991), 243–50. Wrocław was the heir of the faculty and traditions of Lwów University.

insulated from subversive ways of thought. Tadeusz Lachowicz, who acted as associate dean of natural sciences in Wrocław in 1968, has recorded his amazement that "students who had been indoctrinated and lied to, who at every step encountered the discrepancy between theory and practice and as such were demoralized, suddenly, from one day to the other, showed a different face, that of patriotism, idealism, and solidarity, as well as a readiness to make sacrifices."[58] Indeed, the students surprised themselves. At the beginning, most took action impulsively, out of an elemental sense of community with their colleagues who had been injured in Warsaw. Almost as automatic was their outrage over the press coverage of student protest. None had ever experienced such distortion and manipulation of activities they themselves had been involved in. This was an important learning experience of the deeper realities of People's Poland.[59]

Over several weeks, student demands escalated, from calls for "democratic freedoms" and "freedom of press and association," to appeals for the foundation of "oppositional clubs of parliamentary deputies," respect for the freedoms guaranteed by the constitution (for example, of artistic production), unimpeded circulation of information, and the abolition of censorship. In the judgment of Andrzej Friszke, what began as a motley "collection of grievances" grew to the fullest statement of the democratic opposition seen since 1956.[60] Some controversy arose after the fact about whether the student movement was "left" or "right." Student speakers' constant references to "socialism" convinced Zygmunt Bauman that they desired a reform of socialism above all else.[61] Critics responded that students had no choice but to argue in these terms, but that what was really new in their resolutions were demands for democracy and freedom.[62]

58. "Mój marzec 1968," in *Studia i materiały z dziejów Uniwersytetu Wrocławskiego* (Wrocław: Wydawnictwo Uniwersytetu Wrocławskiego, 1994), 3:215.

59. For demands from Kraków, see Eisler, *Marzec 1968*, 257; for those from Wrocław, Edward Czapiewski, "Marzec 1968 roku i jego następstwa w moich wspomnieniach," in *Studia i materiały z dziejów Uniwersytetu Wrocławskiego* (Wrocław: Wydawnictwo Uniwersytetu Wrocławskiego, 1994), 3:222–35.

60. Paczkowski, *Pół wieku dziejów Polski*, 367, and the declaration adopted at a student meeting in Warsaw on 28 March 1968, drafted by Jakub Karpiński, Andrzej Mencwel, and Jadwiga Staniszkis, in Friszke, *Opozycja polityczna*, 245.

61. For example, one resolution drafted in Wrocław stated that "we want an improvement of our system . . . the discussions we are holding proceed from socialist positions." Eisler, *Marzec 1968*, 245. For Bauman's argument see his introduction to *Wydarzenia marcowe 1968* (Paris: Instytut Literacki 1969).

62. For a recapitulation and deepening of his disagreement with Bauman, first stated on the pages of *Kultura* (Paris) in 1969, see Jakub Karpiński's "'Krótkie spięcie' i obrazy marca 1968 roku," in *Marzec 1968: Trzydzieści lat później*, 314–28.

The reminiscences of one Wrocław student suggest an explanation that combines elements of both. Students argued in terms of socialism, not so much out of an internalized Marxist worldview, but rather because "socialism" was the major organizing concept of political life in postwar Poland, and the only idiom in which they might petition the government. Unlike their professors, many students had a naive faith in this government, something only police truncheons could beat out of them. To call them protoliberals suggests a different but also valid interpretation; resolutions did indeed demand essential civil liberties. What is striking, in other words, was not that students were antisocialist or anticapitalist, but that they entered confrontation politically unformed.[63] Thus the story of students in 1968 is a story, not only of how Polish regime permanently alienated many left-leaning intellectuals, but also of how it also disillusioned many more who had a basic yet amorphous sympathy for the goals of the government.[64] In this sense the March events signaled an even more dramatic erosion of the legitimacy of Polish Communism than we customarily assume from accounts focusing on the genesis of a new dissidence in the 1970s.

That these losses are not more broadly acknowledged among historians has to do with the "peace" that seemed to enter university life in Poland after 1968. Political peace was purchased at a high price: after the police and militia had broken up centers of student protest throughout Poland, many university departments, especially in the humanities, were closed for a time, and their students forced to reapply for admission. In all, some fifteen hundred Polish students thus lost their right to study.[65] The minister of education, historian Henryk Jabłoński, dismissed a number of famous supporters of the student protest, including philosopher Leszek Kołakowski, historian Bronisław Baczko, economist Włodzimierz Brus, and the sociologists Maria Hirszowicz, and Zygmunt Bauman.[66] At Warsaw University alone, 128 cases were later registered of academic employees (*pracownicy naukowi*) terminated for "other than academic reasons."[67] An estimated one thousand Jewish students and five hundred Jewish academics also left the world of Polish higher education and made

---

63. For these recollections see Czapiewski, "Marzec 1968," 222–35, esp. 227.
64. Paczkowski, *Pół wieku dziejów Polski*, 368.
65. Friszke, *Opozycja polityczna*, 247–49; Paczkowski, *Pół wieku dziejów Polski*, 366.
66. Friszke, *Opozycja polityczna*, 248.
67. Eisler, *Marzec 1968*, 446.

their way to Israel or the West in order to escape officially fomented anti-Semitism.[68] Subsequently historians would blame a number of university deans and rectors for demanding expulsions; more widespread was the practice of accepting dismissals of colleagues and students without protest.[69] At best some university authorities made it possible for persecuted colleagues to continue teaching at other universities.[70]

In the supposedly more liberal 1970s the regime attempted to control universities through more delicate means. Rather than dismiss ideologically troublesome faculty, the ministry now simply refused to extend contracts, or rejected professors' choices for doctoral students, or delayed applications for promotion. A basis for such operations was the higher education laws of 1968, which significantly reduced the university autonomies secured by laws of a decade earlier. For example, universities again lost their right to select rectors. This and other "reforms" were introduced in the name of technocratic efficiency. In fact, their goal was to make universities fully serve the state, above all by "training cadres," while keeping the voice of the academic community as weak as possible.[71]

As a result, universities of the 1970s were places of subtle intimidation, where conformism was rewarded and uncritical servility toward authorities held up as an ideal. In this atmosphere mediocrities advanced, most notoriously the "March docents," some 575 assistant (adjunct) professors who were made docents without *habilitacja*.[72] Few opposed state arbitrariness outright. Late in the decade, initiatives in dissent emerged within the Polish intelligentsia, most famously in KOR (Committee for the Protection of Workers), but university communities failed to be drawn in. Precisely for that reason Adam Michnik and his collaborators set up "flying universities," which met in private apartments and treated subjects that could not be taught at universities, especially in history, law, and literature.

---

68. Paczkowski, *Pół wieku dziejów Polski*, 371.
69. These condemnations were voiced during the Solidarity period in the fall of 1980. Eisler, *Marzec 1968*, 446. For the case of a dean demanding the expulsion of a doctoral student who had been expelled from the party for a "hostile attitude toward party and government," see Jacek Kochanowicz, "Marzec 1968 i życie intelektualne Uniwersytetu," in Kula, Osęka, and Zaremba, *Marzec 1968. Trzydzieści lat później*, 134.
70. Kochanowicz, "Marzec 1968," 139.
71. Ibid., 137–38.
72. Ibid., 137. At this time there was a total of 4,500 professors and docents in Poland.

Conclusion

Despite dictatorship, Polish universities maintained and defended academic freedoms to a degree that was not matched in other countries surveyed in this volume, with the possible exceptions of Czechoslovakia in the period 1965–69, and Spain in the 1960s. The question is why. It would be a mistake to accord Polish academics some inherently superior appreciation of the values of autonomy and freedom. Rather, what becomes clear in comparative study is the importance of a university's place in relations between state and civil society. In Poland the decisive question for legitimation of the state was control over the discourse of the nation.[73] Because of Poland's special history—in particular the crushing of Polish cultural institutions under Russian rule in the nineteenth century—universities were able to lay claim to a special role in articulating the interests of the nation. That role was strengthened during World War II, when university faculty and students took leading roles in the anti-Nazi resistance. In contrast to the situations in Hungary or Germany, the war had intensified the legitimacy of universities in the public eye. The Communists understood this fact and moved tentatively against them, fearful that by crushing these Polish cultural institutions they might come to occupy the space in the national memory associated with tsarism, Bolshevism, and Nazism—the enemies of Poland.[74]

Chinese or Russian Communists did not have comparable concerns. In China and Russia considerations of national interest made academic freedom appear secondary. Primary was rapid industrialization. In Wilhelmine Germany too, higher education was valued as a means to help assert national pride. In Poland, however, early industrialization had taken place under foreign auspices. Unlike Chinese counterparts, who saw in Communism a chance to emerge from a history of underdevelopment, Polish intellectuals after World War II feared a new round of exploitation in an expanding imperial system. This wariness translated into low numbers of Polish students and professors in the PZPR, which though Polish was seen as serving Russian interests.

---

[73]. On the efforts expended by Poland's Communists to lay claim to the national discourse, see Marcin Zaremba, *Komunizm, legitymizacja władzy komunistycznej w Polsce* (Warsaw: Wydawnictwo TRIO, 2001).

[74]. It was commonplace for Polish students in the postwar period to vilify Polish riot police as "Gestapo," for example.

The upshot of the party's relative restraint was persistence of the university community as a place where people could ask questions that could not be imagined elsewhere in Polish society. In this perhaps most important sense, Polish universities were more a threat than a support to the Polish dictatorship. They were outposts of freethinking in the relatively freest society in the Soviet sphere. Polish students experienced a kind of shock upon enrollment, and became gradually sensitized to injustices and hypocrisies that had lain beyond their intellectual horizons, given the media restrictions of provincial Poland. Equally important, universities schooled the young in alternative visions. For five years, they could read forbidden texts in university libraries (professors provided permission slips) and probe uncensored ideas within seminars, consultations, and student clubs. Polish universities were not "mass" universities like their counterparts in the West, and generally students got to know their professors, especially those who guided undergraduate theses (students referred to these professors as "promoters" or "masters").[75] These theses often tackled difficult and politically problematic issues, and therefore did not find wide readerships, but students found broader audiences through underground publications such as journals, pamphlets, and books. State-funded university dormitories of major universities harbored thousands of illegal publications, tucked away in closets and desk drawers.

Professors supported students who were endangered because of such activities (or the occasional public demonstration), by refusing, for example, to cancel their student status. Academics did not view their activities in narrowly professional or apolitical terms. As Warsaw historian Jacek Kochanowicz has written, despite the devastations of 1968, "a certain characteristic model of intellectual and scholar could continue to operate, someone who, while representing a high professional level, did not limit himself to professional activities, but rather via newspaper articles, essays, public readings, or simply at the table of a cafe continued to influence the thinking of people beyond his specialty."[76] And despite the influx of "March docents" a sense of community solidarity survived at universities that minimized the ability of the party to impose its own nominees upon universities. This solidarity made it harder for the regime to divide and rule, pitting students against faculty, in the way counterparts did in Russia, China, or Czechoslovakia: never did a massed "red studentry" or

---

75. Kochanowicz, "Marzec 1968," 131.
76. Ibid., 132.

studentocracy threaten to overthrow established university hierarchies.[77] In Poland students or workers were more likely to see their (national) enemy in Communist functionaries than in the old professors.

Paradoxically, this argument about Polish nationalism makes the least sense in Poland itself: precisely the national discourse causes the nuances of international comparison to seem trivial. Poles don't compare the sovietization of Poland to the sovietization of other countries. In their view, the transformations of Polish higher education, even if less severe than in Hungary or East Germany, were devastating enough. This seems particularly true for observers on the right, where concern for the suffering of historic Poland approaches an obsession. Certainly up to the Solidarity period, their arguments appear convincing: a visitor to Poland in 1979 might well have said that Polish universities were producing an intelligentsia of the sort described by Milovan Djilas or George Konrad and Ivan Szelenyi. Far from subverting socialism, universities solidified it; they graduated "clerks" who betrayed Poland. Polish universities performed well the task that American activist Mario Savio accused all universities of doing, of "turning out people with all the sharp edges worn off, the well-rounded person."[78]

That pessimistic view makes less sense when one considers what happened the following year: after the trade union Solidarity was legalized, the intelligentsia entered and massively supported it. Allowed to vote freely, professors and students elected colleagues who represented democratic reform; historians and other social scientists explored unknown pasts and probed unimagined futures; university senates rehabilitated the victims of 1968; and in December of 1981, trade union cells at universities were among the last to surrender to martial law. They were far from pacified when the strikes broke down, but rather resisted attempted "restructurings" throughout the 1980s. Like the reforms of the 1970s, these were meant to effect better state control in higher education.

Still, it would be a simplification to speak of universities as saboteurs of socialism. Universities, like the overwhelming majority of Polish citizens, supported the regime in an "objective" sense: they worked for it, out of

---

77. This issue is dealt with at greater detail in my *Captive University: The Sovietization of East German, Czech and Polish Higher Education* (Chapel Hill: University of North Carolina Press, 2000).

78. Leora Maltz, *The Cold War Period, 1945–1992* (Farmington Hills, Mich.: Greenhaven Press, 2003), 154.

necessity, but not without frequent, sometimes severe misgivings.[79] Even the bulk of the party's cadres served the regime out of perceived necessity, as is suggested by the relatively smooth transition of that party to social democracy after 1989. One might helpfully distinguish between the roles in politics and economy played by university graduates, and those played by university communities, in particular students. Like cohorts in other societies, the former group, suddenly compelled to make a living on their own, found itself amenable to compromises. If these were made with the state, that was because the state was practically the sole employer in Poland. It also was the primary supplier of apartments, health benefits, vacations, and university education for the "new class's" children.

These children, however, once students, tended to act with little regard for the practical consequences of their actions. Here one sees evidence of Poland's romantic tradition, which had emerged under foreign rule in the nineteenth century, and made calculating consequences seem almost immoral, provided that the cause seemed a grand one: the protection of national culture, defense of the university's corporate rights, or solidarity with those suffering persecution. One might speak of a reinforcement of conventional forms of academic autonomy by particular historical traditions. In a broader context, one is again reminded about what was strange in the Polish situation: not so much a particular love of freedom on the part of academics, but an institutional and discursive context that gave this concept meaning and force.

---

79. Hirszowicz, *Bureaucratic Leviathan*, 195.

8

Resistance to the Sovietization of Higher Eduction in China

DOUGLAS STIFFLER

Shall we make Beijing University into a recreation hall, perhaps a rendezvous for a few men of culture, or a training center for revolutionary cadres?
—CCP historian He Ganzhi, 1949, quoted in Maria Yen, *The Umbrella Garden*

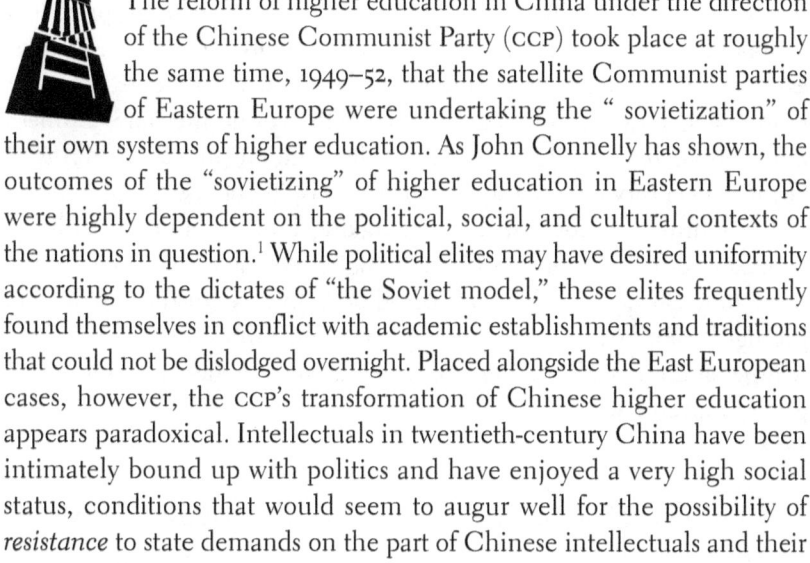

The reform of higher education in China under the direction of the Chinese Communist Party (CCP) took place at roughly the same time, 1949–52, that the satellite Communist parties of Eastern Europe were undertaking the " sovietization" of their own systems of higher education. As John Connelly has shown, the outcomes of the "sovietizing" of higher education in Eastern Europe were highly dependent on the political, social, and cultural contexts of the nations in question.[1] While political elites may have desired uniformity according to the dictates of "the Soviet model," these elites frequently found themselves in conflict with academic establishments and traditions that could not be dislodged overnight. Placed alongside the East European cases, however, the CCP's transformation of Chinese higher education appears paradoxical. Intellectuals in twentieth-century China have been intimately bound up with politics and have enjoyed a very high social status, conditions that would seem to augur well for the possibility of *resistance* to state demands on the part of Chinese intellectuals and their

---

1. John Connelly, *Captive University: The Sovietization of East German, Czech, and Polish Higher Education, 1949–1956* (Chapel Hill: University of North Carolina Press, 2000).

institutions. The historical record of the CCP's transformation of higher education in the early 1950s suggests, however, that Chinese institutions of higher education and the intellectuals associated with them were "transformed" without significant resistance (contrary to the cases of Poland and the Czech lands), and with only minimal input from the institutions and intellectuals concerned. How can we explain the seeming paradox, in the Chinese case, of sociopolitically *significant* intellectuals, and their apparent failure to defend their interests and the interests of their institutions in the early 1950s?

In what follows, I will attempt to show that Chinese university leaders *did* try to defend their interests in a relatively brief (and heretofore overlooked) "window of opportunity" for negotiation with the regime that lasted from the entry of the CCP armies into Beijing in early 1949 to the hardening of the regime's stance toward the politically suspect bourgeoisie that resulted from Chinese entry into the Korean war in October 1950. Given the experiences of Chinese intellectuals immediately prior to 1949, their ability to negotiate with the triumphant Chinese Communist state was quite limited. Finally, I will suggest that in the cultural context of China, *institutionally based* resistance to the state was inherently suspect, thus, Western observers of the Chinese scene should not necessarily look to the universities *as institutions* to be the defenders of a nascent "civil society." Rather, Chinese universities should be seen as providing sociopolitical space for the nurturing of intellectuals whose *moral protests*, expressed individually or in the form of student movements, are their most effective means of bringing pressure to bear on the state. Chinese intellectuals have typically expressed these moral protests in terms of twentieth-century nationalist discourse, that is, in defense of the interests of the Chinese nation. In this way, taking into account the cultural context of CCP-led reform of Chinese higher education, we may understand how Chinese intellectuals could be both weak institutionally and yet highly significant and potentially powerful, a thorn in the side of the regime, and especially influential when acting together in spontaneous protest movements.

Chinese Higher Education Before the Communist Takeover

Two dictatorial regimes in succession attempted to reorganize the system of higher education that had developed in the early Republic, the first—

the Guomindang (GMD) (1927–49)—with only modest success and the second—the CCP (1949–present)—taking up and completing what the first regime had begun. In its origins and outlook, the GMD had much in common with the CCP. The GMD had been reorganized into a conspiratorial, Leninist party under the guidance of Soviet political and military advisers in the early 1920s. GMD cadres received training in the Soviet Union during the First United Front period (1924–27); some members were former anarchists and Trotskyites. The GMD, like the Communists in the early 1950s, pressed an agenda of central control and social transformation that included an extension of control over the Chinese system of higher education.[2]

The system of higher education that both GMD and CCP reformers sought to transform had developed in uneven and piecemeal fashion. The first modern, Western-style university in China was the Imperial University (*jingshi daxue tang*), founded after the otherwise abortive Hundred Days' Reform.[3] In April 1912, after the fall of the Qing dynasty, the university was renamed Beijing University (Beijing daxue xiao, or "Beida"). Under the leadership of Cai Yuanpei, who served as president of Beijing University from January 1917 to 1919, Beida underwent a transformation as Cai encouraged some of China's most reform-minded and radical intellectuals to take up professorships.[4]

In the early part of the Republican period (1912–27), there existed several basic types of institutions. Beijing University was the only national university, and fell directly under the jurisdiction of the Ministry of Education. Private schools founded by Chinese educators may be considered a second category. In this group was Tianjin's highly respected Nankai University, an institution founded by Zhang Boling (1876–1951), a graduate

---

2. On Guomindang rule during the Nanjing decade (1927–37), see Hung-mao Tien, *Government and Politics in Kuomintang China, 1927–1937* (Stanford: Stanford University Press, 1972); Lloyd Eastman, *The Abortive Revolution: China under Nationalist Rule, 1927–1937* (Cambridge: Harvard University Press, 1974); and Parks Coble, *Facing Japan: Chinese Politics and Japanese Imperialism, 1931–1937* (Cambridge: Council on East Asian Studies, Harvard University, 1991).

3. Timothy Weston, "Beijing University and Chinese Political Culture, 1898–1920" (Ph.D. diss., University of California, Berkeley, 1995), 14–33.

4. Cai was a holder of the *jinshi* degree, the highest examination degree under the imperial examination system, and had spent the years 1907–11 in Germany, where he graduated with a bachelor of arts from the University of Leipzig. As minister of education, Cai promoted the Humboldtian university model, which called for the spiritual cultivation of the "whole person," the encouragement of scholarship, and the autonomy of the university vis-à-vis the state. Ibid., 85–101.

of the Beiyang Naval Academy. Fudan University in Shanghai rose to prominence under the leadership of the Catholic layman Ma Liang (1840–1939). These institutions were generally founded by a charismatic educator who forged ties with local, modernizing elites. Some technical schools, such as the Beiyang College of Engineering, also resulted from the combined energies of charismatic founders and modernizing elites. Finally, the missionary institutions such as the American-funded Yenching University played a most important role in Republican higher education. Christian missionary schools such as Yenching in Beijing, St. John's in Shanghai, and Jinling University in Nanjing educated the children of a wealthy, semi-Westernized urban elite. The English spoken on many of the campuses gave these institutions something of the character of an alien cultural overlay on Chinese society. In all, there were some thirty-seven colleges and universities in China in 1922, and more than half of them were concentrated in the Beijing-Tianjin and Shanghai areas.[5]

The GMD-led Republican state asserted formal control over higher education by reorganizing the Ministry of Education in 1928. GMD-sponsored legislation supplied a new nationalist, modernizing credo for higher education: "Universities and professional schools must emphasize the applied sciences, enrich the scientific content of their courses, nurture people with specialized knowledge and skills, and mould healthy character for the service of nation and society."[6] In accordance with this new emphasis on higher education serving the nation, the GMD regime required all institutions of higher education to register with and be certified by the Ministry of Education. This process of winning accreditation forced the universities to comply with government regulations regarding financial strength and academic qualifications. The Ministry also required that the missionary colleges cease religious proselytizing and teach the new state ideology—Sun Yat-sen's Three Principles of the People. With the exception of St. John's University in Shanghai, all of the religious institutions complied with the new government directives.[7]

---

5. Et-tu Sun-Tzu, "The Growth of the Academic Community 1912–1949," in *The Cambridge History of China*, ed. Denis Twitchett and John K. Fairbank, vol. 13, *Republican China 1912–1949, part 2* (Cambridge: Cambridge University Press, 1983), 361–420.

6. "Zhongguo jiaoyu nianjian" [China Education Yearbook] (Shanghai: Kaiming shudian, 1934), part A, 16, quoted in Ruth Hayhoe, *China's Universities, 1895–1995: A Century of Cultural Conflict* (New York: Garland Publishing, 1996), 52.

7. Wen-hsin Yeh, *The Alienated Academy: Culture and Politics in Republican China, 1919–1937* (Cambridge: Harvard University Press, 1990), 167–82.

Believing that the Chinese education system was in serious need of rationalization and reform, the Chinese government asked the League of Nations to appoint a commission to study the education system and make recommendations. The commission, led by the German professor C. H. Becker, visited China in 1932 and identified a number of problems in Chinese higher education, most of which had, in fact, already come to the attention of Chinese educators themselves. These included serious geographical imbalances in the distribution of universities and colleges nationally, wasteful duplications in research and teaching, and an over-emphasis on politics, law, and humanities which seemed to indicate the continuance of the traditional view of higher education as a route into the civil service. Recommendations served to promote a continental European-style system (in contrast to American and British models) involving more state control and regulation of the universities to set priorities and assure academic standards, recommendations which the statist Guomindang regime was already inclined to find congenial.[8]

Besides the modest successes achieved in asserting a measure of state control over the private and missionary institutions, the Guomindang regime managed to address some of the other issues that had been raised by the commission. In 1930 approximately 59 percent of the 28,677 university and college students were studying in the fields of law, politics, and liberal arts, and only 21.2 percent were studying engineering and the sciences. In 1937, out of a total student body of 31,188 college and university students, only 32 percent were majoring in humanities and law and the percentage majoring in engineering and the basic sciences had increased to 36 percent.[9] The decrease in the percentage of students studying politics and law reflects increasing ideological control exerted by the Guomindang, just as the increase in the study of engineering and the basic sciences reflects the state's modernizing imperatives. Both of these trends were to continue and reach their consummation in the first years of the People's Republic.

Yet another trend started by the GMD that the CCP would continue was the establishment of party universities. One side of this process of

8. Suzanne Pepper, *Radicalism and Education Reform in 20th-century China: The Search for an Ideal Development Model* (New York: Cambridge University Press, 1996), 37–45; Hayhoe, *China's Universities*, 53–54; League of Nations' Mission of Educational Experts, *The Reorganization of Education in China* (Paris: League of Nations' Institute of Intellectual Co-operation, 1932).

9. Hayhoe, *China's Universities*, 52, 54.

"partification" (*danghua*), the assertion of a measure of ideological control over the universities, was the closure of institutions representing the greatest threat to the GMD's ideological hegemony. Shanghai University, founded with the help of the CCP in the early 1920s, and which emphasized Marxist social sciences, was closed in the GMD purge of Communists in 1927.[10] Subsequently, the anarchist-inspired National Labor University was established on the former campus of Shanghai University. This experiment was brought to an end in 1932 when the Labor University was shut down.[11]

The GMD sought to create a network of regional, party-controlled universities in its strongholds of central and southern China. These institutions included National Central University (Zhongyang daxue) in Nanjing, Zhejiang University in Hangzhou, and Zhongshan University in Guangzhou (Canton).[12] In particular, Zhongshan University became a model for other institutions to emulate in the "partification" process. Zhongshan's president, Zhu Jianhua, who would become minister of education in the early 1930s, established an Office of Political Education at the university that was directly responsible to the Central Committee of the GMD.[13] In other institutions, the state required that students be familiar with Sun Yat-sen's Three Principles of the People (nationalism, democracy, and the people's livelihood). The national flag, portraits of Sun Yat-sen, Sun Yat-sen uniforms, and party publications appeared on every campus. Military training for students became compulsory. Further, party youth organizations established branches on campus, and the GMD installed loyal cadres into school administrations.[14]

The GMD regime made these initial inroads into the universities and colleges in the 1930s amidst a deepening national crisis brought on in

---

10. Yeh, *Alienated Academy*.

11. Ming K. Chan and Arif Dirlik, *Schools into Fields and Factories: Anarchists, the Guomindang, and the National Labor University in Shanghai, 1927–1932* (Durham: Duke University Press, 1991).

12. Ruth Hayhoe, "Chinese Universities and the Social Sciences," *Minerva* 31, no. 4 (winter 1993): 478–503.

13. "The partification of higher education was not merely a question of gaining control. In theory, the *Three Principles of the People* was a comprehensive system that encompassed a unique approach to education. In reality, there was the experience of Zhongshan University for the Party to draw upon. In terms of concrete measures and programs, therefore, the partification of higher education amounted to an effort to remake China's colleges and universities in the image of Zhongshan University, as it emerged from the purification struggles of 1926." Yeh, *Alienated Academy*, 174.

14. Ibid., 176–79.

large part by the pressure of the Japanese military. The Japanese military's attempt to detach North China from the Chinese central government in 1935 caused renewed student activism and a tide of discontent with Chiang Kai-shek's policy of appeasement. On 9 and 16 December 1935, students and other urbanites demonstrated in Beijing, and a public National Salvation movement arose which called for resistance to Japan.[15] Despite the "partification efforts" on campuses in the 1930s, the limitations of Guomindang control became obvious in this period. Support for the party among faculty and students of institutions of higher education would erode even further during the course of World War II and especially during the Chinese civil war.

During World War II many institutions of higher education in GMD-controlled areas, like the national government itself, undertook epic evacuations to the interior of the country. The faculty, staff, and students of China's three most prestigious universities, National Beiping (Beijing University), Tsinghua, and Nankai universities, embarked on a journey from Beijing in the northeast to Kunming, Yunnan province, in China's far southwest, where they established National Southwest Associated University (Guoli xinan lianhe daxue, often abbreviated "Lianda").[16] Through these evacuations of entire institutions to China's interior, the Guomindang government aimed to preserve "national treasures," the intellectual elite who remained important to the legitimacy of any regime in China, and to deny the Japanese any chance of winning the allegiance of this elite.

Having made such efforts in wartime to maintain the allegiance of this intellectual elite, starting in the last several years of the war the Guomindang Party gradually lost their allegiance, together with that of students and urbanites. Wartime inflation, fueled by official corruption, served more than any other factor to undermine support for the Guomindang regime. Intellectuals spoke up against the Guomindang's dictatorial policies and corruption in the final years of the war, and the regime responded with crude repression. Meanwhile, the CCP in wartime, under the slogan of the United Front and resistance to Japanese aggression, had succeeded in recruiting patriotic students to its cause and had spread its control to one-quarter of China's rural population.[17]

15. Coble, *Facing Japan*.
16. John Israel, *Lianda: A Chinese University in War and Revolution* (Stanford: Stanford University Press, 1998).
17. James Yick, *Making Urban Revolution in China: The CCP-GMD Struggle for Beijing-Tianjin, 1945–49* (Armonk, N.Y.: M. E. Sharpe, 1995).

In all of the chaos and dislocations of the 1930s and especially the war years, it is nonetheless quite remarkable that the number of institutions of higher education and total enrollment grew markedly, testimony in part to the emphasis that the Guomindang had put on the growth of universities as a mark of national pride in the face of Japanese aggression. Whereas there had been a total of eighty-five colleges, universities, and professional schools enrolling 37,566 students in 1930, in 1945 the total number of institutions stood at 141, enrolling 83,498 students. Just two years later, the number of institutions of higher education grew to 207, with a total enrollment of 154,612 students.[18]

Even more salient than GMD support, however, was the growth of an urban middle class in the 1930s and 1940s which sought new education opportunities and a voice in politics. The growth of the popular press in these years is one index of the expansion of a politicized citizenry that had begun to link its own interests to those of the Chinese nation. This new, urban China tied to industry, commerce, and the modernizing state had been fostered by the GMD regime during the decades of its rule. During the civil war period, however, the GMD lost the support of this rising urban middle class: the years of war and general sense of exhaustion made this group hungry for a political alternative. In numbers and influence this group was too small to be decisive, but they were literate and politically aware, and occupied administrative and professional positions that were essential to the governmental machinery of any Chinese regime.[19] The growth in higher education shows that change had rapidly accelerated in the decades leading up to the Communist victory.

Regime Attitude on the Eve of the Takeover

In reforming Chinese higher education, the CCP could draw on several legacies. The most important legacy was that of the Republican-period institutions themselves, with which Chinese Communist leaders were familiar as graduates of some of these institutions. CCP leaders were also familiar with Soviet universities and cadre-training schools, since many had studied in the Soviet Union in the 1920s.[20] Finally, the CCP also founded its

---

18. Hayhoe, *China's Universities*, 56.
19. Coble, *Facing Japan*, 289–96.
20. In the 1920s two Soviet cadre-schools trained large numbers of Chinese Communists: one was the Communist University of the Laborers of the East (1921–36), and the other was

own schools, most notably Anti-Japanese University (Kangda), North Shaanxi Academy (Shaanbei gongxue), and North China University (Huabei lianhe daxue). These were not universities in the usual sense, but cadre-training schools which served to indoctrinate CCP cadres in current party policies, Western and Chinese revolutionary history, and organizational techniques of use in the war against Japan (1937–45) and the Chinese civil war (1946–49).[21] Such cadre-training schools offered a possible model for the reorganization of universities after 1949.

In adopting policies toward the Republican-era institutions, however, the Communists had to take into account the nature of these institutions and the class basis of the new regime. In his 1949 essay "On the People's Democratic Dictatorship," Mao Zedong stated that the new regime would be a coalition of four classes—workers, peasants, national bourgeoisie, and petite bourgeoisie—under the leadership of the working class. The Chinese Communist Party, as the vanguard embodying the class interests of workers, would lead the coalition. In Marxist-Leninist terms, this formulation was entirely orthodox for a colonized or semi-colonized country that had been engaged in a national revolutionary struggle.[22] The important thing about this formulation was that it implied moderate policies in the realm of higher education. The CCP leadership saw the universities both as important bases of support and as creatures of the national and petite bourgeoisie and determined not to disturb them too much in the immediate aftermath of the CCP victory. Winning over the urban middle classes, of whom the intellectuals formed a key part, would be required in order to successfully establish an urban-based regime.

The regime's basic policies in the cultural and education realm first took shape in the "Common Program of the Chinese People's Political

---

Sun Yat-sen University (1925–30). Famous Chinese revolutionaries who attended the latter include Deng Xiaoping, who attended in late 1926 and worked with Jiang Jingguo in the Communist Youth League organization, as well as Yang Shangkun, Dong Biwu, Ye Jianying, and Wang Ming. Miin-ling Yu, "Sun Yat-sen University in Moscow, 1925–1930" (Ph.D. diss., New York University, 1994), 90, 177–78.

21. For Communist Party training schools, see Jane L. Price, *Cadres, Commanders, and Commissars: The Training of the Chinese Communist Leadership, 1920–45* (Boulder, Colo.: Westview Press, 1976), and John Seybolt, "Yenan Education and the Chinese Revolution, 1937–1945" (Ph.D. diss., Harvard University, 1969).

22. The Chinese had discussed the four-class composition of the new state, and Stalin had expressed his approval of the formulation. See the section of Liu Shaoqi's 4 July 1949 letter to Stalin, "The New Political Consultative Council and the Central Government," in Andrei Ledovsky, "The Moscow Visit of a Delegation of the Communist Party of China in June to August 1949," *Far Eastern Affairs* 4 (1996): 73–78.

Consultative Conference," which served as the basic document establishing the regime's legal authority pending the adoption of a constitution. The first article of the Cultural and Educational Policy section reads as follows: "Article 41. The culture and education of the People's Republic of China are New Democratic, that is, national, scientific and popular. The main tasks of the cultural and educational work of the people's government shall be the raising of the cultural level of the people, training of personnel for national construction work, liquidating of feudal, compradore, fascist ideology and developing of the ideology of serving the people."[23] Excepting the reference to compradore and fascist ideology, the nationalist, technocratic thrust of this statement is in most respects identical to the Guomindang regime's educational ideals.[24] Leaders of institutions of higher education hoped for, and were led to expect, considerable moderation in the CCP's cultural and educational policies. Intellectuals were given further encouragement by the CCP leadership's appointment of noncommunist leftist intellectuals to prominent positions in the educational and cultural organs of the new regime.[25]

The Chinese Communist leadership made the inevitable decision that China would "lean to one side" both in international affairs and in its domestic policies, areas which—as Chen Jian has recently shown—were tightly intertwined.[26] The Chinese Communists carefully planned their takeover of mainland China, and their transformation of state and society. Domestically, the Chinese Communist leadership's goals were to quickly extend and consolidate control over Chinese society, to revive the

---

23. "Common Program of the Chinese People's Political Consultative Conference," in *Toward a New World Outlook: A Documentary History of Education in the People's Republic of China, 1949–1976*, ed. Shi Ming Hu (New York: AMS Press, 1976), 9–11.

24. For a helpful overview of Guomindang-era higher education policies, see Hayhoe, *China's Universities*, 42–60. See also Pepper, *Radicalism and Education Reform*, 37–45, 86–117.

25. Ma Xulun, appointed minister of education in 1949, was one such sympathetic "democratic personage" who had a long history of leftist political activity. Ma had served as vice-minister of education under the Guomindang in 1928–29, but resigned over personal differences with then minister of education and future Beijing University president Jiang Menglin. Ma continued to be a popular philosophy professor at Beijing University from 1931 to 1936, but his difficulties in getting along with Hu Shi and others resulted in his leaving. After the war, Ma was active in the Chinese Democratic League and fled to Hong Kong and then to Communist-held areas in northeast China when the GMD banned the democratic parties in 1947. Biography of Ma Hsu-lun, in *Biographical Dictionary of Republican China*, ed. Howard Boorman, 5 vols. (New York: Columbia University Press, 1967–79), 2:465–68.

26. Chen Jian, *Mao's China and the Cold War* (Chapel Hill: University of North Carolina Press, 2001), 1–16.

war-ravaged economy, and to prepare the ground for the industrialization of the People's Republic of China. Like Stalin, CCP leaders understood that national power and international recognition depended, ultimately, on industrialization. Further, the orthodox (Marxist-Leninist-Stalinist) conception of the building of socialism, and eventually of Communism, presupposed material abundance. Thus, it was entirely logical that the CCP leadership set their sights on Soviet-style industrialization, as this was necessary from both the ideological standpoint and for China's future (restored) role as a world power.

The main reason that the CCP leadership emphasized a speedy and successful takeover of the universities was their conviction that only the institutions of higher education could be counted on to produce cadres capable of building a powerful state and an industrialized nation. Without cadres, the CCP government would be weak and the nation poor. In their attention to higher education, the CCP leaders had learned well Stalin's dictum: "Cadres decide everything."

Other reasons for the CCP's attention to institutions of higher education are more closely linked to the Chinese sociopolitical context. Since the May Fourth Movement of 1919, university students in Beijing had taken the lead in calling for political and cultural transformations in China. Indeed, the Communist Party itself had gotten its start in the politically charged atmosphere of the post-1919 period, and many of the CCP's early leaders were university professors, students, and employees, in contrast to Eastern Europe, where many communist leaders were actively hostile toward universities and intellectuals.[27] Hence, the party was favorably disposed toward universities, seeing them as fertile grounds for recruits and for the building of support for CCP policies.

On the eve of the Communist takeover, student support for the Communists on the campuses of North China, particularly in Beijing-Tianjin, was strong, and Chinese university students took the lead (encouraged by underground Communist operatives) in agitating against American involvement in the Chinese civil war.[28] Anti-American demonstrations swept Chinese campuses in 1946–47 and were yet another factor that served to weaken the legitimacy of Chiang Kai-shek and the GMD regime. The Communists could thus count on strong support among activist

27. Connelly, *Captive University*, 114–17. On early CCP leaders, see Hans J. Van de Ven, *From Friend to Comrade: The Founding of the Chinese Communist Party, 1920–1927* (Berkeley and Los Angeles: University of California Press, 1991).

28. Yick, *Making Urban Revolution*, 94–111.

students, and the well-developed networks of Communist operatives, to bring the universities quickly under control.

Most teachers were ambivalent about the CCP. The nation's intellectual elite, concentrated in the universities of Beijing/Tianjin and Shanghai, had turned overwhelmingly against the GMD regime in the civil war years but were cautious about the Communists, adopting, in effect, a "wait-and-see" attitude. Institutions of higher education had been deeply influenced by American models and American culture, so the campuses were in many ways culturally alien to the peasant troops and lower-level Communist cadres who marched into Beijing in early 1949.

The Takeover

Chinese Communist armies surrounded the city of Beijing in December 1948. There the peasant soldiers of the CCP halted, awaiting the outcome of negotiations for the peaceful surrender of what was then a walled city. Yenching and Tsinghua universities were located in Haidian, outside the city walls and thus were the first to encounter Communist forces. As is reported in memoir literature of the period, students felt considerable excitement and enthusiasm about the arrival of the CCP armies.[29] An American teacher at the missionary-sponsored Yenching University described first contacts with Chinese Communist cadres:

> The day [Monday, 13 December 1948] was dull and overcast. . . . Our gates were guarded by both students and members of the faculty, but they were still open, and a steady stream of refugees, tugging bundles, was coming in. . . . Late on Wednesday, we learned that Communist troops were outside our gates and so we knew the change-over had taken place. [The next day] Lucius Porter was on twenty-four hour duty at the West Gate where he was in telephone communication with all parts of the campus. . . . He ordered the gate unbarred and found a very young political cadre accompanied by two soldiers. The cadre was unarmed, but the guards were fairly draped with weapons.

---

29. Philip West, *Yenching University and Sino-Western Relations, 1916–1952* (Cambridge: Harvard University Press, 1976), 136–72; Yen, *Umbrella Garden*, 1–22.

The first question asked was most disarming. "Has Yenching been hit during the fighting?" No. "Does Yenching need anything?"

The next day, a Chinese Communist cadre, a graduate of an American missionary middle school, spoke to the entire school at a meeting in Bashford Hall—today, the main administration building of Beijing University:

> The auditorium was crammed, for there were servants, and work people like gatemen and janitors, as well as students and us teachers. It was obvious that the speaker was ill at ease. He had probably never completed the work in our Middle School, and here he was talking to learned university students and their tremendously learned professors! So he was sweating profusely and began rather stumblingly. But . . . he soon recovered his self-confidence and gave us a glowing picture of our future, along with a proper pep talk about the virtues of our new masters. He was received with cordial applause, but the audience was not as thrilled as I expected us to be. The young man bowed, and went away followed by the two guards.[30]

The faculty, staff, and students of American-sponsored Yenching University had ample reason to be nervous during the Communist takeover, but the moderate behavior of the Communist cadres did much to allay initial fears.

In fact, the CCP takeover of institutions of higher education had been carefully thought out, as the party knew that intellectuals were a group absolutely critical to their success in the cities. Mao himself had ordered careful treatment of Yenching and Tsinghua universities during the seizure of power.[31] The party established military control committees to manage the takeover of civilian organs in the cities. In Beijing, the committee established a cultural subcommittee, which was chaired by Qian Junrui, a party education specialist soon to become vice-minister of education and head of the Ministry's party committee; this subcommittee in turn had sections for education, literature and arts, museums, and the press. Qian also headed the education section.

---

30. West, *Yenching University*, 90–91.
31. Mao Lirui and Shen Guangqun, eds., *"Zhongguo jiaoyu tongshi," di liu juan*, 2d ed. (Jinan: Shandong jiaoyu chubanshe 1995), 6:18–19.

The takeover process at other universities resembled that at Yenching University. First, school leaders, faculty, and staff were called to a meeting by the Communist cadres, informed of CCP takeover policies, and asked for suggestions. Then, the entire school was convened and informed of the takeover in a like manner. The universities were then overseen by several CCP military and civilian cadres, under the authority of the military control committees. The CCP overseers quickly began to provide financial support in the form of food; to organize the students, staff, and faculties; and to begin initial curricular reform, which in practice meant the abolition of Guomindang-sponsored political ideology courses and, where possible, the beginning of a CCP political ideology course. Such was the basic situation at Beijing-area institutions in early 1949. Takeover of universities in Shanghai and other areas in central and west China took place in basically the same manner in the summer of 1949.[32]

Student activists who had been underground party members played critical roles in mobilizing support for the new regime. Maria Yen, a senior at Beijing University in 1949–50 who subsequently fled to Hong Kong, detailed the enthusiasm with which many students greeted the Communists, and the process by which the CCP expanded its influence among students.[33] Because of substantial underground activity at Beijing universities from the mid-1940s the CCP could count on a large numbers of student cadres, as well as formerly underground party and Youth League members.[34] In the 1949–50 academic year, amid the excitement surrounding the Communist takeover, or "liberation" (*jiefang*, the word most often used in Chinese Communist discourse), and the establishment of the People's Republic on 1 October 1949, activist students in Beijing organized their classmates to provide input on conditions of university life. Students were required to join various "progressive" organizations based on the dormitory, department, academic specialty, and

---

32. Ibid., 15–24.
33. Maria Yen, *The Umbrella Garden: A Picture of Student Life in Red China* (New York: Macmillan, 1954). This memoir is loosely based on Maria Yen, *Hongqi xiade daxue shenghuo* (Hong Kong: Youlian chubanshe, 1952). The Chinese version is written in uncompromisingly negative, anticommunist terms, and uses harshly pejorative language. In contrast, the English memoir narrates the hopefulness of students during the Communist takeover, the students' participation in CCP-led activities, and the author's and other students' growing disillusionment with the political demands put on students by activist CCP and Youth League members at the university.
34. Yen, *Umbrella Garden*, 34. Here Yen describes the interest and surprise among students when it was revealed who had been an underground party or Youth League member in the late 1940s.

other university structures. These student-run committees, in turn, helped make decisions on such critical issues as student stipends, evaluations of professors and course content, and opportunities for further student work and study. Professors were criticized as thoroughly "bourgeois" and urged to reform their attitudes and serve the people.

As described by Maria Yen, professors were under considerable suspicion and enormous pressure in the first months of the People's Republic. On the eve of the Communist takeover, "activist" students had appealed to wavering professors and convinced some that the CCP needed them in the new society, and that they should not retreat with the Guomindang but remain at their posts. There had been many encouraging signs in the first months of Communist rule, especially the relatively high salaries, paid in grain coupons, that the new rulers offered the professors.[35]

But the CCP's reliance on the activist students, as well as pro-CCP faculty and staff, forced the professoriate into almost complete passivity from the outset of Communist rule. Many professors had memories of student activism in Republican-era universities, and some had participated in demonstrations, and therefore when faced with student activists in the late 1940s, they were apt to be cautiously supportive. But professors also acted out of self-protection in a situation in which they were defined as a large part of the problem. Most, whether out of guilt, sympathy, or self-preservation, claimed a desire to engage in political study, to make "progress," and keep up with the times. More than a little professorial guilt came across to Maria Yen in her conversations with professors, a sense that the liberal democratic ideals that many professors had become committed to while studying abroad, had ultimately failed. For many, it seemed, there was no alternative but to try to cooperate with the new regime and hope for the best.[36]

Reforms were clearly coming, having begun already in some areas, but it was as yet unclear to administrators and professors just how thorough reform would be, that is, just how much of the pre-1949 legacy would be negated. Professors were encouraged by "activist" students to attend extra "thought reform" meetings, and some resisted in time-honored ways: they failed to show up, or when they did show up to meetings aimed at party-directed reform of the universities, just sat in silence, saying that they had just come to the meetings to "listen" and "learn."[37] This kind of

35. Ibid., 37–38, 140.
36. Ibid., 138–40.
37. Ibid., 143.

withdrawal from active political engagement is clearly understood in Chinese society as a protest against leaders. By a strategy of "passive" resistance, professors could individually express their disapproval of change.

Responses to the new regime among professors varied, however, depending on individual belief and institutional circumstance. Up to the Chinese intervention in the Korean War in the fall of 1950, there is considerable evidence that university professors maneuvered to preserve prerogatives and liberal ideals despite intense pressure.[38] With hindsight, this was of course a losing battle, and Western scholarship on Chinese universities and intellectuals, constrained as it is by source limitations and the limitations of hindsight, seems to have overlooked this brief "window" in the first two years of the PRC, when intellectuals were struggling to define their relationship to the new regime.[39]

The First All-China Conference on Higher Education

The First All-China Conference on Higher Education, held in Beijing from 1 to 9 June 1950, brought together university leaders and their new masters in the Ministry of Education.[40] For the attendees from the "old" universities, the questions were, What would reform mean for their institutions and educational traditions? What was the attitude of the new regime toward the universities, and the higher education, of the old regime?

---

38. Closer examination will show a direct relationship between this period of relatively moderate CCP policies, which allowed some room for negotiation with the state, and the Hundred Flowers campaign of 1956–57, in which intellectuals finally spoke up in anger and frustration about what they had endured since the final closing of this "window" in the fall of 1950.

39. Pepper, *Radicalism and Education Reform*; Hayhoe, *China's Universities*. Neither of these two important works on Chinese higher education see the years 1949–50 as essentially differing from what came later, that is, Chinese universities were reorganized without resistance or input from university administrators or professors. Commenting on decisions at the First All-China Higher Education Conference in 1950, Pepper writes: "These decisions had already been made at the highest levels, and the academic community, without realizing it, was not being asked but told what lay in store." Pepper, *Radicalism and Education Reform*, 174. On the same key conference, Hayhoe writes: "Neither autonomy nor academic freedom were at issue in these deliberations, with the overriding emphasis being on how higher education could be shaped to serve the new socialist economy and polity." Hayhoe, *China's Universities*, 76. A careful examination of the materials of this conference, however, shows the process of reform to have been much more complicated than has been realized.

40. Zhongyang jiaoyu kexue yanjiusuo, ed., *Zhonghua renmin gongheguo jiaoyu dashiji, 1949–1982* (Beijing: Jiaoyu kexue chubanshe, 1983), 19.

Minister of Education Ma Xulun spoke to the conference on its opening day and made it clear that higher education must now serve the needs of the state. In his speech, Ma reviewed initial accomplishments in the academic year 1949–50 and outlined regime goals for the near future. Thus far, change had basically been limited to "curricular and administrative reform." This meant that politically offensive courses had been abolished and, where possible, courses with political content in line with the ideology of the new regime had begun to be taught. This was quite similar to the GMD's earlier effort at "partification" in the 1930s. Ma stated that higher education must unequivocally serve national purposes: "First and most important, our higher education must closely correspond to the needs of the national economy, politics, culture, and national defense. It must first of all serve the needs of economic construction, because economic construction is the basis for all other types of national construction."[41] These goals could be achieved through work in two important areas, the first of which was curricular reform. Curricular reform in the old institutions, Ma stated, should emphasize scientific and technical subjects, combining theory and practice. Specialists should cooperate in proposed curricular reforms, and each school would have to submit curricular reform plans to the Ministry of Education before the coming academic year. These statements echoed the GMD's efforts to centralize control over higher education, and to promote engineering and technology over training in the humanities.

A second important arena of effort, Ma stated, would be newly created institutions and courses:

> In order that our higher education serve economic and other types of construction needs, the second critical task is, in cooperation with the Ministry of Education and every government institution engaged in these tasks, to strengthen the educational facilities of Chinese People's University and other new-style higher educational institutions, to create all types of specialized schools, and to add to all our universities and institutes short-term specialized courses and training classes in accordance with our practical needs.[42]

41. Ma Xulun, "Diyici quanguo gaodeng jiaoyu huiyi kaimuci," *Renmin jiaoyu* 1, no. 3 (1950): 11–14.
42. These new institutions were the Harbin Institute of Technology, promoted as the model of Soviet-style higher education in science and technology, and Chinese People's

Ma added several more points in his instructions to the conference. China's new system of higher education must welcome workers and peasants and give them special attention and help in institutions of higher education so as to create a new group of intellectuals (*zhishifenzi*, lit. "knowledgeable elements"). Finally, Ma called for the Ministry of Education to assume the leadership of all institutions of higher education in regard to policies, administrative structure, institutional planning, hiring and firing, curriculum, teaching materials and teaching methods. The Ministry would assume control over comprehensive universities (namely, the most prestigious universities—Beijing, Tsinghua, Nankai) as well as normal universities, while leaving some specialized and technical institutes under the jurisdiction of their respective functional government departments. Also, recognizing the reality of limited resources, Ma allowed that the educational departments of China's six military-administrative regions would have to handle educational affairs in their respective areas until the Ministry of Education could exercise direct control.[43]

Ma's speech was, in effect, a prescription for the eventual sovietization of higher education in China. In this, Ma was fully backed by the Soviet adviser to the Ministry of Higher Education, A-er-xin-jie-fu, who also addressed the conference. A-er-xin-jie-fu's speech gave little comfort to academics from the American-modeled universities, as he described the overriding importance of specialist, technical education in the Soviet Union and asserted that Soviet experience was completely applicable in the new People's Republic of China. He went on to explain the role that higher education played in the Stalinist plan for national wealth and power:

> Now, how do we catch up to and surpass the advanced countries in technology and industry? First, build modern heavy industrial enterprises, light industrial enterprises, smelting enterprises, mines, and railroads, and so on. Second, cultivate our own cadres—scientific, technical, medical, educational, and so on.
> Soviet institutions of higher education must, first, provide higher education to worker-peasant youth. [They] must raise the

---

University, the model for Soviet-style training in economic-managerial specialties, political ideology, and other state-related specialties. Mao and Shen, "*Zhongguo jiaoyu tongshi*," *di liu juan*, 6:89–94. On the latter institution, see Douglas A. Stiffler, "Building Socialism at Chinese People's University: Chinese Cadres and Soviet Experts in the People's Republic of China, 1949–57" (Ph.D. diss., University of California, San Diego, 2002).

43. Stiffler, "Building Socialism," 13.

cultural level of the people. They must cultivate from among the people cadres with a high level of technical mastery. Only from a nation of literate and cultured people, from the people, from the workers and peasants, from the laborers—only from these can high-level cadres be cultivated, and only such a nation as this cannot be defeated.

Second, Soviet universities must not train lofty but useless generalists but should train specialist talent—engineers, doctors, teachers, economists, agricultural specialists, statisticians, mining resource specialists, scientific workers, and so on and so forth.

Third, the old universities existing before the October Revolution had to change their goals, change their courses of study, in order to suit the country's new tasks.

Fourth, [we had to] establish new institutions of higher education, primarily higher technical schools. . . .

I believe that all the tasks faced by the People's Republic of China . . . are in principle the same as those faced by my motherland, the Soviet Union, after the October Revolution. I believe that all the tasks faced by Chinese higher schools are in principle the same as the tasks faced by the higher schools of the Soviet Union after the Great October Revolution.[44]

Chinese university leaders must have found disturbing the low priority accorded in the Soviet Union to comprehensive universities, as opposed to specialist institutes. The Soviet adviser stated that China's prerevolutionary universities, like Russia's, had developed under "feudal," and in China's case—semicolonial—conditions, and so naturally could not be expected to shoulder the tasks of a developing socialist state. The Soviet higher education expert further noted the irrationality of concentrating comprehensive universities in the capital city and stated that this was undoubtedly a legacy of China's semicolonial status. In the Soviet Union, A-er-xin-jie-fu pointed out, there were only thirty comprehensive universities (with no more than one to a city), while there were some eight hundred specialist institutions of higher education. In conclusion he said: "I think that the People's Republic of China should also develop higher education

---

44. A. P. A-er-xin-jie-fu, "Cong Sulian gaodeng jiaoyu de jingyan luetan jige wenti . . ." [A General Discussion of Several Questions Based on the Soviet Union's Experience in Higher Education], *Renmin jiaoyu*, 1 July 1950, 25.

in institutes, and these institutes should have the same position in higher education as universities."[45]

Minister of Education Ma's closing remarks conceded no ground to conference participants who wanted pre-1949 higher education to be treated as progressive in some aspects, and who wanted to exert influence in the process of post-1949 reform of higher education. Chinese scholars who have examined the relevant Ministry of Education archives have revealed, however, that liberal educators spoke up in a way that was sure to have antagonized party officials.[46] The main objections centered on the oft-repeated principle that institutions of higher education must serve the "construction" needs of the new state and society. If this was true, academics objected, would not all universities simply be turned into technical schools? In response to another regime goal, that of opening the doors of institutions of higher education to workers and peasants, some academics objected that this would mean a drastic lowering of university standards. Some proposed that the universities be put in charge of the "theoretical," leaving the "practical" to technical schools, a proposal obviously designed to retain the leading role—and the lion's share of state resources—for the prestigious Republican-era institutions like Beijing and Tsinghua universities. However, on the other side, "some people" (probably party educators) questioned the need for what they probably saw as elitist, time-consuming higher education and proposed that the whole system emphasize practical, short-term education of the cadre-school type.[47] In closing remarks the minister revealed the existence of serious disputes:

> Both before and in the course of the conference, many of our comrades held all types of differing opinions. For instance, before the conference [in preparatory meetings] there were sharp disagreements about curricular reform, and in conference discussions there were heated disputes on policies, responsibilities, courses of study, and regulations. Also, all sorts of differing opinions and methods have been aired in the newspapers. This is a very positive phenomenon. . . . At the same time, people have respected the Common Program of the CPPCC [Chinese

---

45. Ibid., 26–27.
46. Mao and Shen, "*Zhongguo jiaoyu tongshi*," *di liu juan*, 6:10–12.
47. Ibid., 11.

People's Political Consultative Conference] . . . [and] spoken out with all kinds of differing opinions. Through discussion we have solved problems in the spirit of "seeking truth from facts." When we have been able to achieve unanimity, we have reached conclusions to be followed by action; when we were unable to reach agreement, or when the subjective or objective conditions are not yet right, we have put off reaching conclusions and will all continue to study [the question].[48]

It seems likely that the disputes at this conference arose in part out of frustrations that academics had experienced during the first year and a half of CCP rule, as well as the hope that individual academics and perhaps the institutions themselves could influence the course of reform of higher education. At the conference, lines seem to have been drawn between those advocating the continued importance of the comprehensive, elite universities like Beijing and Tsinghua, and those who would downgrade these prestigious universities and emphasize a technical, mass-based approach.

Resistance in the University

Maria Yen's anecdotal description of curricular reform at Beijing University, beginning on a limited scale in the spring of 1949, adds considerable support to the view that university administrations, faculties, and student bodies were not entirely passive in the face of the new demands. The spring semester of 1949, beginning just after the Communists took Beijing, was a testing period for CCP control of universities. The university introduced one new course, "The History of Social Development," taught by He Ganzhi, a course which Yen described as heavily enrolled despite the fact that it was not compulsory.[49] In this semester, nearly all the law courses were abolished for "reactionary" content, and many social science courses were also canceled. More sweeping, according to Yen, were changes in "viewpoint" adopted in various courses in the departments of economics,

---

48. Ma Xulun, "Diyici quanguo gaodeng jiaoyu huiyi bimuci," *Renmin Jiaoyu* 1, no. 1 (1950): 15–16.
49. He Ganzhi was a prominent party historian who had taught at CCP cadre-training schools since the Yan'an period. After 1949, he taught party history at Chinese People's University.

social sciences, philosophy, and Western languages, which involved the substitution of Maoist materials and anti-imperialist rhetoric for Western-oriented curricula.[50]

At the beginning of the fall semester of 1949, however, even more concerted efforts were made to reform the Beijing University curriculum. Professors were expected to consult their students on changes in course content. According to Yen, the more self-confident professors made only perfunctory attempts to do this, while others deferred to the students completely.[51] Nevertheless, problems persisted. Because of the lack of Marxist texts in the social sciences and humanities, professors taught from the new viewpoint using the old materials. Some "esoteric" or politically suspect required courses were made optional, such as Shakespeare in the English department.[52] The Ministry of Education ordered that the entire department of philosophy be abolished.[53]

Resistance could be perceived in the offhand remarks of professors, one of whom said: "Do they want well-educated men? Or are they just after cadres who can read, write, run an office, and handle a foreign language?" According to Yen, party activists organized a meeting of students to approve the curriculum reforms, but several students immediately stood up and questioned the reforms. In response to a request for student opinions on the reforms, the first speaker said:

> "I really don't think the changes should be as sweeping as the last two government orders have called for. After all, isn't a university supposed to be a place for academic study and research? Is Beida [Beijing University] the right place to use materials better designed for a short-term intensive training course?"
>
> "I agree," his friend chimed in, "I don't think these last changes are so good, either. Keeping our standard up is as important as

50. Yen, *Umbrella Garden*, 124.
51. Ibid., 130–31.
52. Some, however, would regret their denunciations of Shakespeare, as the first shipment of Soviet literary magazines were full of articles lauding Shakespeare, an example of how revolutionary China and the Stalinist Soviet Union were initially out of sync in cultural matters. Classical music and ballroom dancing were two other bourgeois avocations initially censured by activist students who later had to eat their words when they found that both the socialist world and the CCP's own leadership enjoyed both. Mao Zedong, Zhou Enlai, and others in the top leadership held Saturday-night ballroom dances in the Communist base-area capital of Yenan. On Shakespeare, ballroom dancing, and classical music, see Yen, *Umbrella Garden*, 172–73, 90–93, 172–76.
53. Ibid., 132.

introducing the new materials. In my opinion the university should be kept as a place for training 'higher' talents."

"These last changes are simply too much." The third speaker was even braver. "If all you want to do now is extend applied political training, why don't you just abolish all the universities?"[54]

It is striking that the objections raised by these students are congruent with those raised during the Conference on Higher Education, namely, the importance of academic standards in rapidly changing institutions, the possibility of universities continuing in their role of training in "theoretical" or otherwise nonpractical areas, and the danger of the university's demise in the face of state demands.

In the course of this opposition to reform in the 1949–50 academic year, two prominent "democratic figures," Zhang Dongsun, a professor of philosophy at Yenching University, and Zhang Xiruo of the Social Sciences Department at Beijing University approached Chairman Mao Zedong and asked that the "over-leftist" curricular reforms be slowed down. Mao then sent a handwritten note to the Ministry of Education asking that proposed changes be deferred for one year.[55] Chinese scholars who have examined Ministry of Education archives corroborate this account. They state that, during the Conference on Higher Education, Beijing and Tsinghua University professors did *not* agree with proposed institutional reforms, and instead advocated the expansion of their own institutions. As a result, institutional reforms that might have been carried out in 1950–51, were delayed until 1952.[56] It should be recalled that academic leaders in institutions of higher education were frequently the very "democratic personages" who headed the token democratic parties which Maoist theory held to be representative of the bourgeois classes. Regime policy was to conciliate these individuals and the interests they were presumed to represent, so it is not at all surprising that such higher education leaders would attempt to take their concerns to Mao.

The modes and depth of resistance to proposed reforms in higher education in the first two years of the People's Republic of China remain to be investigated.[57] What is sure is that any "window of opportunity" for

54. Ibid., 133.
55. Ibid., 133–34.
56. Mao and Shen, "*Zhongguo jiaoyu tongshi*," *di liu juan*, 6:46.
57. More research needs to be done on this issue. Access to Ministry of Education archives will be critical; in the meantime researchers must, as in most areas of research on the

universities to speak up in favor of liberal democratic values was shut in October 1950, when China entered the Korean War. University professors, always under suspicion as the carriers of "bourgeois" ideology, were subjected to a series of campaigns which forced them out of any stance of passivity into humiliating acts of self-denunciation and contrition. The Thought Reform Campaign, targeted at intellectuals on a nation-wide scale, began in December 1950, and continued for months. During this campaign, famous professors published their life histories and confessions one after another, denouncing their previous attraction to pro-American bourgeois thinking and announcing their new willingness to serve the people and to learn from the Soviet Union.[58] This campaign, together with the Resist-America and Aid-Korea Campaign and the Campaign to Suppress Counterrevolutionaries, both of which were carried out as mass movements in the wider society, contributed to an atmosphere of regimentation and fear among intellectuals, an atmosphere which made further attempts at defending prerevolutionary or "bourgeois" practices and beliefs completely untenable.

The Soviet-Inspired Reform of Universities in 1951–1952

In this ideologically regimented atmosphere Chinese Communist leaders finally carried out their sweeping, Soviet-inspired reorganization of all institutions of higher education, a reorganization which closed old universities, established new ones, and consolidated prerevolutionary departments and institutions into new departments and institutions, sometimes by moving entire faculties to different regions.[59]

PRC, depend on Chinese scholars, who themselves may have limited archival access. Interviews with participants in these events are a promising avenue of research in China.

58. Theodore H.E. Chen, *Thought Reform of the Chinese Intellectuals* (Hong Kong: Hong Kong University Press, 1960).

59. Mao and Shen, "Zhongguo jiaoyu tongshi," di liu juan , 6:27–28. See also West, *Yenching University*, 195–243. Institutional reform of institutions of higher education had been going on since 1949, as we saw with the closure of Beijing University's philosophy department. In the first year, some schools described as "reactionary," such as Tianjin's Deyu Institute—a school allegedly run by Guomindang intelligence services—were shut down, and commercial diploma mill–type schools were also ordered to close. The new regime encouraged private institutions, including missionary colleges, to continue but required that they register with the central authorities, something the Guomindang had also done in the early stages of its assertion of control of universities.

This massive reform began in November 1951, when a national Conference of Engineering Institutes was convened. What started as the reorganization of engineering institutes resulted in the dismantling and restructuring of three-quarters of the universities, colleges, and institutes in China. The idea was to establish, at last, regional balance by relocating institutions and to emphasize engineering and other technical disciplines by downgrading the prestigious comprehensive universities. Regional reorganization took China's six big military-administrative regions as the basis, and aimed to maintain a minimum of one, or at the most two, comprehensive universities in each region. Thus, Tsinghua University was remade into a technical university, and its social sciences and humanities programs were transferred to Beijing University. As Suzanne Pepper has pointed out, this reorganization enacted changes that Chinese academics—and the League of Nations' educational consultants—had called for in the early 1930s.[60]

The 1952 reorganization created three types of institutions: comprehensive universities, specialized institutes, and specialized schools. The reorganization affected three-quarters of all schools, and resulted in the closure of 49 old institutions and the establishment of 31 entirely new ones.[61] Engineering universities and institutes were established in key centers of the six regions by concentrating talent and consolidating departments of the former comprehensive universities. These new specialized institutes, in turn, were designated to serve as models for higher education in their fields in their respective regions. From a total of 227 such institutions in 1949, at the completion of reorganization in 1952 there were 181 tertiary-level institutions.[62]

Missionary-run universities had played a prominent role in Republican-era Chinese higher education, and were also a bastion of American influence. Predictably, these universities did not survive the Korean War era and the university reform of 1951–52, although they did endure for a surprisingly long time. One of the first missionary schools to fall afoul of the new regime was Catholic Furen University, one of the four most prestigious universities in Beijing. Furen University was taken over by the Ministry of Education in October 1950, allegedly because the school's

---

60. Pepper, *Radicalism and Education Reform*, 37–45.
61. Mao and Shen, "Zhongguo jiaoyu tongshi," *di liu juan*, 6:75–77. See 6:87–88 for contributions of Soviet advisers in the Ministry of Higher Education.
62. Hayhoe, *China's Universities*, 80–81.

foreign missionary advisers had resisted state control.⁶³ The outbreak of the Korean War and the Chinese confrontation with America spurred the government to take action on American missionary-sponsored institutions. In early 1951, twenty foreign-supported institutions of higher education were nationalized, including the prestigious Yenching University, and in the sweeping reforms of 1952–53, even the names of these institutions were eliminated.⁶⁴

This radical reorganization of higher education was aided by the presence of "Soviet experts" (*sulian zhuanjia*) at some of the leading universities and in the Ministry of Higher Education. The first Soviet adviser to the Ministry was A-er-xin-jie-fu, who was in China for much of 1950, and who, as discussed above, explained the Stalinist rationale for higher education to the participants in the First All-China Higher Education Conference. The adviser A. A. Fomin served at the Ministry during the critical period of reform in 1952–53.⁶⁵ Although these men did not stay long in China (especially in comparison to later advisers, who stayed three years), they served during the most critical period of reform. This was the time in which Soviet experts' opinions were most eagerly sought, and the Chinese most enthusiastic in enacting their suggestions.

A-er-xin-jie-fu and Fomin consistently emphasized the rationality and practicality of the Soviet system, and this advocacy met an enthusiastic response in Ministry and party.⁶⁶ Chinese educational administrators had been grappling with the irrationality and impracticality in the Chinese system of higher education since the century began, but especially in the late 1920s and 1930s.⁶⁷ In the fall of 1952, Fomin participated in the large-scale reorganization of Chinese higher education and the simultaneous creation of the Ministry of Higher Education.⁶⁸ In a speech to the

63. Mao and Shen, "Zhongguo jiaoyu tongshi," *di liu juan*, 6:33–34. Most of Furen University became part of Beijing Normal University.

64. Ibid. Still, it is remarkable that even after three years of CCP rule, Yenching University in the winter of 1951–52 still existed as a (now state-supported) Christian institution, even sponsoring, during the height of the Korean War, a Christmas performance of Handel's *Messiah*, in Chinese. West, *Yenching University*, 219.

65. Mao and Shen, "Zhongguo jiaoyu tongshi," *di liu juan*, 6:87–88.

66. Both A-er-xin-jie-fu and Fomin addressed important central educational conferences, and both had their speeches printed in *People's Education* (*Renmin jiaoyu*), the monthly journal of the Ministry of Education, and therefore we are in a position to know something of what Soviet advisers at the Ministry advocated in the early 1950s.

67. Pepper, *Radicalism and Education Reform*, 37–45, 86–117.

68. We can assume that Fomin was deeply involved in this process, but until access to the Ministry of Education archives is gained, we will not know the details: what input and resistance, if any, were offered by the universities themselves.

Conference on the Reorganization of Beijing-Tianjin Institutions of Higher Education, published in *People's Education* in September 1952, Fomin emphasized the leading role of specialist, technical institutes in the Soviet Union. He stressed the *practicality* of this system, in which engineers could immediately go to work in their specialties, in contrast to the situation in capitalist countries, where generalist training meant that newly graduated engineers were unequipped for immediate work. He further emphasized the comprehensive, planned, and eminently *rational* nature of this system, with 436 specialties all with education plans, approved by the Ministry, and specifying the precise numbers of hours to be devoted to each subject, exams to be taken, theses to be written. Again, Fomin contrasted this rationality with the presumed chaotic variations of capitalist educational regimes.[69]

Reorganization in higher education was accomplished without significant protest after the "window of opportunity" for negotiation with the regime closed in the fall of 1950. Sovietization of the Chinese higher education system, however, ran counter to the tendencies of the many Western-trained professors who resented what they saw as both a lowering of standards in "opening the doors to workers and peasants," and the devaluing of pure academic research and personal and institutional autonomy in favor of an exclusive focus on practical service of the state.

The Thought Reform campaign directed against intellectuals, which began in the fall of 1950, disabused university administrators and professors of the notion that they would have significant input in defining their role and the role of their institutions in the new society. Professors and universities spent the next four years engaged in thought reform and in trying to follow the Soviet model in higher education, which was meant to serve the nation's need for technical and engineering talent during the First Five-Year Plan (1952–56).

In 1956–57, however, the tide turned, and in the Hundred Flowers Campaign intellectuals were asked by Mao himself to criticize the reforms that had taken place along Soviet lines since the CCP entered the cities in 1949. After initial hesitation, professors, students, and other intellectuals responded in early 1957 with devastating and potentially destabilizing critiques. Many focused on the sovietization of institutions

69. A. A. Fu-min, "Sulian gaodeng jiaoyu de gaige—zai jingjin gaodeng xuexiao yuanxi tiaozheng zuotanhui shang de jianghua" [The Reform of Higher Education in the Soviet Union—Speech at the Conference on the Reorganization of Beijing-Tianjin Higher Education Institutions], *Renmin Jiaoyu*, September 1952, 10–11.

of higher education and the damage that this had done in some areas. They echoed the objections raised by university professors during the First National Conference on Higher Education in the summer of 1950.[70] Liberal-minded professors had been effectively silenced from late 1950 to 1957, but the Hundred Flowers campaign persuaded many to speak out.

The party and Mao, however, responded vengefully to those questioning Communist Party rule and socialism. More than a million individuals were labeled "Rightists" and sent down to the countryside to reform themselves through labor. Some would spend the next twenty years in the countryside in forced internal exile, or in prison during the Cultural Revolution (1966–76). The Anti-Rightist Movement finally broke the back of prerevolutionary intellectuals and initiated an era of even more radical change in higher education, in the Maoist direction of "massification" and the hegemony of Maoist revolutionary ideology.[71]

Conclusion

Overall, this analysis suggests that Chinese universities did not present an obstacle to consolidation of the Chinese Communist regime in the early 1950s, and institutions of higher education made only a weak effort to defend themselves against the extension of state control.[72] How can we explain this, especially when we recall that Chinese universities were no strangers to American and European ideals of academic autonomy? Chinese universities had defended their prerogatives in the Republican period, and yet, in the first years of the People's Republic, few institutions protested their consolidation or dissolution.[73]

One of the main reasons that university leaders accepted the demands of the new state, I would argue, is that many of the reforms were simply extensions of what the Guomindang regime had been trying to accomplish, and what even foreign observers had recommended. Analysts of the

---

70. Roderick MacFarquhar, *The Hundred Flowers Campaign and the Chinese Intellectuals* (New York: Praeger, 1960).
71. Pepper, *Radicalism and Education Reform*, 278–301.
72. In John Connelly's study, Poland is the outstanding example of resistance to the sovietization of the universities. Connelly, *Captive University*, 71–77.
73. Hayhoe, *China's Universities*, 50–52.

Chinese system of higher education, including the League of Nations Commission, had called for a more rational and equitable geographic distribution of institutions of higher education and for these institutions to teach subjects that were more immediately relevant to China's practical needs.[74] When an education official of the new People's Republic like Ma Xulun, who also happened to have been an important education official under the old regime, set out to accomplish exactly these tasks, many educational leaders agreed that such change was necessary and inevitable.

The political and social contexts of the civil war years further explain the ease with which Chinese universities were reformed. Inflation, corruption, and war had undermined support for the old regime and exhausted the urban middle class and the intellectuals who were desperate for economic stability and clean government, which the Chinese Communists seemed to offer. Those who would not be reconciled to the new regime, however, retreated with the Guomindang to the island of Taiwan. Hu Shi, the postwar president of Beijing University and luminary of the May Fourth Movement, evacuated Beijing for Taiwan as CCP armies prepared to enter the city in early 1949. Hu, seeing the future more clearly than most, said that under a right-wing regime he would at least enjoy the luxury of silence without having to "reform" himself. Thousands of intellectuals voted with their feet and escaped to Taiwan, leaving behind those who were willing to give the new regime a chance.

Finally, at a deeper level, the relationship between intellectuals and the state has always been close, from imperial China to the PRC, even as the position of intellectuals vis-à-vis the state and the nature of the intellectuals as a group have changed. Chinese intellectuals of the late twentieth century are not Chinese literati in new garb, but they nonetheless maintain some of the old Chinese literati's status concerns and orientation to public affairs. One cannot, after all, throw off long-standing cultural preoccupations and habits of thought overnight. The Chinese literati's concern with public affairs, however, has been transmuted in the twentieth century into concern for *the nation*.

Chinese intellectuals are sometimes thought of as "failing" because, when faced with a choice between a semi-Westernized "enlightenment" (implying reason, intellectual autonomy, democratic values, and human

---

74. Pepper, *Radicalism and Education Reform*, 44; League of Nations' Mission, *Reorganization of Education in China*.

rights) and a strong Chinese nation, they have most often chosen the latter.[75] This is to misread the context in which Chinese political discourse has developed from the late imperial period to the present. Universities, like the old Confucian academies, have only posed a serious challenge *as institutions* when the state has been weak. In the face of a strong state, and especially vis-à-vis modernizing regimes such as that of the Guomindang and the Communists, institutional resistance can be and has been effectively labeled self-interested and unpatriotic. With few exceptions, twentieth-century Chinese intellectuals have professed a concern for the nation as a value overriding all others, and institutional resistance to the state remains taboo insofar as the state has been able to identify itself with the interests of the nation.

In the Chinese context, it is when intellectuals challenge the state individually, in moral terms, that they are at their most effective and are most dangerous to state hegemony.[76] This is, perhaps, the most profound inheritance of the past in contemporary Chinese political discourse. Universities in China have been able to serve as incubators for intellectuals of a wide variety of political persuasions in the twentieth century, but it

---

75. Chow Tse-tsung, *The May Fourth Movement: Intellectual Revolution in Modern China* (Cambridge: Harvard University Press, 1960); Vera Schwarcz, *The Chinese Enlightenment: Intellectuals and the Legacy of the May Fourth Movement of 1919* (Berkeley and Los Angeles: University of California Press, 1986). Both Chow and Schwarcz conclude that Chinese intellectuals retained a primary commitment to the nation, which tended to make enlightenment instrumental to national ends.

76. Students and intellectuals who took part in the 1989 Tiananmen Square protests were at their most effective when they confronted the state symbolically, in ways which made it appear corrupt and unresponsive to societal demands (often ironically phrased in traditional, moral terms).

77. Exemplars of righteous protest include (1) Hai Rui (d. 1587), a late Ming official who criticized the emperor's extravagance and was praised in 1959 as man of "courage for all times," who "remained unintimidated by threats of punishment"; such praise was taken as criticism of Mao and helped to launch the Cultural Revolution; (2) Lu Xun (1881–1936), a leftist writer whose short stories satirized Chinese society and government, and was often at odds with CCP literary policies; (3) Wen Yiduo (1899–1946), a romantic poet and Lianda literature professor whose membership in the Democratic League and criticisms of GMD policies resulted in his assassination by GMD agents; (4) Peng Dehuai (1898–1974), a CCP general and hero-leader of Chinese forces in the Korean War, who in 1959 attacked Mao's Great Leap policies and spent the rest of his life under house arrest; (5) Ma Yinchu (1882–1982), a Beijing University president and economist who advocated population control policies in the late 1950s, at a time when party leaders—particularly Mao—held that more is better; (6) Fang Lizhi (1936–), an astrophysicist and former vice-president of the Chinese University of Science and Technology, who supported Chinese student demonstrators in 1986 using the language of scientific rationalism; (7) Wei Jingsheng (1949–), a Beijing worker and former People's Liberation Army soldier who called for a Fifth Modernization—democracy—to support the other Four Modernizations, which aim at making China a modern and powerful nation.

has seemed as though all roads have led to the Rome of the modern Chinese nation. Intellectual dissent has broken out precisely in the context of arguments over China's future as a nation, and universities have played an important role in fostering this kind of individual moral dissent.[77] It is likely, then, that new dissenters will arise, from the universities and elsewhere, challenging the state precisely on the grounds that it is potentially most vulnerable: as guardian of the Chinese nation.

9

Between Control and Collaboration: The University in East Germany

RALPH JESSEN

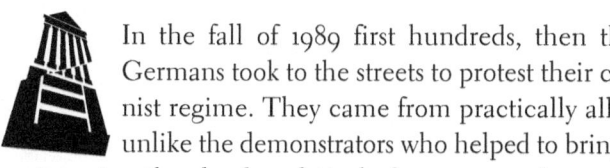
In the fall of 1989 first hundreds, then thousands of East Germans took to the streets to protest their country's Communist regime. They came from practically all walks of life, but unlike the demonstrators who helped to bring down dictatorial regimes in other lands, relatively few were professors or students. East German artists, writers, and pastors indeed assumed the classical role of "intellectual" in times of political upheaval, but the same cannot be said of academics. The few who did participate neither initiated nor contributed to the intellectual ferment of the citizens' movement. Such exceptions as the biomathematician Jens Reich were few and far between.[1] There was for the German Democratic Republic (GDR) no such symbol as Beijing's Tiananmen Square, either in the positive sense, as an emblem of a student democracy movement, or in the negative as the locus of brutal suppression. Even the grassroots movement of peace initiatives and citizens' rights groups, which had played a dangerous cat-and-mouse game with the Secret Police (Stasi) for almost a decade, had virtually no contact with universities. If there was an institution that afforded a space for

---

1. Jens Reich, *Abschied von den Lebenslügen: Die Intelligenz und die Macht* (Berlin: Rowohlt, 1992). See also the interview with Reich in Guntolf Herzberg and Klaus Meier, *Karrieremuster: Wissenschaftlerporträts* (Berlin: Aufbau Verlag, 1992), 406–44.

nonconformist thinking in East Germany, then it was *nolens volens* the Protestant Church, not the university.[2]

Initially it was neither self-evident nor predictable that the universities would represent a safe haven for routine accommodation and loyalty during the GDR's collapse. There had, after all, been next to no contact between universities and the political left in earlier German history. On the contrary, until 1945 the universities were the exclusive preserve of the educated bourgeoisie, despite cautious attempts during the years between the wars and during the Nazi years to open them up socially. Politically, most academics oscillated between liberalism and conservatism, until, at the end of the Weimar Republic, significant numbers of students and younger researchers embraced the promises of National Socialism. After 1933 their numbers were swelled by the many professors and docents who had fortuitously discovered sympathy for the "Third Reich."[3]

But irrespective of how the intelligentsia thought of itself politically, one thing it certainly was not: Communist. To this extent it is self-evident that East German universities would not play a pioneering role in grounding the East German dictatorship; what is not self-evident is that they themselves would become the objects of an extraordinary political transformation. By 1989 students and professors had become so loyal that they continued to support the Socialist Unity Party of Germany (SED) even when its end was well within sight. How was that extraordinary shift—from decidedly anticommunist, to a pillar of support for a Communist regime—possible?

The following chapter sets out to find explanations among the specificities of early East German history and in the changes that continued into the 1960s. Historians have already sketched out competing versions of this

---

2. Erhart Neubert, *Geschichte der Opposition in der DDR, 1949–1989* (Berlin: Christoph Links, 1997); Detlef Pollack, "Religion und gesellschaftlicher Wandel: Zur Rolle der evangelischen Kirche im Prozess des gesellschaftlichen Umbruchs in der DDR," in *Der Zusammenbruch der DDR: Soziologische Analysen*, ed. Hans Joas and Martin Kohli (Frankfurt: Suhrkamp, 1993), 246–65; Wolfgang Bialas, "Die protestantische Revolution und der 'Geist des Sozialismus,'" *Deutschland-Archiv* 26 (1993): 417–25.

3. Michael Grüttner, *Studenten im Dritten Reich* (Paderborn: Schöningh, 1995); Rainer Hering, "Der 'unpolitische' Professor? Parteimitgliedschaften Hamburger Hochschullehrer in der Weimarer Republik und im 'Dritten Reich,'" in *Hochschulalltag im "Dritten Reich." Die Hamburger Universität, 1933–1945*, ed. Eckhart Krause et al. (Berlin: Dietrich Reimer, 1991), 85–111; Helmut Heiber, *Universität unterm Hakenkreuz*, part 1, *Der Professor im Dritten Reich: Bilder aus der akademischen Provinz* (Munich: Saur, 1991); Hellmut Seier, "Die Hochschullehrer im Dritten Reich," in *Deutsche Hochschullehrer als Elite, 1815–1945*, ed. Klaus Schwabe (Boppard am Rhein: H. Boldt, 1988), 247–95.

story. Some have related it as a tale of conquest and subjection, in which universities appear as passive victims of an aggressive occupying force and its collaborators. Such a narration provides instructive details about the ruthless Soviet Military Administration (SMAD) and the Communist public education administration, but tends to ignore the National Socialist prehistory of universities, during which many students and professors willingly collaborated with the Nazi regime. Without this background one cannot understand the success of the SMAD in forcing purges upon universities in 1945–46.[4] Other historians have emphasized more positive aspects of early postwar university history, for example, the voluntary steps taken toward denazification and toward a shattering of structures that had kept universities the domain of a single class. Such readings were promoted by the SED,[5] but also by some historians writing after the fall of the Berlin Wall, who were eager to identify "opportunities" for democratic socialism supposedly missed because of Stalinism and the Cold War.[6]

It goes without saying that such apologetic interpretations miss the core of the problem. A third set of stories are structured around resistance and victimhood. They accentuate the conflict between Communist pressure to reorganize universities and the resistance of the academic milieu, for example, the escalating power struggle at Berlin University, which led to the founding of the Free University in the American sector of the city in 1948, the activities of the Protestant "young parish" among students, or the local protests against the politicization of studies in 1956.[7] This version

---

4. See, for example, classics that still reward reading: Marianne Müller and Egon Erwin Müller, ". . . *stürmt die Festung Wissenschaft": Die Sowjetisierung der mitteldeutschen Universitäten seit 1945* (Berlin: Colloquium, 1953); Max Gustav Lange, *Wissenschaft im totalitären Staat: Die Wissenschaft der Sowjetischen Besatzungszone auf dem Weg zum "Stalinismus"* (Stuttgart: Ring, 1955); Thomas Ammer, *Universität zwischen Demokratie und Diktatur: Ein Beitrag zur Nachkriegsgeschichte der Universität Rostock* (Cologne: Wissenschaft und Politik, 1969); and Karl Wockenfuss, *Einblicke in Akten und Schicksale Rostocker Studenten und Professoren nach 1945* (Rostock: Association of former Rostock Students [VERS], 1995).

5. Soja Fiedler, "Die Politik der Partei der Arbeiterklasse zur Durchsetzung ihrer führenden Rolle an den Universitäten der DDR (1945/46–1955)" (Ph.D. diss., Humboldt University, Berlin 1986); Walter Mohrmann, *Geschichte der Humboldt Universität zu Berlin von 1945 bis zur Gegenwart: Ein Überblick* (Berlin: Humboldt-Universität, 1980); Roland Köhler et al., *Geschichte des Hochschulwesens der Deutschen Demokratischen Republik (1945–1961)* (Berlin: Institut für Hochschulbildung, 1976).

6. For example, Roland Köhler, "Die verpasste Chance: Streit um eine demokratische Hochschulverfassung in der sowjetischen Besatzungszone, 1946–1949," *Hochschule Ost* 3, no. 4 (1994): 72–84.

7. Ilko-Sascha Kowalczuk, *Die Niederschlagung der Opposition an der Veterinärmedizinischen Fakultät der Humboldt-Universität zu Berlin in der Krise 1956/7: Dokumentation einer Pressekonferenz des Ministeriums für Staatssicherheit im Mai 1957* (Berlin: Der Berliner

reveals the conflicts caused by the transformation of higher education, but tends to underestimate the willingness of professors to collaborate, as well as the advantages that some could derive from this situation.

In contrast to the views sketched above, this chapter attempts to join two perspectives: on the one hand, it portrays the university as an object of political intervention from above and from outside—a key institution of modern society, whose organizational structure, personnel, and content-based functions were reorganized from the ground up by the SED and the Soviet occupation forces. On the other hand, it presents the university as an arena of action, in which the rules of academic life and the rules of the new power coexisted. This approach permits consideration of the internal limits of transformation. Throughout, attention will be directed to the decisive role of historical and geopolitical preconditions: the National Socialist past, Soviet occupation, and the emerging division within Germany.

"Storm the Fortress of Academia": The Replacement of Elites and Structural Discontinuities in the 1940s and 1950s

Soviet and East German Communists had no trouble justifying the reorganization of higher education that they orchestrated in 1945–46: they argued that the Nazi past and the willing collaboration of many professors between 1933 and 1945 necessitated radical change. As recent research has shown, the reactions of the various groups within the university to the Nazi seizure of power were anything but homogeneous: under the surface of the "brown university" different modes and stages of involvement were possible depending upon generation, discipline, and status group.[8] But during the immediate postwar years no one in the new administration was interested in differentiation or historical complexity. To the contrary, the undeniable necessity of an antifascist purge served as a catch-all

---

Landesbeauftragte für die Unterlagen des Staatssicherheitsdienstes der ehemaligen DDR, 1997); Patrick von zur Mühlen, Der "Eisenberger Kreis": Jugendwiderstand und Verfolgung in der DDR, 1953–1958 (Bonn: Dietz, 1995); Waldemar Krönig and Klaus-Dieter Müller, "Der Greifswalder Studentenstreik, 1955," Deutschland-Archiv 27 (1994): 517–25; Hermann Wentker, "'Kirchenkampf' in der DDR: Der Konflikt um die junge Gemeinde 1950–53," Vierteljahrshefte für Zeitgeschichte 42 (1994): 95–127; James F. Tent, The Free University of Berlin: A Political History (Bloomington: Indiana University Press, 1988).

8. See Michael Grüttner's contribution to this volume.

argument for the deepest cuts in personnel that German universities have ever seen.

Altogether the loss of academic personnel at the six universities in the Soviet Occupied Zone amounted to 83 percent of the staffing levels of the winter semester of 1944. Only 17 percent of all professors and docents who had taught before the end of the war remained in office two years later.[9] The departments of mathematics, natural sciences, medicine, and law suffered above-average losses (the last retained 7 percent of its 1944 faculty into the postwar period). There was stronger continuity in the faculties of philosophy, agriculture, and above all theology. Younger faculty members were affected disproportionately by the waves of purging: of all docents in 1944 only 9 percent were able to continue their activities; for the associate professors the figure is only 14 percent. Of the full professors (*ordentliche Professoren*) 28 percent survived the first large cut. The break in personnel at the beginning thus particularly affected the younger generation in the natural sciences, which had been disproportionately involved in National Socialism,[10] while the representatives of the traditional university subjects were less affected.

Only after 1947, with the onset of the socialist reorganization of higher education, did priorities in personnel policies shift significantly. Now the remaining representatives of the traditional humanities and social sciences came under strong pressure to leave. In unison with the SED

---

9. The academic literature refers to this blood-letting as "denazification," but this term does only partial justice to the chaotic events of these months. Beside political purging, the deportation of several hundred academics by the American and Soviet occupation forces and migrations to the Western zones of occupation also played significant roles. Ralph Jessen, *Akademische Elite und kommunistische Diktatur: Die ostdeutsche Hochschullehrerschaft in der Ulbricht-Ära* (Göttingen: Vandenhoeck & Ruprecht, 1999), 261–79. See Damian von Melis, *Entnazifizierung in Mecklenburg-Vorpommern: Herrschaft und Verwaltung, 1945–1948* (Munich: Oldenbourg, 1999); Hans-Uwe Feige, "Zur Entnazifizierung des Lehrkörpers an der Universität Leipzig," *Zeitschrift für Geschichtswissenschaft* 42 (1994): 795–808; Alexandr Haritonow, "Entnazifizierung an der Bergakademie Freiberg, 1945–1948," *Bildung und Erziehung* 45 (1992): 433–41; Clemens Vollnhals, ed., *Entnazifizierung: Politische Säuberung und Rehabilitierung in den vier Besatzungszonen, 1945–1949* (Munich: Deutscher Taschenbuch Verlag, 1991); Helga A. Welsh, "Entnazifizierung und Wiedereröffnung der Universität Leipzig, 1945–1946: Ein Bericht des damaligen Rektors Professor Bernhard Schweitzer," *Vierteljahrshefte für Zeitgeschichte* 33 (1985): 339–72.

10. See Michael H. Kater, *The Nazi Party: A Social Profile of Members and Leaders, 1919–1945* (Oxford: Basil Blackwell, 1983), 69, 109f. See also Mitchell G. Ash, "Wissenschaftswandel in Zeiten politischer Umwälzungen: Entwicklungen, Verwicklungen, Abwicklungen," *Intern. Zeitschrift für Geschichte und Ethik der Naturwissenschaften, Technik und Medizin* 3 (1995): 1–21.

leadership in Berlin, Communist education administrators in the individual states of the Soviet Zone stirred up ill-will toward the "bourgeois" academics in the humanities. Pseudo-plebeian mobilization among Communist students mixed with administrative pressures to force the dismissal, premature retirement, or departure for the West of those who had been identified as class enemies.[11] Representatives of disciplines within which the SED maintained a monopoly on truth—such as philosophy, history, and law—were particularly hard hit. The law department at the University of Rostock was closed completely. By 1951 more than half of all professors in the humanities were "new people," who did not come from the traditional academic milieu. In the social sciences, including law and economics, 80 percent of the professors were recently installed. They had either completed their doctoral degrees after 1945 or, even more frequently, had been appointed without completing any degree whatever.

The picture was quite different in the natural sciences and in the medical and technical schools. Just as a second wave of dismissals was crippling the humanities and social sciences, here authorities began rehabilitating and reintegrating those academics who had been dismissed during denazification. Those who had not fled to the West now had a good chance of being reinstated. During the 1950s professors who had completed their training during the Weimar Republic or the Nazi years became the dominant force in these faculties. Only by the beginning of the 1960s did a generation trained after 1945 begin asserting itself.[12]

Thus, despite the unparalleled dismissals of 1945–46, teaching staffs of the early 1950s displayed a differentiated picture. Widespread discontinuity in the social sciences contrasted with a high degree of continuity in the natural sciences and in medicine, with the humanities fitting somewhere in between. As the weight of denazification had been distributed in precisely the opposite manner, that is, heavier in the natural sciences and medicine, lighter in the social sciences and humanities; this asymmetry

---

11. See, for example, the University of Jena: Peter Schäfer, "Die Jenaer Universitätskrise von 1948," in *Universität im Aufbruch: Die Alma mater Jenensis als Mittler zwischen Ost und West*, ed. Herbert Gottwald (Jena: Academià & Studentica Jenensia, 1992), 325–31; Günter Zehm, "Repression und Widerstand an der Universität Jena, 1949–1989," *Bildung und Erziehung* 45 (1992): 453–65.

12. Ralph Jessen, "Diktatorischer Elitewechsel und universitäre Milieus: Hochschullehrer in der SBZ/DDR (1945–1967)," *Geschichte und Gesellschaft* 24 (1998): 24–54; Anna-Sabine Ernst, "Von der bürgerlichen zur sozialistischen Profession? Ärzte in der DDR, 1945–1961," in *Die Grenzen der Diktatur: Staat und Gesellschaft in der DDR*, ed. Richard Bessel and Ralph Jessen (Göttingen: Vandenhoeck & Ruprecht, 1996), 25–48.

must be explained by personnel policies adopted in the sovietization that took place from 1947–48 onward.

Once the division of Germany had assumed inexorable momentum, the SED and SMAD had been able to drop all tactical considerations and conclude the expulsion of their ideological adversaries in the humanities. Yet Germany's division also meant that they had to build a viable university system in the half of Germany they were to rule; that, in turn, meant retaining and attracting much-needed experts in the natural and technical sciences. As easy as it had been in the chaos of Germany's collapse to dismiss academics implicated in National Socialism, so now was it difficult to find qualified, politically acceptable successors. In practice, therefore, a pattern of recruitment established itself with marked differences according to discipline. In medicine, the natural sciences, agriculture, forestry, and the technical disciplines the traditional methods of recruitment remained for the most part intact and the faculties were largely restored. The decimated ranks in these subjects could hardly be filled by the few returning émigrés from National Socialism, and the efforts to entice West German experts remained largely fruitless.[13] Therefore the Communist university administration did not hesitate to reinstate in large numbers those natural and medical scientists who had been dismissed for their collaboration with the National Socialists only shortly before. These "gold fillings from the mouths of the reactionaries"[14]—as Robert Rompe, one of the few physicists close to the SED, characterized them in 1948—became intensely courted in the emerging East-West conflict. They were to shoulder the burdens of building East German science, and the state lavished upon them countless privileges. Between 1947 and 1952 the monthly salary for East German professors multiplied between four and five times;[15] and natural scientists in particular began negotiating "individual contracts" regulating the equipping of institutes, funds for conference travel, additional income, and assistance with

---

13. Marita Krauss, *Heimkehr in ein fremdes Land: Geschichte der Remigration nach 1945* (Munich: Beck, 2001); Herbert A. Strauss and Werner Röder, eds., *International Biographical Dictionary of Central European Emigrés, 1933–1945*, vol. 2, *The Arts, Science, and Literatur* (Munich: Saur, 1981).

14. See Robert Rompe's contribution to the discussion in the stenographic record of the Seventh (Twenty-first) Conference of the Party Leadership of the SED, 11–12 February 1948, in Stiftung Archiv der Parteien und Massenorganisationen der DDR im Bundesarchiv (SAPMO BA) DY 30/IV 2/1/40, folio 126.

15. "Verordnung über die Erhaltung und die Entwicklung der deutschen Wissenschaft u. Kultur v. 31.3.1949," in *Zwei Jahrzehnte Bildungspolitik in der Sowjetzone Deutschlands:*

children's educations.[16] A few particularly prominent scientists received "special salaries" of up to fifteen thousand marks per month. The "National Prize," introduced in 1949 and commanding purses of up to a hundred thousand marks did its part to keep the precious experts in the country; so did the "Committee for the German Intelligentsia," which was founded in the same year and administered countless perks for East German academics, ranging from apartments to heating fuel to holiday accommodations.[17]

If the SED attempted to integrate supposedly apolitical scientists by granting them privileges—turning a blind eye to their lack of sympathy for Soviet-style socialism—the approach in the humanities and social sciences was different. Here the party undertook a systematic and politically motivated reconstruction of the faculties, with little to no reintegration of those previously "denazified." Instead, a small group of leftist intellectual émigrés came from the West and played key roles in the reconstruction of new, politically correct faculties in the humanities. Often they had been appointed to professorships in spite of resistance from the old faculty. This group comprised a couple dozen intellectuals and scientists close to the German Communist Party (KDP) who had spent the war years in Turkey, Great Britain, Switzerland, Mexico, or the United States (rarely the Soviet Union), and who, in the years to come, undertook tremendous burdens in the training of a new generation of academics.[18] Their impact on this generation was due not only to their professional profile but also to their political credit in the party and moral capital derived from their status as victims of Nazism or as émigrés. Some representatives of this type of scholar were also present among the founding generation of the social sciences, and a large proportion came from the SED's own cadre reserve. In the 1950s a number were appointed to professorships in economics,

---

Dokumente, ed. Siegfried Baske and Martha Engelbert, vol. 1, 1945–1958 (Berlin: Freie Universität Berlin, 1966), 105–12; Henner Wolter, *Zusatzversorgungssysteme der Intelligenz: Verfassungsrechtliche Probleme der Rentenüberleitung in den neuen Bundesländern* (Baden-Baden: Nomos, 1992).

16. In 1960 87 percent of professors of medicine and 64 percent of professors in technical and natural science disciplines, but only 22 percent of their colleagues in the humanities and social sciences held individual contracts. Figures in the Bundesarchiv (BA) DR-3, 822.

17. See the quite similar early Soviet strategies of integration in Michael David-Fox's contribution to this volume.

18. Michael F. Scholz, "Sowjetische Besatzungszone und DDR," in *Handbuch der deutschsprachigen Emigration, 1933–1945*, ed. Claus-Dieter Krohn et al. (Darmstadt: Wissenschaftliche Buchgesellschaft, 1998), 1180–88.

journalism, and pedagogy though they had never completed university training. Their main qualification was long-standing activity as journalists or as political instructors for the KDP or SED.[19]

As had been the case with the early purging, interventions in the structure of higher education soon after 1945 were carried out in the name of "antifascism," though here too intentions and repercussions went far beyond simply breaking with the National Socialist past. Two phases can be identified in the mid- to late 1940s.[20] Higher education policy of the first phase can be described as "formal restoration" and "institutional differentiation." The first term alludes to the demonstrative abolition of changes undertaken by the Nazis and a formal return to the legal situation applicable during the Weimar Republic. This return was merely "formal" because, apart from anything else, the administration of the universities was subjected to constant manipulation by the Communist-led public education administration of the individual states and of the central zonal administration, out of which the government of the GDR emerged in 1949. Because the SMAD and—with its support—the Communist-controlled German Education Administration in Berlin (DVV) overruled the restored self-governing organs in cases of conflict, they were able to rebuild the institutional structure of the universities with faculties, deans, senates, and elected rectors according to the traditional pattern.

The decisive structural change in the first five postwar years was in the establishment of new institutions under the control of the KDP/SED, which were either housed at universities or took over the functions of the universities. Among these were the "New Teacher" and "People's Judges" schools in 1945–46, whose crash courses took over most of the training of teachers and lawyers for a few years, thus channeling these people out of the universities.[21] In legal education the "German Administration Academy" in Forst-Zinna (1948) and the "German College for Justice"

---

19. Jessen, *Akademische Elite*, 315–35.
20. See John Connelly, *Captive University: The Sovietization of East German, Czech, and Polish Higher Education, 1945–56* (Chapel Hill: University of North Carolina Press, 2000), 40–45.
21. Petra Gruner, *Die Neulehrer—ein Schlüsselsymbol der DDR-Gesellschaft: Biographische Konstruktionen von Lehrern zwischen Erfahrungen und gesellschaftlichen Erwartungen* (Weinheim: Deutscher Studienverlag, 2000); Brigitte Hohlfeld, *Die Neulehrer in der SBZ/DDR, 1945–1953: Ihre Rolle bei der Umgestaltung von Gesellschaft und Staat* (Weinheim: Deutscher Studienverlag, 1992); Julia Pfannkuch, *Volksrichterausbildung in Sachsen, 1945–1950* (Frankfurt: Lang, 1993); Hermann Wentker, ed., *Volksrichter in der SBZ/DDR, 1945–1952: Eine Dokumentation* (Munich: Oldenbourg, 1997).

(1952) contributed to this trend. In 1953 they were joined into the "Walter Ulbricht German Academy for State and Legal Science" (DASR) and thereafter fell under the strict control of the SED.[22] Within the universities the "Social Science" and "Pedagogy" faculties, founded in 1946, played a similar role—new docents, mostly loyal to the SED, filled departments that were to train successive generations for schools and public administration. The "old" faculties had no say either in the appointment of teaching staff or in the admission of students.[23] The German Education Administration thus softened the initial confrontation with the universities and still wielded decisive influence on the training of future teachers, lawyers, and administrative functionaries, on whose loyalty the establishment and ideological security of the nascent dictatorship largely depended.

While the "New Teacher" courses and "Social Sciences" faculties were being established, both under the strong influence of the SED but nevertheless belonging to the state sector, a totally new type of "institution of higher education" emerged, standing outside state structures, namely, the schooling and training colleges of the SED and of the Free Federation of German Unions (Freier Deutscher Gewerkschaftsbund, FDGB), as well as of the Communist youth organization Free German Youth (Freie Deutsche Jugend, FDJ)—both of which were controlled by the SED. On 14 May 1946 the leadership of the SED elevated the KDP's Party School to Party College "Karl Marx," which began instruction in June that year. In the same year the trade union school of the FDGB (which received its college status in 1952) and the "Youth College" of the FDJ were established.[24] All three colleges served to train the rapidly growing body of functionaries of each organization. Admission to these colleges, curricula, final examinations, and later appointment of graduates were all

---

22. Andreas Herbst et al., *So funktionierte die DDR* (Reinbek: Rowohlt, 1994), 45–46; Gert-Joachim Glaessner, *Herrschaft durch Kader: Leitung der Gesellschaft und Kaderpolitik in der DDR am Beispiel des Staatsapparates* (Opladen: Westdeutscher Verlag, 1977), 304–9; Rudolf Schwarzenbach, *Die Kaderpolitik der SED in der Staatsverwaltung: Ein Beitrag zur Entwicklung des Verhältnisses von Partei und Staat in der DDR (1945–1975)* (Cologne: Wissenschaft und Politik, 1976), 110–15.

23. Hans-Uwe Feige, "Die Gesellschaftswissenschaftliche Fakultät an der Universität Leipzig (1947–51)," *Deutschland Archiv* 26 (1993): 572–83; Karl Wockenfuss, "Professor X: 'Wir bilden gewissermassen Politoffiziere des gesellschaftlichen Lebens aus': Einblicke in Akten und Schicksale von Professoren und Studenten der Philosophischen und Pädagogischen Fakultät von 1950 bis 1968," *Beiträge zur Geschichte der Universität Rostock* 19 (1994): 47–77.

24. See Herbst et al., *So funktionierte die DDR*, 370–71, 438–40, 783–87, and the relevant articles in H. Zimmermann, ed., *DDR-Handbuch*, 3d ed. (Cologne: Wissenschaft und Politik, 1985).

determined exclusively according to political criteria. Several years later, in September 1949, the "Marx-Engels-Lenin Institute" of the SED leadership began its work, operating as the "Institute for Marxism-Leninism" from 1956 onward.[25] Research and training functions were also assumed by the "Institute for Social Sciences of the Central Committee of the SED," the later "Academy for Social Sciences."[26] The SED leadership set its sights on the prestigious insignia of a respectable university for its Party College "Karl Marx": in 1947 the school was divided into four "faculties," each headed by "deans," and their most important docents received the title of "professor" in 1952; from 1953 on the party college had the right to confer degrees.

The SED colleges and those of the "mass organizations" fashioned an independent type of party-controlled institution of higher education alongside the universities, and as such pushed the principle of institutional differentiation to the limit. They enabled the SED to recruit and train urgently needed functionaries without being dependent on the collaboration of politically suspect university faculties. During the radicalization of the late 1940s and early 1950s the Party College also served to train a loyal cadre of docents for the social sciences at the universities. For example, between 1948 and 1950 it organized two docent training programs which prepared party academics to teach "Marxist-Leninist Social Sciences" at the universities.[27] Countless SED historians, philosophers, economists, and social scientists received their ideological shaping here and later made careers at East German universities. In this respect the Party College played an important part in the ideological offensive at the universities at the beginning of the 1950s.

In subsequent years the personal connections between universities and party colleges abated, however. Viewed from a long-term perspective the importance of party institutions for higher education lay less in transfer of personnel than in the ideological formation of the humanities and social sciences as disciplines, a function which became thoroughly institutionalized by the end of the 1960s. At this point "academic committees

---

25. See *Vierzig Jahre Institut für Marxismus-Leninismus beim ZK der SED, 1949–1989* (Berlin: Institut für Marxismus-Leninismus, 1989).

26. Herbst et al., *So funktionierte die DDR*, 41–45; Wilhelm Bleek and Lothar Mertens, *DDR-Dissertationen: Promotionspraxis und Geheimhaltung von Doktorarbeiten im SED-Staat* (Opladen: Westdeutscher Verlag, 1994), 41.

27. See Ernst Richert, *"Sozialistische Universität": Die Hochschulpolitik der SED* (Berlin: Colloquium, 1967), 72.

for social scientific research" were established to coordinate the content and organization of individual research projects. No less than five of these "academic committees" were affiliated with the SED's Academy for Social Sciences, among them the Committee for Philosophy and Sociology. A further two were affiliated with the Institute for Marxism-Leninism (one of these was the Committee for Historiography), and two were affiliated with the Party College and the Trade Union College respectively.[28]

Between 1949 and 1951 the new state put an end to the dual track system of traditional universities on the one hand and separate, politically controlled institutions of higher education on the other. The actual party establishments remained in existence, but the new teacher courses and the people's judge courses were discontinued and the social scientific and pedagogic faculties were shut down and their functions integrated into the ordinary faculties. This was not a sign of diminishing ideologization of higher education, but rather of the reverse, a successful political *Gleichschaltung*. In swift order a series of decrees by the central state education administration destroyed what was left, or what had been reinstated in 1945–46, of the corporate constitution of the universities.[29] Universities were defined as state teaching establishments and subordinated to government supervision. The previous organs of self-governance at the universities remained as a hollow facade that concealed the actual power relations. Even if deans and rectors continued to be elected, only those candidates were considered who had previously been selected by the SED. In 1949 admissions, the disbursement of stipends, and the political control over the course of study were made the responsibility of a "dean of students," nominated by state authorities.[30] Collegial committees, such as the senate or the "inner faculty circle" that had once regulated faculty matters lost their exclusivity and were diluted through the inclusion of politically controlled functionaries. With the establishment of four state-appointed deputy vice chancellors—for undergraduate study in the social sciences, for matters of research, for academic research assistantships (*Aspirantur*), and for student affairs—all important university responsibilities were taken out of the hands of elected committees. Officially, the rector remained the university's representative to the outside world, but real

28. "Wissenschaftliche Räte," in Zimmermann, *DDR-Handbuch*, 1523.
29. The most important decrees are collected in Baske and Engelbert, *Dokumente*, vol. 1.
30. "Vorläufige Arbeitsordnung der Universitäten und wissenschaftlichen Hochschulen der SBZ v. 23.5.1949," in Baske and Engelbert, *Dokumente*, 1:115–22, 21.

power was transferred to state commissars, only barely robed in academic credentials.[31]

Even though the details of university administration were subject to further fine-tuning, the basic structures created in the early 1950s largely remained in place until the major education reform of the late 1960s. Before those incisive changes some room for maneuver remained at universities, through traditional academic chairs, seminars, and institutes, even if university autonomy as such had been destroyed. In everyday life a professor often had more authority and power than a party functionary. This was especially true of medical and natural science institutes.

Last among the dramatic changes of the 1940s and 1950s were the deep interventions in the recruitment of students. These began with a drastic political purge in the student admissions of the first postwar semester. Greatly suspicious of former military officers and members of Nazi organizations who wanted to continue interrupted studies, admissions regulations set high political hurdles for enrollment. All erstwhile members of the Nazi Party (NSDAP), discharged military officers, and the children of formerly prominent Nazis were to be denied access to higher education. Active resistance fighters and members of the opposition were given preference, as were such applicants whom the Nazis had denied higher education on grounds of race or political conviction.[32] This meant that many students who had begun their studies before the end of the war were not able to complete them: in the summer of 1946 half of all Berlin students were freshmen.[33]

After 1947 the emphasis in admissions shifted: it was no longer one's political activities during the Nazi years that determined access to higher education, but rather social background and the political attitudes of the applicants since the end of the war. Applicants from worker or peasant families, graduates of state-supported high school equivalency courses (*Vorstudienanstalten*), and those persecuted by the Nazis were granted preferred admission. Only after all such applicants had been admitted could applicants from the next category be considered: those able to

---

31. Müller and Müller, . . . *die Festung Wissenschaft*, 259; "Vorläufige Arbeitsordnung," 6:1; *Durchführungsbestimmung zur Verordnung über die Neuorganisation des Hochschulwesens* v. 3.3.1951, *Gesetzblatt der DDR*, 1951, 175.

32. On student admissions, see Herbert Stallmann, *Hochschulzugang in der SBZ/DDR, 1945–1959* (Sankt Augustin: Richarz, 1980).

33. Müller and Müller, . . . *die Festung Wissenschaft*, 77.

demonstrate "active participation in the democratic development in Germany," namely, those who had behaved in conformity with the expectations of the SED. Only after this reservoir had been exhausted could any remaining candidates receive consideration.

With this institutionalization of preference for children of the lower classes a dictatorial policy of counterprivileging began which was practiced with remarkable consistency until the early 1960s. This, along with the "worker and peasant faculties" founded in 1949 to prepare young workers for higher education, radically altered the social recruitment for most academic jobs.[34] In the second semester after the war only about 10 percent of students at Berlin University came from worker or peasant families, but by 1950 the figure was 26 percent and by 1955 over 55 percent.[35] The losers in this policy were the children from the middle and upper classes, whose chances for higher education markedly worsened. SED hopes that those born into workers' families would also prove born Communists were not always fulfilled, but the ruthless social selection provided East Germany's Communists with advantages that cannot be underestimated. Both in propaganda toward West Germany and toward its own population the SED could portray itself as the party of historical fairness that had finally broken "bourgeois privilege in education." The "workers and peasant faculties" and the SED's claim for social justice in matters of education as well as its antifascist rhetoric played a crucial role for the positive perception and mystification of the early years of the GDR by many East German intellectuals.[36] So the party achieved long-term dividends in

---

34. Michael C. Schneider, "Grenzen des Elitenaustausches: Zur Organisations- und Sozialgeschichte der Vorstudienanstalten und frühen Arbeiter- und Bauernfakultäten in der SBZ/DDR," *Jahrbuch für Universitätsgeschichte* 1 (1998): 134–76; idem, "Chancengleichheit oder Kaderauslese? Zu Intentionen, Traditionen und Wandel der Vorstudienanstalten und Arbeiter-und-Bauern-Fakultäten in der SBZ/DDR zwischen 1945 und 1952," *Zeitschrift für Pädagogik* 41 (1995): 959–83.

35. Jochen Lippstreu, *Chancengleichheit und studentische Rekrutierung in der Sowjetischen Besatzungszone (SBZ/DDR), 1945–1963* (master's thesis, Freie Universität Berlin, 1995), 21.

36. See Hermann Kant, *Die Aula*, 22d edition (Berlin: Rütten u. Löning, 1981).

37. Lutz Niethammer et al., *Die volkseigene Erfahrung: Eine Archäologie des Lebens in der Industrieprovinz der DDR: 30 biographische Eröffnungen* (Berlin: Rowohlt, 1994), 44–45; Karl Ulrich Mayer and Heike Solga, "Mobilität und Legitimität: Zum Vergleich der Chancenstrukturen in der alten DDR und der alten BRD, oder Haben Mobilitätschancen zu Stabilität und Zusammenbruch der DDR beigetragen?" *Kölner Zeitschrift für Soziologie und Sozialpsychologie (KZfSS)*, 1994: 193–208; Ralph Jessen, "Mobility and Blockage in the Seventies," in *The East German Dictatorship: Ambiguities of Repression and Experience in the GDR*, ed. Konrad H. Jarausch (Providence: Berghahn, 1999), 341–60.

political loyalty by systematically elevating a stratum of upwardly mobile members of the lower classes.[37]

The politicization of instruction began in the fall of 1946, when all students were required to attend a lecture course titled "Political and Social Problems of the Present Age." University instruction as a whole was still largely unaffected by this innovation. In fact, the separation of academic instruction from political schooling remained mostly intact even after 1951, when indoctrination in Marxism-Leninism became a part of the curriculum. After this point, students were required to complete a three-year "Basic Course in Social Studies."[38] Specially trained docents, usually young people without particular academic expertise, were entrusted with this indoctrination, and in short order involved themselves in a draining struggle for authority with the established faculty.

Actual university teaching changed less during the obviously political reforms of the early 1950s—the intensity of which depended upon the discipline and the personality of the instructor—than to the far-reaching organizational changes and a distinct promotion of rote-learning. The higher education reform of 1951 ended the German tradition of a minimally structured "free" course of study. A ten-month academic year was imposed with centrally ordained schedules that were tightly structured by regular intermediate exams. University studies were now characterized by early specialization rather than breadth, and by firm schedules of set classes rather than free choice of lectures and seminars.

Taken as a whole, the five years between the reopening of East German universities in 1946 and the reforms of 1950–51 seem to represent a two-stage process of change that reached nearly all areas of the university—the teaching body, students, the institutional structure, and curriculum (but did not yet affect research). Both phases intersected and interpenetrated each other. Although a clear push to radicalism can be detected in 1947–48, there is little basis for the supposition that the preceding phase of "antifascist" reforms was something like a "good beginning" or a "missed opportunity" for a better development. All too visible behind the antifascist rhetoric was a desire to subjugate the universities politically. During the phase of radical change between 1947 and 1951 it is striking how closely the SED kept to a scenario for change perfected twenty years before

---

38. This was the Gesellschaftswissenschaftliches Grundstudium. See the reminiscences in Waldemar Krönig and Klaus-Dieter Müller, *Anpassung, Widerstand, Verfolgung. Hochschule und Studenten in der SBZ und DDR, 1945–1961* (Köln: Verlag Wissenschaft und Politik, 1994), 50.

in Russia, and repeated elsewhere in postwar Eastern Europe.[39] The fact that East German leaders took building blocks from the Russian revolutionary construction kit without injecting many of their own ideas demonstrates the very close guidance of the SMAD, even if exact scenarios of imitation are not always easy to reconstruct. Whatever the precise route of transfer, all the measures of the SED's higher education policy discussed here, from the partial closing of law schools to the founding of worker and peasant faculties, the political seizing of the university administration, the establishment of independent party colleges, the systematic support of those rising from the lower classes in the student body, the introduction of obligatory Marxist-Leninist courses, the preference of teaching before research, and the provision of material privileges for "bourgeois specialists" had been tested between 1918 and 1920 at Russian universities.[40]

Scope and Limits of Political Penetration: Control and Compromise as Part of the Competition Between the Two Germanies

For those who witnessed the destruction of independent student representations and the strangling of intellectual freedom at East German universities in the years after World War II, there was little doubt that the communist "storming of the academic fortress" had taken its objectives. If anything, events of the early 1950s reinforced such impressions: the visitor to East Berlin could witness pictures of Stalin going up at "Humboldt University," columns of Free German Youth marching up Unter den Linden on official holidays, and hysterical witch hunts against "objectivism" and "cosmopolitanism" encroaching upon university grounds. Obviously the universities, severely damaged in their intellectual substance, self-awareness, and moral integrity after twelve years of National Socialism, did not have much left with which to resist the concerted pressures of Soviet occupiers and native Communists, who took advantage of unusually favorable political circumstances to in a couple of years turn student body, teaching staff, university constitution, and instruction upside-down. Denazification merged seamlessly with Stalinization: those who resisted

---

39. Connelly, *Captive University*, 3ff.
40. See the contribution by Michael David-Fox in this volume.

lost student status or academic position, and frequently escaped to the West. Those who stayed behind adapted, sometimes out of conviction, sometimes not.[41]

This picture of a revolution imposed from without and above reveals much, but not everything. Upon closer inspection, contradictions and conflicts become evident between SED and academic community even in the 1950s. These proved that a total reconstruction of the social microcosm of the university had not been successful. In spite of the best efforts of dictatorship, universities of this period were not subordinated to a single will. Within the natural sciences—though not in the social sciences and humanities—significant spaces remained within which authorities had to negotiate their ambitions. This professorial power derived in part from the open border between the two Germanies. East Germany could not behave as if insulated from the outside world, but rather was forced to interact and compete with the West German "class enemy." In addition, the very nature of scientific research, in which results cannot be preprogrammed, forced the SED to permit research a certain measure of freedom. In theory, the SED could discipline university teaching staff any time it liked, but in practice it had to anticipate the potential repercussions of repressive measures. University teachers were after all researchers too, and the party could not simply dispense with their cooperation if state plans for scientific output were to be met.

From the early postwar years considerable gaps separated the specific disciplines in how they were treated by the SED. These deepened in the 1950s, when, on the one hand, the regime restored medical, technical, and natural scientists to academic positions, while on the other it did nothing to mend the ruptures effected after the war in the social sciences and humanities. One indicator for restoration is the proportion of former NSDAP members in the teaching body. Of university professors active in 1954, 31 percent of the natural scientists, 41 percent of those teaching agriculture, forestry, and veterinary medicine, 42 percent of the engineers, and almost 46 percent of the physicians had belonged to the Nazi Party.[42]

---

41. Just how successful this rebuilding process was in the Soviet Occupied Zone/GDR becomes starkly apparent when it is compared to the developments in the neighboring countries of Poland and Czechoslovakia, where the "sovietizing" of the universities went much less smoothly. See Connelly, *Captive University*.

42. Jessen, *Akademische Elite*, 304–7. Before the building of the wall in 1961 only 13 percent of medical professors were members of the SED. See Anna Sabine Ernst, "Doppelstaatsbürger von Partei und Fach? Das soziale und politische Profil der DDR-Medizinprofessoren in den 50er Jahren," *Hochschule Ost* 6, no. 2 (1997): 26.

As many as 60 percent of university rectors had once possessed NSDAP membership books—and these were found disproportionately in the natural, medical, and technical sciences.[43] Not much changed in these breakdowns until 1962. And even then, between 31 percent and 37 percent of professors in the natural sciences, medicine, agriculture, forestry, and the technical disciplines had once been Nazis, while professors in the humanities and social sciences barely reached half these figures, with 17.5 percent and 15.2 percent respectively.[44]

With these figures in mind, the purges of 1945–46 seem less a major break than a temporary interruption. The GDR also reintegrated academics in a way that was reminiscent of the infamous article 131 of the Basic Law (the *Grundgesetz*) in the Federal Republic, which had made possible the return of many academics dismissed after 1945 for political reasons, though it did so more quietly and to a more limited extent.[45] Rehabilitation in disciplines less affected by ideology was limited less by political scruples than by the fact that many academics had left for the West and were no longer available for reintegration. Thus the initial purging was more effective than higher education officials of the 1950s would have liked.

The major distinction to Western development lay in selectivity by discipline. While those representatives of the "hard" disciplines who had remained in the Soviet Occupied Zone/GDR could assume their professorships once more, their colleagues in the humanities and social sciences remained out in the cold. Contrary to what one might expect, the reintegration of former Nazis did not present the ruling SED with any political risks. As in the West, such individuals behaved with great loyalty to the state.[46]

The emigration of dismissed scientists to the West points to a dilemma that dogged the SED through the 1950s. Alone in the East bloc, the establishment of Communist dictatorship in the GDR implied the splitting

---

43. Jessen, *Akademische Elite*, 306.
44. See "Übersichten der kaderpolitischen Zusammensetzung des Lehrkörpers der Universitäten, Hoch- und Fachschulen der DDR, v. 31.12.1962," in BA DR-3, 6060, and Jessen, *Akademische Elite*, 473–84.
45. See Ulrich Schneider, "Zur Entnazifizierung der Hochschullehrer in Niedersachsen, 1945–1949," *Niedersächsisches Jahrbuch für Landesgeschichte* 64 (1989): 343–46; Wolfgang Langhorst, *Beamtentum und Artikel 131 des Grundgesetzes* (Frankfurt: Lang, 1994); Anikó Szabó, *Vertreibung, Rückkehr, Wiedergutmachung: Göttinger Hochschullehrer im Schatten des Nationalsozialismus. Mit einer biographischen Dokumentation der entlassenen und verfolgten Hochschullehrer* (Göttingen: Wallstein, 2000).
46. Connelly, *Captive University*, 158.

of one nation into two states. This had far-reaching consequences for the development of higher education in the GDR. For one thing, East German institutions of higher education had to form a "nation-state" academic system. For another, a constant moral competition between East and West emerged over who was the legitimate heir to the German academic tradition, as well as over who had convincingly broken with the Nazi past. But the most important aspect of this competition between the two Germanies was the dual labor market within which the SED had to rebuild East German higher education. Unlike their Polish or Hungarian colleagues, East German academics could emigrate to their own country. If professors and students escaped political pressures by leaving for the Federal Republic, this might be seen by the SED as quite advantageous, as it weakened the intellectual potential for opposition.[47] The price of political peace was, however, an uninterrupted brain drain of highly qualified experts.[48] The great purges of the early postwar period had cost East Germany approximately 1,300 professors and docents, yet between 1952 and 1961 some 2,000 professors, docents, and assistant professors left East German universities and colleges for the Federal Republic.[49] As the losses of emigration could hardly be balanced by gains from immigration, and newly trained academics were insufficient to fill the gaps, a chronic shortage of personnel emerged at East German universities during the 1950s. In 1951, 384 professorships, 140 docent posts, and 383 assistantships stood vacant; eight years later there were 156 unfilled professorships, 176 vacant docent positions, and 777 unoccupied assistantships.[50] As is always the case when shortage confronts great demand, those with something to offer profited. This was reflected, not only in the high salaries

---

47. Albert O. Hirschman, "Exit, Voice and the Fate of the German Democratic Republic: An Essay in Conceptual History," A *Quarterly Journal of International Relations* 45 (1993): 173–202; Stefan Wolle, "Flucht als Widerstand?" *Widerstand und Opposition in der DDR*, ed. Klaus-Dietmar Henke et al. (Cologne: Böhlau, 1999), 309–26.

48. Helge Heidemeyer, *Flucht und Zuwanderung aus der SBZ/DDR, 1945/46–1961: Die Flüchtlingspolitik der Bundesrepublik Deutschland bis zum Bau der Berliner Mauer* (Düsseldorf: Droste, 1994); Hartmut Wendt, "Die deutsch-deutschen Wanderungen—Bilanz einer 40jährigen Geschichte von Flucht und Ausreise," *Deutschland-Archiv* 24 (1991): 386–95; H. von zur Mühlen, "Flucht und Eingliederung der Wissenschaftler," *Fachberater für Vertriebene, Flüchtlinge und Kriegsgeschädigte* 15 (1962): 67–71; *Die Flucht des Geistes aus der SBZ* (Bonn: Presse- und Informationsamt der Bundesregierung, 1960).

49. John Connelly, "Zur 'Republikflucht' von DDR-Wissenschaftlern in den fünfziger Jahren," *Zeitschrift für Geschichtswissenschaft* 42 (1994): 331–52; Krönig and Müller, *Anpassung*, 40; Jessen, *Akademische Elite*, 46.

50. Hausmitteilung v. 9.5.1951, in BA DR-3, 1343; Vorlage des SHF an das Sekretariat des ZK der SED v. 23.12.1959, in BA DR-3, 5790.

for technical, natural, and medical scientists, but also in the reduced political pressures exerted upon such individuals. The high numbers of former NSDAP members in these fields clearly reflects the desperation of education authorities: they had no choice but to reappoint the brown sheep. Into the mid-1950s the old professors in these fields controlled the recruitment of successors, and very little of Communist ideology seeped into teaching. When the cadre department of the SED attempted to increase its influence in the natural sciences after 1956, it was soon forced to retreat, fearful of driving more specialists into the West.[51]

Another way of dealing with this dilemma was to compensate for politicization of teaching by granting freedom to research. Such a strategy contradicted ideals of "unity in research and teaching" that had played a central role in the German university system since the beginning of the nineteenth century.[52] Though reality began to depart from such ideals in the first third of the twentieth century, even after 1945 many academics continued to feel they were goals worth striving for. Yet very soon distinct tendencies in the opposite direction became discernible: in the summer of 1946 the former "Prussian Academy of Sciences" was reopened in East Berlin as the "German Academy of Sciences," and a veritable research empire began to evolve under its roof. If initially the basis for research lay in the former "Kaiser Wilhelm Society," soon new establishments were added: in 1948 there were twenty academy institutes, by 1957 seventy-five, and by 1962 one hundred and nine, and the research emphasis was decidedly in the natural sciences.[53] In the second half of the 1950s growth in nonuniversity research establishments exceeded that of university counterparts. And even if education functionaries of the SED seldom addressed the issue, a two-class academic society was slowly emerging: universities became increasingly politicized and focused on teaching, while the Academy of Sciences became a refuge for research. Here even conservative academics without any sympathies for the SED could conduct their research, often under excellent conditions, without placing the ideological education goals of the party at universities in any jeopardy. Those wanting to

---

51. Jessen, *Akademische Elite*, 95–102.
52. Gert Schubring, ed., *"Einsamkeit und Freiheit"—neu besichtigt. Universitätsreformen und Disziplinenbildung in Preussen als Modell für Wissenschaftspolitik im Europa des 19. Jahrhunderts* (Stuttgart: Franz Steiner, 1991); R. Steven Turner, "The Prussian Universities and the Research Imperative, 1806–1848" (Ph.D. diss., Princeton University, 1973).
53. Rudolf Landrock, *Die Deutsche Akademie der Wissenschaften zu Berlin, 1945–1971* (Erlangen: Deutsche Gesellschaft für Zeitgeschichtliche Fragen, 1977), 17–31, 156.

evade the politicized teaching sphere did not, therefore, need to defect to West Germany; instead they could withdraw to fairly comfortable niches, which for many years felt little direct political pressure—provided, that is, that SED research planners valued their research interests.[54]

The development of extra-university research thus shows that Communists did not only thwart the ambitions of East German academics: whoever was involved in economically important research and refrained from open opposition could profit from generous salaries and well-equipped institutes. East German academics also enjoyed an added layer of job security, because Germany's division insulated them from West German competition for scarce positions and research funds. Furthermore, in the second half of the 1950s committees were established for research planning and political consultancy through which ambitious natural scientists influence East German academic policy. The "Research Advisory Council," established in 1957, deserves special mention as a liaison office between academia and politics. It was founded by several prestigious natural scientists who were inspired by the model of the "Imperial Research Council" established by the Nazis: one of its members, Peter Adolf Thiessen, had indeed belonged to this earlier incarnation. They hoped to influence SED science policy and to supervise research and development throughout the GDR. Several key members were natural scientists who had worked in Soviet nuclear and aerospace research after the war and now, having returned home, expected influential posts in the East German academic world. SED academic policymakers willingly fulfilled these hopes, above all because the emerging system of centrally planned research required a central interface between policy and science. By favoring such scientists the SED also seemed pro-science in the face of Western competitors. Finally, the Research Advisory Council helped

---

54. Peter Nötzoldt, "Der Weg zur 'sozialistischen Forschungsakademie': Der Wandel des Akademiegedankens zwischen 1945 und 1968," in *Naturwissenschaft und Technik in der DDR*, ed. Dieter Hoffmann and Kristie Macrakis (Berlin: Akademie, 1997), 125–46; Jürgen Kocka and Peter Nötzoldt, eds., *Die Akademien der Wissenschaften zu Berlin im geteilten Deutschland, 1945–1990* (Berlin: Akademie, 2002); Rüdiger Schroeder, "SED und Akademie der Wissenschaften: Zur Durchsetzung der 'führenden Rolle' der Partei in den fünfziger Jahren," *Deutschland Archiv* 28 (1995): 1264–78; Peter Th. Walther, "Bildung und Wissenschaft," in *DDR-Geschichte in Dokumenten: Beschlüsse, Berichte, interne Materialien und Alltagszeugnisse*, ed. Matthias Judt (Berlin: Christoph Links, 1997), 225–91; idem, "Denkraster- und Kaderpolitik der SED in der Deutschen Akademie der Wissenschaften zu [Ost-]Berlin," in *Deutsche Literaturwissenschaft, 1945–1965: Fallstudien zu Institutionen, Diskursen, Personen*, ed. Petra Boden and Rainer Rosenberg (Berlin: Akademie, 1998), 161–72.

integrate representatives of the old elite in the natural sciences, by holding out the prospect of active input in science policy in return for political allegiance to the GDR. To what extent they actually became involved in formulating such policy is another question.[55]

Radicalization and the Generation Transfer of the Late 1950s

A radicalization in SED higher education policy in the late 1950s showed how equivocal were the signs of reconciliation the party had transmitted to top natural scientists in 1957 through the founding of the Research Advisory Council. As in other East bloc countries, the de-Stalinization crisis after the Twentieth Party Conference of the Communist Party of the Soviet Union in February 1956 generated a certain amount of unrest in the GDR.[56] Yet after the Ulbricht leadership had asserted itself against its critics from within the party and successfully suppressed nascent demands for internal liberalization, a new wave of restructuring commenced that affected nearly all sectors of East German society. In law the infamous "Babelsberger Conference" of 1958 signaled the final subordination of the judiciary to the political. In 1959 the SED unleashed a campaign propagating close ties between artistic work and the "interests of the working class"; soon afterward it launched the forced collectivization of agriculture. The party also focused special attention on universities because they had generated opposition to the ideologization of teaching in the wake of Khrushchev's condemnation of Stalin.[57]

The most visible manifestations of this opposition were student protests against Marxist-Leninist indoctrination and the ever unpopular courses in the Russian language in the spring and fall of 1956. The SED

---

55. Agnes Charlotte Tandler, *Geplante Zukunft. Wissenschaftler und Wissenschaftspolitik in der DDR, 1955–1971* (Freiberg: Technischer Universität Bergakademie, 2000), 79–83.
56. Karl Wilhelm Fricke, "Widerstand und Opposition von 1945 bis Ende der Fünfziger Jahre," in Deutscher Bundestag, *Materialien der Enquete-Kommission "Aufarbeitung von Geschichte und Folgen der SED-Diktatur in Deutschland,"* vol. VII/1 (Frankfurt: Suhrkamp, 1995), 15–25; Helga Grebing, "Die intellektuelle Opposition in der DDR seit 1956: Ernst Bloch—Wolfgang Harich—Robert Havemann," *Aus Politik und Zeitgeschichte* B45/46 (1977): 3–19; Armin Mittler und Stefan Wolle, *Untergang auf Raten: Unbekannte Kapitel der DDR-Geschichte* (Munich: Bertelsmann, 1993), 163–295.
57. Kowalczuk, *Niederschlagung*; Klaus-Dieter Müller, "Studentische Opposition in der SBZ/DDR," in *Widerstand und Opposition in der DDR*, ed. Klaus-Dietmar Henke et al. (Köln: Böhlau, 1999), 93–124.

did not content itself with suppressing such protests and expelling the most active participants from the university. Rather, it used the crisis as a pretext to stage a new assault on universities, aimed at realizing the "continuing socialist reconstruction of technical and higher education."[58] Until that point the facade of university tradition had been maintained and many in the older generation of professors had been kept on out of necessity; but now the remnants of university autonomy were to be eliminated. For those observing this process from the outside, the radicalization manifested itself above all in the spectacular disciplinary measures taken against individual instructors. These measures were supposed to achieve the "removal of all openly oppositional elements from the teaching body" and to "completely neutralize all bourgeois influence" in the humanities and social sciences, as was explained to the SED leadership by the state secretary responsible for higher education, Wilhelm Girnus.[59] One of the best-known cases concerned the Leipzig philosopher Ernst Bloch. In 1948, Bloch had been appointed as a Marxist to a professorship in philosophy at Leipzig against the wishes of a conservative majority in the faculty. However, during the 1950s he had aroused the suspicions of party ideologues with his independent thinking. When in 1956 former Stalinist Bloch made remarks critical of the SED and its higher education policy the party instigated a propaganda campaign against him, which culminated in his forced retirement in August 1957.[60] Other professors suffered similar fates, even if their cases did not make such large waves.

The ideological offensive against individual nonconformist academics was, however, only the tip of the iceberg. In fact the SED wanted finally to gain complete control over the academic recruitment process. While the selection of students according to social background and political affiliation had been practiced relatively successfully since the 1940s, the personnel planners of the SED repeatedly ran into difficulties in altering the composition of the teaching body. They had mostly replaced the staff in the humanities and social sciences in the late 1940s and early 1950s,

---

58. "Verordnung über die weitere sozialistische Umgestaltung des Hoch- und Fachschulwesens v. 13.2.1958," in Baske and Engelbert, *Dokumente*, 1:353–58.
59. Girnus to Schirdewan v. 9.11. 1958, in BA DR-3: 215.
60. Hans-Uwe Feige, "Ketzer und Kampfgenosse—der Leipziger Ordinarius für Philosophie Ernst Bloch," *Deutschland-Archiv* 25 (1992): 697–717; Volker Caysa et al., *"Hoffnung kann enttäuscht werden": Ernst Bloch in Leipzig* (Frankfurt: Hain, 1992); Michael Franzke, ed., *Die ideologische Offensive: Ernst Bloch, SED und Universität* (Leipzig: Leipziger Universitätsverlag, 1993).

but in the natural sciences and medical disciplines a mostly conservative professorial establishment continued to decide upon the success or failure of academic careers. In these fields the traditional university milieu (*Ordinarienuniversität*) remained relatively intact, and the possession of an SED party membership card could in some cases impede rather than foster the hiring of an assistant professor or docent. In order to alleviate the shortage of qualified professors the SED leadership was even forced, in some cases, to accept the appointment of West German candidates, who certainly harbored no sympathies for Communism.[61]

In the late 1950s top SED functionaries came to believe that the time had come for fundamental change: in all professorial appointments the "interests of the worker and peasant state" was supposed to become "the determining factor."[62] Even the medical faculties, which had been treated with kid gloves until then, were forced to accept the appointments of scholars loyal to the SED, often in the face of professorial resistance.[63] The medical faculty at the University of Rostock was to become the "first socialist faculty" in this discipline.[64] Higher education authorities proudly reported appointing SED members to twenty medical professorships from 1957 to 1959. This was a significant increase over the preceding decade, during which only nine comrades had supposedly been appointed.[65]

At the end of the 1950s nonacademic criteria became ever more decisive for academic appointments. Aside from SED membership and lower class background, activities and successes in nonuniversity "practice" gained in importance. In 1959 the following "principles for cadres" were stipulated by the State Secretariat for Higher Education: "In order to systematically improve their class composition, universities and technical colleges are to train and employ competent people with practical experience from the

---

61. Jessen, *Akademische Elite*, 297–301.

62. "Punkt I, 2m der Verordnung über die weitere sozialistische Umgestaltung des Hoch- und Fachschulwesens v. 13.2.1958," in Baske and Engelbert, *Dokumente*, 1:353–58.

63. See the report by Prof. Dr. Kurt Winter, "Betr. Berufungspolitik auf dem Sektor Medizin v. 13.6.1958," in BA DR-3: 219. See also Anna-Sabine Ernst, "*Die beste Prophylaxe ist der Sozialismus*," *Ärzte und medizinische Hochschullehrer in der SBZ/DDR, 1945–1961* (Münster: Waxmann, 1997), 212.

64. "Bericht der Parteikommission zur Überprüfung der Arbeit der Genossen der Abt. Medizin v. 24.3.1958," in BA DR-3: 344.

65. "Thesen zum Bericht der Gruppe Medizin über die politisch-ideologische Situation auf dem Gebiet der Medizinischen Fakultäten und Medizinischen Akademien, Vorlage zur Dienstbesprechung am 10.2.1959," in BA DR-3: 175.

working classes, socialist agriculture, and the intelligentsia."[66] Elsewhere the demand was made for "bolder efforts to employ seasoned experts as professors even when they do not have the second dissertation [*Habilitation*]."[67] In the same year, higher education authorities were able to report to the Council of Ministers the appointment as professors of "members of the working classes," despite the resistance of the medical and natural science faculties.[68]

Attempts by the party to establish control of graduate training provoked serious conflict. Within German higher education, academic careers had progressed up till then in close, long-lasting dependence upon the established professors. Beginning with the bond between doctoral student and adviser, through the assistant professorship, right up to the *Habilitation* and the appointment to a professorship, the entire academic recruitment process ran along lines of dependence and networks of personal contacts.[69] As long as professors were scarce and attractive career alternatives were to be had in West Germany, the SED continued to fall short of its ambitions because of these informal career structures.

This is the point at which the SED exerted pressure. In 1957 a new regulation for assistant professors increased the emphasis on political criteria for acceptance into the professoriate and took away from professors the power to appoint successors.[70] Simultaneously, a rolling wave of purges through the universities removed politically unreliable junior academics and showed those who remained that the protection of their "bosses" would no longer do them much good if they did not conform to the will of the SED. At Humboldt University alone twenty-three assistants were

---

66. "Grundsätze der sozialistischen Kaderpolitik" (circa 1959), in BA DR-3: 1578.
67. "Entwurf eines Kommissionsberichts zu den Thesen zum wissenschaftlichen Nachwuchs v. 24.6.1959," in SAPMO BA DY 30/IV 2/9.04/605, folios 5–49, here folio 14.
68. "Bericht an den Ministerrat über die Durchführung der Anordnung v. 13.2.1958 über die weitere sozialistische Umgestaltung des Hoch- und Fachschulwesens," in BA DR-3: 172; "Entwurf einer Kaderkonzeption v. 21.4.1960," in BA DR-3: 1569.
69. Peter J. Brenner, "Habilitation als Sozialisation," in *Geist, Geld und Wissenschaft: Arbeits- und Darstellungsformen von Literaturwissenschaft*, ed. Peter J. Brenner (Frankfurt: Suhrkamp, 1993), 318–56; Jürgen Wilhelm, "Die Stammeskultur der Ordinarienuniversität," in *Soziologie: Entdeckungen im Alltäglichen. Festschrift für Hans Paul Bahrdt zum 65. Geburtstag*, ed. Martin Baethge and Wolfgang Essbach (Frankfurt: Campus, 1983), 477–95.
70. "Anordnung über die Tätigkeit der wissenschaftlichen Assistenten und Oberassistenten an den Universitäten und Hochschulen v. 26.11.1957," in *Gesetzblatt der DDR*, part 1, no. 76, 620–23.

dismissed for political reasons in 1958.[71] The SED had to soften this measure after a short time because of a drastic increase in numbers of assistant professors defecting to the West, but it did not abandon its basic decision to politicize the recruitment of junior professors.

These interventions were supplemented by an increasing politicization of university teaching. During the first big push in this direction in the early 1950s the party had separated ideological indoctrination from instruction in the academic disciplines and restricted its propagation to docents in the "Basic Course in Social Sciences." Yet beginning in 1957 professors and docents were themselves supposed to begin politically "schooling" students. A new regulation of 1957 determined that teaching, research, and political schooling (*Lehre, Forschung und Erziehung*) were equally important tasks for university staff. The "assistant professor regulation" mentioned earlier assigned junior staff "a particularly high responsibility for the socialist schooling and education [*Erziehung und Ausbildung*] of students" and demanded of each new academic that his professional achievements as well as "political attitude" should exhibit a willingness and ability "to support the education and schooling of students in the spirit of socialism."[72] In order to make them able to do this, an additional obligatory course in Marxism-Leninism of at least three hours per week was ordered by the State Secretariat.[73] The SED even tried to force remedial education in the new ideology upon professors, for example in the "Marxist Colloquium" that was established at the University of Leipzig. By the end of the 1950s the party had thus subjected professors to massive political pressure, intended to bridge the division between subject-specific instruction and political "schooling" that was established ten years earlier.[74] The political encumberment of teaching was all the

---

71. "Anlage zum Schreiben Prorektorat für den wissenschaftlichen Nachwuchs der Humboldt-Universität zu Berlin an Staatssekretariat für das Hoch- und Fachhochschulwesen v. 16.9.1961," in BA DR-3: 5790.

72. "Präambel der Anordnung über die disziplinarische Verantwortlichkeit der Hochschullehrer v 8.2.1957," in *Gesetzblatt der DDR*, part 1, 177–80; "Präambel und Para. 2 der Assistentenordnung v. 26.11.1957," in *Gesetzblatt der DDR*, part 1, 620–23.

73. "Anweisung Nr. 112 v. 6.6.1958, Studium des Marxismus-Leninismus durch die Angehörigen des wissenschaftlichen Nachwuchses," in Baske and Engelbert, *Dokumente*, 1:386–87.

74. See Peter Paul Straube, "Zur Einführung eines Erziehungsauftrages an den Universitäten und Hochschulen in der DDR," in *Universitäten im Umbruch. Zum Verhältnis von Hochschule, Studenten und Gesellschaft*, ed. Friedrich W. Busch (Oldenburg: Isensee, 1992), 29–61.

more dramatic as the party was simultaneously expanding the German Academy of Sciences by diverting ever more research capacities from the universities. In 1959, Humboldt University rector Kurt Schröder found pithy words to describe the new trend: "We face the danger that science will be practiced only in the Academy, while universities will concern themselves with nothing beyond pedagogy, politics, and polytechnics."[75]

There were two reasons why the SED was better able to carry out this incursion in the late 1950s rather than the late 1940s. First, the party and the higher education authorities it controlled now had a certain amount of experience in handling the universities. In the early years it had relied upon the Soviet Military Administration, Communist-controlled education ministries (in the now defunct *Länder*), a relatively small group of SED functionaries at the universities, and crucially, the Communist youth organization FDJ with its ability to mobilize students. Political "purging campaigns" had provided a gruesome but necessary backdrop. However, the apparatus had lacked both the technical expertise and the power to fine-tune staffing policy. By the late 1950s, however, cadre departments—whether at universities, the State Secretariat, or the SED Central Committee—were well enough developed to implement long-term "cadre plans," through which the growth of teaching faculties could be carefully controlled.

Second, just ten years after SED policies had initiated a departure toward a different kind of university, there were now a notable number of politically loyal and technically qualified junior academics at the disposal of the SED. From the late 1940s the party had paved ways to the professoriate around those dominated by the old guard. Above all, the research assistantship (*Aspirantur*), introduced in 1951 on the Soviet model, was supposed to carry dozens of ideologically correct candidates to academic careers. The graduate and postdoctoral students who received state stipends within the framework of the *Aspirantur* were subject to a political selection process and required to attend political educational events during their time of support. Certainly not all of these research assistants in the 1950s were political careerists. But now that the SED steered toward a new escalation in the political struggle, it found plenty of accomplices willing to take advantage of the new situation. Almost every time it launched a campaign against a "bourgeois" professor, a candidate loyal to the SED

---

75. As quoted in a letter from Girnus to Ulbricht dated 16.12.1959, in SAPMO BA DY 30/IV 2/9.04/605: folio 394.

stood in the wings, ready to fill the soon-to-be vacant position.[76] The dynamic of radicalization in the late 1950s was fueled as much by the career interests of a generation of political protégés as it was by the determination of the political leadership to sweep away remnants of the "bourgeois" universities.

The 1960s: Technocratic Reforms and Perfection of Control

The building of the Berlin Wall on 13 August 1961 had far-reaching implications for the conditions under which East German higher education policy was executed. Prior to this point representatives of supposedly "apolitical" disciplines had profited from an academic job market that included both East and West Germany. Now that market was cut in two; renowned professors in the natural scientists could no longer exert pressure upon the SED in negotiations affecting their positions, nor, conversely, did the party have to concern itself with the interests of the older generation of academics. A sort of forced normality crept in behind the wall. The confrontation between the Germanies lost something of its drama, and the citizens of the GDR had little choice but to make peace with the country's political and social system. And now that it had secured the status of the GDR by force, the regime could dedicate itself to policies of modernization.[77]

Both impulses—efforts toward modernization and toward more effective control—shaped the development of East German universities until the end of the 1960s. This ambivalence was apparent even before the building of the wall. At a time when the shrill tones of cultural revolution were frightening the academic community, a careful listener might also detect sounds that were more to the liking of scientists. In 1959 the GDR government launched a seven-year plan that was supposed to effect the final breakthrough to economic prosperity. The plan did not content itself with merely reaching the level of West Germany, the eternal rival,

---

76. See, for example, the cases of the German studies professor Hildegard Emmel and of the historian Heinrich Sproemberg, in Hildegard Emmel, *Die Freiheit hat noch nicht begonnen: Zeitgeschichtliche Erfahrungen seit 1933* (Rostock: Reich, 1991), and Veit Didczuneit et al., *Geschichtswissenschaft in Leipzig: Heinrich Sproemberg* (Leipzig: Leipziger Universitätsverlag, 1994).

77. See Andre Steiner, *Die DDR-Wirtschaftsreform der sechziger Jahre: Konflikt zwischen Effizienz- und Machtkalkül* (Berlin: Akademie, 1999).

by 1961, but went further: by 1965 the production of consumer goods was to be increased by 177 percent.[78] Such steep growth rates were to be achieved above all through the "high tech" fields, such as the chemical and electrical industries. For a few years there were even dreams of airplanes "made in the GDR." Hopes placed in the growth potential of modern, "intelligence-intensive" branches of the economy helped sustain enthusiastic debates in the 1960s about an imminent or even nascent "scientific-technical revolution."[79]

The more important science and technology became for the further development of the socialist society, the more prominent higher education became, for it was higher education that was to train the necessary experts. Thus even universities found themselves in the swell of far-reaching growth projections in the late 1950s and early 1960s. For example, the number of students was to increase from 56,000 in 1959 to 73,000 by 1965. The projections for instructional and research staff were even more ambitious: the "Research Council," under the leadership of the chemist Peter Adolf Thiessen, urged a doubling of the teaching body by 1965. This goal had hardly become official policy when Thiessen pushed his demands further: "Actually," he said in February 1960 during a meeting with the Central Committee of the SED, "the goal of doubling the teaching body ought to be achieved by 1963."[80] Even if the development of the universities progressed in markedly smaller steps in practice, the outlook seemed promising for many scientists. It may even have assuaged the pain of a closed border.

The technicist "magic spell of systems theory and cybernetics"[81] could be detected throughout the 1960s and, along with continued political

---

78. Herman Weber, *Geschichte der DDR* (Munich: Deutscher Taschenbuchverlag, 1986), 298–301; Christoph Klessmann, *Zwei Staaten, eine Nation: Deutsche Geschichte, 1955–1970* (Göttingen: Vandenhoeck & Ruprecht, 1988), 313.

79. Hartmut Zimmermann, "Politische Aspekte in der Herausbildung, dem Wandel und der Verwendung des Konzepts 'Wissenschaftlich-technische Revolution' in der DDR," *Deutschland-Archiv, Sonderheft: Wissenschaftlich-technische Revolution und industrieller Arbeitsprozess* 9 (1976): 17–51; Arnold Buchholz, "Die Rolle der wissenschaftlich-technischen Revolution (WTR) im Marxismus-Leninismus," *Wissenschaftssoziologie—Studien und Materialien* (= *KZfSS*, Sonderheft 18) (Opladen: Westdeutscher Verlag, 1975), 457–78.

80. Girnus to Ulbricht 16.12.1959, in BA DR-33, 221; "Abt. Wissenschaften v. 27.2.1960: Beratung v. 26.2.1960 bei Gen. Gross u.a.," in BA DR-3, 5332. "Forschungsrat der DDR: Empfehlung zur raschen Steigerung der Ausbildung von naturwissenschaftlich-technischen Fachkräften an Universitäten und Hochschulen v. 9.8.1960, als Vorlage für das Politbüro beim ZK der SED am 9.12.1960," in SAPMO BA DY 30/IV 2/9.04/17, folio 134–36.

81. Tandler, *Zukunft*, 324–30.

pressures and ever more perfectly organized cadre policies, shaped the last great structural changes in the East German university system, the so-called third university reform.[82] The changes of the late 1960s had five basic components: first, there was now a definitive break with the traditional model of German university organization, in that the faculties and institutes were dissolved and replaced by new organizational units called "sections." Second, the system of academic exams was reconstructed, which, third, had a significant impact on the recruitment of university teachers. Connected to this there was, fourth, an improved "cadre planning" that led, fifth, to a last great shift in personnel at the end of the 1960s, during which the remaining representatives of the old generation of academics were removed.

The abolition of faculties and institutes in 1967–68 is a good example of how closely goals of modernization and interests of power were intertwined during the 1960s. Officially, the reform served to create larger organizational units for research, teaching, and education called "sections," which lay beyond the boundaries of faculties and institutes, and gathered together different institutes in the same discipline. These were designed to suit the demands of the "scientific-technical revolution" by for example focusing on complex economic tasks and connecting scientific fields that used the same methods or large-scale scientific tools. The benefits expected from the new organizational structure included, among other things, cost savings, an interdisciplinary integration of the sciences, more rational use of research tools, libraries, laboratories, and closer cooperation with nationalized enterprises.[83] Sometimes the American system of departments was mentioned as a model.

Accompanying this program of modernization were also deep incursions into the social micromilieu and the staff structure of the university, which strengthened the SED's influence considerably. Until this point the institutes, as the smallest units of the university, had been under the control of the older generation of professors, and they had often decided about the training of graduate students on their own. These small spheres of independence now ceased to exist. The new "section directors" were

---

82. Hubert Laitko, "Das Reformpaket der sechziger Jahre—wissenschaftspolitisches Finale der Ulbricht-Ära," *Naturwissenschaft und Technik in der DDR*, 35–57; Siegfried Baske, ed., *Bildungspolitk in der DDR, 1963–1976: Dokumente* (Berlin: Harrassowitz, 1979).

83. See, for example, the case of the University of Jena in Tobias Kaiser et al., "Modell- oder Sündenfall? Die Universität Jena in den Kontroversen und die 'Dritte Hochschulreform,'" *Jahrbuch für Universitätsgeschichte* 8 (2005): 45–69.

appointed by the rector, and the old institute directors were left with hardly any role to play. Section directors, like other influential functionaries, were usually selected from the ranks of loyal SED members.[84]

The reform of academic examinations and appointment procedures took a similar course. Again, considerations of efficiency stood in the foreground, while in the background power relations shifted. The most important reform concerned the abolition of the *Habilitation*. In the traditional German university system this had been more than simply a second doctoral dissertation; it was a prerequisite for appointment to professorship. As long as the *Habilitation* was a precondition for appointment, the academic community had a veto in staffing matters. In practice this principle had been weakened by political interventions: now it was abolished completely. In place of the *Habilitation* a second examination was introduced according to Soviet models, the "doctor of sciences." Unlike the *Habilitation* it did not count as a professional examination for aspiring professors, but rather as a second academic degree, divorced from the demands of university research and teaching.

The consequences of this change were soon revealed in another area that was subjected to sweeping reformation: professorial appointments. Beginning in 1968 candidates had to produce a new certificate, the "facultas docendi," which confirmed their political, pedagogic, and disciplinary suitability. Because the new degree of "doctor of sciences" was not a prerequisite, this measure decisively diminished the influence of professors on the appointment of their successors. It also intensified the politicization of professorial recruitment: candidates had to prove, among other things, that they would fortify students' "socialist state consciousness."

In general, SED university policies of the 1960s were much better organized than those of earlier years. Where the party had once had to improvise because of very thin staffing levels, now it introduced centralized cadre policies. Behind a sealed border functionaries were able to draft a plan for academic personnel development that covered the entire GDR and coordinated all subjects for all universities. Planning staff in the SED Central Committee apparatus and in the Ministry for Higher Education now systematically registered positions as they became vacant, catalogued the up-and-coming academics who might fill these positions,

---

84. See Hans Joachim Meyer, "Zwischen Kaderschmiede und Hochschulrecht," in *IV. Hochschulreform: Die ostdeutsche Wissenschaftslandschaft, 1989/90. Eine Retrospektive*, ed. P. Pasternack (Leipzig: Leipziger Universitätsverlag, 1993), 116–35.

sorted candidates according to political and scholarly criteria, and developed central plans for filling these positions over several years. While universities initially retained strong influence on this Kafkaesque planning process, from 1965 onward, with the cooling off of technocratic reform impulses and the general increase in political pressure, it increasingly evolved into political selection process. Candidates were assessed according to their "efforts to school students" (*Erziehungstätigkeit*), with schooling understood to mean ideological indoctrination. In early 1966 the Ministry even required that "proposals for appointment that mention only scholarly competence" be "corrected." It continued: "Future professors and higher education officials must above all be socialist educators."[85]

The combination of well-coordinated organizational changes, copiously staffed ministries, and altered appointment criteria explain how SED functionaries finally realized a dream in the late 1960s: in 1969 approximately 83 percent of all newly appointed professors belonged to the SED, and the "bourgeois" remnants of the old body of professors had been pushed from their posts. Tight political control was secured down to the ground level of each section. Even at the tip of the policy-advisory committees there was no longer a need to integrate power-conscious "bourgeois" geniuses. The "research advisory board," in which the grand old men of the natural sciences had set the tone since its founding in 1957, lost its place of privilege step by step, ceding power to various circles of experts and working groups: "The special position which individual scientists had enjoyed in the 1950s gradually came to an end in the late 1960s."[86]

Conclusion: Repression and Collaboration

By the early 1970s the dust stirred up by the higher education reforms of the 1960s had settled; the reconstruction of East German universities was complete. It had taken a good twenty years and run through various phases: from the massive losses of staff during the denazification phase to the Stalinist "storming of the academic fortress" in the early 1950s; from a second thrust of cultural-revolutionary radicalizing at the end of the

---

85. "Es ist davon auszugehen, daß die künftigen Leiter und Hochschullehrer in erster Linie sozialistische Erzieher sein müssen." *Erste Auswertung der Kaderprogramme von den Universitäten und Hochschulen o.J.* (1966), in BA DR-3, 3112.

86. Tandler, *Zukunft*, 333.

decade to the reforms of the 1960s, beneath whose technocratic surface the political penetration of the university was perfected. There would be no more notable changes until the collapse of the GDR. There were, of course, occasional signs of resistance against this political reformation from the professoriate and student body—usually muttered quietly, but on odd occasions expressed vociferously. Measured against the reach and severity of the Communist reconstruction of the universities, these protests were astonishingly rare. After the founding of the GDR the majority of both students and professors behaved loyally toward the political system. At no point was there any real danger to the regime emanating from the universities: neither during the uprising of June 1953 nor during the terminal crisis of the SED dictatorship in 1989 did students or academics play a significant part. From the point of view of the regime this was a remarkable success; it can be accounted for by willful political interventions, the specificities of East Germany's postwar situation, and certain elements of the academic community's political culture.[87]

These factors cannot be viewed in isolation from each other; in fact they were mutually reinforcing. Yet most decisive were the regime's political interventions, the gist of which is captured by three words: selection, repression, and integration. The exercise of power always has something to do with the choice of personnel, and for a Communist regime obsessively fixated upon "cadres" this was especially true. From 1945 until 1989 the selection of undergraduate and graduate students, and of teaching staff, played a prominent role in the higher education policies of the SED. At issue was always who should decide, and according to which criteria, about inclusion or exclusion in the academic community. As comparison with the Polish and Czech cases shows, the SMAD and SED very effectively controlled access both to the teaching body and the student population.[88]

Yet challenges did remain, especially in supposedly apolitical subjects, where a balance had to be struck between political control, professional standards, and informal cultural and social career patterns within the academic "guild." In the 1940s and 1950s Communist higher education authorities had used crude methods to influence academic recruitment, usually intervening massively from the outside, for example in the purging

---

87. John Connelly analyzes the key role played by the national political culture for the actual course taken by the "sovietizing" process in *Captive University*, 282–91, his comparison of university development in Poland, Czechoslovakia, and in the Soviet Occupied Zone/GDR.

88. Ibid., 126ff., 226ff.

waves after the end of the war, the late 1940s, and after 1956. But during the 1960s their techniques became more sophisticated. The initial separation of political from subject-related criteria for academic advancement was now bridged by an increasingly "professional" cadre administration, as well as by new examination regulations and altered appointment procedures. At the same time the border between the two Germanies, which had acted as a social and political pressure valve and decisively shaped processes of academic recruitment, was now closed. Previously, members of universities who did not want to cooperate with the regime had been able to leave the country without great risk. There can be little doubt that the mass emigration of "bourgeois" academics to West Germany throughout the 1950s weakened the basis for intellectual opposition to the SED for many years to come.

Political control and repression were important aspects of Communist staffing policies from the early postwar years, which saw a massive exclusion of academics tainted by association with National Socialism (1945–46) and then the displacement of liberal and conservative humanists (1947–50). After this point the regime settled into a pattern of selectively but regularly disciplining recalcitrant students and docents. All sorts of institutions had a part in this, though fears of delayed careers were more important in manufacturing conformity than the harsh attacks by the party or the State Security Police (Stasi), which were directed against individuals. Among the peculiarities of the SED dictatorship in comparison to other Communist regimes was the great success in penetrating society with a plethora of organizations that depended ultimately on the leadership of the party. That was also true in higher education.

Still, repression alone was no guarantee for success. The SED regime had few supporters at universities during the early years, but it quickly established practices encouraging collaboration. In much of the natural sciences, medicine, and the technical disciplines the relationship between regime and academics was a process of interaction; a kind of negotiation process between unequal partners, in which the SED could always assert itself by force in individual cases, but in which structurally it was dependent on the willingness of the other side to collaborate.

The successful integration of East German natural scientists, physicians, and engineers therefore hinged largely on positive incentives. Competition from the "main enemy" in the West also played a vital role. The SED attempted to gain the allegiance of valued "bourgeois" specialists of the old generation with an abundance of privileges, and it enjoyed no mean success. The younger generation was attracted by the career prospects of an expanding university system and the monies lavished on members of the "new intelligentsia." Indeed, the broad-based upward mobility of the 1950s figured among the most effective means of social integration and, in a sense, represented a correlate to the defection of the old academic elite to the West. An entire generation of social climbers saw Communism as a source of patronage. This was a basis for long-lasting loyalty. Furthermore the SED offered respectable opportunities even to those academics who viewed themselves as politically neutral specialists. The dearth of professional experts right after the war combined with protection from Western competition to radically improve their career conditions; later they benefited from the vision propagated in the late Ulbricht-era of a "scientific-technical revolution."

Members of the successor generation also profited to some extent from structural changes made to academic professions in the GDR. The more career development became the target of long-term political planning and emphasis shifted from academic examinations to political loyalty, the more the younger generation severed ties of dependence to the academic establishment. Furthermore, job security rose as the demand-oriented planning guaranteed a job to all who completed their professional training. In short: the risk structure of the academic profession changed. Careers became less dependent on the vagaries of academic roulette or on the established scientific community. The price for this was subservience to political authorities. Whoever conformed and fit in with the system could enjoy security—at the price of unfreedom, intellectual stagnation, and opportunism.

It bears repeating that the restructuring of East German universities depended heavily on certain specifically German preconditions. Promises in the early postwar years of a radical, antifascist "fresh start" provided Communists with a claim to legitimacy that seemed difficult to contest, and would have been impossible to achieve with appeals to Marxism-Leninism alone. More crucially, the younger generation—of whom many would experience the collective social elevation of the 1950s—proved particularly receptive to the SED's antifascist founding myth. Their earliest collective experience had been as members of the Hitler Youth, whose hopes and illusions had suddenly collapsed in 1945. The SED offered them the chance to switch to the "right" side of history, if only they subordinated themselves to the most consistent of all adversaries of fascism: the Communist Party. This offer proved highly attractive and a very effective basis for integration.

Among the conditions specific to Germany was national division, the effects of which have been mentioned above. This division made possible politically and socially selective processes of migration and weakened the potential for opposition. It also eased the integration of those who remained, some of whom found themselves in an advantageous negotiating position with the state. Taken together, both of these circumstances—the National Socialist past and the present German division—decisively frustrated the possibility that oppositional, anticommunist thought might avail itself of nationalist arguments, with all the political momentum that might have implied. This circumstance distinguished the East German universities, as John Connelly has convincingly argued, from those of neighboring Poland, where the pressure to sovietize came from the outside and met with a largely homogenous academic milieu that cherished an unbroken national self-consciousness.

Finally, into the explanation of the relative calm at the East German universities one must include long-standing traditions of academic-political culture. Not without reason was the GDR sometimes referred to as the "more German" of the two states. The milieu of the German universities was overwhelmingly conservative, or at least national-liberal since the founding of the German Empire in 1871, and many academics had looked upon the Weimar Republic with hostility. Such a history placed the academic community at a great distance from the Communist movement. But beneath the surface of manifest political attitudes one can also discern mental patterns that eased conformism. The tradition of the German "educational institution" (*Bildungsuniversität*) provided ready models of apolitical scholars, dedicated to "pure" science. Though this image of the academic in an ivory tower did not match the socialist ideal, many members of older academic milieus allowed themselves to be integrated in this way, especially as the SED liked to be cast as the true heir of humanist legacy. That party derived even greater benefits from the traditional allegiance to the state held by German educational elites.

If the SED was relatively successful until the end of the 1960s in politically integrating the universities and academic elite, then this success without doubt rested on dictatorial methods. But repressive measures alone would not have sufficed. Academic work does not survive without a modicum of independence and initiative. Therefore, the success of integration depended in part on the extent to which the SED was able to encourage the willingness to cooperate actively. Roughly speaking, two modes of integration were at work here. The humanities and social sciences were integrated normatively via replacement of personnel, "Marxism-Leninism," a politicized understanding of scholarship, and the founding myth of antifascism. The integration of the natural, medical, and technical scientists, by contrast, was based on a distinct continuity in personnel, and on the results of an asymmetrical "negotiation process" in which material and symbolic rewards, the recognition of limited freedoms, and implied possibilities of codetermination were "negotiated." Until 1961 the open border secured the "negotiating position" of the academics involved, but even in the following decades the relationship between academic elite and dictatorship rested not only on totalitarian rule, but also on the willingness to engage in active collaboration.

Translation: Hilary Collier Sy-Quia and John Connelly

Concluding Reflections:
Universities and Dictatorships

MICHAEL GRÜTTNER

I

For the ruling elites of dictatorships, universities have various functions to fulfill: they are potential multipliers of the reigning ideology, but also institutions for training future elites such as doctors, scientists, teachers, and engineers. In addition, they offer research potential that can be useful in realizing political, military, and economic objectives. Regardless of ideological differences, control over the universities was therefore a vitally important goal for every dictatorship. The essays in this volume suggest five different paths to this goal:

1. Aligning research and teaching with the ideas of those in power, especially through the founding of institutes, fields of study, and lecture courses that propagate ideology in the guise of science. The essays collected here contain numerous examples of this approach: while university institutes for Marxism-Leninism, political economy, and the history of the workers' movement appeared in the Soviet Union and its satellite states, in Mussolini's Italy the new subjects included corporatism, colonialism, and racial science. Under the National Socialists, racial hygiene, folklore, military science, and prehistory enjoyed special support from the regime.

In addition, existing institutes and chairs came under pressure to adopt the official ideology or at least to avoid anything that might place them in opposition to that ideology, especially in fields traditionally close to politics, like the humanities. But in some regimes examined in this volume there was also a tendency to subject the natural sciences to the dominant ideology. The best-known examples are "German physics" during the Nazi period, and the theories of the Soviet agro-biologist T. D. Lysenko, which were promoted by Stalin himself.

2. Ideological purging of teaching staffs and student body. With the exception of Poland, the dictatorships examined here witnessed mass dismissals of university professors on political grounds. As we learn from Miguel Ángel Ruiz Carnicer, these were particularly destructive in a country like Spain, where the establishment of the Franco dictatorship had involved three years of bloody civil war, leaving over half the professorships in Spain vacant. In addition, the dictatorships examined here attempted with varying success to consider only "politically dependable" candidates in making appointments.

3. Exerting political control over access to the university. Political selection of students was an important instrument for controlling universities, especially for Communist parties who were initially confronted by skeptical or hostile students from the traditional elites. Communists therefore attempted to recruit a student body loyal to state and party that was drawn chiefly from previously underprivileged social strata. Similar projects are also found in noncommunist dictatorships, although in these instances—as for example the "Langemarck program" in the Third Reich—they remained marginal.

4. Restricting or abolishing the self-government of the universities. To ensure that the governance of the universities was in the hands of "politically reliable" individuals, the free election of rectors and deans was de facto abolished. Instead, either rectors were appointed by the state or the actual governance of the universities was handed over to party functionaries. To the outside world universities therefore presented themselves as an integral component of the regime.

5. Restricting the international contacts of universities. The motivations for doing this varied. In the case of National Socialism, it resulted from nationalistic and racial resentment against the idea of "international scholarship and science." In Communist states, by contrast, intensive contact with the West was suspect because it was perceived as a potential source of ideological deviance. Astoundingly, even within the Eastern bloc, exchanges of professors and students did not get under way until ten years after the end of World War II, as Jan Havránek highlights in his essay.

For a number of reasons, attempts to harness universities to the agendas of the powerful have encountered repeated obstacles. University-based higher learning consists of a multitude of disciplines whose inner workings can be assessed only by specialists. By its nature, scholarship continually changes, and the direction of change cannot be predicted. For their part, professors, especially in the natural sciences, are frequently integrated in an international scientific community, and few are willing to dispense entirely with the recognition and approval of that community. Restrictions or interruptions of these contacts can easily lead to scientific stagnation and provincialism. All these factors make it difficult to get a solid political grip on the universities. Under dictatorships, therefore, universities were better able to preserve a certain measure of independence and autonomy than other institutions, for example schools.[1]

II

It has occasionally been claimed that true science can flourish only in democracies. Such a view cannot be reconciled with the facts. Precisely under Stalinism a huge scientific system emerged at great cost, which left such evidence of its high performance as atomic weapons and spectacular successes in space travel.[2] For various reasons, German science in the 1930s lost the international position of leadership that it had early in the century. Nevertheless, German scientists during the Nazi period were still capable of important scientific innovations, such as the rocket program pursued during the Second World War.[3]

Should one therefore conclude that democratic and dictatorial regimes are equally capable of scientific accomplishments?[4] In my view the factors just mentioned speak against such a conclusion: in almost all the regimes

---

1. Thus Tracy H. Koon, *Believe, Obey, Fight: Political Socialization of Youth in Fascist Italy, 1922–1943* (Chapel Hill: University of North Carolina Press, 1985), 73. Although Koon's observation refers only to Italian Fascism, it is presumably of more general relevance.
2. Loren R. Graham, *What Have We Learned about Science and Technology from the Russian Experience?* (Stanford: Stanford University Press, 1998), 52ff.
3. Michael J. Neufeld, *The Rocket and the Reich: Peenemünde and the Coming of the Ballistic Missile Era* (New York: The Free Press, 1995).
4. Michael Gordin et al., "'Ideologically Correct' Science," in *Science and Ideology: A Comparative History*, ed. Mark Walker (London: Routledge, 2003), 58f.

studied in this volume, purging of scholarly institutions caused significant damage. Compared to the innumerable victims of political repression in the Soviet scientific system or the massive expulsions from German universities after 1933, the consequences for higher education of the McCarthy Era or the German "Berufsverbote" pale in significance. Likewise, a personnel policy influenced by ideological criteria keeps gifted scholars away from universities, thus damaging their productive capacities. Even a leading National Socialist like Joseph Goebbels recognized such facts during the Second World War and voiced vigorous criticism of his party's personnel policy. Similarly, attempts to regulate university admissions by political standards run the risk of squandering a country's intellectual potential. That is why the Soviet leadership abandoned preference for workers' children in university admissions for many years after 1935, as Michael David-Fox has shown. Similar developments took place in other socialist states.[5] The enforcement of political dogmas can easily lead to the ossification of a university's intellectual life. The consequences are most visible in the humanities and social sciences, but evident also in the natural sciences, for example in Lysenkoism or "German physics."

Thus there are good reasons to believe that despite spectacular accomplishments, higher education and science in dictatorships are far less successful than they would be without purges, without political selection of professors and students, without fruitless dogmas. The interest of modern dictatorships in producing ideological uniformity and enforcing political loyalty necessarily detracts from the productivity of the scientific system and therefore stands at odds with a country's need for qualified scientists, doctors, teachers, and engineers. Such needs define the limits of dictatorial regimes, which, after all, cannot sacrifice completely scientific, technological, and military effectiveness. Those who make science policy in these regimes thus confront the basic question of whether universities should produce ideology and loyal functionaries or create indispensable knowledge. Dictatorships that subjected universities to rigorous political control reduced scholarly productivity, but if institutes of higher learning are left with too much autonomy, the danger arises that they may go astray politically. In practice these alternatives often lead to radical vacillations between a course of ruthless politicization and a strategy that courted specialists even if their political loyalty was rather suspect.

5. See John Connelly, *Captive University: The Sovietization of East German, Czech, and Polish Higher Education, 1945–1956* (Chapel Hill: University of North Carolina Press, 2000), 68.

III

Since dictatorships launch attacks on the freedom of science, one might presume that universities stubbornly resist the consolidation of dictatorships. However, the essays in this volume have shown that this was nowhere the case. To be sure, criticism of state interference was voiced in every case analyzed here, and in every country there were efforts to preserve the autonomy of the universities. Occasionally, as in Prague, there were even street demonstrations. But in general only scattered individuals or smaller groups spoke up, while the universities as institutions either adapted themselves or became incapable of action.

None of this is meant to deny the significant differences between the countries represented in these essays. In some cases universities kept the respective regime at arm's length for a rather long period. That was especially true in Soviet Russia, where a large segment of the professors sympathized with the liberal democrats, but also in Poland, where the Communist takeover of power was seen as the beginning of another episode of foreign rule. In the other countries, however, the new rulers rapidly subjected universities to their will, most easily in states like the German Democratic Republic or Hungary, where the universities had been morally discredited by their collaboration with the recently overthrown dictatorships.

Almost everywhere sections of the university were willing to support the new regime. The three radical right-wing dictatorships in Italy, Nazi Germany, and Spain benefited greatly from students' enthusiasm for fascism in the interwar period. By contrast, Communism did not enjoy comparable support from the students, at least not until the 1960s. Only at Chinese and Czech universities, as the essays by Douglas Stiffler and Jan Havránek show, was the Communist seizure of power supported by many students. In some dictatorships politically active students were invested with extraordinary powers, a condition referred to in Czechoslovakia as "studentocracy."

Not only students proved willing to back dictatorship, however. In Nazi Germany many younger academics also served the new rulers, as did eminent professors like Carl Schmitt and Martin Heidegger. In Fascist Italy, as Ruth Ben-Ghiat emphasizes, many intellectuals provided scientific legitimacy for the racial laws of 1938. In some Eastern European countries academics initially welcomed the Communists as liberators from Nazi occupation. A number of eminent Czech academics decided to join the Communist Party under the influence of such sentiments. In Hungary, Nobel prize–winning biochemist Albert Szent-Györgi became the Communist Party's most important ally in its efforts to transform the scientific establishment.

Throughout the twentieth century, the idea that intellectuals resist dictatorship because they suffer from dictatorship has repeatedly proved an illusion. Motivations for "the treason of the clerks" (Julien Benda) varied. Alongside occasional ideological agreement and frequent career aspiration stood the expectation that one's own research would profit. Others hoped to take leading roles in the new system. Another reason for the universities' attitude was their position as state institutions financed almost entirely by the government. Last but not least, mass dismissals produced winners alongside the losers, namely those who moved in to fill the vacancies.

IV

The dictatorships described in this book differed in many regards. Their differences were not only ideological in nature, but also manifested themselves in their stability, duration, and willingness to use violence against real and supposed enemies. Such differences appear not only when we contrast Communist and "fascist" dictatorships; they are also visible when we compare the Soviet Union of the 1930s to the Hungary of the 1960s, or Hitler's Germany and Mussolini's Italy. Can we nevertheless speak of a Communist or a fascist university model?

This question can be most readily answered—or so it would seem, at least—in the case of Soviet Communism and its satellite states. When Marxism-Leninism spread to encompass one-third of the world between 1945 and 1949, Soviet universities provided a model for the Communists in other countries. One characteristic element of this model was the demotion of most universities to second-rate scientific institutions. Top-level research in the Soviet Union centered on the Academies of Sciences, while the chief task of universities lay in teaching. In practice this amounted to a separation of research and teaching, a bifurcation that was replicated throughout Eastern Europe after the Second World War.

A second element of the Soviet model that was copied all across Eastern Europe was the establishment of "workers' and peasants' departments" (so-called *rabfaki*), in which youth from the lower classes that were considered politically reliable received preparation for a regular university education. The *rabfaki* trained new cadres, but they also helped extend the party's political grip upon universities because both the teachers and the students of these departments were chosen primarily on political lines. Other features of the Soviet university model included the attempt to steer all university life through long-term planning, and the introduction of obligatory basic courses in Marxism-Leninism, which took up a considerable portion of the overall time that students devoted to their studies.

The Communist states established after World War II therefore possessed a model of a Marxist-Leninist higher education that—it would seem—merely had to be copied. But the essays collected here show that the university landscape in Eastern Europe was more varied than outside observers had once thought. For example, the Polish universities, as John Connelly emphasizes, were fundamentally different from those in other Communist states in that they largely avoided political purges. As in agriculture, where the expected collectivization did not take place, the new Polish rulers shied away from a radical implementation of their ideas in higher education. The result was an academic elite that mostly rejected politicization.

Special developments occurred also in other East European countries. For example György Péteri, in his study of Hungary, describes a liberalization in the 1950s which profoundly altered the relationship between higher education and politics. Hungarian universities, including their humanistic faculties, acquired a remarkably high degree of autonomy by East European standards. Even institutes that had been created to legitimate the ruling system were able partly to emancipate themselves from assigned tasks. A critical Marxist philosophy arose whose most important representatives, among them Ágnes Heller, ceased to see their task as that of justifying the actual socialist ruling system. Comparable developments in Poland and Czechoslovakia were cut short in 1968 when the state made a show of force.

The situation was different in the three dictatorships we have examined that could be labeled "fascist" (Germany, Italy, and Spain). There was no international center of "Fascism" with a guiding function like the one exercised by the Soviet Union in the Communist sphere of power. Consequently there was also no generally accepted "Fascist" model of the university that could have served as a blueprint for other countries. There is no question, though, that the dictatorships in Italy, Germany, and Spain drew inspiration from one another. For example, the politics of the

Falangist student organization Sindicato Español Universitario (SEU) in Spain was clearly influenced by the Italian Gruppi Universitari Fascisti (GUF), while the labor services of Italy and Spain were clearly imitations of institution of the same name in Hitler's Germany.

Yet we can also recognize substantial differences among the three right-wing dictatorships. While German National Socialists and Spanish Francoists used their seizures of power immediately to initiate mass dismissals at the universities and destroy their autonomy, Italian Fascists were initially rather restrained. To be sure, in Italy as well the autonomy of the institutions of higher learning was slowly curtailed after the Fascists came to power, but for many years it was not possible to speak of a fundamental reshaping of Italian universities. A radicalization of university policy began later, with the loyalty oath of 1931, but above all the racial laws of 1938, which claimed many victims among the professoriate. Whether this radicalization was the product of internal or external factors remains a subject of debate, as Ruth Ben-Ghiat shows. What is beyond debate, though, is that Italian Fascism drew closer to German Nazism with the racial laws of 1938.

A comparable development was not evident in Spain. Although the country's new political elite had been anti-Jewish in attitude since the civil war, anti-Semitic measures were largely absent—mostly because practically no Jews were left in Spain after the civil war.[6] In other respects, as well, the policy of Francoism toward the universities was clearly different from that of National Socialism. As Miguel Ángel Ruiz Carnicer shows, Spanish policy on higher education was dominated not by the fascist Falange, but by conservative Catholicism. In stark contrast, Germany was ruled by a party whose hostility toward the Catholic Church emerged more and more clearly during the 1930s. By 1938 the regime had decided to "dismantle" the departments of theology. Nevertheless, this intention was carried out only in part because direct action against the churches seemed politically too risky during the war.

On the whole, what stands out in a comparison of university policy in the three right-wing dictatorships we have analyzed are differences rather than similarities. A "fascist" university common to all three dictatorships did not exist.

6. See Michael Grüttner, "Faschismus, Franquismus und Antisemitismus in Spanien," in *Vorurteil und Rassenhass: Antisemitismus in den faschistischen Bewegungen Europas*, ed. Hermann Graml et al. (Berlin: Metropol, 2001), 95–118.

V

Once the dictatorships were ensconced, university teachers focused primarily on defense of their professional interests[7] — a difficult undertaking in regimes characterized by strong anti-intellectual or antibourgeois sentiments. Defending professional interests meant several things: maintenance of scholarly standards, as well as efforts to obtain more funding and personnel for research, higher salaries for university teachers, and greater prestige. Such a defense should not be misread as resistance to a dictatorship; nevertheless, a professional representation of academic interests could, *nolens volens*, take on a political dimension if, for example, it emphasized the relevance of scholarly criteria in opposition to a personnel policy with a political focus. The defense of professional interests became thoroughly political when it tried to prevent politically motivated paradigms from infiltrating into scientific research and teaching. We know that the doctrines of T. D. Lysenko encountered the same kind of resistance among Russian geneticists as the theories of "German physics" did among most physicists in Nazi Germany.[8]

One can interpret the effort at defending professional interests as contributing toward a constraint on dictatorial power. From a functional perspective, however, this kind of behavior also helped to preserve or enhance the productivity of science and thus the efficiency of the entire system. Moreover, a strategy of defending professional interests in totalitarian dictatorships like Nazi Germany and the Soviet Union, which had a largely instrumental relationship to science, could be successful only if those who pursued it were able to persuade the new political elite that universities and science were indispensable for the implementation of their political, military, and economic plans. To mount an effective defense of their professional interests, universities thus had to emphasize their usefulness. Accordingly, the critics of "German physics" in Hitler's Germany as well as the opponents of Lysenko in Stalin's Russia pointed emphatically to the military importance of their field in order to gain the ear of the political rulers.[9]

---

7. See Dietrich Beyrau, ed., *Im Dschungel der Macht: Intellektuelle Professionen unter Stalin und Hitler* (Göttingen: Vandenhoeck & Ruprecht, 2000), 32ff.

8. See Nikolai Krementsov, *Stalinist Science* (Princeton: Princeton University Press, 1997); Alan D. Beyerchen, *Scientists Under Hitler: Politics and the Physics Community in the Third Reich* (New Haven: Yale University Press, 1977).

9. See Beyerchen, *Scientists Under Hitler*, 176ff.; Krementsov, *Stalinist Science*, 251ff.

This provided the basis for the emergence of a frequent modus vivendi between dictatorship and science, one from which science also benefited. For example, the essay on Nazi Germany shows that universities were given greater leeway beginning in 1937. The number of political appointments declined, and the influence of the departments on personnel decisions grew. During the war, the basic anti-intellectual sentiment in the party was replaced by a propaganda campaign intended to enhance the standing of science and by generous funding for "war-critical" research. A turnaround in the policy on higher education that was even more dramatic occurred in the Soviet Union in 1931–32, as the essay by Michael David-Fox reveals. The breakup of the Soviet universities that had begun in 1929 at the initiative of the Communist student leadership was halted and largely reversed. At the same time, "bourgeois specialists" were rehabilitated, and generous privileges were bestowed on segments of the intelligentsia.

A similar process took place after 1945 in Communist-dominated Eastern Europe. As Ralph Jessen shows in the case of the GDR, some East German university teachers were given an abundance of material benefits—even though many of them had little sympathy for socialism in its East German incarnation. In 1952, the top income of an East German professor was ten times that of the average worker. However, it was chiefly natural scientists who enjoyed such privileges, which were unquestionably remarkable in a "workers' and peasants' state."

Clearly, the strategy of defending professional interests by pointing to one's indispensability for the system was often a successful strategy. It would therefore be false to see universities as merely passive objects of dictatorial exertions. After a period of disorientation, they generally adapted to the new political conditions and tried to make them work for their own interests. However, universities could never be certain whether a new, favorable direction in university policy would last or fall victim to the next shift in the political winds. Not only in Maoist China were the policies of the ruling party toward scholars characterized by "wide swings between liberalization and harsh tightening," as a recent comparative study has shown.[10] And as Michael David-Fox highlights in his contribution, the Soviet academic intelligentsia was disproportionately affected by the purges of the 1930s in spite of many material privileges. Moreover, in

---

10. See Gordin et al., "'Ideologically Correct' Science," 55.

the Communist countries such privileges were usually regarded as transitional measures to be employed until a truly "socialist intelligentsia" emerged. And so, when the German Democratic Republic closed itself off from the West by erecting a wall in 1961, some of the privileges for professors were revoked. But in 1988, the top salary for an East German professor was still three times the average income for a worker. That was almost exactly equivalent to the usual ratios in West Germany.[11]

VI

The question of whether consideration of professional interests also led to a political integration of universities cannot be answered in a general terms. As a number of essays in this volume have shown, one did not automatically lead to the other. To the extent that the dictatorships studied here were threatened or overthrown by popular movements, it almost always happened with the active participation of the universities.

In Spain beginning in the 1960s, the active segments of the student body (often in cooperation with the younger generation of academics) were, alongside the workers and the autonomist movements in some regions, the most important force in the resistance to the Franco regime—an obvious symptom that after three decades, Francoist university policy was bankrupt. As Györgi Péteri highlights in his essay, in the uprising in Hungary in 1956, the most important anti-Stalinist mass movement of the 1950s, the universities—and here especially the students—also played an important role. And they included, remarkably enough, many students from families of workers and peasants, that is, students whose new academic status was largely the product of Communist higher education policy. Jan Havránek notes that the Prague spring of 1968 drew strong support from the universities, and in 1989–90, as well, universities played a crucial role in the collapse of the Communist dictatorship. Polish universities can point to an especially long tradition of political protest, as we learn from John Connelly's essay. This development already began in May of 1946 with student demonstrations that were supported by professors. It reached a high point in the 1960s with the movement of solidarity with the dissidents Jacek Kuroń and Karol

---

11. See Ralph Jessen, *Akademische Elite und kommunistische Diktatur: Die ostdeutsche Hochschullehrerschaft in der Ulbricht-Ära* (Göttingen: Vandenhoeck & Ruprecht, 1999), 207ff.

Modzelewski and in the large student demonstrations in March of 1968. In 1980–81 Polish universities lent enthusiastic support to the workers' movement Solidarity. A last, spectacular example of this kind of student activism was the Chinese student movement in 1989, which ended with the massacre in Tienanmen Square in Beijing.

In the face of this impressive record, however, we must make two qualifications. First, the statement that universities played an active or even leading role in opposition movements does not apply to all the dictatorships studied here. Especially notable is the case of the GDR, where universities played no appreciable role either during the uprising of 17 June 1953, or during the death throes of the SED dictatorship in the fall of 1989. Ralph Jessen has analyzed the reasons for this exceptionalism and emphasizes the role of a border with the West that was relatively open for a long time and ensured a continual exodus of potential oppositional elements. But second, and more generally it was certainly not the case that all members of universities participated in the opposition movements that arose from universities. Quite often, it would be more correct to speak of student movements that were occasionally supported by segments of the faculty.

The willingness of students to take up the cause of opposition movements was an international phenomenon that pervades the entire history of the twentieth century. Students belong to an age group in which the readiness to take a stand on ideals is especially high. Until the expansion of higher education in the 1960s, most lived with an awareness of belonging to an elite. That created the necessary self-confidence which allowed them to assume a leadership role in times of political upheaval and change. Traditionally students also enjoy a high degree of independence; they are no longer subject to parental authority and not yet tied to professional hierarchies or familial responsibilities. This generally increases the readiness to assume risks.

While these factors explain the willingness of students to engage in political protest, they say nothing about their political goals, which in actuality were quite diverse. In the past century, student activism has lacked a clear political profile, and the direction of its thrust was influenced by highly disparate political and cultural factors. It would therefore be quite wrong to assume that twentieth-century students as such were antidictatorial in general. In the period between the two world wars students spearheaded fascist opposition movements in many European countries—not only in Italy, Germany, and Spain, but also in Portugal and Rumania.[12] Yet the essays on Italy, Germany, and Spain in this volume have shown that student activism quickly waned where fascist parties took power and began to regiment the life of the students. The "second generation" of students experienced fascism not as radical opposition but as state power and consequently lacked the enthusiasm of their predecessors.

The essays in this volume make clear how difficult it is to provide an unequivocal statement about the place of universities in the dictatorships of the twentieth century. Universities were undoubtedly victims, for they suffered from purges, the destruction of traditional structures, and the loss of autonomy. But they were also in many cases pillars of the regime and beneficiaries who knew how to use the new political situation to promote their own interests and to accentuate their indispensability. Few institutions have a tradition as old as that of universities. That in itself points to their adaptability, a characteristic that is striking in many of the essays collected here.

Translation: Thomas Dunlap

---

12. See António Costa Pinto, *The Blue Shirts: Portuguese Fascists and the New State* (New York: Columbia University Press, 2000), 122ff.; Armin Heinen, *Die Legion "Erzengel Michael" in Rumänien: Soziale Bewegung und politische Organisation* (Munich: Oldenbourg, 1986), 234ff.

INDEX

AAUP. *See* American Association of University Professors
academic autonomy, 10, 76, 120, 147, 151, 166, 212, 240; defended by fascists, 72; destruction of (in GDR), 256; erosion of, 65
academic clubs (Poland), 189
academic freedom, 2–4, 6–7, 9, 11–13, 52, 71, 151, 153, 172, 228; and nationalism, 209; weakening of after World War II, 146
Academy of Sciences: of Hungary, 140; and compromise with Bolsheviks, 31; of Czechoslovakia, 176–77; German (East Berlin), 264, 271; of Hungary, 146, 150, 158; Imperial (Petrine), 17, 21, 22, 26; of Poland, 198; of Prussia reopened as the German Academy of Sciences (1946, East Berlin), 264; of the USSR, 16, 34, 36, 39, 43
ACNP. *See* Asociación Católica Nacional de Propagandistas (ACNP)
Action N (Poland), 194
A-er-xin-jie-fu, Soviet advisor to the Ministry of Higher Education (China), 230–31, 238
affirmative action, 42, 258
Alicata, Mario, 62
All-Union Council of the National Economy (Vesenkha), 38
American Association of University Professors, 4
anti-fascism, anti-fascists, 47, 54–56, 63, 67, 253, 255, 281, 283
anti-intellectualism, 84, 98; of Nazi movement, 90, 98; in Spain, 122
anti-Semitism, 27, 65–67, 78, 89, 104, 144, 154, 168, 290; laws effecting education (Italy), 66; after March 1968 events (Poland), 208; racial laws in Italy (1938), 66; support for among German students, 80; Warsaw students protest against (March 1968), 205
Arbeitsgemeinschaft Nationalsozialistischer Studentinnen (ANSt). *See* Working Community of National Socialist Women Students

Arias, Gino, 68, 132
Asociación Católica Nacional de Propagandistas (ACNP), 115, 130, 134
Association of German Universities: protest (1930), 79; reservations toward National Socialism (1933), 83

Baczko, Bronisław, 202, 207
Bairati, Alberto, 60
Basic Law (Germany), 262
Basque Country, 137
Bauman, Zygmunt, 7, 202, 204, 206, 207
Becker, Carl Heinrich, 77
Beida. *See* Beijing University
Beijing University, 215
Ben-Ghiat, Ruth, 55, 64, 114, 119–20, 193
Berend, Iván, 159, 160
Bethlen, István, 142
Bibó, István, 146–48, 153
Bloch, Ernst, 266–67
Bobińska, Celina, 199
Bollinger, Lee C., 8
Bolshevik Party. *See* Communist Party of the Soviet Union (CPSU)
Bongiovanni, Bruno, 50
Borgese, Guiseppe, 57
Bormann, Martin, 94, 102
Bottai, Giuseppe, 57, 65–66, 70–72
Bourdieu, Pierre, 12, 141
Bowdoin College, 5
Brno University, 174
Brown University, 5
Brus, Włodzimierz, 202, 207
Bureau of Proletarian Students, 37

Cai, Yuanpei, 215
Campaign to Suppress Counterrevolutionaries (China), 236
Catholic University of America, 5
Catholicism: in higher education, 4–5, 21, 48, 54, 64, 66, 77–78, 115, 117, 122, 129–34, 168, 194–95, 216, 290; in Italian culture, 72
CCP. *See* Chinese Communist Party (CCP)

Central Bureau of Proletarian Students (Soviet Union), 30, 36
Central Commission for Improving the Life of Scholars (Soviet Union) (TSEKUBU), 31
Central Qualification Commission for Scientific Workers (Poland), 194–95
Central University (Madrid), 118, 132
centralization: in higher education, 30, 41, 48, 65, 118; of higher education, 17, 190, 256
Chałasiński, Józef, 196
Charles University (Prague), 171, 173, 174, 176, 178, 179, 180, 181, 182
Charter 77, 180
Chiang Kai-shek, 219, 223
Chinese Communist Party (CCP), 33, 213, 214, 215, 217, 218, 219, 220, 221, 222, 223, 224, 225, 226, 227, 228, 233, 234, 238, 239, 241, 243
Christian missionary schools in China, 216
civil society, 3, 13, 19, 21, 133, 209, 214; Russian social estate system (*soslovie*), 22
Civil War (Chinese), 224
Civil War (Russian), 26–29
Civil War (Spanish), 113–19, 122, 128, 132, 135, 284
Club of Seekers of Contradictions (Poland), 203
Club of the Burning Tomato, 200
Club of the Independent Intelligentsia (Prague), 180
Cold War, 1, 117, 211, 222, 247
Colegios Mayores Universitarios. *See* university residences (Spain)
collaboration of scholars, 13, 54, 107, 119, 134, 247–48, 251, 255, 276, 278, 281, 287
Commissariat of Enlightenment (Narkompros), 27, 36, 38–41; of Ukraine during the Civil War, 29
Committee to Protect Workers (KOR) (Poland), 208
Committee for the Extension of the Syllabus (Spain), 118
Committee for the German Intelligentsia (East Germany), 252
Communist Party of Czechoslovakia (KSČ), 170, 172, 174, 179, 181–82
Communist Party of the Soviet Union (CPSU), 10, 17, 19, 22–37
conformism, 48
Consejo Superior de Investigaciones Científicas (CSIC) (Spain), 126, 130–33

conservatism, as tempering right radicalism, 127
continuities: of higher education, 210; of university personnel, 281; of university policy, 26, 50, 131; of university traditions, 20, 188, 191, 249, 250
crimes of Nazi regime, and scholars, 108
Croce, Benedetto, 50–52, 54
Crooked Circle Club (Poland), 201
CSIC. *See* Consejo Superior de Investigaciones Científicas (CSIC) (Spain)
Cultural Accord between German and Italy (1938), 69–70
Cultural Revolution (China), 240, 243
Curran, Charles E., 5
curricular reform, 31, 39, 45–46, 51, 58, 60, 65, 155, 172, 190, 226, 229, 232, 234–35, 259

Dalton plan, 34
David-Fox, Michael, 17, 26, 29, 32, 34–35, 43, 140, 165, 193, 252, 260
De Santis, Giuseppe, 62
De Vecchi, Cesare Maria, 64–65
denazification of higher education (East Germany), 248, 250
deprofessionalization of universities, 12, 51, 193
desarrollismo, 117
Deutsche Demokratische Partei. *See* German Democratic Party (DDP)
Deutsche Volkspartei. *See* German People's Party (DVP)
Deutschnationale Volkspartei. *See* German National People's Party (DNVP)
discontinuities: of disciplines in Poland, 196; in East German social sciences, 250; in higher education, 132, 154–55, 261; in Hungary, 156; of personnel in Spain, 121; in professoriate, 177
dismissals of professors, 3–7, 10, 54, 81–82, 85, 88–91, 102, 123, 172, 195, 208, 250
Djilas, Milovan, 186, 211
Dobrowolski, Kazimierz, 196
Domin, Karel, 176
Dubček, Alexander, 178
DVV. *See* German Education Administration in Berlin (DVV)

economics as university subject, 11, 30, 95, 124, 132, 154–55, 157, 159, 164, 174, 177, 181, 193, 194, 233, 250, 252
Ehrlich, Ludwik, 196, 197

Index   299

elitism, 24, 49–50, 52, 115, 118, 122, 126, 232
Erdey-Grúz, Tibor, 149, 150
Erziehung und Ausbildung. *See* socialist schooling and education (GDR)
Ethiopia, 65; student support for conquest, 64
eugenics, 133

Falange (Spanish), 114–16, 119, 122, 124–27, 129, 135–36; and imitation of other fascist regimes, 115; limits of university policy, 128; supposedly moderate fascism of, 116
Falange Española de las Juntas de Ofensive Nacional-Sindicalista (FE de las JONS). *See* Falange (Spanish)
Fascism: clerical, 122; and creative autonomy, 55; Italian, as imperfect totalitarianism, 46; and overtures to youth, 61; as shaping Italian youth, 73; as subject of study, 58
Fascist Association of the School. *See* National Federation of Fascist Universitarians (FNUF) (Spain)
Fascist Grand Council, 56
Fascist National Party (PNF), 45, 53–56, 61, 68
Fascist University Groups (GUF), 47, 54, 59–64, 69, 71, 73, 124; and cultural resources for population, 61; *Littorialli della cultura e dell'arte*, 62, 63, 125
fascisticization of higher education, 54, 122
Federación de Estudiantes Católicos, 118
Federación Universitaria Democrática de Estudiantes (FUDE) (Spain), 137
Federación Universitaria Escolar (FUE), 118–19
Fehér, Ferenc, 155
females in student body, 51–52, 60–61, 91, 100–101, 123–24, 133
First All-China Conference on Higher Education, 228, 238
Fischl, Otto, 174
flying universities (Poland), 208
Fomin, A. A., 238
former NSDAP members: in East German professoriate, 262
Franco y Bahamonde, Francisco, 47, 61, 113–23, 129, 132–35, 138
Frankly Speaking (*Po Prostu*) (Poland), 200–201
Free Trade Union of the Hungarian Teachers, 149

freedom: of learning, 3, 139, 177; of teaching, 3, 139
Frente de Juventudes (Youth Camps) (Spain), 136
FUE. *See* Federación Universitaria Escolar (FUE)
Furen University (China), 237

generation: crisis of younger generation, 75, 81; gap, 35–36, 58–59; socialized by fascism, 45, 56, 61, 72–73
generational conflict, 35–36, 45, 56, 58–59, 61, 73, 75, 81, 84–85, 89, 91, 95, 102, 120, 135, 137, 199, 248–52, 272, 274, 279, 293, 295
Gentile, Emilio, 46, 50, 54, 72; reform program (1923), 56
German Communist Party (KPD), 252–53, 254
German Democratic Party (DDP), 79
German Education Administration (DVV), 253–254
German Labor Front, 98
German model in higher education, 66, 75, 125, 129
German National People's Party (DNVP), 79
German People's Party (DVP), 79
German physics, 284
Giner, Salvador, 122
GMD. *See* Guomindang (GMD) (China)
Goebbels, Joseph, and respect for science, 109
Gomułka, Władysław, 187, 199, 201, 203–04
Gorbachev, Mikhail, 179
Gottwald, Klement, 171
Great Break in Soviet higher education, 15–16, 39–41
Great Purges (Soviet Union), 43
Great Reforms in imperial Russia, 18, 21
Grinko, G. F., 30
Gross, Jan T., 203
Gross, Walter, 93
Grüttner, Michael, 80–81, 114, 120, 139
Grzybowski, Konstanty, 192
Günther, Hans F. K., 79
Guomindang (Nationalist Party, GMD) (China), 215–20, 222–27, 229, 240–43

Härtle, Heinrich, 106
Hass, Ludwik, 202
Hauser, Arnold, 155
Havel, Václav, 181

He Ganzhi, 233
Heidegger, Martin, 84
Heidelberg University, 79, 82
Herbert, Zbigniew, 186, 251, 257
Herrera Oria, Cardinal Ángel Herrera Oria, 134
Hess, Rudolf, 86, 94
higher education: expansion of, 18, 21, 26, 43, 65, 128, 235, 294; mythologies about, 120 (Spain), 139 (Hungary); in the Third Reich, institutions created for oversight of, 85
higher technical institutes (VTUZY) (Soviet Union), 39
Hirszowicz, Maria, 187, 207, 212
historiography, Nazi, 105
Hitler Youth generation, 279
Hitler, Adolf, 9, 63, 69, 87, 91, 98, 102
Hlinka, Andrej, 168
Hobza, Václav, 177
Holland, Henryk, 201
Holy See, and Franco's regime, 117
Hora, Antonín, 177
Horthy, Admiral Miklós, 152
Hrbek, Jaroslav, 178
Hu Shi, 222, 241
humanities, 12, 29, 31, 38, 41–43, 51, 106–7, 118, 131, 133, 144, 149, 154, 176, 198, 207, 217, 229, 234, 237, 249–52, 255, 261–62, 267, 281, 284, 286
Humboldt, Wilhelm von, 6, 12
Humboldtian university, 2, 149, 215
Hundred Flowers Campaign, 239
Hungarian Institute of Economic Research, 154
Hungarian Institutes (Collegium Hungaricum), 142
Husák, Gustav, 179, 181

Ibáñez Martín, José, 121, 131
idea of the university, 12
ideology, 11, 13, 15, 18, 47, 49, 67, 69–70, 88–89, 91, 100–101, 104, 107–8, 116–17, 192, 194, 216, 222, 226, 229, 236, 240, 262, 264, 270, 283–84, 286
Imperial Univeristy, renamed Beijing University (1912), 215
indoctrination, 29, 56, 101, 120, 126–27, 175–76, 192, 259, 270, 276; protests against in GDR, 266
informers and higher education. in Italy, 47
Institución Libre de Enseñanza (Spain), 130

Institute of Red Professors, 30
intelligentsia: academic, 43, 165; accommodation of, 43, 57, 186, 211, 214; and Communist Party, 25, 187, 193, 246; Communist repression of, 28, 174; dissent among, 187, 204; and dissent, 208, 211; and higher education, 19–23, 36, 186–87, 201; high social status of (China), 213; and Italian fascism, 65; liberal, 25; networks of, 201; new, 42, 61, 153, 158, 162, 269, 271, 279; and 1968, 204; non-Party intelligentsia and Bolshevik state, 36; old, 41; privileges of, 187; proletarian, 36; and specialists, 25; technical, 187; urban, 158
Italian model, in higher education, 61, 115, 117, 129
Italian-German relations, 69, 70

Jabłoński, Henryk, 207
JAE. See Junta de Ampliación de Estudios e Investigaciones Científicas (Spain)
Jagiellonian University (Kraków), 190, 197, 199
Jászi, Oskar, 155
Jewish exiles from Nazi Germany, in fascist Italy, 47
Joven Academia, 129
Junta de Ampliación de Estudios e Investigaciones Científicas (Spain), 131
Junta para la Ampliación de Estudios. See Committe for the Extension of the Syllabus (Spain)

Kádár, János, 153–54, 160–63
Kadlec, Karel, 177
Kaganovich, Lazar', 38
Kalista, Zdeněk, 177
Karl Marx University of Economics (Budapest), 160–61
Katětov, Miroslav, 182
Klebelsberg, Count Kuno, 142, 143, 144, 152
koła naukowe. See academic clubs (Poland)
Kołakowski, Leszek, 203, 207
Konopczyński, Władysław, 193
Konrad, George, 186, 211, 259
KOR. See Committee to Protect Workers (KOR) (Poland)
Kornis, Gyula, 143
Kors, Alan, 6
Kosík, Karel, 178
Kotarbiński, Tadeusz, 202
Kovács, István, 159

KPD. *See* German Communist Party (KPD)
Krauss, Werner, 83, 101, 251
Krieck, Ernst, 87, 95, 96, 104
Kula, Witold, 197, 202
Kuroń, Jacek, 186, 200, 202, 205

labor service for students, 71, 83, 100, 102, 290
Lande, Jerzy, 196, 198
Lateran Accords, 51
Law of the Organization of Universities (LOU), 126–28
League of Nations, 65, 70, 217, 237, 241
Lehrfreiheit. *See* freedom of teaching
Leningrad, students at, 34
Leningrad State University, 39–40
Lernfreiheit. *See* freedom of learning
Ley de Ordenación de la Universidad (LOU). *See* Law of the Organization of Universities (LOU)
Ley, Robert, 98
Littoriali della cultura e dell'arte. *See* Fascist University Groups (GUF)
Lowell, Abbott Lawrence, 9
loyalty oath in Italy (1931), 47
Lukács, György, 146, 151, 155, 159
Lunacharskii, Anatolii Nikolai, 22, 36
Lysenko, T. D., 284, 291

Maria Castiella, Fernando, 134
Ma Xulun, 216, 222, 229–30, 232–33, 241–43
Machovec, Milan, 178
Mączak, Antoni, 202
Main Committee on Professional Education (*Glavprofobr*), 28
Main Council (Poland), 190–91
Manifesto of Racial Scientists (Italy). *See* racial laws
Mannheim, Karl, 155
Mao Zedong, 221–22, 225, 234–35, 239–40, 243
Marburg, 83, 89, 92, 95, 100–101
Marchlewski, Teodor, 192
Markov, M., 37
Martial Law (Poland), 187, 211
Martín-Artajo, Alberto, 134
Marx-Engels-Lenin Institute (East Germany), 255
Marxism-Leninism, 11, 38, 41–42, 137, 155–56, 164, 175–77, 192, 194, 196, 198, 221, 223, 255–56, 259–60, 270, 279, 281, 283, 288–89; protests against compulsory instruction in, 266

MCP. *See* Ministry of Popular Culture (Italy)
medicine, 64, 67, 70, 124, 133, 135, 174–75, 249–52, 261–62, 278
Meinecke, Friedrich, 97
Metzger, Walter, 3, 7
Michnik, Adam, 203, 204, 208
Mickiewicz, Adam, 204
military industrial complex, 1
military service for students, 96, 102, 108
Miłosz, Czesław, 186
Ministry of Education (Spain), 128
Ministry of Higher Education (Poland), 203
Ministry of National Education (Italy), 66
Ministry of National Education (Spain), 124
Ministry of Popular Culture (Italy), 65
Ministry of Public Instruction (Italy), 49, 52
Moczar, Mieczysław, 204
Model Gymnasium (of Budapest), 154
modernization in higher education, 20, 71, 142, 144, 146, 151, 163, 216–17, 272, 274
Modzelewski, Karol, 200, 202, 204, 294
Molotov, Viacheslav M., 36, 203
Mommsen, Theodor, 9, 103
Moro, Aldo, 54, 62
Moscow Higher Technical School, 28
Moscow State University, 16, 22, 38–39, 41
Moscow State University, 33
Mussolini, Benito, 45–50, 52, 53, 59, 62, 64–65, 72, 73, 119, 122

Nagy, Imre, 159
National Fascist Party (PNF), 45
National Federation of Fascist Universitarians (FNUF), 55
National Institute of Fascist Culture, 54
National Prize (East Germany), 252
National Scholarships Council (Hungary), 142
National Socialism, 10, 75, 92, 98, 100, 102, 108, 147, 249, 251, 260, 278; and East German professoriate, 246; student resistance to, 102
National Socialism (German), 12, 54, 59, 61, 66–68, 75–76, 80–85, 87, 90, 93, 98–100, 102, 104, 107, 114–15, 120, 127, 133, 168, 180–81, 246, 248, 250–51, 253, 257, 262–63, 280; ambivalence of professors toward, 85; attitudes toward scholarship, 103; contempt for intellectuals, 98; imitation of, 66, 71; impact on students, 100; institutional clashes, 87; Nazi party members at universities, 79, 92; personnel

National Socialism (German) (*continued*)
  policies in higher education, 91; phases of university policy, 90; professoriate's support of foreign conquest, 97; and reverse in anti-intellectualism, 109; student enthusiasm for, 80; students in Party organizations, 100; university policy of, 88, 91
National Socialist German League of Lecturers (NSDDB), 85, 94, 104
National Socialist German Student League (NSDStB), 102; strongest political force in German universities, 80
National Socialist German Studnet League (NSDStB), 99-01, 119
National-Syndicalism (Spanish), 116. *See also* Falange (Spanish)
natural sciences, 70, 95, 144, 149, 206, 249–51, 261–62, 264, 266, 268, 276, 278, 284, 286
Nazi students, and influence on professorial appointments, 109
Negrisoli, Bortolo, 57
new class, 64, 186, 188, 212
New Economic Policy (NEP), 30–31, 33, 35
Newman, John Henry, 1
Nicholas I, Tzar of Russia, 21
Novikov, Mikhail, 22, 25
NSDAP. *See* National Socialism (German)
NSDDB. *See* National Socialist German League of Lecturers (NSDDB)
NSDStB. *See* National Socialist German Student League (NSDStB). *See* National Socialist German Student League (NSDStB)
Nuremberg laws, effect on Italy, 66

objective scholarship, rejection of by Nazis, 103
Office of Political Education (China), 218
Oncken, Hermann, 82, 97
Opletal, Jan, 180
Opus Dei, 115, 118, 130–31, 134
Organización Sindical, 116
Ortega y Gasset, 133
Ossowska, Maria, 194, 202
Ossowski, Stanisław, 194
overproduction of university graduates, 48, 50, 51, 144

Palach, Jan, 178, 180
Partido Comunista de España, 137

Partito Nazionale Fascista. *See* Fascist National Party (PNF)
Party College (East Germany), 254–56
Party schools, 34
Pellizzi, Camillo, 59
People's Judges, 253
Peter the Great, Tzar of Russia, 17, 23
Péteri, György, 12, 17, 43, 140, 152, 153, 157, 164, 165
Petőfi Circle, 158, 160
philosophy, as university subject, 51, 124, 132–33, 155, 164, 170–71, 174–75, 177, 181, 194, 196, 203, 222, 234–36, 249–50, 256, 267, 289
physical education, 126
physics, 91, 105, 108, 286, 291
Pieńkowski, Stefan, 191
Planning, in higher education, 126, 135, 143, 150–53, 192, 194, 230, 265, 274–76, 279, 289
Po prostu. *See Frankly Speaking*
Pokrovskii, Mikhail, 22, 28, 38
Polányi, Karl, 155
Polish United Workers Party (PZPR), 193–97, 198, 199, 203, 207
political science, 58, 124, 156, 164
politicization: as part of Soviet model, 192; of higher education, 12, 35, 46, 47, 58, 79, 83, 120, 247, 259, 264, 270, 275; rejection of by professors, 289; of student admissions, 139
Pomian, Krzysztof, 200
Post, Robert, 6, 8, 145
Poznań, 76, 91, 189, 196, 198–99, 205
premilitary education, 126
Preobrazhenskii, Evgenii, 28
Primo de Rivera y Saenz de Heredia, José Antonio, 115, 118, 120, 124, 136
professionalism, 12, 156, 162
professoriate: Communists among (GDR), 276; and Communist Party, 25, 193; composition of in Germany, 76; conservatism of, 78, 79, 143, 188; continuity of, 188, 191; decline in social status of, 98; and defense of university, 40, 277; delegitimized by war, 145, 190, 247; denominational structure of in Germany, 77; fascist party members among, 55; informal networks among, 165; integration of former Nazis, 262; invites state intervention, 148; legitimation through anti–Nazi resistance, 209; nationalist (in Hungary), 145; Nazi Party

members among, 80, 85, 93; Nazi Party members in East German, 261; old, 38, 193, 195, 198; opposition to Communism among, 182; and opposition to Franco Regime, 138; passivity of, 56, 227, 240; politicization of appointments, 93; and prerogatives, 32; prerogatives of, 34; recruitment into, 172, 195, 267, 269, 271; red, 29; resistance to Sovietization of, 171, 233; surveillance of, 33; and tsarist regime, 22; in Weimar Germany, 78
purging: of Communists by GMD (China), 218; failure of in Poland, 191; of professors, 119 (*See also* dismissals of professors); of students, 173, 257; at universities, 11, 20, 32, 33, 46, 53–54, 57, 67–68, 71, 88, 102, 122, 128, 171, 174, 179, 188, 203, 204, 208, 247, 251, 262–63, 269, 284, 286, 289, 292, 295
PZPR. *See* Polish United Workers Party (PZPR)

Qian Junrui, 225

rabfaki. *See* workers' faculties
race, 59, 68–69, 89, 104, 108, 133, 257
racial laws: in Germany (Nuremberg laws), 66; in Italy (1938), 48, 66–68. *See also* anti-Semitism
racial science, 105, 283
racism, 5, 46, 48, 62, 66–71, 73, 79, 89, 102, 133, 155, 283–84, 287, 290
Reich Ministry of Education (Germany), 85–87, 93–94, 102; competes with University Commission of the NSDAP, 86; Office on Scholarship, 86
Reich, Jens, 245
REM. *See* Reich Ministry of Education (Germany)
research, 16, 22, 67, 88, 108, 164, 235; freedom of, 9, 12; freedom of in GDR, 265; organization of, 34, 144; planning of, 34; separated from teaching, 2, 149; subcontracted by government, 7
Residencia de Estudiantes (Spain), 130
Resist America and Aid Korea Campaign (China), 236
Respighi, Ottorino, 62
Riappo, Ian Petrovich, 30
Ritter, Gerhard, 96
Rockefeller Foundation, 142
Rompe, Robert, 251
Rosenberg, Alfred, 27, 86–87, 90, 94–95, 104, 106, 265

Rudzińska, Anna, 202
Ruffini, Francesco, 55
Ruiz-Giménez, Joaquín, 134
Rust, Bernhard: Reich Minister of Education, 86
Ryba, Bohumil, 177

Sakulin, Pavel N., 27
Sándor, Pal, 154, 157, 161
Sauckel, Fritz, 88
Scheel, Gustav Adolf, 106
Schmitt, Carl, 84
Scholarship, limits to politicization of, 93, 106, 122, 127, 179, 197
School Charter (1939), 70–72. *See* Gentile, Emilio Reform program (1923); as revision of Gentile reform, 66
Schramm, Percy Ernst, 96, 97
Schultze, Walter, 86
Second Moscow University, 39
SED. *See* Socialist Unity Party of Germany (SED)
Servicio Español del Profesorado de Enseñanza Superior (SEPES), 122, 127
SEU. *See* Sindicato Español Universitario (SEU)
Shakhtii show trial, 35
Shmidt, Otto Yulievich, 38
Sieradzki, J., 199
Silió, César, 118
Silnicki, T., 197
Silverglate, Harvey, 6
Sindicato Español Universitario (SEU), 119–20, 122, 124–28, 136–37; hopes to use German and Italian models, 129
Sindicatos Democráticos de Estudiantes (SDE) (Spain), 137
Sławińska, Irena, 194
SMAD. *See* Soviet Military Administration
Smend, Rudolf, 78
social advancement, 50
social leveling, 98
social mobility, 13, 42, 46, 50, 59, 192
social sciences, 10, 11, 27, 29, 32, 38, 41–43, 144, 149, 154, 165, 177, 198, 201, 218, 234, 237, 249–50, 252, 255–56, 261–62, 267, 281; politicization of in GDR, 252
socialist schooling and education, 270
Socialist Unity Party of Germany (SED), 246–56, 258–81
Solidarity (Poland), 211
Sottsass, Ettore, 62

Soviet Military Administration (SMAD), 247, 251, 253, 260, 277
Soviet models, 231; in GDR, 260; in higher education, 10, 35, 165, 192, 213, 239, 271, 275, 288
sovietization, 10, 31, 35, 165, 211, 213, 230, 239–40, 251, 253; in Chinese universities, 237; of higher education, 163
specialization, in higher education, 30, 38–40, 104, 259
speech codes in the U.S., 5–6, 8
Speer, Albert, 109
SS (Schutzstaffel), 86–88, 94, 95, 99, 105–06
St. John's University (China), 216
Stalin, Joseph, 15–16, 18, 20, 36, 39, 42–43, 156, 200, 221, 223, 260, 266
Stalinism, 35, 43, 153, 166, 174, 186–87, 191, 200, 247
Stasi (Staatssicherheitsdienst), 45, 278
Stiffler, Douglas, 10
Stomma, Stanisław, 194
Strasbourg, 76, 91, 97
student activism, 219, 227, 294
student admissions, 171, 257
student fraternities, 100–102
student life: in Nazi Germany, 99, 102; obligatory activities, 29, 32, 42, 100–101, 127, 175, 260, 289; regimentation of, 54, 124
student movements, 22–24, 27, 31, 36–38, 118, 137, 204, 206, 214
students, 22, 31–32, 35–36, 49, 50, 54, 72, 82, 91, 118, 124–25, 136, 139, 160, 173–74, 182, 200, 204, 206–8, 217, 226, 243, 257, 260, 269, 277; and affirmative action, 27, 153, 258; anti-fascist, 54; and attack on universities, 30; Communists among, 32, 36, 199; and Communist Party, 25; continuities of, 188; dissent among, 203; erosion of critical faculties among, 47; and hostility to democracy, 80, 119; Impact of Nazi policy on, 100; increase in numbers, 123; independent organizations of, 189; indoctrination of, 61, 120; informers among, 47; and limits to politicization of, 127; and Nazi organizations, 100; Nazi Party membership among, 80; opposition to Communism of, 189; and opposition to Hungarian Stalinism, 158; opposition to Nazism, 102, 168; organizational membership of, 32, 99, 100, 119, 200, 227, 271; political socialization of, 72; power of, 34–35, 37, 90, 171, 180; and purges, 102,
173; purges of, 32, 171; and resistance to National Socialism, 102; and struggle against Franco regime, 137; subcultures among, 35; and support for Communists (China), 223; and support for Czech Communism, 170; supported by professors, 210
Students' Central Organization (SVS) (Czechoslovakia), 169
Sun Yat-sen, 216, 218, 220
SVS. *See* Students' Central Oranization (SVS) (Czechoslovakia)
Szekfü, Gyula, 149
Szelényi, Ivan, 186, 211
Szent-Györgyi, Albert, 144, 148–50, 153

Tatarkiewicz, Władysław, 194
Teatro Español Universitario (TEU), 125
technical higher education, 10, 12, 24, 26, 30, 35–36, 38–40, 42–43, 48, 51, 53, 95, 108, 118, 128, 130, 167, 177–178, 182, 187, 216, 229–33, 237, 239, 250–52, 261–62, 264, 267–68, 271, 273–74, 278–81
technocratic reforms in GDR, 272
TEU. *See* Teatro Español Universitario (TEU)
theology, 5, 90, 131–33, 249, 290
Thought Reform (China), 236, 239
Three Principles of the People. *See* Sun Yat-sen.
Trade Union College (East Germany), 256
Treaty of Trianon, 142, 144
Trznadel, Jacek, 186
Tuka, Vojtech, 168

unemployment, of university graduates, 48, 49, 61, 65, 70, 73
Ungaretti, Giuseppe, 62
Union of Polish Writers (ZLP), 204
Union of Polish Youth (ZMP), 199–200
Union of Socialist Youth (ZMS) (Poland), 201
Universitarian Battalions, 64
universities: as ideological training grounds, 126; break–up of, 30, 39; as medieval fortresses, 37; passivity of (in China), 240; passivity of (in East Germany), 246; passivity of (in Spanish Civil War), 120; regression of in Spain, 121, 127, 130; resurrection of in the USSR, 43
University: Beijing University, 219, 222, 225–26, 233–35, 237, 241, 243; Catholic Furen University (China), 238; Charles University (Prague), 168–71, 182; Free

University (West Berlin), 247; Humboldt University (East Germany), 260; idea of, 10, 41, 121, 141; Jagiellonian University (Kraków), 190, 197; Karl Marx University of Economics (Budapest), 156; Law School of the Loránd Eötvös University (Budapest), 156; Moscow State, 15, 22; Nankai (China), 219; National Central University (Nanjing, China), 218; National Labor University, closed in 1932 (China), 218; Shanghai University, 218; Shaniavskii People's University (Soviet Union), 22; Tsinghua University (China), 219, 224, 232, 235, 237; Yenching University (China), 216, 224, 226; Zhongshan University (Guangzhou, China), 218

university autonomy, 18, 22, 25, 28, 33, 46, 79, 83, 118, 121, 139, 153, 161, 165, 189, 257; final elimination of in GDR, 267; as formality, 143; made indefensible through collaboration, 151

University Commission of the NSDAP, 85–86

University Federation of Italian Catholics (FUCI), 54

University of Barcelona, 128
University of Berlin, 247
University of Bonn, 88
University of Bratislava, 167–68
University of Economics (Prague), 171
University of Fudan (China), 216
University of Kazan', 39
University of Lublin (Poland), 198
University of Massachusetts, 5
University of Michigan, 6, 8
University of Nankai (China), 215
University of Pavia, 64
University of Pennsylvania, 5
University of Perugia, 58
University of Poznań (Poland), 193
University of Rome, 53, 67
University of Rostock (East Germany), 250, 268

University of Szeged (Hungary), 142, 144
University of Technology (Budapest), 159
University of Toruń (Poland), 189, 194, 195, 199
University of Turin, 53, 55, 60
University of Warsaw, 190, 191, 200, 202, 205, 207
University of Wisconsin, 4, 6, 116
University of Wrocław (Poland), 186, 189, 191, 193, 199, 205–07
university reform, as rationalization, 40, 239, 241, 274
university residences (Spain), 124; as forms of discipline, 124

Valencia, 119
Venturi, Lionello, 57
Vígh, Károly, 149, 151
Violence, on campuses, 50, 54, 66, 119, 122, 137, 205, 288
vocationalism in higher education, 29, 30, 36, 38
Volpicelli, Luigi, 63
Vydvizhenie (affirmative action, Russia), 42, 192

Wacker, Otto, 93, 94
Weber, Max, 78
workers' faculties (*rabfaki*), 32
Working Community of National Socialist Women Students (ANSt), 100
World War Two: and Chinese higher education, 219; and German universities, 97; and Italian universities, 63

Yen, Maria, 213, 226–27, 233–34

Zhang Boling, 215
Zhang Dongsun, 235
Zhang Xiruo, 235
Zhdanov, Andrei A, 43
Zhu Jianhua, 218
ZMP. *See* Union of Polish Youth

www.ingramcontent.com/pod-product-compliance
Lightning Source LLC
Chambersburg PA
CBHW021936290426
44108CB00012B/854